New Horizons in Tourism

Strange Experiences and Stranger Practices

New Horizons in Tourism

Strange Experiences and Stranger Practices

_____

Edited by

Tej Vir Singh

Centre for Tourism Research and Development
A-965/6 Indira Nagar, Lucknow 226016, India

CABI Publishing

CABI Publishing is a division of CAB International

CABI Publishing
CAB International
Wallingford
Oxfordshire OX10 8DE
UK

CABI Publishing
875 Massachusetts Avenue
7th Floor
Cambridge, MA 02139
USA

Tel: +44 (0)1491 832111
Fax: +44 (0)1491 833508
E-mail: cabi@cabi.org
Website: www.cabi-publishing.org

Tel: +1 617 395 4056
Fax: +1 617 354 6875
E-mail: cabi-nao@cabi.org

A catalogue record for this book is available from the British Library,
London, UK.

Library of Congress Cataloging-in-Publication Data

New horizons in tourism : strange experiences and stranger practices /
edited by Tej Vir Singh.
    p. cm.
  Includes bibliographical references (p.).
  ISBN 0-85199-863-1 (alk. paper)
  1. Tourism. 2. Adventure and adventurers. 3. Heritage tourism.
  I. Singh, Tejvir, 1930–   II. Title.
  G155.A1N429   2005
  338.4′791—dc22   2004004676

ISBN 0 85199 863 1

Typeset by Servis Filmsetting Ltd, Manchester
Printed and bound in the UK by Biddles Ltd, King's Lynn

Contents

Contributors

J.R. Aramberri, *Department of Hospitality Management, Drexel University, Academic Building, Office 110, 33rd and Arch Streets, Philadelphia, PA 19104, USA*

C. Ashley, *Overseas Development Institute (ODI), 111 Westminster Bridge Road, London SE1 7JD, UK*

G.J. Ashworth, *Heritage Management and Urban Tourism, Department of Planning, Faculty of Spatial Science, University of Groningen, Post Box 800, 9700AV Groningen, The Netherlands*

R. Buckley, *International Centre for Ecotourism Research, Griffith University, Parklands Drive, Southport, Australia*

P. Chauhan, *Government of Himachal Pradesh, Block-1, Set-4, Type V, Richmond Hill, Shimla – 175001, India*

M. Cleaver Sellick, *Central Washington University, College of Business, 400 E. 8th Avenue, Ellensburg, WA 98926-7485, USA*

G.I. Crouch, *School of Business, Faculty of Law and Management, La Trobe University, Melbourne, Victoria 3086, Australia*

D.A. Fennell, *Department of Recreation and Leisure Studies, Brock University, St Catharines, Ontario L2S 3A1, Canada*

H. Goodwin, *International Centre for Responsible Tourism, University of Greenwich, 6 Preston Malthouse, St Johns Road, Faversham, Kent ME13 8EW, UK*

R.K. Headland, *Scott Polar Research Institute, University of Cambridge, Lensfield Road, Cambridge CB2 1ER, UK*

J. Laing, *School of Business, Faculty of Law and Management, La Trobe University, Melbourne, Victoria 3086, Australia*

D. Landau, *International Association of Antarctica Tourism (IAATO), Office of the Secretariat, IAATO, PO Box 2178, Basalt, CO 81621, USA*

J.J. Lennon, *Moffat Centre for Travel and Tourism Business Development, Glasgow Caledonian University, Cowcaddens Road, Glasgow G4 0BA, UK*

T.E. Muller, *Griffith University, PO Box 905, Runaway Bay, Qld 4216, Australia*

B. Prideaux, *School of Business, James Cook University, Townsville, Qld 4811, Australia*

D. Roe, *International Institute for Environment and Development (IIED), 3 Endsleigh Street, London WC1H 0DD, UK*

P. Schofield, *Management Research Institute, University of Salford, M6 6PU, UK*

A.V. Seaton, *Luton Business School, Department of Tourism and Leisure, University of Luton, Putteridge Bury, Hitchin Road, Luton, Bedfordshire LU2 8LE, UK*

S.S. Seop-Kim, *Department of Hotel Management and Tourism, Sejong University, #98 Gunja-Dong, Kwangjin-Gu, 143-150 Seoul, Republic of Korea*

S. Singh, *Department of Recreation and Leisure Studies, Brock University, 500 Glenridge Avenue, St Catharines, Ontario, Canada L2S 3A1*

T.V. Singh, *Centre for Tourism Research and Development, A-965/6 Indira Nagar, Lucknow – 226016, India*

T.H.B. Sofield, *Tourism Program, University of Tasmania, Locked Bag 1-340G, Launceston 7250, Tasmania, Australia*

J. Splettstoesser, *PO Box 515, 433 West Fifth Street, Appt 202, Waconia, MN 55387, USA*

D.J. Timothy, *Department of Recreation Management and Tourism, PO Box 874905, Arizona State University, Tempe, AZ 85287-4905, USA*

About the Contributors

Julio Aramberri is Professor at the Department of Tourism, Drexel University, Philadelphia, USA. Between 1985 and 1999 Aramberri worked for the Spanish Tourism Administration in different capacities. He was Director General of the Spanish National Tourism Administration (Turespaña) from 1987 to 1990. Aramberri has authored or co-authored eight books on different sociological subjects, as well as on marketing research, and has published over 35 articles in different scholarly magazines. He is a member of the International Academy for the Study of Tourism and Editor of *Annals of Tourism Research*. He also belongs to the Editorial Board of *Annals en Español*, and of *Tourism Recreation Research*.

Caroline Ashley is a Research Fellow at the Overseas Development Institute in London and part of the Pro-Poor Tourism Partnership. Research interests include: pro-poor tourism strategies; rural livelihoods; diversification and growth; community-based natural resource management; community–private partnerships. Caroline was previously working in Namibia with the Ministry of Environment and Tourism as a Resource Economist. She particularly focused on CBNRM issues in Namibia and elsewhere in southern Africa.

Gregory Ashworth is Professor of Heritage Management and Urban Tourism in the Urban and Regional Studies Institute, University of Groningen, The Netherlands. His research interests include, heritage, tourism and place marketing within the context of urban management and planning. Recent publications include *Retrospect and Prospect on the Tourist Historic City* (2000), *European Heritage Planning and Management* (2000), *A Geography of Heritage* (2001).

Ralf Buckley is Director of the International Centre for Ecotourism Research at Griffith University, Gold Coast, Australia. He has worked in over 40 countries worldwide and has published over 200 journal articles and a dozen books, including five in ecotourism. His most recent publication is *Case Studies in Ecotourism* (2003).

Purnima Chauhan is a Ph.D. student at the University of Himachal Pradesh, Shimla, India. She is Secretary in Ministry of Urban Planning and Development, Government of Himachal Pradesh, India. Purnima has published several papers on resort destination in research journals and international conference proceedings.

Megan Cleaver Sellick was an Assistant Professor of Business Administration, at the College of Business, Central Washington University, in the USA. She died in July 2004, at the age of 29, after battling liver cancer and undergoing treatment in Gold Coast, Australia. Her research on the travel consumption of seniors and ageing Baby Boomers has been published in the *Journal of Travel and Tourism Marketing, the Journal of Vacation Marketing*, the *Journal of Sustainable Tourism*, the *Journal of Hospitality and Tourism Research* and *Social Indicators Research*.

Geoffrey I. Crouch is Professor of Marketing in the School of Business, La Trobe University, Melbourne, Australia. He specializes in tourism marketing with particular interests in destination marketing and competitiveness, tourist choice modelling, tourism psychology and consumer behaviour, and space tourism. He is co-author of *The Competitive Destination* and co-editor-in-chief of the journal, *Tourism Analysis*. Geoffrey is also currently Treasurer of the International Academy for the Study of Tourism.

David A. Fennell is Professor at Brock University, St Catharines, Canada. His main area of research is ecotourism which he has explored for many years, primarily in the lesser developed regions of the world. David has undertaken research and conducted workshops in many countries. He is the author of *Ecotourism: an Introduction* (1999), *Ecotourism Programme Planning* (2002), and co-editor of *Ecotourism Policy and Planning* (2003). Fennell is the founding Editor-in-Chief of the *Journal of Ecotourism*, and is an active member on the editorial boards of other academic journals in tourism and leisure research. Most recently he has undertaken research on tourism ethics, with a new book, *Tourism Ethics*, on the horizon.

Harold Goodwin is Director of the International Centre for Responsible Tourism at the University of Greenwich, UK, and part of the Pro-Poor Tourism Partnership. He works on tourism and poverty reduction and recently completed a Department for International Development-funded project on tourism in The Gambia and co-chaired the 2002 Cape Town Conference on Responsible Tourism in Destinations. He is a co-founder of responsibletravel.com and the Responsible Tourism Partnership.

R.K. Headland is a polar historian and Archivist at the Scott Polar Research Institute. He has served with the British Antarctic Survey in the South, and Scott Polar Research Institute in the North. He has lectured on many scores of cruises to the Antarctic and Arctic, has led tourists to the South Pole, and was taken prisoner on the Argentine invasion of South Georgia in April 1982.

Samuel Seongseop Kim is Assistant Professor of Hospitality and Tourism Management, Sejong University, Korea. Trained at Texas A&M University, USA, he has published about 25 papers in international research journals. His research interests include impacts of tourism, marketing and tourism resources development. He is on the editorial board of *Journal of Travel and Tourism Marketing*.

Jennifer Laing is a Ph.D. scholar looking at the motivations behind frontier travellers. Jennifer has presented papers on space tourism at several conferences, and is co-author of a paper on space tourism at the 'Tourism: State of the Art II Conference' in Glasgow in 2004. She is a recipient of a scholarship from the Australian CRC for Sustainable Tourism.

Denise Landau is Executive Director of the International Association of Antarctica Tourism (IAATO), and has a variety of experience in the tourism industry for more than 20 years. She manages the activities of some 50 member companies of IAATO, compiles environmental impact assessments and coordinates documents required for visits to Antarctica. She also represents IAATO as a delegate to the Antarctic Treaty Consultative Meetings and, time permitting, teaches skiing in Colorado.

John Lennon is Professor and Chair at the Moffat Centre for Travel and Tourism Business Development, Glasgow Caledonian University, Scotland. The Moffat Centre (1998) is responsible for the production of national and international consumer and market research and business development consultancy. John has extensive experience within the tourism and hospitality industries and has undertaken tourism and travel projects in Fiji, the USA,

Egypt, Nepal, Romania, Poland, Germany, Czech Republic, Singapore, Ireland, Russia and the UK. Author of six textbooks and over 50 articles on the travel and tourism industry, his best known titles are *Dark Tourism* with M. Foley (2000), *Current Trends in International Tourism Statistics* (2001) and *Museums and Galleries: Alternative Approaches to Funding and Revenue Generation* with M. Graham and I. Baxter (2001).

Thomas E. Muller is the Distinguished Professor of Consumer Psychology, at Hagoromo University of International Studies, in Osaka, Japan and Adjunct Professor and Foundation Chair in Marketing, at Griffith University, in Australia. The author/co-author of 80 published articles in scientific journals and books, he has travelled in 63 countries – and on all seven continents – and is fluent in six languages. He is currently writing two books, one on visits to Antarctica by senior tourists, the other on sustainable tourism at remote coral reefs.

Bruce Prideaux is Professor of Marketing and Tourism Management at the Cairns campus of James Cook University, in Queensland, Australia. He has published widely in the tourism field particularly in the areas of tourism transport and destination development. He is currently undertaking research into destination development, the mechanisms for diffusing research findings and co-edits a number of special issues of international journals including *Tourism Recreation Research*.

Dilys Roe is Senior Research Associate at the International Institute for Environment and Development in London and part of the Pro-Poor Tourism Partnership. In addition to work on pro-poor tourism, current research interests include the role of government in establishing an appropriate policy and institutional framework for sustainable tourism, the potential of company–community partnerships in the tourism industry and the impacts of tourism certification schemes.

Peter Schofield is Senior Lecturer and consultant in the Management Research Institute at the University of Salford, where he teaches quantitative and qualitative research methodology and tourism marketing. His research and consultancy interests include visitor decision-making and behaviour, urban and cultural heritage tourism management, service quality management and tourism impacts.

A.V. Seaton is Whitbread Professor of Tourism at the University of Luton, UK. He has published over a dozen books including the recent title (with G. Dann) *Slavery, Contested Heritage and Thanatourism* (2002); and about 100 research papers in tourism journals. Seaton has lectured, researched and consulted in over 30 countries. His main research interests are: tourism marketing and behaviour, tourism history, book town tourism and dark tourism.

Shalini Singh is Associate Professor (Tourism) at Brock University, St Catharines, Canada. She is Executive Editor of *Tourism Recreation Research*, India. Her research interests focus on and around Himalayan tourism, policy and planning (India), education, community and volunteer tourism. She has authored/co-authored/edited several books, with the most recent publication being *Tourism in Destination Communities* (2003). Singh also serves on the editorial board of *Tourism Management* (UK), *Tourism Development Journal* (India).

Tej Vir Singh is Professor and Director, Centre for Tourism Research and Development, Lucknow, India. Singh is founding Editor-in-Chief of the Centre's research journal *Tourism Recreation Research* that won the Emerald Golden Page Award 2003, UK. He has published over two dozen books on tourism and related themes. He was Senior Research Fellow Ford Foundation, ICIMOD, Kathmandu (1987–88); consults for several world organizations in tourism including UNEP, Rockefeller Foundation, National Geographic Society (Washington, DC). He chairs the India Chapter of Asia Pacific Tourism Association (Korea). Singh is member-emeritus of the International Academy for the Study of Tourism and was awarded a Lifetime Honorary Professorship in Tourism and Hospitality by the Bundelkhand University, Jhansi, India in 2002.

Trevor Sofield, is Professor and Inaugural Chair, Tourism Programme, University of Tasmania, and Tasmania Coordinator, Australian Cooperative Research Centre for Sustainable Tourism. He is on the Board of Management of CIRET, France; Director, Board of Australian Tourism Research Institute; Australian National Representative, APTA. Sofield has published several important books on tourism; his most recent publication is *Empowerment for Sustainable Tourism Development* (2003)

John Splettstoesser is a geologist with field experience in Antarctica that began in 1960, and was employed at three major US universities for 25 years. He also lectures on tour vessels to both polar regions, totalling some 100 cruises to Antarctica and 35 to the Arctic. John has edited five books on polar

subjects and guest-edited *Antarctic Tourism* (with Valene Smith), a special issue of *Annals of Tourism Research* (1994). He has been an Advisor to the International Association of Antarctica Tour Operators since its founding in 1991, and has two geographic features (a glacier and a mountain) named for him in Antarctica.

Dallen J. Timothy is Associate Professor at Arizona State University, USA, and Visiting Professor of Heritage Tourism at the University of Sunderland, UK. His work in tourism focuses on heritage, consumption, borderlands, developing world issues, supranationalism, and collaborative development. His most recent books include *Heritage Tourism* (2002), *Shopping Tourism, Retailing and Leisure* (2003) and *Tourism, Diasporas and Space* (2003).

Preface

This book is an attempt to capture the multi-faceted nature of tourism in all its wide-ranging experiences and activities, which are often amazing and bizarre. Much tourism revolves around novelty-seeking; and modern technology has made it talismanic for the tourist to seek out the white virginity of the polar regions, to fly into space, and to discover the exoticism of the 'other'. Tourism today offers a strange world of experiences that needs to be studied thoroughly. This volume presents a few out-of-the-ordinary instances of peripheries overtaken by tourism and the experiences they offer. It is often difficult, and perhaps too early, to record what happens when tourism finds access to such unparalleled and unspoilt ecospheres of beauty. In any case, impact assessment was not within the purview of this project; none the less, the thought that tourism often defiles such supernal environments did re-echo in the mind, crying out for some convincing answers.

The book, therefore, is also about the good (though uncommon) practices in tourism that give it a fair name – that tourism results in expansion of the mind and adventure of the soul; it promotes peace and amity in this strife-torn world; it is an exercise in deontology to conserve the resources; an environmental pilgrimage; and can also work for the benefit of the poor and destitute. No longer mere rhetoric, these dynamic concepts are considered the green shoots of recovery that promise revival of the lost art of travel. This book, I hope, will help to nurture these ideas and encourage their development.

It was a joy to gather together such themes for this project, although it was indeed challenging to select the right authors; still more difficult was to convince the publisher of the marketability of a title that carried such poetic and dreamy overtones – so different from the run of the mill. I am glad that this dream has come true, opening 'new horizons' for serious scholars to work upon and to establish new realities on themes such as *space tourism*, *volunteer tourism*, *pro-poor tourism*, *deep ecotourism*, *dark tourism*, *senior tourism* and many other similar themes that have emerged in the post-modern era. These topics have been little explored in research journals, and book chapters dealing with them have appeared only occasionally and sporadically. The idea for this book took its inspiration from these publications to organize an anthology where the reader may have easy 'one-stop' access to these ideas. I feel that this is one more important reason for a book like this to exist. I am sure that scholars of tourism will have a better grasp of what the idea of 'new horizons' entails after reading this book, as most of the contributors have spent years exploring the theme and can rightfully claim great expertise in the subject. If *New*

Horizons goes down well with the tourism print market, I should also thank Ralf Buckley, who suggested this title while I was seeking 'new skies'.

Tej Vir Singh
Centre for Tourism Research and
Development
Lucknow, India

Acknowledgements

I acknowledge the cooperation, help and expertise received on this book from many people from all over the world. To name them individually would not be possible, though I wish I could, but the list is too large for the space available. Certainly, I owe much to all the contributors, who agreed to participate in this project despite their other commitments. I particularly appreciate their timeliness in meeting deadlines. Many of the authors gave freely of their expertise to assess various chapters of this volume. Valene Smith, G.J. Ashworth and John Splettstoesser, in particular, acted as referees for more than one chapter – my special thanks to them. I am no less grateful to the other referees, who willingly cooperated in reviewing the other chapters. My thanks go to Frances Brown (UK), William Richter (USA), Joan Henderson (Singapore), Tony Seaton (UK), Ross Dowling (Australia), David Fennell (Canada), Melanie Smith (UK), Carl Jenkins (UK), Michael Leitner (USA), Philip Pearce (Australia), Alastair Morrison (USA), Sue Broad (Australia), Stephen Wearing (Australia), Nancy McGehee (USA), John Fletcher (UK), Erik Cohen (Israel) and Michael Hall (New Zealand).

I also thank my colleagues at the Centre for Tourism Research and Development, who were of constant assistance, despite the pressures of their day to-day routine. Shalini Singh and Sagar Singh helped me in the development of the project with fruitful discussions on the theme, leading to the selection of this title. Masood A. Naqvi and Prachi Rastogi dealt efficiently with the computer work and final assemblage of the material as it flooded in from all corners of the world. I appreciate their lively spirit and enthusiasm for this project of the Centre.

Rebecca Stubbs of CAB International has been of immense help, from the beginning of the proposal of this project to its completion. I appreciate her exemplary professionalism.

Tej Vir Singh

1 Tourism Searching for New Horizons: an Overview

Tej Vir Singh

*Centre for Tourism Research and Development,
A-965/6 Indira Nagar, Lucknow – 226016, India*

I am a part of all that I have met;
Yet all experience is an arch wherethrough
Gleams that untravelled world, whose margin
  fades
For ever and for ever when I move.

Alfred Lord Tennyson: *Ulysses*

The Ulyssean spirit of wanderlust seems to have seized today's tourists, who seek novel experiences and dream of impossible destinations offering strange practices in unusual habitats. With modern science and advanced technologies at hand, it is no more a mirage to chase the stars and sleep beneath the glacier, or to walk in space. All this may sound like a tale from the *Arabian Nights*; but it is happening. Incredible as it may seem, an American businessman, Dennis Tito, became the first paying space tourist when he travelled on board the Russian Soyuz vehicle for a visit to the International Space Station in April 2001. Jules has offered another life-changing experience by constructing his 'Undersea Lodge' at the bottom of the Emerald Lagoon in Key Largo, Florida, where guests must scuba-dive to reach their underwater accommodation. The unique Sheraton Wild Horse Pass Resort and Spa in Phoenix, Arizona, is a collaboration between the Sheraton Group and the Maricopa and Pima tribes from the Gila River Indian Reservation, which offers an experience of Pima and Maricopa culture in

an authentic setting. There is a growing appetite for the extreme and unusual environments that the industry is offering to tourists who are interested in bizarre experiences.

Theme hotels are also growing in number, particularly in the developed world. Examples include Coober Pedy ('opal capital of the world') in Australia, The Nordic Inn Medieval Brew and Bed in Crosby, Minnesota, and the Library Hotel in New York City, which all have some unique experiences to offer. Bolivia has the Salar de Uyuni Hotel, made of salt, and there are ice hotels in several countries. Many resorts offer self-improvement programmes for fitness freaks. Centres in Tucson, Reno, Baja California and Anguilla are successfully operating life assessment management programmes (WTO, 2001). Kerala in India and some Himalayan resorts have developed holistic health centres, where they offer 'yoga tourism'. Even more strange things are happening in tourism that combine to make it a many-splendoured phenomenon. Helber (1988: 21) indicates trends towards 'experience-oriented holidays' with the emphasis on action, adventure, fantasy, nostalgia and exotic experiences. The more sanguine travellers of today, as Frew (1989) observes, no longer want to spend their time sunbathing beside a five-star hotel pool, but seek out new and unforgettable experiences that will become part of them; something curiously unusual to be told by the fireside when they are back at home. In fact, these memories are their precious travellers' mementos. Mindless hedonism and pleasure-seeking are no longer fashionable; contemporary tourists choose to use their leisure time quite differently. Changing socio-economic patterns have given rise to new patterns in holiday-taking, drawing from an expanding range of interests (Holloway, 1985: 39). Ousby (1990: 5) remarks that patterns of travel are related to movements in tastes generally. Weiler and Hall (1992: 4) consider that 'special-interest tourism' is characterized by the tourist's search for novel, authentic and quality experiences.

Since novelty can soon wear off (Bello and Etzel, 1985: 26), there is a constant need to find more exotic customs, cultures and peoples 'especially when they are remote in both time and space' (Wang, 2000: 115). Novelty does not exist at home but is always found elsewhere. Cohen (1995: 23) comments that

> the distance is of sociological as well as spatial significance, and it implies exposure to the strangeness of an unaccustomed environment along with the experience of novelty and change for the tourist. It is a search for 'something-out-thereness.'
> (Dann, 2002: 66)

To celebrate the 'difference' in people and places (MacCannell, 1976), tourism has to search for new horizons of experiences that are bizarre and pregnant with curiosity. Thus, a destination that desires repeat business from novelty-seekers must continuously adjust in order to offer some new opportunities for novel experiences (Bello and Etzel, 1985: 26). Curiosity and exploration have much in common, in that both relate to what Aristotle calls the 'desire to see' those things that our mundane everyday lives and boring domesticity cannot offer.

The Lure of the Pleasure Peripheries

Western tourists in search of novel experiences look for remote Utopian places – the Himalayan Shangri-las, the pyramids of Egypt, the buried cities of the Incas and the fantasy world of Eden (Rousseau and Porter,

1990) – to be discovered beyond their shores, possibly in the distant East. The 'primitivism' and 'strangeness' of these places are hard to resist and the travellers set forth to discover these pleasure-domes and lands of enchantment.

> The Western attraction to the exoticism of the East has been fundamental to the formulation of many tourism packages, commencing with those to Egypt of Thomas Cook.
> (Boniface and Flower, 1993: 39)

'Orientalism', with all its promise of exotic, sensuous and erotic delights (Said, 1991), attracted multitudes of visitors to the developing societies that hailed tourism with great euphoria, but this honeymoon period did not last long. Tourism, in its conquest of new peripheries, has left many 'tourist-cores' behind.

Prosser (1994) explains how, in the early 1950s, most tourism spread out globally from the tourist growth-poles existing in Western Europe and the eastern USA as a 'tidal wave of pleasure periphery'. He identified five peripheral regions of the world that tourism overtook 'for novelty, uniqueness and exclusivity of experience'. Prosser believes that it was a perpetually enthusiastic search,

> encouraged by the tourism industry, which derives the pleasure periphery rippling outwards over time from tourist-generating regions to envelop ever new destinations.
> (1994: 24)

His spatio-temporal model of tourism spreading out might sound somewhat descriptive, but it is a fact that modern tourism had firmly established its mighty presence in the developing and less-developed regions of Asia, Africa and Latin America by the 1980s and had started spreading its tentacles into the remote and forbidden lands of the Arctic and Antarctica to seek new domains of touristic experiences. Society Expeditions' (1990) invitation to its 'World Discovery' holiday is worth savouring, as it sounds so enticing to take a joyride into the utopia of exoticism, where a tourist would enter into an authentic 'novelty zone'.

> (T)he great explorers ventured from the familiar to lands that were little more than whispered

tales and outlines on a map. The adventure is continued today on Society Expeditions' 1990 voyages to Antarctica, the Arctic, South America, the South Pacific, Indonesia and Australia . . . it will take you far away from the beaten track, one like all great discoveries, you won't just pass by, but will land and explore destinations that most people miss.

(Society Expeditions, 1990)

The Rise of Mass Tourism

All too many people were to be attracted to these hitherto less travelled or untravelled land-scapes of beauty, leaving them scarred and even ruined, consuming their uniqueness. 'Man kills the things he loves', was never more true than this tragedy of mass tourism.

Mass tourism as a worldwide phenomenon has had tremendous sway in changing the atti-tudes of the host societies, particularly of peripheral regions of extreme marginality and vulnerability. The tribal ethnic groups of the 'Fourth World' (Graburn, 1976) have been largely the victims of modern tourism. Tourism impact – socio-economic, ecological and polit-ical – has been extensively recorded in the tourism literature (see Boorstin, 1964; Noronha, 1979; Cohen, 1978, 1995, 2003; Mathieson and Wall, 1982; Singh, 1989). Cohen (1995) provides a comprehensive cri-tique of the changing nature of tourist attrac-tions and places noting their 'shift from the natural to the artificial and contrived, besides related changes in tastes and preferences of tourists in different societies'. Tourists differ as do societies.

The momentous issue raised in the sociol-ogy of tourism – 'authenticity of experience' (MacCannell, 1973, 1976; Cohen, 1989, 2003; Pearce and Moscardo, 1986; Turner and Manning, 1988) – warrants a brief com-ment here, as it is quite relevant in the context of the curiosity that goes with the tourist expe-rience. MacCannell (1973) believes that modern Western tourists are on a quest for the 'exotic other', the authentic, which they seek to experience vicariously as the hosts 'stage them-selves' to meet the expectations of the guests. This lure of consumption eventually leads to the commoditization not only of tangible objects but also of intangible services, activities and

experiences. As Graburn quips: 'Tourism is a form of commoditization of experience' (1983: 27). Fairclough further elaborates:

The commodity has expanded from being tangible "good" to include all sorts of intangibles: educational courses, holidays, health insurances, and funerals are bought and sold on the open market in packages, rather like soap providers.

(1989: 35)

The true purpose of travel (to experience otherness) is often defeated because the prod-uct is fake or adulterated. Boorstin (1964) con-demns mass tourism as a 'collection of pseudo-events', where a packaged tour pro-vides only 'insulated experience' from con-trived attractions. Tourists, perhaps for this reason, are moving away from 'tinsel and junk' (Poon, 1989: 75) to the search for more real, natural and authentic experiences, although Wang (2000: 76) laments that even Nature is no more a masterpiece of God. Cohen's post-tourists are more pragmatic in their search for the 'real' and 'original', as they hold that authenticity, like the primitive, has largely van-ished from the contemporary and post-modern world, and hence it is fruitless to go looking for it (2003: 6). Boorstin (1964) in his chapter 'From traveller to tourist: the lost art of travel' considers mass tourism as the decline of the traveller and rise of the tourist (1964: 84–85); the former has a high taste and the latter a low taste in travel (Rojek, 1993), to the extent that tourism is often denigrated as 'vulgar'. Barrett argues that 'tourist' is the worst kind of insult (1990: 3).

The New Wave Tourism

While conventional tourism served as an opiate to the 'masses', the 'classes' were disillusioned with its severe negative consequences. This dis-quietude in society was responsible for the emergence of what Wheeler (1992) calls the new wave tourism. New forms of tourism appeared as a result of a

wide variety of economic, socio-cultural and environmental factors that showed a structural economic shift from Fordist to post-Fordist

mode of production accompanied by cultural shifts characterized as moving from modernism to post-modernism.
(Mowforth and Munt, 1998: 320)

Since the concept was considered as an alternative to mainstream mass tourism, it was given the umbrella term, 'alternative tourism'. Although it refuses to be contained in definitional boundaries, this term was particularly fashionable during the 1970s and 1980s (Cazes, 2000: 20). Alternative tourism (AT) now overflows into various somewhat synonymous names, such as responsible tourism, authentic, green, integrated, adventure, ethnic, and nature-based tourism – the list is constantly growing. Indeed, all these terms mean different things to different people according to the role they have within the activity. Ecotourism, another form of alternative tourism, had better resonance, with a wide range of usage in praxis and parlance.

The quintessential attributes of these new forms of tourism were, briefly, smallness in size and scale, low impact on environments leading to resource sustainability, conservation, equity, empowerment and local control. To many scholars of tourism, it was the foundation for 'R.E.A.L. tourism' as it was to be a *rewarding, enriching, adventuresome* and *learning* experience (Read, 1980: 202). To Cohen it was 'Counter-cultural Alternative Tourism that attempts to invert the values, motives, attitudes and practices associated with conventional mass tourism' (1989: 271). Weaver (1998: 31) simplistically observes that it was a 'shift in focus from the well-being of the tourist industry to the well-being of the host community'. Both MacCannell (1976) and Cohen (1979, 1985) refer to post-modern travellers as 'experimental' and 'experiential' tourists.

These new forms of tourism ushered in an era of abandonment, bringing back the true spirit of the traveller, and holidays moved beyond sheer relaxation and indulgence towards the opportunity to 'study', 'learn' and 'experience' the world. 'To strive, to seek, to find and not to yield' seems to be the motto of these post-tourists. Disgusted with those aspects of modern living that appeared to be materialistic, empty, stale, meaningless and culturally unfulfilling, characterized by ennui and

boredom, these tourists searched for existential realities, to be discovered in the realm of Nature that still had retained some 'bliss of solitude'. This wanderlust grew insatiably, much like Cohen's 'drifter' (1987) or Plog's (1987) 'allo-centric'. The tourist sought in Nature what was sublime and beautiful, savage and sombre – climbed mountain summits, trekked into remote cultures, encountered 'First Peoples', relished their organic food, enjoyed their archaic lifestyle, and shared their traditional knowledge. Ecotourism, the new avatar of AT, made all this possible within its travel framework. This was perhaps the best thing that had happened to tourism as an experience and activity. Thus, people started moving to 'undisturbed' and 'uncontaminated' natural areas, softly and cautiously for the specific objectives of 'studying', 'admiring' and 'enjoying' the biophysical and cultural diversity of this planet (Ceballos-Lascuráin, 1996). What had been regarded as a forbidden resource for tomorrow, as being too good for tourism, was now within the reach of an average tourist.

The concept was delightful as it was subtle and hard to practise because it implied a 'scientific', 'aesthetic' and 'philosophical' approach to travel. Besides building a perfect green management system at the local level, it demanded 'dedicated' and 'hardcore' ecotourists (Lindberg, 1991: 3), who should be immersed in Nature and all that it stands for. The movement has gathered momentum worldwide with a fair degree of success, particularly in national parks and protected areas of the south, but was not without problems. Ecology is a science of conservation where everything is related to everything else. The good will come out when 'eco-development' philosophy is practised in its true essence. Certainly tourism has widened its horizons as ecotourism embraces other subtypes of AT such as adventure, nature and culture tourism (Fennell, 2002: 13). Fennell's ACE (adventure, culture and ecotourism) conceptual framework finds support in Graburn's (1989) earlier work where he argued that nature tourism and cultural tourism are not mutually exclusive. Given all the controversy raging around the practice of ecotourism, it is now considered as an appropriate technique for sustainable development that has respect for environment and resource parsimony and, perhaps for this reason, multinational hotel chains are gradually adopting these green strategies the world over (Green Horizon Travel, 1995). The much berated mass tourism can now be given a better face. Weaver argues that ecotourism, AT and sustainable tourism may be interpreted as inter-related manifestations of a much larger trend, evident within the tourism industry and, indeed, within society as a whole (1998: 29–30).

Couched firmly in the philosophy of conservation ethics, ecotourism development, particularly in the Third World societies, asks for effective empirical research into the dynamics of 'ecosystems' (both natural and human) for achieving sustainability. Too much of the 'touristification' that inevitably goes with the growth of a destination, meddles with natural systems, resulting in erosion of resources and consequently the impairment of experience.

Lafant and Graburn hold that AT

> expresses the concept of a 'New Order Tourism' as it is a force aimed at social change. It signifies quality, respectability and responsibility.
>
> (1992: 90–91)

Proponents of New Tourism hope that the ugly experiences associated with mass tourism, especially in developing societies; such as 'dehumanization', 'subjugation' and 'servility', will be overcome. This promise may not prove a social therapy or panacea for all these experiences, but it is true that tourism mills are busy inventing new activities, trends and innovative experiences to meet the ever-changing tastes of the tourists. To this scenario may be added emerging global forces of change such as environmentalism, diversification within a homogeneous world, evolution of a knowledge-based society, demographic shifts, massive advances in technology, shifting value systems, and change from a 'service' to an 'experience' economy (Goeldner et al., 2000). Hall (2000), in his PEST (political, economic, social, technology) analysis, projects possible future trends that point to new horizons in tourism, with quite a few of them being practised now.

Demand for such peak consumers is growing and is likely to grow, especially from knowledge-based economies, as travellers from these countries are more 'experienced, discerning and demanding' in individualized experiences. Such travellers, according to Forbes and Forbes (1992), are more interested in enriching their lives with experiences than being passive consumers of entertainment. They seek interactive, highly involved quality experiences, focusing on special interest destinations. Providers of such special services have to be highly knowledgeable, imaginative and innovative entrepreneurs.

Dramatic advances in technologies, especially in areas of transport and information, have made such iconic experiences possible. Inter-planetary space travel is no longer an unattainable dream while electronically simulated travel experience is a 'virtual reality'. Travellers with the spirit of serendipity can discover amazing earth features and wondrous wildlife in forbidden polar regions; they dive with killer whales in dark icy seas; experience timeless cultures preserved in some unknown mountain cave. For that fascination with the macabre, they trip out on death; visit war-zones for first-hand experience in destruction; indulge in altruistic pursuits to redress ailing humanity; and espouse the cause of deep ecotourism for greening the industry. The list of such strange experiences and stranger practices is endless. This brave new world has so much to offer.

New Horizons: Experiences, Trends and Practices

This volume is an effort to document some of these new trends, experiences and practices that make it such an interesting study within the framework of the tourism industry. The core hypothesis behind this project is that old tourism, largely based on 'sea, sun and sand' shall, in future, experience a marked shift to exotic and bizarre practices in unusual habitats. Amazing tourism developments are already happening all over the planet which need to be thoroughly studied and gathered together for easy reference. Out of the myriad unusual experiences and novel trends that are happening within the industry, only illustrative themes have been included for examination. No effort has been made to study them from the marketing standpoint, nor have the demand and

supply sides been focused on, due to many constraints, especially data crisis in these fields of
enquiry. Episodic and sporadic as they are in
nature, it will take some time to attract the
attention of serious scholars.

This book, in five parts, illustrates the
tremendous outreach of tourism in search of
extraordinary and spectacular experiences,
both 'bright' and 'dark'. Practices in tourism
that aim to correct the harm previously done to
the destination locations and societies in the
name of 'conventionalism', popularly known as
mass tourism, and the humanization process
which is often neglected in the lure of consumerism, are also examined.

Part 1, 'The Edge of Tourism', has four
interesting themes. Geoffrey Crouch and
Jennifer Laing (Chapter 2) discuss space as the
ultimate frontier experience for the 21st century, combining danger, thrills and romance.
Vacationing in space is already a reality. Dennis
Tito did it in 2001, Mark Shuttleworth followed
a year later. Currently a tourist can visit only
the International Space Station (ISS), about
400 km above the Earth, at the prohibitive cost
of US$20 million. At present, accommodation
is spartan but functional. The authors report
that in the near future a wheel-shaped space
hotel would have features such as a casino,
restaurant and a cinema. Visitors will be able to
play basketball or tennis, view the Earth and
stars, and go for spacewalks. More dramatic
experiences are in store as the century wears
on.

John Splettstoesser, Denise Landau and
R.K. Headland (Chapter 3) explore the forbidden Antarctica that now 'remains as one of the
most attainable destinations for tourists' and at
a reasonable cost to the client depending upon
objective and duration of itinerary. They inform
us that the continent is still incompletely
explored, particularly its ice-sheet interior and
the ice–rock interface, where lakes have been
discovered by radar. Most tourists visit only
those coastal areas that are accessible by ship,
where wildlife and scenery are abundant. Since
its discovery, Antarctica has been much
explored and trekked. Although dedicated to
science and research, tourism is not forbidden
and, in some respects, is even tolerated as a
commercial enterprise, as long as the rules of
entry are followed, particularly those that

involve environmental practices and conservation. John (with his co-authors) is a superb sto-
ryteller who reveals interesting facts about the
continent through juicy anecdotes to satisfy the
curiosity and excitement of travellers.

Ralf Buckley (Chapter 4) dwells on the cutting edge of tourism and moves into remote
areas and high places for an exploration of
high-risk commercial adventures. Adventurism
is not new, but these activities are now performed with the help of highly skilled professionals. The essential features of so-called
'extreme adventure tourism' are remote and
relatively inaccessible areas, high individual skill
requirements and significant individual risk. He
remarks: 'no guts, no glory'. This chapter
examines what the extreme adventure sector
does, how it has risen in popularity and how it
is linked to individual outdoor recreation, luxury
expedition tourism and remote-area backpacker travel.

Tourism in quest of the unique has often
made serious inroads into the precious natural,
cultural heritage of the destination. As access to
beauty is made easier, the splendid environments fall into decay. This has happened in the
Himalayan Kulu Valley, where a sequestered
hermit village, Malana, which has jealously preserved its 'little culture' over the centuries, has
been taken over by those seeking novelty.
Considered to be the oldest living republic in
the world, Malana is famous for its monadic
existence, having its own systems of law-
making, administration and policing; local tri-
bunals, strange language, and quaint rituals all
combine to make it an object of curiosity. T.V.
Singh, Purnima Chauhan and Shalini Singh
(Chapter 5) describe how an isolated mountain
community has fallen into a tourist trap and lost
its distinctive uniqueness. The authors suggest
some remedial measures for the conservation
of heritage and development of indigenous
tourism.

Novelty is not all about bright and beautiful things; the dark, dismal and disturbing can
also arouse tourist curiosity. **Part 2** deals with
'The Macabre in Tourism'. Chapters 6, 7 and
8 are devoted to this theme.

A.V. Seaton and John Lennon (Chapter 6)
examine the phenomenon of 'thanatourism'
and travel associated with death, and suggest
why it is likely to become a more significant

force in the third millennium. This chapter explores the diverse motivations behind thanatourism and the ways in which it can evolve spontaneously without the activation of tourism entrepreneurs. The authors argue that the motivation for thanatourism is ill-understood and contentious. Motives, however, are discussed from religious, social and anthropological perspectives. The chapter discusses issues and dilemmas posed by thanatourism sites to public administrators besides ideological and ethical problems that produce tension. Focusing on the future, the authors look at the nexus of circumstances that are likely to expand thanatourism as an industry and as a tourist practice.

Dallen Timothy, Bruce Prideaux and S.S. Seop-Kim (Chapter 7) take up war zones and demilitarized boundaries (ceasefire lines) by drawing their material from Bosnia Herzegovina and demilitarized boundaries on the Korean peninsula and in Cyprus. Bosnia, despite the lingering effects of war, still attracts what they call 'war tourists'. Similarly, wars in Cyprus and Korea have not officially ended but the demarcated ceasefire lines are important tourist attractions. The authors discuss the dynamics of tourism to these types of war-related places and the relationship between war and tourism.

G.J. Ashworth (Chapter 8) deals with the management of atrocity heritage sites for tourism. The chapter takes into account the nature of the product, the nature of the demand for it, and finally the management. He argues that atrocity heritage contains many intrinsic elements that 'inspire curiosity for being unique, unusual, and out-of-the-ordinary and mundane'. However, the management of these sites is riddled with difficulties because of the multiple uses of the site, of which tourism is only one, as well as the problem of the emotions evoked by such sites, which impose constraints and responsibilities on their management for tourism. Two cases are used for illustration; non-site or event-specific monumental commemoration (Jewish holocaust monuments, slavery and the Atlantic slave trade), the management of specific sacralized sites and spaces of atrocity from the recent or more distant past.

Much has been said against conventional forms of tourism and the good that AT augurs,

particularly ecotourism which has a healing influence on the habitat and the communities that are involved in the tourism industry. **Part 3** has three chapters (9, 10, 11) which expand on 'The Unconventional in Tourism'. David Fennell (Chapter 9) examines some of the crucial issues involved in the practice of 'deep ecotourism' and expounds on theoretical and practical reverence, responsible for a sound and sustainable industry. The chapter includes a discussion of the role and relationships between different actors (government, industry, tourists and communities) as well as contrast between hard and soft path-forms of ecotourism. Underlying this inspiring discussion is the belief that researchers and decision makers have failed to incorporate a values- and ethics-based approach in ecotourism and thus have floundered in their attempt to maximize ecotourism potential as a model of sustainable tourism development.

Trevor Sofield (Chapter 10) attempts to demonstrate how subtly and ingeniously structured ecotourism practices can bring about desirable results even in highly sensitive and fragile ecosystems. He presents the Tasmanian wilderness experience in two contrasting locations; the mountainous inland wilderness of Cradle Mountain Lake, St Clair National Park, and the rugged coastal wilderness of the Bay of Fires. This unique experiment is designed, structured, operated and managed by a noted architect, Ken Latona. The experience that has been created in these two locations is, *par excellence*, where 'one touch of Nature makes the whole world kin'.

Peter Schofield presents an interesting experience in health tourism (Chapter 11) offered by Soviet salt-mine holidays in the Kyrgyz Republic (Kyrgyzstan). This resort attracts tourists from far and wide for health cures. The Soviet Salt World is situated approximately 5 km away from Chon Tuz in Naryn Oblast where salt is extracted from the lower of the two levels. The upper, a 1-km tunnel, has been creatively re-used for health tourism because of its bronchial healing properties. One can stay at the Salt World resort for 16 days for a price of US$180.00. Visitors acclimatize for the first 2 days in the disused mines. The rest of the time is spent in underground mine chambers decorated with archaeological remains of bears, camels and birds. Other facilities include table tennis, cable television, a library and disco-bar. The author hopes that such innovative trends in tourism will help promote development in a backward region.

Tourism has often been charged with being an elite activity that caters only for the younger and richer members of society, and that it is a 'last-resort-industry' for the developing and the less developed nations of the world. **Part 4** attempts to dispel some of these criticisms and has three chapters devoted to 'poverty tourism': 'Tourism for the Poor, the Old and Humankind'. Dilys Roe, Harold Goodwin and Caroline Ashley (Chapter 12) plead for pro-poor tourism (PPT), an approach that generates net benefits for poor people. This development approach attempts to enhance the linkages between tourism business and poor people in order to increase tourism's contribution to poverty reduction. According to the authors, PPT can involve any type of concern – a small lodge, an urban hotel, a tour operator, an infrastructure developer and links with many different types of people such as staff, neighbouring communities, landholders, producers of food, fuel and other suppliers, operators of microtourism businesses as well as other users of tourism infrastructure and resources. The chapter reviews the effectiveness of nine strategies developed for pro-poor tourism and presents six case studies from the developing societies to demonstrate that although PPT may have limited impact at the national level, at the local level its interventions can be invaluable. The authors believe that if opportunities for the poor could be opened up in all places where tourism is significant in the South, millions of people could benefit from an industry which currently tends to take more than it gives.

The world population is rapidly aging, particularly in the Western nations, and many developed nations in the East, such as Japan. By 2025 the elderly will represent a very significant proportion of a nation's entire population. These nations have a steadily growing proportion of people who are leading longer, healthier and more productive lives than was the case in the past. The ageing of travellers from traditional tourism-generating countries will lead to a demand for new experiences

and new facilities. Megan Cleaver Sellick and Thomas Muller address these challenges and opportunities in Chapter 13, and establish some useful findings based on their empirical researches into the senior market. Contrary to popular thinking, the senior tourist group is far from homogeneous and hence the infrastructure and facilities will be differently tailored to meet their needs. The chapter offers insight on how underlying travel motives, personal value orientations and the concept of self-perceived age or self-identification can reveal unique segments within the senior tourism market for new tourism product development, destination positioning and branding.

Stemming out of eco-vision have emerged more sustainable tourism practices in the name of 'volunteerism' which embody in them the true spirit of travel – a kind of journey in personal discovery and caring for humanity. Volunteer tourism is a new travel phenomenon, introduced by a range of institutions such as Earthwatch, WWF, 'One World Travel', and 'Community Aid Abroad', who play an active role in promoting this kind of experience through sponsoring youthful volunteers to the Third World, whose serious leisure focuses on conservation projects and community development, besides encouraging support at a local level. Shalini Singh and T.V. Singh (Chapter 14) discuss the emergence of volunteer tourism in the remote Himalayan regions of India. Two case studies: Kanda in Uttaranchal and the Ananda Project in the Kulu Valley (Himachal Pradesh) have been reported. The authors believe that such projects will benefit the laggard areas socio-economically and provide growth impulses for further development, as well as promoting fellow feeling and brotherhood among the guest and host communities.

Part 5 is devoted to 'The Future': Julio Aramberri speculates on the shape of things to come. 'The future is a different world' as Prideaux crisply observes, 'where today is tomorrow's yesterday' (2002: 319). Taking a cue from Dean MacCannell, the author argues that the expansion of the Internet and easy access to information on tourist attractions will eventually limit our curiosity for remote destinations to the virtual world. In future, he suspects, people will be happy visiting developed

Internet sites, forgetting about the actual world. Overtaken by this element of uncertainty, Julio soliloquizes much like Shakespeare's Hamlet: 'Will Travel Vanish?' He embarks on a long discourse on the 'to-be and not-to-be' state of mind and finally concludes that cyber-travel will be a poor substitute for 'real travel', as physical travel satisfies another human need – the need for distinction. Future travel might be reserved for couch potatoes in terms of knowledge but there may still be reason to leave the couch, 'out-performing the Joneses'. Voyeurs of the cyberworld would certainly go for sex tourism. Some survey reports confirm that sex sites have become the most popular use of the Internet. Julio discusses this hot issue further and hopefully concludes that the untimely demise of actual travel has been highly exaggerated; none the less one has to look for new horizons in tourism – maybe somewhere on the Moon or Mars!

References

Barrett, F. (1990) The independent guide to real holidays abroad. *Independent*, London.

Bello, D.C. and Etzel, M.J. (1985) The role of novelty in the pleasure travel experience. *Journal of Travel Research* 24(1), 20–26.

Boniface, P. and Flower, P.J. (1993) *Heritage and Tourism in the Global Village*. Routledge, London.

Boorstin, D. (1964) *The Image: a Guide to Pseudo-Events in America*. Harper and Row, New York.

Cazes, G. (2000) Alternative tourism. In: Jafari, J. (ed.) *Encyclopedia of Tourism*. Routledge, London, pp. 20–21.

Ceballos-Lascuráin, H. (1996) *Tourism, Ecotourism and Protected Areas*. IUCN, Gland, Switzerland.

Cohen, E. (1978) The impact of tourism on the physical environment. *Annals of Tourism Research* 5(2), 215–237.

Cohen, E. (1979) Rethinking the sociology of tourism. *Annals of Tourism Research* 6(1), 18–35.

Cohen, E. (1985) Tourism as play. *Religion* 15, 291–304.

Cohen, E. (1987) Alternative tourism: a critique. *Tourism Recreation Research* 12(2), 13–18.

Cohen, E. (1989) Primitive and remote hill tribe trekking in Thailand. *Annals of Tourism Research* 16(1), 30–61.

Cohen, E. (1995) Contemporary tourism: trends and challenges. In: Butler, R. and Pearce, D. (eds) *Change in Tourism: People, Places and Processes*. Routledge, London, pp. 12–29.

Cohen, E. (2003) Contemporary tourism and the host community in less developed areas. *Tourism Recreation Research* 28(1), 1–10.

Fairclough, N. (1989) *Language and Power*. Longman, London.

Fennell, D.A. (2002) *Ecotourism Programme Planning*. CAB International, Wallingford, UK.

Forbes, R.J. and Forbes, M.S. (1992) Special interest travel. *World Travel and Tourism Review*, Vol. 2. CAB International, Wallingford, UK.

Frew, W. (1989) On the trail of adventure travel. *Australian Financial Review*, May 17.

Goeldner, R.G., Ritchie, J.R.B. and McIntosh, R.W. (2000) *Tourism: Principles, Practices, Philosophies*, 8th edn. John Wiley and Sons, New York.

Graburn, N.H.H. (1976) Introduction: the art of the Fourth World. In: Graburn, N.H.H. (ed.) *Ethnic and Tourist Arts*. University of California Press, Berkeley.

Graburn, N.H.H. (1983) The anthropology of tourism. *Annals of Tourism Research* 10(1), 9–33.

Graburn, N.H.H. (1989) Tourism: the sacred journey. In: Smith, V.L. (ed.) *Hosts and Guests: The Anthropology of Tourism* 2nd edn. University of Pennsylvania Press, Philadelphia, pp. 21–36.

Green Horizon Travel (1995) *Holidays That do Not Cost the Earth*. Information pack. Green Horizon Travel.

Hall, C.M. (2000) The future tourism: a personal speculation. *Tourism Recreation Research* 25(1), 85–95.

Helber, L.E. (1988) The roles of government in planning in tourism with special regard for the cultural and environmental impact of tourism. In: McSwan, D. (ed.) *The Roles of Government in the Development of Tourism as an Economic Resource*. Seminar Series No.1, Centre for Studies in Travel and Tourism, James Cook University, Australia.

Holloway, J.C. (1985) *The Business of Tourism*. Pitman, London.

Lafant, M.F. and Graburn, N.H.H. (1992) International tourism reconsidered: the principle of the alternative. In: Smith, V. and Edington, W.R. (eds) *Tourism Alternatives: Potential and Problems in the Development of Tourism*. University of Pennsylvania, Philadelphia, USA.

Lindberg, K. (1991) *Policies for Maximizing Nature Tourism's Ecological and Economic Benefits*. World Resource Institute, Washington, DC.

MacCannell, D. (1973) Staged authenticity: arrangement of social spaces in tourist settings. *American Journal of Sociology* 79(3), 589–603.

MacCannell, D. (1976) *The Tourist: a New Theory of the Leisure Class*. Macmillan, London.

Mathieson, A. and Wall, G. (1982) *Tourism: Economic, Physical and Social Impacts*. Longman, London.

Mowforth, M. and Munt, I. (1998) *Tourism and Sustainability: New Tourism in the Third World*. Routledge, London.

Noronha, R. (1979) Paradise reviewed: tourism in Bali. In: deKadt, E. (ed.) *Tourism: Passport to Development*. Oxford University Press, Oxford.

Ousby, I. (1990) *The Englishman's England: Taste Travel and the Rise of Tourism*. Cambridge University Press, Cambridge.

Pearce, P. and Moscardo, G. (1986) The concept of authenticity in tourist experiences. *Australia and New Zealand Journal of Sociology* 22(1), 121–132.

Plog, S. (1987) Understanding psychographics in tourism research. In: Ritchie, J.R.B. and Goeldner, C.R. (eds) *Travel, Tourism and Hospitality Research: a Handbook for Managers and Researchers*. John Wiley and Sons, New York, pp. 203–213.

Poon, A. (1989) Competitive strategies for a "new tourism". In: Cooper, C. (ed.) *Progress in Tourism, Recreation and Hospitality Management,* Vol.1. Belhaven, London.

Prideaux, B. (2002) The cybertourist. In: Dann, G.M.S. (ed.) *The Tourist as a Metaphor of the Social World*. CAB International, Wallingford, UK.

Prosser, R. (1994) Societal change and growth of alternative tourism. In: Cater, E. and Lowman,

G. (eds) *Ecotourism: a Sustainable Option?* John Wiley and Sons, Chichester, UK, pp.19–35.

Read, S.E. (1980) A prime force in expansion of tourism in the next decade: special interest travel. In: Hawkins, D.E., Shafer, E.L. and Rovelstad, J.M. (eds) *Tourism Marketing and Management Issues*. George Washington University, Washington, DC, pp. 193–202.

Rojek, C. (1993) *Ways of Escape: Modern Transformations in Leisure and Travel*. Macmillan, London.

Rousseau, G.S. and Porter, R. (1990) Introduction. In: Rousseau, G.S. and Porter, R. (eds) *Exoticism in the Enlightenment*. Manchester University Press, Manchester, UK.

Said, E. (1991) *Orientalism*. Penguin, London.

Singh, T.V. (1989) *The Kulu Valley: Impact of Tourism Development in the Mountain Areas*. Himalayan Books, New Delhi, India.

Society Expeditions (1990) *Invitation to a World of Discovery*. World, London

Turner, C. and Manning, P. (1988) Placing authenticity – on being a tourist: a reply to Pearce and Moscardo. *Australia and New Zealand Journal of Sociology* 24(1), 136–139.

Wang, N. (2000) *Tourism and Modernity: a Sociological Analysis*. Elsevier Science, Oxford.

Weaver, D.B. (1998) *Ecotourism in the Less Developed World*. CAB International, Wallingford, UK.

Weiler, B. and Hall, C.M. (1992) Introduction. In: Weiler, B. and Hall, C.M. (eds) *Special Interest Tourism*. Belhaven, London, pp.1–14.

Wheeler, B. (1992) *Eco or Ego Tourism: New Wave Tourism – a Short Critique*. Insight, English Tourist Board, UK.

WTO (2001) *Newsletter No. 2*. WTO, Madrid.

2 Vacationing in Space: Tourism Seeks 'New Skies'

Jennifer Laing and Geoffrey I. Crouch

*School of Business, Faculty of Law and Management,
La Trobe University, Melbourne, Victoria 3086, Australia*

It was paradise. I just came back from paradise.
Dennis Tito, first space tourist (Tyler, 2001)

Space is the ultimate frontier experience for the 21st-century tourist, combining danger, thrills, novelty, romance and social cachet, as well as spiritual and personal fulfilment. People have dreamed about visiting space throughout the millennia, but until recently it was purely in the realm of the science-fiction novel or movie, or reserved for the professional astronaut or cosmonaut.

The early pioneers of space travel spent days and sometimes weeks in space. Missions then were highly structured and task-driven, as are most Space Shuttle flights today, but there was still time for the astronauts to gaze around and appreciate the stark beauty that is space. Astronaut Al Bean wrote of viewing the tiny Earth from space as 'a wondrous moment' (Bean, 1998), while Buzz Aldrin – the second man to walk on the Moon and a present-day proponent of space tourism – similarly referred to the 'magnificent desolation' of the lunar surface (Aldrin and Warga, 1973).

The next challenge was to see how long human beings could survive in space. Sending people to live on space stations for 3–14 months at a time has taught us to deal with problems such as isolation or physiological changes, although further research is needed before we can safely cope with longer journeys, such as a mission to Mars. These people were, and are, living in space for the purposes of work rather than play, but their experiences and the lessons learned from them have paved the way for the future space tourist.

The Space Tourism Market

Space tourism can be said to have had its genesis in April 2001, with American millionaire Dennis Tito's visit to the International Space Station (ISS), an orbiting laboratory, on a Russian Soyuz spacecraft (Crouch, 2001b). Non-astronauts had previously flown in space, such as a Japanese journalist on the Russian Space Station *Mir* in 1989, but Tito was the first to pay his own 'fare' and travel for pleasure. He was followed a year later by South African Internet millionaire Mark Shuttleworth. No longer was space purely the domain of the career astronaut or scientist, although it did come with a reputed price tag of US$20 million per flight (Crouch, 2001a).

While Tito was labelled the world's first 'space tourist', Earth-based space tourism is well-entrenched, and orbital travel by the average citizen has been anticipated for years (Goodrich, 1987; Ashford, 1990). While the popular image of 'space tourism' generally encompasses human beings flying to and perhaps staying for short periods of time in space, it can in fact be defined more broadly. The space tourism market can be broken down into the following categories (after Crouch and Louviere, 2001):

* Virtual
* Terrestrial
* Near-space
* Sub-orbital
* Low-orbital/high-orbital.

There is a paucity of academic literature on space tourism in general, let alone examining these potential market segments. Thorough and rigorous research is required to examine the level of current market activity, as well as estimating future market demand (Crouch, 2001a).

Virtual space tourism

Not all space tourism experiences planned for the future will require an active participant. Some will utilize the latest technology to give tourists the sense of visiting space without leaving the comfort of their armchairs. 'Virtual reality' has been put forward as 'a logical progression in the use of technology in tourism' (Cheong, 1995) and a possible alternative to going into space for those who either can't afford or who fear the orbital space tourism experience (Pearce et al., 2000). It could be used as a way to stimulate interest in or market space flight to a wider audience, by making the experience 'come alive' for the general public. Virtual reality could also be seen as the ultimate 'staged experience' for the tourist (MacCannell, 1999), or an example of Eco's (1986) 'travels in hyper-reality'.

LunaCorp[1] in the USA is looking at using virtual reality for commercial and tourism purposes when it plans to send its Icebreaker Moon Rover vehicle to the Moon (LunaCorp, 2003). The idea is that 'tourists' would watch the Rover's progress on the Moon live on the Internet, on television networks and at science centres. Additional vehicles are subsequently planned for a 'Grand Apollo Tour' of historic lunar landing sites. There is a possibility that future Earth-bound tourists may watch the journeys of those in space via web-cams or cameras mounted on a helmet. People would be given a 'bird's-eye view' of a trip into space through the helmet, so that the observer has the sensation of seeing what the 'tourist' would see.

Virtual reality, apart from its potential advantages of increasing accessibility for those who otherwise couldn't afford to pay the price of a trip to space and as a method of marketing future spaceflight opportunities, also promotes sustainability, as a way of limiting the impact on the fragile space environment and the amount of fuel used to take people into space. The same type of technology has been mooted for the site of the Titanic, 12,000 feet (3658 m) below the sea, with lights and high-definition digital and video cameras enabling people to watch the wreck through a computer and view it up close from a variety of angles (Handwerk, 2002).

Terrestrial space tourism

Terrestrial space tourism incorporates space camps, theme parks and other activities where members of the public can enjoy a space-related experience without actually leaving the Earth's surface. Examples include visits to Cape Canaveral in Florida to view rocket and Space Shuttle launches, and the National Air and Space Museum at the Smithsonian in Washington, DC, to see exhibits such as the Apollo 11 command module and the suit that astronaut John Glenn wore in 1962 when he became the first American to orbit the Earth. Tourists visiting Space Center Houston at NASA's Johnson Space Center can observe the activities of Mission Control, where flights of the Shuttle and ISS missions are coordinated, and see mock-ups of the Space Station modules used for astronaut training (Fig. 2.1). In Australia, space enthusiasts can visit a permanent space exhibit at the Powerhouse Museum in Sydney, watch the Parkes Radio Telescope observing the heavens, as shown in the recent movie The Dish (2000) or enjoy a show on stars and the Milky Way at a local planetarium.

Private companies such as Space Adventures and Incredible Adventures are pro-

Fig. 2.1. *Saturn V* rocket at Johnson Space Center, Houston, Texas (photo by Jennifer Laing).

viding a variety of terrestrial space tourism activities or packages, sometimes in conjunction with a space industry partner. Space Adventures,[2] while taking bookings for future sub-orbital flights, have developed their own land-based space and space training 'adventures' which incorporate the use of training and flight simulators, Russian parabolic flights to experience short periods of weightlessness, and visits to launches. Other programmes they have promoted over the past few years include a science expedition to the Antarctic in January 2002 to recover lunar and Martian meteorites, led by Apollo astronaut and geologist Dr Harrison Schmitt, and a tour of the Australian Outback in December 2002, guided by a former astronaut, to observe a total eclipse. Space Adventures also helped to broker the flight of the second space tourist, Mark Shuttleworth. Incredible Adventures[3] are taking reservations for their 'Space Cruiser' vehicle, which they hope will fly tourists into space in several years time. Meanwhile, their suite of space tourism programmes provides individuals with the opportunity to undertake cosmonaut training in Russia's Star City.

Space camps are an example of space tourism experiences particularly directed at young people. For example, SPACE CAMP[4] has been operating in Alabama, USA, since 1982 and offers a 5-day programme with activ-

ities such as simulated Space Shuttle missions, large-format IMAX movies, training simulators, scientific experiments, and talks about space exploration – past, present and future.

Near-space tourism

Near-space experiences include flights that permit a person to experience short periods of weightlessness, or very high-altitude supersonic 'joy rides' and sightseeing trips. For some time now, the Russians have been taking tourists on microgravity ('zero-g') flights aboard the Ilyushin-76 cosmonaut training aircraft. Tourists can also take a flight in a high-performance jet like the MiG. It flies to about 82,000 feet (25 km), nearly three times the altitude of Mt Everest. A trip in the MiG-25 'Foxbat' is advertised as allowing the tourist to see a horizon stretching 715 miles (1151 km) across, while flying at Mach 2.5 (1 mile every 2 seconds).

Sub-orbital space tourism

This category of space tourism is not yet a reality, but is the most active in terms of the variety of concepts on the drawing board. This tourist does not attain orbit, only reaching an altitude sufficient for them to see the curvature of the Earth and the blackness of space for a brief period. They may also be able to enjoy a minute or two of weightlessness. The whole experience may only last about 15 minutes from launch to landing. At this stage, space tourists like Tito and Shuttleworth are flying to the ISS, necessitating a longer-duration flight.

New forms of transportation, which are efficient, reliable and reusable, will be required, as well as enough paying tourists to cover the high initial R&D costs (Aldrin, 2001). Technological challenges are, however,

> the least of the problems confronting space tourism entrepreneurs . . . the most difficult problem remains not in design and implementation, but in raising needed investment funds.
>
> (Simberg, 2000)

The ability to build a sustainable industry is therefore dependent on the establishment of market demand for space tourism (Crouch, 2001a; Crouch and Louviere, 2001). There is also the possibility that the X-Prize (see section on Industry Overview) will encourage private sector investment and innovation, which will in turn help to foster this form of space tourism.

Low-orbital and high-orbital experiences

This category, the most costly form of space tourism activity, as well as potentially the riskiest, covers actual orbital experiences lasting anywhere from a day, to several days, weeks or even longer. Currently it would include accompanying 'official' crews on missions, or a residential stay in a Space Station, as Tito and Shuttleworth did. In the future, it might include holidays on specially built orbiting hotels, or visits to a permanent tourist facility or resort on the Moon or Mars.

The Hilton Hotels Group disclosed a few years ago that they were looking into the feasibility of constructing a space hotel, perhaps 15–20 years down the track (*Florida Today*, 1999), while Virgin Atlantic Airways has considered a long-range plan which includes the development of a hotel on the Moon as a destination for Virgin Galactic Airways, a future fleet of space-liners (Kiger, 2001). While some

of these ideas may never become actuality, they are indicative of the innovativeness, determination, and entrepreneurial and technical talent being applied to these endeavours.

Industry Overview

The failure of the Space Shuttle *Columbia* during re-entry to the Earth's atmosphere in February 2003, leading to the tragic loss of seven astronauts' lives, did not appear to have signalled the end of most forms of space tourism. It highlighted the risks of space travel, which tend to be overlooked by the public in the face of seemingly routine space flights, but in fact might be a motivating factor for future space tourists. Media coverage and the speech of the President of the USA immediately after the tragedy also demonstrate the high level of goodwill which exists both politically and socially for the continuation of space exploration and space activities in general. The Russian space agency initially suspended tourist flights to the ISS, as the Shuttle has been grounded until late 2004. Russian Soyuz seats have been needed to ferry rotations of the ISS crew, although there are plans to take another space tourist to the ISS in 2005. Other events over the past few years have increased the likelihood that a space tourism industry beyond terrestrial bounds will develop, albeit possibly in the long term.

NASA appears to have overcome its reluctance to allow space tourists to visit the ISS, following the widely publicized controversy over Dennis Tito's visit. The Russian and American space agencies entered into an agreement to allow future space tourists to the Space Station, which involved setting guidelines for the selection of space tourists (*SpaceRef*, 2002). People could be disqualified from consideration if they abuse alcohol or drugs, have indulged in dishonest, criminal or 'notoriously disgraceful' conduct, or belong to organizations that reflect poorly on partner nations in the ISS project. They must also meet the agreed-upon medical criteria, including medical aspects of behavioural assessments. Several further prospective space tourists commenced training for a flight, among them guitarist Lance Bass and former NASA administrator Lori Garver, although their

Fig. 2.2. The *Thunderbird* spacecraft; Starchaser Industries' entry for the X-Prize.

flight opportunities were ultimately quashed due to a failure to raise the necessary funds via sponsorship. Other high-profile individuals who have indicated an interest in space travel include James Cameron, the *Titanic* director.

Space tourism conferences and workshops are now held on a regular basis and organizations and associations throughout the world, such as the Space Tourism Society[5] and Space Frontier Foundation[6], actively support and lobby for development of the industry. Media coverage on the topic has increased since the flight of Tito, and there appears to be a corresponding growth in general public interest in space tourism.

The private sector appears to be slowly laying the groundwork for a future space tourism industry. Kinki Nippon Tourist, one of Japan's largest travel agencies, has set up a branch to develop and market space travel (*Space Daily*, 2001). They state that they would like to offer a variety of experiences, from a 10-minute sub-orbital flight to a week in orbit staying at a space hotel. A number of private organizations are also developing commercial vehicles which are designed to transport tourists into space. Examples include Bristol Spaceplanes from the UK with their Ascender vehicle; the USA's Kelly Space and Technology with their Astroliner launch vehicle; the Russian Cosmopolis XXI Aerospace System (C-21), a next-generation spacecraft

specifically designed for sub-orbital space tourist flights in conjunction with Space Adventures; and the Thunderbird spacecraft being developed by the UK aerospace company Starchaser Industries.

Over 20 teams around the world have registered in the lucrative X-Prize,[7] a competition run by a private foundation in the USA to stimulate competition in space tourism. The X-Prize of US$10 million will be awarded to the first non-government organization which can fly three people into space and back (defined as 100 km up) and repeat the feat within a period of 2 weeks. Starchaser Industries, whose *Thunderbird* spacecraft (Fig. 2.2) is one of the entrants for the X-Prize, sees winning the Prize as a catalyst for developing a long-term sustainable space tourism business (*ABC Online*, 2002). Other front-runners include Scaled Composites with its airborne launcher, the *White Knight*, and space ship, *SpaceShip One* (Fig. 2.3); Pioneer Rocketplane with the *Pioneer XP*; Kelly Space and Technology with the LB-X spacecraft; Bristol Spaceplanes; and the Canadian Arrow team. A similar prize, known as the Orteig Prize, was awarded to Charles Lindbergh in 1927 for being the first man to fly solo from New York to Paris in the *Spirit of St Louis*, which aimed at fostering a fledgling aviation industry. In a neat twist, Lindbergh's grandson is vice-president of the X-Prize foundation (David, 2002).

Fig. 2.3. View of Scaled Composites' *White Knight,* intended to be used to provide a high-altitude airborne launch of their manned sub-orbital spacecraft, *SpaceShip One* (courtesy: Scaled Composites).

Historical and Cultural Background to Space Tourism

Human beings have long dreamt of travelling in space, which now has a special place within popular culture (Wessels and Collins, 1989; *Florida Today*, 1997; Kozinets, 2001). Even as far back as AD 160, the Greek satirist, Lucian of Samosata, wrote *Vera Historia* (*True History*), which includes the story of Icaromenippus, who seeks to fly to the Moon using a wing from an eagle and another from a vulture; a variation on the Greek myth of Icarus. Space travel was a popular subject for 19th-century literature such as Jules Verne's *From the Earth to the Moon* (1865), which spawned a play, *A Trip to the Moon* (1877) and 'pulp fiction' such as *Six Weeks in the Moon* and *The Rocket; or Adventures in the Air*, both of which sold widely (Burrows, 1998). Verne's novel tells the tale of young man, Michel Ardan, who persuades the 'Gun Club', a fictitious group of artillery enthusiasts, to fire him and his crew to the Moon from a massive cannon. It gripped the public imagination, as did Martian-themed popular novels such as H.G. Wells' *War of the Worlds* (1898) and Edgar Rice Burroughs' *A Princess of Mars* (1912). Much of this interest was fanned by the work of Percival Lowell, who set out to prove that lines or grooves viewed on the surface of Mars from the telescopes of the 19th-century astronomer Giovanni Schiaparelli were in fact canals filled with water, built by intelligent life on Mars in a desperate attempt to stave off the effects of drought. The search for life on Mars continues to this day (Walter, 1999).

The post-WWII years

left the American public with an almost insatiable desire for space-related science fiction. In countless movies and stories space warriors suited with fish bowl helmets focused their ray guns on creatures from outer space.
(Wright, 1993)

The *Collier's* magazine series of illustrated articles on space, featuring rocket scientist Wernher Von Braun's vision for the US space programme, including space stations and a mission to Mars, hit a circulation of 4 million. Von Braun later served as adviser to Walt Disney, who produced several space-related movies in the early days of television, to promote 'Tomorrowland', a section of the Disneyland theme park.

When the Russian cosmonaut Yuri Gagarin became the first man to fly in space in 1961, human space flight was no longer confined to the realms of fiction or media fantasy. In 1969, Neil Armstrong set foot on the surface of the Moon and millions around the world watched him do this; vicariously experiencing space travel from their lounge-rooms and workplaces via the television coverage.

In the late 20th century, television programmes such as *Lost in Space* (1965–1968) and *Star Trek* (1966–), films such as *Star Wars* (1977) and even cartoons like *The Jetsons* (1962–1987) were built around our human desire to venture beyond the Earth's surface and, in the words of *Star Trek: the Next Generation*, 'to boldly go where no one has gone before'. The 1969 film *2001: a Space Odyssey*, based on an Arthur C. Clarke science-fiction novel, showed people staying in orbiting 'hotels', which they reached and departed from in modified Pan Am space 'jets'. When the first Space Stations were built in the 1970s, such as *Skylab* and *Salyut*, fantasy became fact. The impact of these movies and literature as an inducement to travel in space could be a fruitful area of research (Riley *et al.*, 1998; Busby and Klug, 2001).

Modern space-related science fiction such as *Red Mars* (1993) and *The Martian Race* (2000) is created around characters who are almost entirely career scientists, astronauts or cosmonauts, rather than the curious amateur of Verne's and Wells' novels. This emphasis on space being the natural domain of the professional rather than 'Joe Average' may perhaps be traced back to the 'cult' of the astronaut in the late 1950s and 1960s, the impact of which is traced in Tom Wolfe's *The Right Stuff* (1979). Selection of the first astronauts in 1959 saw the men treated like heroes by the public, even before they had left the ground. Wolfe explains how these former test pilots reached their exalted status; as the 'elite who had the capacity to bring tears to men's eyes', resulting in the phrase 'the right stuff' becoming a household word and a myth inextricably linked with the space traveller. It will be interesting to see whether opening up space to the public ultimately affects the enduring power of this myth and makes space travel a less attractive and desirable pursuit in the minds of some people.

The Space Tourism Experience

Tito has spoken of his space flight as

> the greatest experience of my life . . . It's hard even with words to explain the euphoria that took place in space.
>
> (*ABC News*, 2001)

The emphasis on the 'experiential' nature of the activity may place space tourism within the growing number of 'extraordinary' hedonic experiences that are attracting attention from tourism researchers (Arnould and Price, 1993; Celsi *et al.*, 1993). The former astronaut Charles D. Walker observes:

> Really what I want to say is that space . . . is a place. But it is not only a place, it is an experience. And it is an all-encompassing physical and psychological experience. And that has to be borne in mind when we talk about passengers, tourism in space, when we talk about a large, widespread representation of humanity taking that opportunity to leave the Earth's surface.
>
> (David *et al.*, 1987)

Motivations of space tourists, both actual and potential, to undertake space flight, and their perceptions of experience once in flight, have yet to be studied in depth. Risks associated with space travel have long been acknowledged (Smith, 2000; Berinstein, 2002) and riskiness as a motivation for tourism, particularly in the adventure tourism context, has been the subject of much research (Celsi *et al.*, 1993; Shoham *et al.*, 1998; Jones *et al.*, 2000). Other motivating factors might be the drive to be 'first' (Smith, 2000), novelty (Bello and Etzel, 1985) or prestige (Riley, 1995).

The nature of the space tourism experience also has not been fully explored, and research might consider the relationship with 'flow' (Csikszentmihalyi, 1975, 1990) or 'edgework' (Lyng, 1990). Flow or 'optimal experience' (Csikszentmihalyi, 1975) refers to the 'complete involvement of the actor with his activity', where the skills possessed by the participant and the challenges posed by the activity are balanced, ultimately leading to intense enjoyment and pleasure. Flow can be an important element in the 'adventure tourism' experience (Celsi *et al.*, 1993; Jones *et al.*, 2000; Ryan, 1997; Gnoth *et al.*, 2000). Lyng's study of 'edgeworkers' looked at voluntary risk-taking behaviour such as taking part in high-risk sports, using the term coined by the author Hunter S. Thompson for those engaging in

> anarchic human experiences . . . Activities that can be subsumed under the edgework concept have one central feature in common: they all involve a clearly observable threat to one's physical or mental well-being or one's sense of an ordered existence.

The 'edgework' construct has also been applied to tourism activities (Arnould and Price, 1993; Celsi *et al.*, 1993).

Sacred Space: Space Tourist or Pilgrim?

One possible motivation behind space tourism may be to find a spiritual dimension or self-actualization in the activity. Yiannakis and Gibson (1992) characterize these tourists as 'seekers', described as individuals 'who through travel, seek to learn more about themselves, and ultimately, the meaning of existence'.

MacCannell (1976, 1999) argues that all tourists are essentially pilgrims, in that they seek 'authentic' experiences. While some have disagreed with his premise (Cohen, 1979; Selwyn, 1996), the parallels between tourists and pilgrims are undeniable (Graburn, 1989; Shackley, 2001; Smith, 1992). Throughout history, people have taken part in pilgrimages to sacred places, to find spiritual enlightenment (Graburn, 1989) or to liberate themselves from 'profane social structures . . . The point of it all is to get out, go forth, to a far holy place approved by all' (Turner and Turner, 1978). Modern equivalents of the religious pilgrimage include some forms of movie-induced tourism (Busby and Klug, 2001) and even adventure tourism.

> The new forms of adventure tourism establish new tourist paths, movements to new places, new spaces, where all roads lead to some kind of shrine (the Sacred Way).
>
> (Zurick, 1995)

Space is acknowledged as a spiritual or sacred place (Belk *et al.*, 1989), perhaps in part because of its associations with 'the heavens', but also because of its extraordinary beauty and unique cultural associations. When talking about his feelings in space, space tourist Dennis Tito was open about the sacred nature of his journey. 'From a spiritual standpoint,' he says, 'it was like I died and went to heaven' (*ABC News*, 2001). When told by a journalist (Clash, 2001) that space sounds like 'heaven', he noted,

> In fact, that's how I've described it. Religious art depicts angels with little wings that could never lift their weight. I see that as the weightlessness. Then the earth is below, because in heaven you're above earth.

Future research may seek to explore this spiritual side of the space tourism experience.

Preparing for Space Travel

Part of the attraction of space tourism also may lie in the extensive pre-training or 'anticipatory' phase (Clawson and Knetsch, 1966; Fridgen, 1984). Tourist behaviour during this phase has been addressed widely in the tourism psychology literature (Berno, 1999), but not with respect to the space tourism experience.

Dennis Tito, for example, spent 9 months training in Russia's Star City, but was still considered to be 'undertrained' by NASA, who attempted to stop his flight to the ISS in part on that basis (*SpaceRef*, 2001). Mark Shuttleworth was also required to train at Star City and NASA's Johnson Space Centre over a period of 8 months, and has described the process as initially 'frightening' (Unsworth, 2002) but ultimately rewarding. The training involved Russian language, MiG-25 and MiG-29 high-altitude supersonic jet flights, survival training, zero-gravity testing, extensive medical exams and Soyuz simulator training. Shuttleworth, like Tito, passed the full cosmonaut board medical certification for space flight. Potential space tourists will need to factor in the lengthy pre-training phase into the cost of the flight.

The Space Hotel

Tourists wishing to visit a permanent facility in space have been limited so far to visiting the ISS, about 400 km above Earth. They travelled there by Russian Soyuz spacecraft, with a total habitable volume of 10 m^3, and accommodation on the ISS was spartan but functional, as befits a working space station rather than a 'space hotel'. This type of 'vacation' is likely to change radically in the future, if current plans take shape.

Concepts being considered include the building of reusable spacecraft to take large numbers to a space hotel, which would then be made to spin, creating artificial gravity. This would prevent some of the physiological changes associated with periods in microgravity. The California-based Space Island Group wants to use empty Space Shuttle fuel tanks to build a wheel-shaped orbiting hotel similar to the space Hilton depicted in the film *2001: a Space Odyssey*. These hotels could contain features such as a casino, restaurants, viewing area and movie theatre, while rooms in a non-rotating central section would enable guests to try out weightlessness. Hand-rails and supports will help novice space travellers move around in those sections without artificial gravity.

Resistance to the harmful effects of space debris will need to be an integral part of new space hotel designs, as will shielding against space radiation for long-term guests and staff.

The high cost of transporting materials into space has led to inflatable modules being mooted for accommodation in space, which could be transported in a compressed state and inflated when they reach their intended location. Shimizu, a Japanese construction firm, spent US$3 million in 1997 developing plans for lunar condominiums and envisages transporting four-storey inflatable buildings to the Moon, then anchoring them on the surface (Kiger, 2001). NASA has been working on a concept for inflatable modules for the ISS, known as TransHab (Laing, 2000). The inflated volume of TransHab is comparable to a 1500 ft^2 (139.35 m^2) home, and is extremely durable, with its layers said to provide greater protection against space debris than metal does.

Problems Associated with the Space Tourism Experience

Those paying high prices for space travel should not expect the luxury of a typical cruise ship or resort hotel. The early space hotels are likely to be sparsely furnished and utilitarian, due to the high cost of transporting construction materials into space. Apart from the basic facilities, privacy will be an important issue in space flight and space holidays. Spacecraft are notoriously cramped, as will be the accommodation at any space hotel, unless inflatable modules can help boost the volume available. There may, however, be ways to minimize the feeling of confinement in space in the design elements (Wichman, 2002).

Life in space can have its downsides, many of them stemming from the existence of zero gravity. Examples include:

> . . . difficulty going to the bathroom, separating your urine from your faeces [for recycling purposes] and having to drink everything through a straw. [You have] to be very careful about what you eat. You mustn't have things that can come off and go drifting away.
> (Wichman, 2002)

Many people experience space sickness (space adaptation syndrome) in the first few days of flight, with nausea and sometimes vomiting and diarrhoea. This is thought to be due to disorientation when the fluid and small bones in the inner ear do not detect the pull of gravity, such as is experienced on Earth. The Share Space Foundation estimate that 60–70% of first-time space travellers will have space sickness for the first 24–36 hours they spend in space, which has implications for short-duration flights of a couple of days or less (Berinstein, 2002).

Longer duration stays in space, of a month or more, may result in more serious physiological changes. A reduction in bone mass after a long time in space mainly affects the bones which take the load of the body's weight on Earth, such as the heels, legs, pelvis and spine. This loss of bone density increases the likelihood of fractures, while release of calcium from the bones into the bloodstream leads to a greater risk of kidney-stone formation ('renal stones'). There appears to be a link between loss of bone mass and fluid shifts in the body in space. These fluid shifts can also have adverse effects on the human cardiovascular system. Aside from anaemia and reduced cardiac mass, astronauts returning home after long flights may experience problems in standing upright (known as 'orthostatic intolerance') and it can take them days to return to their pre-flight exercise capability. Problems with the muscular system include deterioration of tendons and ligaments and wasting away or 'atrophying' of muscles. Coordination problems may persist for weeks when back on Earth.

Exercise, using a treadmill or exercise bike, is one method being used to reduce the severity of this physiological de-conditioning among long-duration space travellers, as is the use of drugs. However, more research is needed, and these countermeasures are not totally successful based on current knowledge and techniques. The majority of the problems associated with zero gravity could be minimized or eradicated by the use of artificial gravity in spacecraft and space hotels. This, however, could destroy many of the 'unique' characteristics of being in space for potential tourists. A solution might be to have a special area set aside for experiencing weightlessness.

Activities in Space

Typical tourist activities in space are likely to be variations of popular terrestrial pursuits, but in an unparalleled and astonishing setting. For example, taking photographs in space may be popular, if professional astronauts and the early space tourists are any guide.

> Now when tourists start going places, of course one of the first things you do is to take pictures of your mates. You take pictures of everybody that is on board the ship, or on board the airplane, or in the expedition, or on board the Space Shuttle . . . You have to take pictures of yourselves while you're there just so you can remember it, and put it in the photo album. Everybody will be taking pictures. This happens today; it has always happened. I think probably even [the] Mercury astronauts put the camera out in front of themselves and took a picture of themselves; there wasn't anybody there to hold the camera for them.
>
> (David *et al.*, 1987)

Before his flight, Dennis Tito, in an interview (Karash, 2001) spoke of his goals 'to photograph the Earth, [and] do a lot of photographs inside the station [ISS]', and took close to 1000 during his short stay in space.

The sheer joy of experiencing weightlessness may also be an attraction, leading to games in space like ball sports, using modified equipment and rules (Thornton and Collins, 2001). Viewing Earth and the stars from a prime vantage point with the assistance of guides, or carrying out spacewalks outside the hotel, wearing a spacesuit, could also be popular pursuits.

The question of sex in space is one that is often raised in the context of space tourism. 'What we've referred to as the romantic possibilities of zero gravity always comes up', says Executive Director of the Space Island Group, Gene Meyers (*ABC News*, 1999). Anecdotally, space travellers are believed to have tried it, although this has been denied by official channels (Interfax, 2001; Pesavento, 2000; Gallagher, 2000).

Researching the Market for Space Tourism

A number of preliminary studies have already been carried out in the space tourism field. For example, a joint NASA/Space Transportation Association (STA) survey (NASA/STA, 1998) asked 1500 US families whether they would be interested in Space Shuttle flights (34%) or travel aboard a space cruise vehicle with similar amenities and programmes to those provided on luxury cruise ships (42%). They found that 7.5% of respondents would be prepared to pay US$100,000 or more for these types of experiences. Rather than comparing space tourism facilities to those provided currently by 'ocean-going cruise ships', it might have been more illuminating to have asked whether these individuals would be prepared to pay this amount of money for relatively simple, basic accommodation, which is a more likely scenario with respect to the early space hotels.

In Japan, Collins *et al.* (1994a,b) examined the demand for space tourism, surveying 3030 people. They found that 80% of Japanese people under 60 years of age would like to go to space. This survey was then repeated by Collins *et al.* (1995) in the USA and Canada. Results of the survey showed that 61% of the population was interested in space tourism. Abitzsch (1996) used these results in comparison with the German market demand for space tourism, which was estimated at 43%.

Most recently, the Futron Corporation commissioned Zogby International to poll 450 wealthy Americans about their interest in space travel, and their willingness to pay for various space travel options. They also gathered data on lifestyle choices, spending patterns, and attitudes towards risk. The sample for the survey was limited to individuals who could potentially afford these high price excursions, selected from adults whose yearly incomes exceeded US$250,000 and/or whose net worth exceeded US$1 million (*SpaceDaily*, 2001). Results showed that 7% of those surveyed would pay US$20 million for a 2-week orbital flight, while 19% would pay US$100,000 for a 15-minute sub-orbital flight. Based on these findings, Futron has forecast that, by 2021:

- Over 15,000 passengers could be flying sub-orbitally annually, representing revenues in excess of US$700 million.
- Sixty passengers may be flying annually on an orbital flight, representing revenues

in excess of US$300 million (Futron Corporation, 2002).

This estimate is based on the fact that the 15,000 people interested in annual sub-orbital flights would be prepared to pay between US$25,000 and US$250,000 for a 15-minute trip, while the 60 people would pay from US$1 million to US$25 million per annum for a 2-week journey to a destination such as a Space Station (Carreau, 2002).

Futron also developed a public space travel forecast as part of a study they did for NASA Marshall Space Flight Center (Analysis of space concepts enabled by new transportation (ASCENT) study). They found that even assuming a cost of US$20 million per flight, and use of the Russian Soyuz spacecraft, in a scenario similar to the Tito and Shuttleworth flights,

> public space travel launches are a significant contributor to launch demand . . . [public space travel] is one of the few areas where growth can be predicted for the launch industry.
> (Futron Corporation, 2003)

These studies, and others like them, indicate a general interest in space tourism and a potential market, but there are many gaps. Extensive and rigorous research is required to establish the nature and size of this market.

Future Research Needs

We have yet to characterize the type of person who would be willing and able to go into space, and whether this varies across international boundaries, gender, age groups or levels of education or income. The industry needs to understand whether the accepted models of consumer behaviour apply to this new and emerging market. Rate of growth and competitiveness might be estimated by using other industries as analogues, such as the adventure tourism or early aviation industries.

The drivers of demand in the space tourism market need to be evaluated, and may include the price or cost of transportation, income levels, safety and perceived level of risk, the duration of the experience, or its unique qualities. Price is clearly a major consideration,

with both Tito and Shuttleworth said to have paid huge sums each for the 'ride of a lifetime'. Much of this research will revolve around surveying people as to their stated choices or preferences, given the low numbers who currently have direct experience of space tourism activities involving space flight. New research methods such as choice modelling could be used to obtain this information, allowing the researcher to build a scenario of a typical space tourism experience and ascertain the attributes that participants require for different cost structures, as well as the trade-offs that would be acceptable to them. This work would help to provide a platform for commercial investment in the space tourism industry.

Industry or Fad: What's on the Horizon for Space Tourism?

Recent marketing studies into space tourism have demonstrated some interest in space travel but have yet to establish the level of market demand required by commercial investors. The development of cheap, reliable transportation into space will also be required in order to make these activities economically viable. While the level of growth in space tourism is hard to predict, it seems very likely that it will become an important component of the tourism industry before the end of the century.

The current hiatus in space tourism activity, as a consequence of the *Columbia* disaster, may encourage the development of the next generation of reusable space vehicles and result in safer forms of transport in space. Other factors which may influence the sustainability of space tourism in the long term include the number of space 'accidents', whether there is a winner of the X-Prize, and the level of government and private sector support for space tourism. There will also be important regulatory issues to be considered.

> A myriad of legal and regulatory aspects of public space travel and tourism must be resolved before viable large scale businesses can emerge. This is especially true of those public agencies with the responsibility to regulate in the interest of public safety. This includes identification of public policies and/or

laws that exist or must be enacted to enable
business formation, licensing, certification and
approval processes for both passengers and
vehicles, clearance and over-flight
considerations, and environmental and safety
issues including atmospheric pollution, solar
radiation (flares) and orbital debris.

(NASA/STA, 1998)

Given, however, the predilection of the
post-modern tourist for novelty, the special
place that space has in popular culture and
public consciousness, and the trend towards
tourism in the 'unlikeliest of places' (Urry,
2002), it would seem that space travel is the
logical next 'hot' destination for the rich and
famous. Whether its reach extends beyond that
rarefied group remains to be seen, and the
time-frame for development appears likely to
span decades. Making space accessible to more
than just a fortunate few, or those with 'the
right stuff' is the way forward to a sustainable
future for space tourism, qualified by environmental concerns if the numbers escalate
beyond the level required to ensure that space
is not sullied. But, in doing so, will space lose
some or all of its mystery, appeal and 'sacred'
qualities?

Acknowledgements

The authors would like to acknowledge the support and assistance of Starchaser Industries for
research conducted in space tourism at La
Trobe University.

Notes

1. http://www.lunacorp.com   (accessed   30
September 2003).
2. http://www.spaceadventures.com (accessed 30
September 2003).
3. http://www.incredible-adventures.com/
(accessed 30 September 2003).
4. http://206.166.131/spacecamp/welcome.jsp
(accessed 30 September 2003).
5. http://www.spacetourismsociety.org   (accessed
30 September 2003).
6. http://www.space-frontier.org   (accessed   30
September 2003).
7. http://www.xprize.org (accessed 30 September
2003).

References

ABC News (1999) Hilton looks to space, September
    22, 1999. *ABCNews.com* website at http://
    abcnews.go.com / ABC2000 / abc2000travel /
    spacehotel_990922.html (accessed 30 Sep-
    tember 2003).
ABC News (2001) Mission accomplished: Dennis
    Tito shares views from space, May 17, 2001.
    ABCNews.com website at http://more.abc-
    news.go.com/sections/primetime/2020/prim
    etime_010517_dennistito_feature.html
    (accessed 30 September 2003).
ABC Online (2002) Woomera counts down to space
    prize, May 4, 2002. http://www.abc.net.au/
    news / scitech / 2002 / 05 / item 20020502
    140747_1.htm (accessed   30   September
    2003).
Abitzsch, S. (1996) Prospects of space tourism.
    Presented at the *9th European Aerospace
    Congress: Visions and Limits of Long-
    Term Aerospace Developments*, May 15,
    Berlin.
Aldrin, B. (2001) Space tourism and the evolution of
    rocket science: a symbiotic partnership in the
    making. In: *Proceedings of the 32nd Annual
    Conference of the International Travel and
    Tourism Research Association: A Tourism
    Odyssey*. Fort Myers, Florida.
Aldrin, E.E. and Warga, W. (1973) *Return to Earth*.
    Random House, New York.
Arnould, E. and Price, L (1993) River magic: extra-
    ordinary experience and the extended service
    encounter. *Journal of Consumer Research* 20
    (June), 24–45.
Ashford, D.M. (1990) Prospects for space tourism.
    Tourism Management 11(2), 99–104.
Bean, A. (1998) *Apollo: An Eyewitness Account by
    Astronaut/ Explorer/ Artist/ Moonwalker*.
    Greenwich   Workshop   Press,   Sheldon,
    Connecticut.
Belk, R.W., Wallendorf, M. and Sherry, J.M. (1989)
    The sacred and the profane in consumer behav-
    iour: theodicy on the odyssey. *Journal of
    Consumer Research* 16 (June), 1–38.
Bello, D.C. and Etzel, M. (1985) The role of novelty
    in the pleasure travel experience. *Journal of
    Travel Research* (Summer), 20–26.
Berinstein, P. (ed.) (2002) *Making Space Happen:
    Private Space Ventures and the Visionaries
    Behind Them*. Plexus Publishing, Medford,
    New Jersey.
Berno, T. (1999) Psychology of tourism. In: Earl, P.E.
    and Kemp, S. (eds) *The Elgar Companion
    to Consumer Research and Economic
    Psychology*.   Edward   Elgar   Publishing,
    Cheltenham, UK.

Burrows, W.E. (1998) *This New Ocean: The Story of the First Space Age*. Random House, New York.

Busby, G. and Klug, J. (2001) Movie-induced tourism: the challenge of measurement and other issues. *Journal of Vacation Marketing* 7(4), 316–332.

Carreau, M. (2002) 'Wealthy would fly in rocket for $25 million,' study says. *Houston Chronicle*, October 18, 2002. See http://www.chron.com / cs / CDA / story.hts / front / 1622097 (accessed 30 September 2003).

Celsi, R.L., Rose, R.L. and Leigh, T.W. (1993) An exploration of high-risk leisure consumption through skydiving. *Journal of Consumer Research* 20 (June), 1–23.

Cheong, R. (1995) The virtual threat to travel and tourism. *Tourism Management* 16(6), 417–422.

Clash, J.M. (2001) Just do it, December 11, 2001. *Forbes.com* website at http://www.forbes.com / global / 2001 / 1112 / 092_print.html (accessed 30 September 2003).

Clawson, M. and Knetsch, J.L. (1966) *Economics of Outdoor Recreation*. Johns Hopkins Press, Baltimore, Maryland.

Cohen, E. (1979) A phenomenology of tourist experiences. *Sociology* 13, 179–201.

Collins, P., Iwasaki, Y., Kanayama, H. and Ohnuki, M. (1994a) Potential demand for passenger travel to orbit, engineering construction and operations in space IV. In: *Proceedings of Space '94, American Society of Civil Engineers*, Vol. 1. ASCE, Reston, Virginia, pp. 578–586.

Collins, P., Iwasaki, Y., Kanayama, H. and Ohnuki, M. (1994b) Commercial implications of market research on space tourism. *Journal of Space Technology and Science* 10(2), 3–11.

Collins, P., Stockmans, R. and Maita, M. (1995) Demand for space tourism in America and Japan and its implications for future space activities. *Space Future* website at http://www.spacefuture.com/archive/demand_for_space_tourism_in_america_and_japan.shtml (accessed 30 September 2003).

Crouch, G.I. (2001a) The market for space tourism: early indications. *Journal of Travel Research* 40, 222–228.

Crouch, G.I. (2001b) After Tito, where to from here?: marketing issues in the development of space tourism. Paper presented at *2001 Conference of the International Academy for the Study of Tourism*, 10–14 July, Macau.

Crouch, G.I. and Louviere, J. (2001) Space tourism marketing research: issues and methodological considerations. Unpublished discussion paper.

Csikszentmihalyi, M. (1975) *Beyond Boredom and Anxiety*. Jossey-Bass, San Francisco, California.

Csikszentmihalyi, M. (1990) *Flow: the Psychology of Optimal Experience*. Harper and Row, New York.

David, L. (2002) Lindbergh's grandson's flight to promote space tourism, April 19, 2002. *SPACE.com* website at http://www.space.com / news / xprize_lindbergh_020419.html (accessed 30 September 2003).

David, L., Citron, R., Rogers, T. and Walker, C.D. (1987) The space tourist. In: Hecker, F. (ed.) *Science and Technology Series*, Vol. 68: *Proceedings of the Fourth Annual L5 Space Development Conference* held April 25–28, 1985. American Astronautical Society, AAS 85–771 to 85–774, p. 183. See http://www.spacefuture.com / archive / the_space_ tourist.shtml (accessed 30 September 2003).

Eco, U. (1986) *Travels in Hyper-Reality*. Picador, London.

Florida Today (1997) America starry eyed as space dominate popular culture, July 8, 1997. See http://www.floridatoday.com/space/explore/stories/1997b/070897j.htm (accessed 30 September 2003).

Florida Today (1999) Hilton Hotels studies feasibility of building hotel in space, September 23, 1999. See http://www.flatoday.com/space/explore/stories/1999b/092399e.htm (accessed 30 September 2003).

Fridgen, J. (1984) Environmental psychology and tourism. *Annals of Tourism Research* 11, 19–39.

Futron Corporation (2002) Futron releases new space tourism publications, October 7, 2002. *Futron Corporation* website at http://www.futron.com / news / pressrelease / default.htm (accessed 30 September 2003).

Futron Corporation (2003) The top ten things we learnt during the ASCENT study, April 10, 2003. *Space Daily* website at http://www. spacedaily.com/news / futon-ascent-whitepaper- 03a.pdf (accessed 30 September 2003).

Gallagher, B. (2000) No space sex? *Scientific American* 282 (January), 22.

Gnoth, A.H.Z., Lengmueller, R. and Boshoff, C. (2000) Emotions, mood, flow and motivations to travel. *Journal of Travel and Tourism Marketing* 9(3): 23–34.

Goodrich, J.N. (1987) Touristic travel to outer space: profile and barriers to entry. *Journal of Travel Research* 16 (2), 40–43.

Graburn, N.H. (1989) Tourism: the sacred journey. In: Smith, V.L. (ed.) *Hosts and Guests: The Anthropology of Tourism*, 2nd edn. University of Pennsylvania Press, Philadelphia, pp. 21–36.

Handwerk, B. (2002) Retrieval of Titanic artifacts stirs controversy. *National Geographic News*, April 12, 2002 at http://news.nationalgeographic.com/news/2002/04/0408_020412_titanic.html (accessed 30 September 2003)

Interfax (2001) 'Sex in space forbidden,' says Russian cosmonaut, June 1, 2001. *SPACE.com* website at http://www.space.com / news / cosmonauts_sex_010601.html (accessed 30 September 2003).

Jones, C.D., Hollenhorst, S.J., Perna, F. and Selin, S. (2000) Validation of the flow theory in an on-site whitewater kayaking setting. *Journal of Leisure Research* 32(2), 247–261.

Karash, Y. (2001) Dennis Tito talks with SPACE.com's Yuri Karash, April 24, 2001. *SPACE.com* website at http://www.space.com / peopleinterviews / tito_Q_and_A-1.html (accessed 30 September 2003).

Kiger, P. (2001) Destination future: part II: space tourism. *The Learning Channel* at http://tlc.discovery.com / convergence / spaceexploration / dispatches/tycoons_02.html (accessed 19 December 2002).

Kozinets, R. (2001) Utopian enterprise: articulating the meanings of Star Trek's culture of consumption. *Journal of Consumer Research* 28(1), 67–88.

Laing, J. (2000) TransHab: over-inflated idea or home sweet home? November 13, 2000. *Universe Today* website at http://www.universetoday.com/html/special/transhab.html (accessed 30 September 2003).

LunaCorp (2003) Broadband lunar exploration: the LunaCorp initiative. *LunaCorp* website at http: // www. lunacorp. com / home. html (accessed 30 September 2003).

Lyng, S. (1990) Edgework: a social psychological analysis of voluntary risk taking. *American Journal of Sociology* 95 (January), 851–886.

MacCannell, D. (1976) *The Tourist: A New Theory of the Leisure Class*. Schocken, New York.

MacCannell, D. (1999) *The Tourist: A New Theory of the Leisure Class*. University of California Press, Berkeley.

NASA/STA (National Aeronautics and Space Administration/Space Transportation Association (1998) *General Public Space Travel and Tourism*, Vol. 1, *Executive Summary*. Marshall Space Flight Center, Huntsville, Alabama.

Pearce, P., Benckendorff, P. and Johnstone, S. (2000) Tourist attractions: In: Faulkner, B., Moscardo, G. and Laws, E. (eds) *Tourism in the 21st Century: Lessons From Experience*. Continuum, London.

Pesavento, P. (2000) From Aelita to the International Space Station: the psychological and social effects of isolation on earth and space. *Quest: The History of Spaceflight Quarterly* 8(2), 4–23.

Riley, R. (1995) Prestige-worthy tourism behavior. *Annals of Tourism Research* 22(3), 630–649.

Riley, R., Baker, D. and Van Doren, C.S. (1998) Movie-induced tourism. *Annals of Tourism Research* 25(4), 919–935.

Ryan, C. (ed.) (1997) *The Tourist Experience*. Cassell, London.

Selwyn, T. (ed.) (1996) *The Tourist Image: Myths and Myth Making in Tourism*. John Wiley and Sons, Chichester, UK.

Shackley, M. (2001) *Managing Sacred Sites*. Continuum, London.

Shoham, A., Rose, G.M. and Kahle, L.R. (1998) Marketing of risky sports: from intention to action. *Journal of the Academy of Marketing Science* 26(4), 307–321.

Simberg, R. (2000) Near-term prospects for space tourism. Unpublished report prepared for the Sophron Foundation by Interglobal Space Lines

Smith, V.L. (1992) The quest in guest. *Annals of Tourism Research* 19, 1–17.

Smith, V.L. (2000) Space tourism: the 21st century 'frontier'. *Tourism Recreation Research* 25(3), 5–15.

Space Daily (2001) Japanese tourist operator opens space division, July 9 2001. *Space Daily* website at http://www.spacedaily.com/news/tourism-01z.html

SpaceRef (2001) NASA holds press conference on the Dennis Tito issue, March 25, 2001. *SpaceRef.com* website at http://www.spaceref.com/news/viewnews.html?id=304 (accessed 30 September 2003).

SpaceRef (2002) Principles regarding processes and criteria for selection, assignment, training and certification of ISS (expedition and visiting) crewmembers, January 31, 2002. *SpaceRef.com* website at http://www.spaceref.com/news/viewsr.html?pid=4578 (accessed 30 September 2003).

Thornton, O. and Collins, P. (2001) On the practical and sporting aspects of football in zero-gravity. Presented at *Symposium on the Popular Commercialisation of Space*, 19 September 2001, British Interplanetary Society, London.

Turner, V. and Turner, E. (1978) *Image and Pilgrimage in Christian Culture: Anthropological Perspectives*. Blackwell, Oxford.

Tyler, P. (2001) Tito finds space paradise, May 8, 2001. *The Age* at http://www.theage.com.au/news/2001/05/08/FFX8QU0UFMC.html (accessed 17 December 2002).

Unsworth, A (2002) Seeing stars where others see limits. *Sunday Times (SA)*, June 2, 2002 at http://www.sundaytimes.co.za/2002/06/02/ insight/in01.asp (accessed 30 September 2003).

Urry, J. (2002) *The Tourist Gaze*, 2nd edn. Sage Publications, London.

Walter, M. (1999) *The Search for Life on Mars*. Perseus Books, Reading, Massachusetts.

Wessels, A.R. and Collins, P. (1989) Space activities and global popular music culture. Presented at the *International Astronautical Federation Congress*, Malaga, 1989, Paper no. IAF-89-671. Available at: http://www.spacefuture. com/archive/space_activities_and_global_pop-ular_music_culture.shtml (accessed 30 September 2003).

Wichman, H. (2002) You can't throw your socks on the floor in a spacecraft. In: Berenstein, P. (ed.) *Making Space Happen: Private Space Ventures and the Visionaries Behind Them*. Plexus Publishing, Medford, New Jersey.

Wolfe, T. (1979) *The Right Stuff*. Farrar, Straus, and Giroux, New York.

Wright, M. (1993) The Disney–Von Braun collaboration and its influence on space exploration. In: Schenker, D., Hanks, C. and Kray, S. (eds) *Selected Papers from the 1993 Southern Humanities Conference*. Southern Humanities Press, Huntsville, Alabama.

Yiannakis, A. and Gibson, H. (1992) Roles tourists play. *Annals of Tourism Research* 19, 287–303.

Zurick, D. (1995) *Errant Journeys*. University of Texas Press, Austin, Texas.

3 Tourism in the Forbidden Lands: the Antarctica Experience

John Splettstoesser[1], Denise Landau[2] and R.K. Headland[3]

[1]PO Box 515, Waconia, MN 55387, USA; [2]International Association of Antarctica Tour Operators (IAATO), Office of the Secretariat, IAATO, PO Box 2178, Basalt, CO 81621, USA; [3]Scott Polar Research Institute, University of Cambridge, Lensfield Road, Cambridge CB2 1ER, UK

Introduction

The discovery of Antarctica and its following exploration has advanced a long way since the time of Ptolemy (AD 150), who endorsed the concept of Greek philosophy that the world was symmetrical, and must, therefore, contain a southern continent (*Terra Australis Incognita*). However, protected by an ice-covered Southern Ocean, with icebergs indicating the presence of a landmass, Antarctica remained elusive until the 19th century before being sighted. Visitors arrived shortly afterwards for commercial and exploratory reasons, but visitors as tourists did not appear until more than a century later. The ability to do so depended then, as now, on a suitable means of transportation, mainly ship, but later, by aircraft.

Thus, three human activities are predominant in the Earth's most remote continent, Antarctica – *exploration*, *science* and *tourism*, and approximately in that order chronologically. Commercial *fishing* can be added as a fourth. The early 1820s included its discovery as a continent, while also exploiting its resources, mainly seals for their pelts. Whaling began in the early 1900s, and continued until the mid-1980s. Both sealing and whaling functioned as long as the resource lasted, ceasing when the animals became close to commercially extinct. Exploration was mainly coastal, being a function

of sea-ice presence and access to locations where bases could be established for inland treks. The attainment of the geographic South Pole was achieved in the early 1900s, and the next phase of activity, further exploration with associated science, began shortly after, especially with the advent of aircraft. Science has become the major reason for human presence on the continent since the 1950s–60s, with tourism following as an ancillary activity, growing in popularity with the passing of each decade. Fishing, some of it with illegal catches, presents a difficult activity to regulate and manage. Preservation of the fragile environment is the theme under which both science and tourism operate, and visitor education continues as a major objective of the tourism industry. The organization known as the International Association of Antarctica Tour Operators (IAATO) provides the management for Antarctic tourism, and liaison with the Treaty Parties that enact legislation to protect the continent and its wildlife (see Notes). What was once an unknown and forbidden part of the planet less than 200 years ago has become more receptive to its recent intruders, although it can also be unforgiving if one becomes careless. Because Antarctica presents itself as 'foreign' and 'forbidden' to nearly all who visit, the visitor/tourist can experience a magical quality unknown nearly everywhere else on Earth. The associated reactions of the visitors are a complementary part of the experience. This chapter discusses the unique experiences of this remote part of the world in the context of a place that no-one owns, but which can be visited and enjoyed by anyone.

Global Commons as a Working Hypothesis

Four environments in our Earth–galactic system are still largely unexplored, and are commonly known as parts of a Global Commons. They are *the oceans, outer space, weather and climate*, and *Antarctica* (Cleveland, 1988). Collectively or separately, they belong to no one person or State, but may be enjoyed or shared by everyone. At least one, Antarctica, has a Treaty dating to 1959 to govern or manage its area (south of 60°S latitude), and others have comparable Treaties that in many respects reserve them for all humankind. Only within the past 30–40 years have three of the Commons developed the means for humans to conduct detailed studies of them as well as to visit them as tourists. Although tourism in Antarctica has more than a century of history, it has become practicable only during the last 30–35 years with the advent of shipborne tourism and, since the 1980s, adventure tourism in the interior of the continent (Headland, 1994). Tourism in two other parts of the Global Commons has a more recent history. For example, since the discovery of the *Titanic* and other sunken vessels, plus visits to deep-sea vents, tourists have been passengers in submersibles to view at close range those objects and features, in parts of the most unknown part of our 'oasis in space' – the deep ocean.

Space tourism is more recent yet, with paying customers (non-astronauts) participating in space travel, visiting space vehicles in orbit. These tourist ventures – Antarctica, the deep sea and outer space – have two things in common: participants range (in general) from being comfortably affluent to very rich.

Antarctica: the Realm of Uncommon Nature

Antarctica continues to be one of the most attainable 'alternative destinations' for tourists,

and at reasonable cost to the client, depending on the objective and duration of the itinerary. The continent is still incompletely explored, particularly its ice-sheet interior and the ice–rock interface (where 'lakes' have been discovered by radio-echo sounding), but nearly all tourists visit only the coastal areas that are approachable by ship, where wildlife, scenery and historic sites are abundant. Because Antarctica is a unique destination for most visitors, their reactions often reflect their unfamiliarity with this part of the planet. A small number of passengers illustrate naiveté, but also thoughtfulness in their questions and comments. After all, polar regions are very different from the usual tourist destinations. Anecdotes of some of the highlights of tourism ventures, and of tourists' impressions of their visits, are related here as part of the history of tourism in this 'forbidden land'. Perhaps it is the remoteness, magnificent scenery, rare wildlife, coupled with confusion between Antarctica and the Arctic, that lead to unusual questions often heard by tour leaders and their staff. Experience by Antarctic tourism operators shows that clients interested in adventure-travel to polar regions are there because they show a higher level of education, and are curious about nature and these unique locations. When someone asks 'Are there still Eskimos living in Antarctica?' it is a sensible question because it seems a likely possibility.

Arctic Comparisons

Many of the tour operators active in Antarctica also conduct cruises and land tours in the Arctic, where many villages and settlements are visited and interactions with the local inhabitants are common. In what might be considered as a trial in this regard were 'family visits' in Russia, in which expedition staff would visit families in coastal settlements on cruises in the Northeast Passage. The families would normally be selected by local agents to ensure that a positive situation would result, with the family providing tea and biscuits, and one or two staff attempting communication in mainly sign language and the few words of Russian they knew. Much smiling and tea-drinking were the result, especially in one instance when the bus driver

Fig. 3.1. Port Lockroy, site of a restored British station in the Antarctic Peninsula, very popular with tourists. A shop and post office are part of the facility operated each summer by British staff.

who dropped off staff at family dwellings forgot some of the addresses, and international relations were at the limit of maintaining a polite situation, perhaps because the schedule for the evening meal was approaching and both the locals and the staff were unsure of the next step to be taken (Frank S. Todd, personal communication, 2000). Interactions of this nature in Antarctic tourism occasionally occur at scientific stations, where English is not always the mutual language, but hospitality is common and passengers appreciate this unique part of an itinerary. For station personnel, it is often welcome when the tour vessel brings the first visitors for the summer after a wintering experience at the station, and fresh fruit and vegetables are often brought ashore as a treat for those who haven't seen either for most of the winter.

'Don't they have their own vegetable garden at the station?'

Some questions from passengers appear to be the result of educational overload, hearing and learning vast amounts of information presented to passengers in lectures and briefings as part of the tour operator's programme. Many comments and questions are focused on the wildlife, seen virtually daily and much of it different from elsewhere in the world.

'Is there such a thing as a female sperm whale?'

'Do penguins bury their dead?'

'Do seals have gills as well as lungs?'

'Do penguins have knees?'

'When penguins migrate, do they fly like other birds, or swim?'

'I heard there were whales sighted, but all I see are fins.'

None of the above were meant as frivolous, but represent reactions and responses to the unique part of the world that tourists visit, in this case, Antarctica. For example, a question about penguins burying their dead is most likely to be asked in response to a naturalist/lecturer stating that chick mortality is often high in penguin colonies. Over many years, then, one would expect to see numerous corpses in the colony, but on a shore visit to a colony, there appear to be relatively few fatalities, and mostly of the current year or past year. Each of these anecdotal questions and comments can thus be analysed as to what the passenger might have heard or seen to derive the response.

An example of confusion that resulted from a southward cruise in Drake Passage, shortly after leaving Beagle Channel, related to a naturalist's meticulously described story of the ship HMS *Beagle*, Captain Fitzroy, Yamana

Indians, Charles Darwin, and intricate details of the voyages of the *Beagle* in that part of southern South America. Following the talk, a passenger commented, seriously, 'Fascinating history, but I didn't know that Darwin had a dog' (Frank S. Todd, personal communication, 1999). This anecdote could well have been the fault of the lecturer trying to include extreme detail in an otherwise straightforward piece about the history of Tierra del Fuego.

Discovery

Antarctica's area is about 13,700,000 km², including all islands and ice shelves (compare Australia, at 7,700,000 km²), and is nearly all ice-covered – only 0.4% of the continent is exposed rock. The maximum known thickness of ice is 4776 m. About 90% of the world's ice is in Antarctica, and 70% of the world's freshwater. The world's lowest recorded surface temperature was at Vostok Station (Russia) in July 1983: −89.2°C.

'If it is July at the South Pole, what month is it at the North Pole?'

Because of its remoteness and position on the planet, the discovery of this last continent is relatively recent, sighted first in 1820 (the planet Uranus was discovered more than 100 years before that, in 1714, by John Flamsteed). Captain James Cook, in his second voyage of discovery in 1772–1775, sailed farther south than anyone before him, crossing the Antarctic Circle, but never saw land. From what he saw, his experiences convinced him that if there were land further south, it would be cold, desolate and inhospitable. If this information were transferred to a tourist brochure today, no one would go.

'What happens to an iceberg when it melts?'

'Is this island completely surrounded by water?'

'Are there any more undiscovered islands?'

Since its discovery and first sighting in 1820, however, it has been explored, traversed (the Norwegian explorer, Roald Amundsen, and his party of four others, were the first to reach the South Pole at 90°S on 14 December 1911), probed with many drillholes to collect ice cores, and its stratosphere has been examined for ozone loss. With the advent of the International Geophysical Year (IGY), 1957–1958, the continent, under the terms of the Antarctic Treaty of 1959, is dedicated to 'science', although it would appear that science and tourism have become compatible in their differing objectives (Splettstoesser, 1996). Tourism is thus not forbidden, but in some respects, is accepted as a commercial enterprise as long as the rules of entry are followed, particularly those that involve environmental practices and conservation of wildlife, for example.

'Will it be easier to open the doors when we leave the magnetic pole?'

Antarctica Visitors and Inhabitants

Unlike its polar counterpart, the Arctic, Antarctica has no indigenous population, and no evidence of one. There are no southern equivalents of Inuit, Lapps or, in the case of the southernmost likely potential inhabitants, the Tierra del Fuegian Indians known as Yamana, Ona, and neighbouring tribes; none of those nomadic populations ever reached the continent or, if they did, authenticated evidence has not been found. Contemporary populations of scientists and support staff have occupied the Antarctic continent at stations continuously since 1944 ('Base A'), and in the offshore South Orkney Islands, since 26 March 1903. Tourists, with only a few exceptions, do not winter, so to speak. Prior to the winter expeditions in 1898 (De Gerlache, on the ship *Belgica*) and 1899 (Borchgrevink, at Cape Adare, mainland Antarctica), the continent and surrounding seas were unoccupied. When the last person leaving Antarctica boarded an expedition ship at the end of summer, one might say that the door to the continent was closed and locked, and the lights turned off (in winter it's dark, anyway) because there was no one else there. The few exceptions were sealers wintering in the South Shetland Islands in 1821 and 1872.

Land-based expeditions, however, starting with Borchgrevink in 1899, had the same method of operation with regard to the seasons. It took most of a summer to navigate a

Fig. 3.2. Pendulum Cove, Deception Island, a popular location for tourists to 'swim' in Antarctica in geothermal waters.

ship through pack-ice to reach a coast, locate a suitable place for a base, place some kind of infrastructure ashore (or live on the ship), spend the winter there and prepare for exploration the following spring and summer, and then, if all went well, leave at the end of the second, or occasionally third, summer. This was the case for Borchgrevink (1898–1900), Scott (1901–1904 and 1910–1913), Nordenskjöld (1901–1904), Bruce (1902–1904), Shackleton (1907–1909) and Mawson (1911–1914), each leaving behind huts to signal their presence and provide an attraction in later years for archaeologists and tourists alike. These historic huts are a major focus for many tourist visits, and also for those involved in the preservation of the huts and their contents (Splettstoesser, 2000a).

'Can Scott's Hut be rented at a reasonable rate, and can we bring our dog?'

How Many Visitors and What Do the Numbers Mean?

History of shipborne tourism

Antarctic tourism is a relatively new phenomenon, and with the exception of sporadic visits it began on a minor scale with a tourist aircraft, a Chilean DC6B, which overflew the Antarctic Peninsula on 23 December 1956. The first tourist ship, *Les Eclaireurs*, an Argentine naval transport carrying paying passengers, visited the same area twice in January and February 1958 (Headland, 1994; Stonehouse *et al.*, 1996). In 1966, the concept of 'expedition cruising', coupled with education as a major theme, began with Lars-Eric Lindblad. Lindblad had the first ice-strengthened tourist vessel built, the *Lindblad Explorer*, and sailed it to Antarctica in the 1969–1970 austral summer. The ship has been there many times since, and has been followed through the next decades by a number of additional tour vessels, some of them Russian. Many of the latter have become available since the political changes in the Soviet Union in 1991. Icebreakers and other vessels have been converted into western-style tour ships and marketed for tourists and itineraries in both polar regions.

'Is it safe to drive the ship at night?'
'Does the crew sleep aboard?'

Mainland Antarctica has had continuous occupation since the start of Operation Tabarin in 1944, and more extensively since the onset of the International Geophysical Year, 1957–1958. Many countries now have winter stations (32 south of 60°S, eight in sub-Antarctic

Fig. 3.3. Esperanza Station (Argentina), Hope Bay, Antarctic Peninsula, site of a research base, a large Adelie penguin colony, and families.

or peri-Antarctic regions), with the continent-wide population being perhaps 1400 individuals, swelling to 3000–4000 or so in the austral summer. By contrast, tourism is virtually a summer activity, November to March, with as many as 14,000 visitors on about 125–130 individual cruises on 15–20 vessels (plus several yachts) during that period, although no shore structures exist for their presence, the ships being their 'hotel', or 'floating station'. Furthermore, not all the visitors actually 'land' on the continent (some ships cruise and sightsee, and over-flights from Chile and Australia conduct scenic flights without landings). The 'residence time' calculated by Headland (1994, and unpublished information, April 2003) shows that tourists spend about 1.0% of their time actually on the continent when compared with Treaty Party activities, which include permanent shore stations and field parties.

Lindblad as a 'claimant'?

The combination of an on-board lecture on Antarctic tourism in the 1990s, plus a follow-up forum on the subject, resulted in an interesting perspective by several passengers who were curious about the beginning of the IGY and 12 countries active in Antarctica gaining a consensus to determine that Antarctica should be dedicated to science, with limitations listed in the 1959 Antarctic Treaty. No one questioned the reasons for the Treaty Articles, and the theme of a land that would be free from strife. However, there were thoughtful and serious comments about the theoretical situation of Lindblad acting earlier than 1969 in starting cruises in Antarctica, landing at McMurdo Sound before 1955 at the site of what is now McMurdo Station (USA), and constructing a base of operations for annual tour ship visits in succeeding summers. Supplies would be left there, and the location, owned by no-one (but claimed by New Zealand as a result of a claim by Great Britain in 1923 that turned the area over to New Zealand to administer), would be dedicated to tourism in the Ross Sea and McMurdo Sound area. Tour ships (the *Lindblad Explorer* and others) could call there each austral summer, drop off their passengers to explore the area locally on foot, see Scott's 1901–1904 hut and the cross on top of Observation Hill, then board the ships to continue on their itineraries. Newly built shore structures would provide shelter, lectures could be given ashore, lunch and coffee could be served, and the facility would be closed for the winter. This could have been pre-1955, when the first US ship arrived to begin construction of McMurdo Station in preparation for the IGY. The theoretical situation invites serious discussion, which amounts to a case of whoever gets there first claims occupancy, if only on a temporary basis. Another way to state it is that McMurdo Station might have ended up being constructed elsewhere, or next door, and 'Lindblad Base' could have persisted through the years as a location to be visited by tour ships. Although the Antarctic Treaty of 1959 placed all seven claims in reserve, their boundaries are unenforceable, and the claims were not surrendered. Lindblad could well have negotiated an arrangement with New Zealand to place a shore facility on Ross Island, much as the USA has presently with New Zealand. Inasmuch as the Ross Dependency was not 'occupied', as it were, since the claim was initiated (1923), if Lindblad got there first, who is to question a presence for tourism on a seasonal basis? It amounts to an international legal issue, which is now only hypothetical. Luckily, tourism has managed to create a place on Earth where there is no commercial fast-food restaurant.

Tourism statistics

Some concern has been voiced about the gradual increase in the numbers of tourists who visit Antarctica each year, with projections approaching 22,000 by the 2006–2007 austral summer (16,000 of those would be involved in land visits, however, with the rest arriving in air over-flights or large-ship cruising only – no shore visits). Within the last decade, numbers of ship-borne tourists have risen from about 6700 in 1992–1993 to nearly 15,000 in 1999–2000, which then decreased slightly to 12,200 in 2000–2001. Fluctuations often occur as a result of 'large ships' with capacities of 500 or more passengers (some with more than 1000) making an occasional cruise to the Antarctic Peninsula, e.g. some without making any landings, thus inflating the tourist numbers for that particular season. When all tourist figures[1] are factored into a total, additional numbers include land-based adventure tourism (135–150 a season) and scenic over-flights

from Australia and Chile without landings adding about 2500–3000 more for that season.

The numbers have to be scrutinized further, though, to determine the number of visitors that actually make shore visits, and further, to estimate the actual time spent ashore. A discussion of a typical shore visit will provide the reasons.

Anatomy of a typical shore visit

Most tourism in Antarctica is concentrated in the Antarctic Peninsula, with some 100 or more known sites that have been visited by tour vessels, some of them sporadically, and others, with more popular attractions such as wildlife and scenery to offer, more frequently. Typically, most shore visits encompass 2–3 hours, rarely more but in some cases less. Weather and ice conditions are a factor in actual time spent ashore, or in fact whether a landing can be made at all. Some visits consist of a combination of time ashore and associated sightseeing by Zodiac boats on the way to shore or from it after the visit. In this way, passenger loading ashore can be kept to a manageable number (IAATO bylaws state that no more than 100 passengers are allowed ashore at any one time). Each landing involves an advance 'scout' boat with Expedition Leader and staff present to locate a suitable landing site, check it for safety and other conditions and then, if satisfactory, passenger transport starts soon after. Upon reaching shore, each boat is met by the Expedition Leader or other staff, and passengers are divided into small groups led by staff (normally 15–20 per staff member) and escorted to points of interest where staff point out the highlights of what is seen. Guidelines are often repeated as a reminder to passengers, especially when wildlife is the attraction.

'*Why do the birds always sit on the white rocks?*'

For various reasons, it is unusual that the entire complement of passengers will go ashore, sometimes due to the difficulty of landing, conditions at the ship (rolling ship), as well as health condition of an individual. Accurate reports of visits are kept by all Expedition Leaders on all vessels, and it can be shown (from the 2000–2001 austral season) that of the nearly 12,240 passengers on tour vessels and yachts, those actually going ashore numbered fewer than 11,000. In addition, not everyone who goes ashore stays for the full time allotted for the visit. By nature of the logistics, not everyone can be transported there at the same time by the small boats (normally Zodiacs) used for the purpose. It normally takes 20–30 minutes to transport 100 passengers ashore using 8–10 Zodiacs, depending on distance from the ship to the landing site, sea conditions, etc., and by the time the last passengers have reached shore, some who arrived earlier often return to the ship. Some passengers stay for the entire time, enjoying what is always a unique experience. Generally, about 75% of passengers stay ashore for about 1–2 hours in a stop scheduled for 3 hours. The remainder return to the ship within 30–60 minutes, or stay for the entire time. The lucky ones who enjoy the entire time allotted would have arrived in the first Zodiac boats.

Tourism activities in the interior

The exception to a lack of land facilities for tourist operations is the summer camp in the interior (Patriot Hills, Ellsworth Mountains, at about 80°20' S, 81°25' W) operated by a private company for adventure tourism – a total of fewer than 150 persons are visitors in that venture annually, but not all at the same time. Popular activities at that site include mountaineering (the four highest peaks in Antarctica are within a short flying range of the camp; Vinson Massif, the highest, reaches 4897 m), visits by aircraft to the geographic South Pole, transfers to an emperor penguin colony to stay for a week or so, adventure-style skiing or sledging trips to the South Pole, or excursions locally. The same private company operates flights from Cape Town to Dronning Maud Land, a near-coastal area in the vicinity of zero-degrees longitude, where the rugged area, once inaccessible because of its remoteness, can be reached by aircraft. Given the capability of aircraft that operate in Antarctica, virtually any location is attainable if fuel depots are placed at strategic locations. The cost of reaching any place on the continent is related mainly to the cost of aircraft fuel and the cost of extending the supply depots ever farther from a base camp. The spectacular angular peaks are a favourite of mountaineers in Dronning Maud Land, and it also provides a starting place for explorers to cross the continent on foot or skis, often using parachutes to take advantage of favourable winds.

'*If all the lines meet at the Pole, how do we know where we are?*'

'*What is the longitude at the South Pole?*'

Sustainability

Given that whatever one needs for visits to Antarctica must be brought in from another landmass and its gateway ports, either by aircraft or ship, can Antarctica ever provide self-sustainability for even a short-term population? Without the option of arable land, strict controls on wildlife conservation, harsh climate, Antarctic Treaty regulations, and a host of other negatives, no 'settlements' are feasible in the normal sense of the word in other parts of the world. Growing certain plants and vegetables by hydroponics has been attempted, but primarily on an experimental or 'hobby' basis. Hunting wildlife for food is forbidden, and no organisms (birds, whales, seals, plants) can be 'taken' without a permit, and always for scientific reasons, or in a life-threatening emergency. The only item necessary for survival that exists in Antarctica is water, for one can always melt glacier ice or icebergs to provide fresh water. Two of the existing stations (one Chilean, the other Argentine) could be considered 'settlements' because they house families, where wives and children of base personnel live, the children attend school, and the inhabitants more or less 'occupy' territory claimed by those countries. In each case the occupants do not actually live there, but are also visitors. After an agreed consignment term, they return to their native countries. The Antarctic Treaty, though, puts the seven claimed areas of Antarctica in abeyance, or a 'deep-freeze', which means that those countries cannot enforce their claims, but do not have to surrender them either. Antarctica is the only landmass in the world that does not require a passport or visa to enter it.

Fig. 3.4. Vinson Massif, Ellsworth Mountains, the highest peak (4897 m) in Antarctica and the site of mountaineering expeditions by private clients annually. Climbers are flown to a nearby base camp from Punta Arenas, Chile, by a private company.

Fig. 3.5. Lemaire Channel, Antarctic Peninsula, a scenic area for tourism vessels (commonly known as 'Kodak Alley' because many thousands of photos are taken on this 10-km-long channel).

Conclusions

Tourism can be projected to be a sustainable activity because of how it operates, as mentioned earlier. Everything required for tourism is brought to Antarctica, and it all leaves when the activity is concluded. The last decade or so has shown a slight progression in numbers of tourists visiting Antarctica, fluctuations depending on the presence or absence of 'large ships' (more than 400-passenger capacity), which conduct an occasional cruise to the Antarctic

Peninsula, but not necessarily on an annual basis. Tour companies active in Antarctic tourism over a period of many years have developed their operations to make them more attractive to clients, initiating activities like diving, kayaking, mountaineering, and the like, or introducing itineraries different from those normally conducted. The survivors are companies that provide good products for clients and capture them for future travel with those companies. Overall, tourism can be sustainable only if the strict bylaws that have been compiled by the umbrella organization known as IAATO (International Association of Antarctica Tour Operators) are followed by all visitors (Splettstoesser, 2000b). IAATO's primary mission is to conduct environmentally responsible, private-sector travel to the Antarctic, and educate passengers in the process. Protection of the environment and adherence to Antarctic Treaty regulations and conventions are mandatory, and tour operators have been shown to follow them as a dedicated group. The objections to tourism presence come from some environmental groups, and also from some of the Treaty Parties, who claim that tourism is not sufficiently regulated, and mishaps or accidents can involve outside logistic support, including search and rescue by Treaty Parties, that detract from the established mission of science. Tour operators, on the other hand, continue to assist the Treaty Parties in their role of conducting scientific research (Splettstoesser, 2000b).

Acknowledgements

Dr Valene Smith's review improved the manuscript, and anecdotal material from passengers was provided mainly by R.K. Headland and F.S. Todd. All the photos were taken by John Splettstoesser.

Note

1. Figures for tourist numbers, cruises, and ships vary depending on the season. Detailed objectives of IAATO include the following:
   - Provide an outreach policy toward the yachting community and to newcomer vessels to ensure that the occasional visitors are aware of environmental requirements and procedures for their activity.

- Support relevant studies that will contribute toward accurate site assessment and monitoring, as exemplified by Project Oceanites. Because of the possibility that wildlife might be adversely affected cumulatively by human presence over a number of years, but the signs of it may not be evident for a long time, tour operators are as eager as others to know whether any detrimental effects are occurring; e.g. breeding changes, behavioural changes, etc., and adjust operations accordingly.
- Maintain high standards of staff training.
- Maintain close supervision of shore excursions.
- Develop a comprehensive system of data recording of tourism statistics to provide information for Treaty Parties and others to monitor and analyse operations.
- Conform to requirements in force for all vessels in Antarctica; e.g. oil-pollution response equipment.
- Participate in Treaty meetings as a means of ensuring that tour operations agree with established practices and regulations.
- Continue dialogue with Treaty Parties to illustrate that science and tourism can truly co-exist in what was once a 'forbidden land', but which is now an area that can be shared for different objectives.

References

Cleveland, H. (1988) Introducing the global commons. In: Cleveland, H. and Burdette, L. (eds) *The Global Commons.* H.H. Humphrey Institute of Public Affairs, University of Minnesota, Minneapolis, pp. 1–13.

Headland, R.K. (1994) Historical development of Antarctic tourism. *Annals of Tourism Research* 21(2), 269–280.

Splettstoesser, J. (1996) Areas of geologic interest in the Antarctic peninsula, and tourism: a case for compatibility. *Korean Journal of Polar Research* **7** (1/2), 116–118.

Splettstoesser, J. (2000a) Centennial of historic huts in Antarctica: a tourist attraction. *Tourism Recreation Research* 25(2), 39–49.

Splettstoesser, J. (2000b) IAATO's stewardship of the Antarctic environment: a history of tour operator's concern for a vulnerable part of the world. *International Journal of Tourism Research* 2(1), 47–55.

Stonehouse, B., Crosbie, K. and Girard, L. (1996) Sustainable tourism in the Arctic and the Antarctic. In: Girard, L. (ed.) *Polar Ecotourism: Proceedings of the 3rd Symposium, St. Petersburg, Russia, 23–26 October 1995,* A. Pas de Loup, Paris, pp. 19–29.

4 Skilled Commercial Adventure: the Edge of Tourism

Ralf Buckley

International Centre for Ecotourism Research, Griffith University, Parklands Drive, Southport, Australia

---

Introduction

If you have the necessary skills, as well as money, commercial adventure tour operators can now take you climbing on 8000 m peaks, kayaking Himalayan rivers in flood, diving under Antarctic ice, parachuting on to the North Pole, or skiing across Greenland. Experiences such as these, which were at the frontiers of human endeavour only a few decades ago, now form a recognizable subsector of the tourism industry. This might be abbreviated as SCARRA (skilled commercial adventure recreation in remote areas).

The bread-and-butter business growth in the adventure tourism sector has been in so-called soft adventure, where unskilled clients show up in street clothes and a tour operator provides transport, equipment, specialized clothing, skilled guides and sufficient on-the-spot training for participants to enjoy a safe and usually short set of thrills (Buckley, 2003b). The broad-scale trend in adventure tourism is thus towards reducing risk, remoteness and skill requirements, so as to broaden market demand. At the same time that one end of the adventure tourism sector is expanding its appeal to mainstream mass tourism, however, the other end is expanding into smaller-volume, higher-cost products which require more advanced prior skills and involve greater individual risk for clients, and operate in more remote and inhospitable areas.

SCARRA seems to be at the edge of the tourism industry structurally as well as geographically. In particular, some commercial adventure activities and destinations have evolved quite rapidly from extreme to soft adventure, whereas others have not. Effectively, this represents the tourism industry continually pressing against its boundaries, sometimes expanding and sometimes meeting resistance. The direction of growth in the tourism sector depends on the balance between the driving pressures of market demand and the resistance of costs and technologies. Worldwide, resistance to growth is decreasing as social and technological changes make it easier and cheaper to visit remote parts of the globe, and reduce at least some of the risks. If SCARRA is seen as one of the edges of the tourism sector, therefore, the factors that determine whether or not a particular activity expands and softens into the mainstream market are significant in determining the future shape of the sector as a whole.

Such expansion, of course, is not necessarily to the advantage of the individual tourism businesses that pioneered the particular products concerned. It moves them from a niche market where they have a strong competitive advantage or even a monopoly, to a larger and broader market where there may be a substantial competition on price. This price competition may exert downward pressures on safety, guiding skills, equipment quality, etc. At the same time, shifting towards a larger but softer adventure tourism market is likely to require changes in accommodation and transport logistics, so as to support more people in greater comfort. Typically, this needs considerably greater capital investment, which may take it beyond the financial reach of pioneer operators.

Skill, Risk, Reward and Remoteness

The critical factors differentiating SCARRA from the adventure tourism sector more generally are skill and remoteness. The skill factor distinguishes it from most commercial nature, eco- and adventure tourism (NEAT) in remote areas, where tour operators strive to make their areas and experiences accessible to unskilled clients so as to maximize their potential market size. The remoteness factor distinguishes it from skilled outdoor adventure recreation in more developed areas, such as heavily-used rock-climbing and scuba diving sites, or so-called park-and-play whitewater kayaking rivers. Associated with the skill requirements and remoteness is an increased level of risk. This, however, is a consequence rather than a defining factor, and tour operators take steps to minimize risks, in order to maintain their future reputation as well as to minimize immediate liability.

From the clients' perspective, SCARRA offers rewards that they cannot obtain at their own local recreational areas, but with greater convenience and efficiency and lower risk than organizing their own private recreational trip. Risk is reduced through the tour operator's local knowledge, guide skills, logistic support and commonly, arrangements for emergency medical assistance and/or evacuation if needed.

As commercial tourism, SCARRA is distinguished from private adventure recreation, competitive adventure sports, etc.; but the distinction can be rather fine. For example, if a private group uses a local commercial outfitter to provide equipment for a particular trip, but provides its own leader, this would be considered as private recreation. If the same group

uses the same outfitter to make the same trip, but with a leader provided by the outfitter, it would be considered as commercial tourism.

Historically, travel in the most remote areas and difficult terrain has nearly always been pioneered by scientific or sponsored expeditions, with commercial tourism lagging far behind. It is only recently that the opportunity to make a first ascent or descent, a first traverse or crossing, or to be the first to carry out a particular recreational activity at a new site, has been marketed as a component of commercial tours. Organizations such as the Explorers Club (2003) in the USA and the World Expeditionary Association (WEXAS, 2003) in the UK, focus on private rather than commercial expeditions. It is only in the last decade or so that organizations such as the Adventure Travel Society (2003) have begun to cater equally for adventure tour operators as well as individuals. Even now, in areas of the world with local populations, transport and accommodation, tourism is commonly pioneered by individual travellers, with commercial tours establishing much later, once the destination is well known.

The way in which adventure tourism has developed thus differs between regions. Broadly, four categories of remoteness can be distinguished:

- *rural areas and parks in developed countries*, typically within a few days from a roadhead and within range of rescue services; human habitation may be restricted by land tenure or economic factors but not by terrain or climate
- *inhabited areas in developing countries*, with purchasable access to local transport, shelter and food supplies
- *sparsely inhabited areas* with no regular mechanized access or local transport, no communications infrastructure and traditional subsistence lifestyles only
- *areas which are uninhabited* because of extreme environments: oceans, poles, some deserts, highest mountain peaks.

In developed nations, SCARRA products typically focus on more and more challenging recreational activities, such as: whitewater kayaking down previously unrun rivers; skiing or snowboarding down previously unrun slopes; ascents of previously unclimbed routes on cliffs and mountains; explorations of previously unvisited caves; or traverses of previously uncrossed terrain. The risk level may be high or extreme, but rescue services are at least potentially available.

Activities such as these are nearly always attempted first by private individuals, sometimes sponsored either for a one-off attempt or as part of professional teams. These are typically followed by other private groups, often from recreational clubs and associations. Once the volume of visitors provides a sufficient market, local outfitters may start to provide on-site equipment rental and/or guiding services. Adventure tour operations can then use these outfitters, or their own gear and guides, to offer commercial trips. Commonly these are sporadic at first, with departure dates customized to individual groups of clients, and trips running only if fully pre-booked. At this stage, prices typically remain somewhat negotiable, calculated trip-by-trip depending on numbers. Only once such charters are well-established will operators begin to schedule routine departures with fixed per-client prices.

Inhabited areas in developing nations are visited routinely by local merchants and other domestic travellers, and their first international tourists are often backpackers relying entirely on local facilities: what might be described as the 'Lonely Planet' market. These, however, are – almost by definition – not engaged in high-risk high-skill recreational activities; firstly because such activities need logistic support, and secondly because they often need access to locally little-used areas, just as in developed nations. As in the latter, therefore, high-skill adventure activities are most often pioneered by private recreational groups, with or without sponsorship. The first commercial adventure tours in these areas are usually self-supported expeditions, bringing all their own equipment. If these are successful, they may lead to the establishment of local operational bases and hiring of local guides, who then pioneer additional new trips. Sometimes, areas with an established industry in one adventure tourism sector may simply expand to add new activities from existing bases. Trekking and mountaineering outfitters and tour operators in Nepal, for example,

branched into whitewater rafting once early descents showed that this activity was both feasible and commercially viable.

In areas occupied by indigenous societies with few links to the rest of the world, almost any travel has a significant adventure element. Worldwide, there are few such societies remaining. There are, however, all possible gradations between complete tribalism and complete urbanization, and there are still many societies where adventure recreation and its associated high-tech equipment are completely unfamiliar. The development of an adventure tourism industry in such areas may be inseparable from other aspects of so-called westernization.

Most remote in perception and practical effect, if not in geographic distance, are the extreme environments where human life cannot be sustained for long without technological means to supply oxygen, warmth or water. These include the so-called forbidden landscapes of the Arctic and Antarctic (Splettstoesser et al., Chapter 3, this volume) and high montane environments above 6000 m, including the so-called dead zone. They also include sections of the world's hyper-arid deserts such as the Rub'al Khali or the Taklamakan, away from the oases which form traditional camel crossing routes. Any human venture into such areas is as a self-supported expedition, and any permanent human base is completely dependent upon continuing re-supplies from outside the region. Independent travel is generally not possible, since all visitors need expedition support; whether through an official, scientific, sponsored, private or commercial expedition.

Within these areas, the degree of skill and risk depend on the activity involved. To visit the Arctic or Antarctic as a passenger on a cruise liner requires neither skill or fitness. To take part in a so-called expedition cruise, with frequent landings by inflatable boats, requires only basic balance and mobility. Multi-day sea-kayaking tours along the shores of Ellesmere Island in the Canadian Arctic are available to any reasonably fit person with some experience in backcountry camping, though prior cold-weather sea-kayaking experience would certainly be an advantage. Diving at the edge of polar ice, cross-country skiing in Greenland, or skydiving on to the North Pole require consid-erable prior skill and experience so as not to endanger either oneself or other members of the group. Beyond this, trips such as unsup-ported sea-kayak journeys in the Antarctic, or ski-mountaineering traverses of the sub-Antarctic South Georgia Island are too difficult even for experienced commercial clients, and have been achieved only by highly skilled and experienced private groups.

Case Studies

High-altitude mountaineering

The first ascent of Mt Everest was an endeavour at the limits of human physical and technical capa-bility. No one had done it before. No machine could get the climbers there or rescue them, and their lives depended daily on their own prepara-tion, capabilities and judgement. The same applies for other high-altitude ascents, notably the other 8000 m peaks. Only a few decades later, commercial clients can pay to be guided to the top of Mt Everest, with transport, porters, camps and all but personal equipment supplied (Boukreev and DeWalt, 1996; Adventure Consultants, 2003).

Arguably, therefore, this is tourism; but at the very opposite end of the spectrum from the con-ventional mass-market tourism destination. Technologies, facilities, logistics and backups may all have improved enormously since the first explorers, but an Everest expedition still involves significant personal risk to life and limb. Most importantly, very few people can make the trip; not just because it costs a lot and it is hard to get a permit, but because few people are fit, strong, skilled and dogged enough either to undertake the training or to withstand an extended period at high altitude. To climb Mt Everest as a commer-cial expedition client may be a new form of tourism, but not one which is currently likely to become mainstream.

The critical aspect is oxygen supply. Oxygen shortage itself, of course, is not an irrevocable barrier, as shown by the large number of recre-ational scuba divers. The limiting factor on high mountains, apart from tradition, costs and climb-ing ethics, is the ability of the human body to carry a sufficient supply of bottled oxygen for a period of days or weeks rather than hours. Shortage of oxygen also places severe constraints on machinery. Whilst jet engines can indeed operate above 10,000 m, the operational limit for most small aircraft is far lower; and only a few helicopters, such as the Swiss-built Lama, can operate safely above 5000 m.

The constraints on softening an Everest ascent are limits of law, tenure, tradition and cost as much as technology. It would, perhaps, not be impossi-ble to build a helipad above the Khumbu Icefall and ladders up the Hillary Step; and to provide clients with so many Sherpas carrying so many oxygen cylinders that any reasonably fit person could make the climb. It would be extremely expensive; but commercial adventure tourism clients include billionaires. It might not receive the sanction of the Governments of Nepal or Tibet; but stranger things have happened. It would greatly offend and interfere with expeditions following current practices; but those practices themselves may have offended the early mountaineers. Guides, fixed ropes and lightweight oxygen bot-tles do not make an Everest ascent easy, but they do make it easier than it was for Tensing and Hillary in 1953. Despite all these possibilities, however, Everest ascents are likely to remain restricted to a fit, elite and well-funded few.

Arctic and Antarctic

The polar environments of the Antarctic and High Arctic have many similarities to high mountains: extreme cold, very high winds at times, difficult terrain, and a landscape of ice and snow. They do, however, have oxygen-rich air. Whilst early explorations of the Arctic and Antarctic were heroic feats of human endurance, illustrated recently by the IMAX movie of Sir Ernest Shackleton's famous voyage, access to polar regions is now a great deal easier. Indeed, there is a permanent scientific base on the South Pole itself. There are blue ice landing strips for aircraft,

(continued)

(Arctic and Antarctic continued)

and there have been proposals to convert the accommodation quarters at an American Antarctic base into a tourist hotel (Buckley, 2003a).

The greatest growth in Antarctic tourism has been in ship-based access. The first commercial boat tour to the Antarctic was operated by a purpose-built, ice-strengthened ship, the *Lindblad Explorer* in 1970; and the same vessel still operates, although now under a different name and ownership (Buckley, 2003a). Over recent years, the number of ship-borne passengers to the Antarctic has increased enormously, as large international cruise liners have begun to include the Antarctic in their routine itineraries.

For the Antarctic environment this growth has been a very mixed blessing (see Splettstoesser *et al.*, Chapter 3, this volume). It does, however, demonstrate that in some harsh remote environments at least, early explorations can lead first to commercial 'expedition' tours and later to mass tourism. Cruise ship passengers need no particular skills or knowledge, and are completely dependent upon the tour operation.

Whilst cruise ships have expanded the Antarctic tourism markets into the mass tourism sector, this has not replaced the smaller-scale specialist adventure sector which is also growing and diversifying. In addition to semi-commercial

expeditions such as that to repair Mawson's Hut, the legacy of an early explorer (APP Mawson's Huts Foundation, 2003), there have been commercial climbing operations at Patriot Hills for a number of years (Adventure Network, 2003; Adventure Consultants, 2003). Recently, tour companies such as Aurora Expeditions (2003) have started to offer Antarctic diving tours.

A similar range of tourist activities has developed in the Arctic. Large luxury cruise ships routinely travel up the west coast of Alaska, though not into the High Arctic. Several companies operate tours using ice-strengthened vessels in the Russian White Sea, Barents Sea and around Svalbard north of Norway. There are boat, sea-kayak and snowmobile outfitters operating in Greenland and Canada's Baffin Island (Tununiq Travel and Adventure, 2003), and commercial hiking and sea-kayak tours which visit Ellesmere Island, even further north (Blackfeather, 2003; Whitney and Smith Expeditions, 2003). For a price, tourists can travel to the North Pole itself in a nuclear-powered icebreaker. They can travel to within 100 km of the Pole by boat, plane and helicopter, and ski the last 100 km in a fully supported commercial tour (North Pole Expeditions, 2003). If they have the necessary skills, tourists can even pay to skydive on to the North Pole (North Pole Adventures, 2003).

Whitewater rafting and kayaking

For whitewater rafters and kayakers, the first descent of a major river is a significant international event, in the same way that the first ascent of a previously unclimbed peak is significant in mountaineering circles. Traditionally, the first person to run each individual rapid gets the right to name it, in the same way that rock climbers name individual routes (through usually less imaginatively).

Whitewater raft and kayak tour companies range in size from a single person with a single raft, to worldwide operations such as Mountain Travel Sobek (2003), a subsidiary of the Microsoft Corporation. The majority of these operators, however, are small- and medium-scale enterprises (SMEs) which own their own rafts and kayaks, operate on a restricted and localized set of rivers which they know well, hire whitewater guides trip-by-trip as required, and get most of

their clients either through multi-activity outdoor tourism retailers such as World Expeditions (2003), or by basing themselves in well-known adventure tourism destinations where they can rely on walk-ins.

Some of these companies add to their repertoire of rivers at intervals by exploring new options; and one or two companies specialize specifically in first descents of significant rivers in remote areas. Since most such first descents are made by experienced private recreational groups, or by professional teams sponsored by major kayak manufacturers, the cachet of a first descent adds significantly to the appeal and value of a whitewater trip for many commercial clients. From an operational perspective, however, a first descent is very different from a routine river-running tour. The river is unknown, the logistics are untested, and the tour is a one-off. Hence the

(continued)

(Whitewater rafting and kayaking continued)

Fig. 4.1. The author entering the first and only kayak run of 'No Exit' rapid on the Mekong River, China. Sponsors: Perception Aquaterra Kayaks, Aleeda Surfsuits, Earth Science Expeditions. Photo: Steve van Beek.

participants, even though they are paying customers, need to have sufficient whitewater and backcountry skills to take part safely and make a net contribution to the expedition, rather than behaving as paid passengers. They also need to be sufficiently good-humoured and flexible to blend well into a group and to adjust to whatever unexpected circumstances may arise.

Whitewater rapids and rivers are classified on an international scale of I–V in degree of difficulty, with Class V subdivided in recent years into V.i, V.ii and V.iii as equipment and techniques continue to improve, and rapids previously considered unrunnable are now being run. Most commercial whitewater rafting tours operate on rivers rated at Class II–III for family trips including children, or Class III–IV for thrill-seeking clients who expect to be flipped into the river at some point. Some commercial rafting trips do run rivers with Class V rapids, but would generally portage the Class V sections, since swimming in Class V whitewater involves a considerable and immediate risk to life.

A small number of companies specialize in Class V whitewater. An example is provided by Expediciones Chile, operating on the Futaleufu

and neighbouring rivers in Patagonian Chile. Whilst the company has now expanded to include fly-fishing and rafting, it started as an experts-only kayak camp, where internationally renowned professional kayak guides would lead skilled kayaking clients down sections of the river ranging from Class IV+ to Class V.iii depending on ability (Buckley, 2003a; Expediciones Chile, 2003). A similar company, Endless River Adventures (Buckley, 2003a; Endless River Adventures, 2003) operates in Costa Rica and Ecuador, but using local accommodation instead of a purpose-built camp. Whilst both these companies offer challenging whitewater, neither offer first descents. The same applies for companies such as Adrift Adventure (2003) in Uganda and Ultimate Descents (2003) in New Zealand and Nepal. The latter, however, now also operates in Bhutan, and their first Bhutan trip a few years ago was offered commercially as a first descent.

A few companies specialize almost entirely in first descents. A prime example is Earth Science Expeditions (2003), run from the USA but specializing in first descents on the big rivers of the Himalayas, in northwest China and southeast

(continued)

(Whitewater rafting and kayaking continued)

Fig. 4.2. The author, Rangitata River, New Zealand. Sponsors: Perception Aquaterra, Aleeda Surfsuits.

Tibet (Buckley, 2003a; Earth Science Expeditions, 2003). Broadly, ESE's owners identify, plan and obtain permission for new first descents, and provide equipment and full logistic support; and then sell a limited number of expedition places to skilled kayakers and rafters.

The rivers run by Earth Science Expeditions are selected for their size, geographical location and global significance rather than degree of difficulty. There are world-famous gorges such as Tiger Leap Gorge on the Yangtze and the Great Bend of the Tsangpo – or indeed the Grand Canyon of the Stikine or Devil's Canyon on the Susitna in Canada – which have been run or attempted by expert private expeditions, in some cases involving loss of life; but which would currently be considered far too dangerous for a commercial trip. On the other hand, to be marketable to experienced whitewater *aficionados*, even a first descent needs a degree of challenge; and besides, first descents are only available on rivers too difficult for local watercraft. In 2003, for example, Earth Science Expeditions is offering a first descent by raft of a section of the Salween, one of the major rivers of the Himalayas; and first descents by kayak only, of a series of smaller but more difficult Class V rivers in China's Gonga Shan area.

Do first descents such as these lead to expansions in commercial adventure tourism? In many cases, yes; but not automatically. Successful operations such as Expediciones Chile (2003) and Endless River Adventures (2003) show that there are skilled recreational kayakers who are prepared to pay for guides and for logistics in unfamiliar areas: the cash-rich, time-poor section of the adventure tourism market (Buckley, 2002a). Similarly, the commercial success of companies such as Adrift Adventure and Ultimate Descents shows that there is a significant market of unskilled adventure tourists prepared to pay for fully guided Class IV whitewater trips in relatively remote areas. The difference between these operations, and the first descents offered by Earth Science Expeditions, is principally one of cost, timing and reliability. First descents command a price premium which generally cannot be maintained in a routine adventure tourism product. In addition, first-descent clients will commonly accept greater uncertainty and less efficient logistics than clients on a routine whitewater trip. For most whitewater rivers, therefore, even challenging rivers in remote areas, it is merely market factors which may restrict rapid growth from a new first descent to a routine tour offering.

Diving

Scuba diving is now a major recreational activity worldwide. In popular diving tourism destinations such as Australia's Great Barrier Reef, commercial tour operators have installed large permanent pontoon structures with giant underwater cages (Quicksilver Cruises, 2003). In these, day tourists with no previous diving practice or qualifications can learn to use a tethered regulator under supervision, either as a stand-alone experience or as a first step in gaining basic dive qualifications (Buckley, 2003a). There are dive resorts and dive charter boats operating throughout the tropics and subtropics.

Indeed, as a commercial tourism activity, diving has a number of advantages over other recreational water sports. Most importantly, since compressors are large, expensive and heavy so that very few divers own one, divers rely completely on commercial dive shops to fill their tanks. Unlike many other adventure tourism activities, therefore, almost all dive tourists are tied in to commercial providers at least for air, even if they have their own equipment, local knowledge and transport. Of course, most dive shops also have an extensive range of equipment and accessories for sale, including high-priced items such as dive computers and underwater photographic gear. In practice, most dive resorts and charter boats now offer standard packages which include guides, equipment rental and even wetsuits as well as air and local transport. Clients can hence arrive completely unequipped, as long as they are appropriately qualified.

The commercial dive tourism industry also benefits from the internationalization of recreational diving qualifications. The international systems operated by PADI, the Professional Association of Dive Instructors (2003), and its US counterpart NAUI, the National Association of Underwater Instructors (2003) are now recognized almost universally for divers and instructors alike. These act as safety certification systems, both for tour operators accepting clients, and for divers seeking reputable tour operators. Dive shops and tour operators are classified by facilities offered and instructor capabilities up to five-star; and individual divers are certified according to capabilities and experience, from basic open-water up to various advanced instructor levels.

As the number of recreational divers has grown, at least partly because of introductory dive tourism, the number of highly experienced recreational divers has also grown. Many of these are constantly seeking new dive locations and experiences as well as specialist diving qualifications. In particular, these include the use of EANx, Enhanced Air Nitrox, for longer deep dives. EANx, commonly referred to simply as Nitrox, is a nitrogen–oxygen mixture with a higher proportion of oxygen than normal air. Many higher-ranked dive shops now offer Nitrox facilities; and new dive tourism operations are constantly exploring increasingly deep and remote destinations. Whereas most commercial dive tours remain above 25 m depth, for example, there are now operators who will lead dives to considerably greater depths at some sites.

Various commercial operators offer dives with sharks, using shark cages for some species and circumstances, but relying on behavioural understanding for other species. Open-water night dives are commonplace, even on completely submerged coral pinnacles far from land.

The most recent addition, perhaps representing the current edge of dive tourism, is diving under the edge of the Arctic and Antarctic ice. Whilst marine scientists have undertaken such dives for decades, it is only recently that logistic support, suitably skilled clients, and sufficient demand has been available for such tours to be offered commercially (Aurora Expeditions, 2003; Smith Diving, 2003; Victory Adventures Diving Expedition, 2003). Perhaps in future, as deep-diving submersible vessels become more commonplace and hence cheaper, these too will be offered as a commercial tourism experience.

Heliskiing and heliboarding

Despite their relatively high cost, heliskiing and heliboarding are established forms of adventure tourism in many parts of the world. The heliski industry seems to be most heavily developed in the Rocky Mountains ranges of southwestern Canada, but there are also well-established heliski operations in New Zealand, Russia, India and in Alaska, Utah and Colorado in the USA. The

(continued)

(Heliskiing and heliboarding continued)

Fig. 4.3. The author, Himalayas. Note avalanche safety pack. Sponsors: Burton Snowboards, Himachal Heliski. Photo: Arnie Wilson.

level of skill required differs between countries and operators, depending partly on terrain and partly on target markets. Advertising by Harris Mountain Heliski (2003) out of Queenstown New Zealand, for example, aims to sell single-day three- or four-run heliski packages to intermediate-level skiers who are already visiting ski resorts in the area. The heliskiing package does not include accommodation or meals, except for lunches on the slopes.

Operators such as Canadian Mountain Holidays (2003) in Canada's British Columbia, in contrast, sell only 1-week all-inclusive packages based in their own backcountry lodges, aimed principally at advanced skiers and boarders, and relying strongly on multiple repeat business from long-established clients. Clients of CMH and its local competitors such as Mike Wiegele Helicopter Skiing (2003) and Selkirk Tangiers Helicopter Skiing (2003) need to be quite fit, strong and skilled skiers or snowboarders simply to keep up with the rest of their helicopter group. In all except the most expensive group charters, heliski tour packages use a single helicopter to shuttle three, four or five groups of skiers and snowboarders in succession. For this system to work safely and efficiently, all the clients need to be able to ski or ride similar terrain at similar

speed. If any skier causes their group to miss its place in the lift cycle, they will not be popular! The skiing is all in backcountry terrain with no avalanche control, and safety depends on the guides' abilities to select runs which are suitably challenging for their clients, but with low risk of avalanche; and the clients' abilities to follow the guides closely down these lines. In some of CMH's operating areas, the terrain is steep and heavily treed, requiring a significant degree of skill from the clients. Indeed, at two of their operating areas, CMH will generally only accept clients who have been prequalified by first visiting one of the company's less demanding areas.

In the Canadian heliski operations, the helicopter lands at the top of each run, and skis are unloaded from a cargo basket by the guide whilst the clients get out of the machine. For at least some heliski operations in Russia, apparently, clients jump from the hovering helicopter on to the snow at the top of each run, adding a further risk factor.

The principal safety concern worldwide, however, is avalanches. As with any form of backcountry skiing, heliskiing involves a greater avalanche risk than skiing within resort areas where potential avalanche slopes are pre-triggered with explosives. Commercial heliski

(continued)

(Heliskiing and heliboarding continued)

operations routinely supply all clients with avalanche transceivers, and train and re-train both new and repeat clients in avalanche search techniques. Commonly, one client in each helicopter group, as well as the guide, carries a snow shovel, avalanche probe and radio. Some operators carry safety precautions even further: Himachal Helicopter Skiing (2003) in the Indian Himalayas issues every skier with an avalanche airbag carried in a small backpack, which is designed to help keep the wearer on the surface of an avalanche flow. Each skier and boarder also carries a small individually coded radio beacon so that they can be located rapidly using a helicopter-based receiver, in addition to ground search. By far the most important safety factor, however, is the skill of the guides. Despite all these precautions, heliskiers are occasionally caught in avalanches or tree wells, and helicopters do occasionally crash. Few of these incidents, fortunately, are fatal but heliskiers and heliboarders do indeed need to remain alert to these risks at all times.

An even greater level of skill is required to maintain safety in new or exploratory heliski operations, where there is no permanent base or associated pool of guide knowledge and where the terrain, snow conditions and weather are less well known. In the last 1 or 2 years, for example, several small operators have begun offering charter heliski tours in Greenland. These are staffed by guides from established heliski operations elsewhere in the world, and rely largely on those operations for their clientele. If these prove commercially successful, they may well lead to the establishment of routine heliski operations in the areas concerned.

As outlined above, different heliski operations involve different degrees of skill and remoteness. Not surprisingly, these are reflected in pricing structures; although, overall, the single most important determinant of price is the number of

groups sharing each helicopter. Heliskiing is expensive, but for many heliskiers price is not a significant barrier. For these individuals, more important factors include: political stability and ease of access to the area concerned; quality and reliability of snowpack; skills and safety qualifications of guides and helicopter pilots and mechanics; and finally, facilities on the ground. In the longer term, the most limiting of these is the quality of the terrain and snow. Given sufficient market demand, and hence funds available, tour operators can provide, control or bypass all the other factors; but clients will only pay this price if the rewards are greater than at the established heliski areas.

Very broadly, the main marketing advantages for heliski operations in the Canadian Rockies are reliable snow and ready access for American clients. In Alaska the principal attraction is particularly steep terrain, not available elsewhere because of avalanche risks. New Zealand is generally less expensive than elsewhere because of currency exchange rates; easily accessible from Japan without significant jetlag; and available in the off-season for northern hemisphere clients. In the Himalayas the principal attraction is the possibility, though by no means the guarantee, of particularly deep, light and dry high-altitude snow, with some of the runs starting at above 5000 m. Russian operations (Heliski Russia, 2003; High Sky Adventures, 2003; Yak and Yeti, 2003) are readily accessible to the European markets; though, in perception at least, facilities and safety may not attain the same standards as elsewhere. A new heliski destination such as Greenland has to compete with all of these. Initially it can do so simply as somewhere different and unknown, and hence attractive to experienced heliskiers looking for a new experience. In the longer term, however, this attraction can only be maintained if Greenland establishes a reputation for high-quality snow at a price comparable to existing destinations.

Surfing

Surf tourism is a relatively recent addition to the commercial adventure sector (Buckley, 2002a). Currently a number of specialist tour operators take experienced surfers to a variety of relatively remote and hence uncrowded surfing destinations, especially in South Pacific island nations

(Buckley, 2002b). The surf at these sites ranges from relatively mellow to highly challenging, with most being coral reef breaks where a wipe-out, especially in big surf at low tide, carries a significant risk of injury. Most of these tours are based in live-aboard charter boats, and more

(continued)

(Surfing continued)

recently also in small specialist surf lodges on various islands (Buckley, 2002a,b, 2003a). Surfing is a highly skilled activity, and these tours certainly qualify as SCARRA.

Examples include: Great Breaks International (2003), Indies Trader Marine Adventures (2003) and the Surf Travel Company (2003) in the Mentawai Island of Sumatra Indonesia; surf resorts in Samoa (Salani Surf Resort, 2003; Sa'moana Resort, 2003; Savaii Surfaris Operations, 2003), Tonga (Ha'atafu Beach Resort, 2003) and Fiji (Nagigia Surf Resort, 2003; Tavarua Island Resort, 2003); tours to Tari and Lohifushi Islands in the Maldives by Atoll Travel (2003); and more.

The world population of surfers is growing, ageing, and becoming more wealthy. This is increasing crowding at mainland continental surf breaks, and fuelling the demand for surf tours. The limiting factors are largely social: the response of local communities in the destination areas; and the interactions between surfers themselves, both tour clients and independent surfers, as the more remote destinations become more crowded (Buckley, 2003a).

As with other forms of outdoor recreation, it is generally private groups and professional teams which first discover new surf breaks, ride larger and more difficult waves, and develop new techniques and variations such as tow-in surfing, hydofoil surfing and kitesurfing (Buckley, 2003b). To date, for example, the giant waves of the Cortez Bank, in the Pacific Ocean 170 km west of San Diego, have been ridden only by professional surfers in boats chartered by their sponsors, not by clients of surf tour companies. The reasons for this certainly include skill, safety and cost. Additionally, however, these waves break only occasionally, when weather conditions generate particularly large ocean swells. Only professional surfers, in general, have both the resources and the flexibility to join a charter boat to the Cortez Bank at short notice.

Conclusions

SCARRA is a significant and growing component of the tourism sector. It is generally not at the edge of the recreational activities involved, whose boundaries are expanded by individual professional athletes and competitions; but it is at the edge of the commercial tourism industry, structurally as well as geographically. The factors that determine whether various types of SCARRA expand and soften into mainstream adventure tourism, or remain as elite, low-volume activities, differ between geographical areas and recreational activities. In some cases the critical factors are geographical or environmental, in other cases social or political, and in other cases economic and financial.

The case studies above are by no means comprehensive. Mountaineering, whitewater rafting and kayaking, diving, heliskiing/heliboarding and surfing are important components of the SCARRA sector, but certainly not the only ones. Other activities include rock and ice climbing, caving, sailboarding and kiteboarding, sailing and ice-yachting, cross-country skiing and snowshoeing, in-line skating, horse riding, mountain biking, ice-biking, parachuting, hang-gliding and more. All of these are offered as commercial adventure tour products in various parts of the world and deserve equal consideration in future analyses.

The economic scale of the SCARRA sector has apparently not been quantified, but is not insignificant. SCARRA's greatest significance for mainstream tourism, however, is that it defines one of the edges of the sector and the directions in which that edge moves in future.

References

Adrift Adventure (2003) http://www.adrift.com (accessed 31 March 2003).

Adventure Consultants (2003) http://www.adventureconsultants.co.nz (accessed 4 April 2003).

Adventure Network (2003) http://www.adventure-network.com (accessed 4 April 2003).

Adventure Travel Society (2003) http://www.adventuretravelbusiness.com (accessed 2 April 2003).

APP Mawson's Huts Foundation (2003) http:// www. mawsons-huts. com. au / expeditions.html (accessed 2 April 2003).

Aurora Expeditions (2003) http://www.auroraexpeditions.com.au (accessed 2 April 2003).

Atoll Travel (2003) http://www.atolltravel.com (accessed 3 April 2003).

Blackfeather (2003) http://www.blackfeather.com/hiking1.html (accessed 2 April 2003).

Boukreev, A. and DeWalt, W. (1996) *The Climb: Tragic Ambitions on Everest.* St Martins Press, New York.

Buckley, R.C. (2002a) Surf tourism and sustainable development in Indo Pacific Islands. I. The industry and the islands. *Journal of Sustainable Tourism* 10, 405–424.

Buckley, R.C. (2002b) Surf tourism and sustainable development in Indo Pacific Islands. II. Recreational capacity management and case study. *Journal of Sustainable Tourism* 10, 425–442.

Buckley, R.C. (2003a) *Case Studies in Ecotourism.* CAB International, Wallingford, UK.

Buckley, R.C. (2003b) Adventure tourism and the clothing, fashion and entertainment industries. *Journal of Ecotourism* 2, 126–134.

Canadian Mountain Holidays (2003) http://www.cmhski.com (accessed 2 April 2003).

Earth Science Expeditions (2003) http://www.shangri-la-river-expeditions.com (accessed 2 April 2003).

Endless River Adventures (2003) http://www.endlessriveradventures.com (accessed 31 March 2003).

Expediciones Chile (2003) http://www.kayakchile.com (accessed 31 March 2003).

Explorers Club (2003) http://www.explorers.org (accessed 2 April 2003).

Great Breaks International (2003) www.greatbreaks.com.au (accessed 31 March 2003).

Harris Mountain Heliski (2003) http://www.heliski.co.nz (accessed 2 April 2003).

Ha'atafu Beach Resort (2003) http://www.surfingtonga.com/index.htm (accessed 3 April 2003).

Heliski Russia (2003) http://www.heliski.ru/en/ (accessed 3 April 2003).

High Sky Adventures (2003) http://www.highskyadventures.com (accessed 4 April 2003).

Himachal Helicopter Skiing (2003) http://www.himachal.com (accessed 3 April 2003).

Indies Trader Marine Adventures (2003) http://www.indiestrader.com (accessed 3 April 2003).

Mike Wiegele Helicopter Skiing (2003) http://www.wiegele.com/main.htm (accessed 3 April 2003).

Mountain Travel Sobek (2003) http://www.mtsobek.com (accessed 2 April 2003).

Nagigia Surf Resort (2003) http://www.fijisurf.com (accessed 3 April 2003).

National Association of Underwater Instructors (2003) http://www.naui.org (accessed 4 April 2003).

North Pole Adventures (2003) http://www.northpole.ru/eng/skydive.htm (accessed 2 April 2003).

North Pole Expeditions (2003) http://www.north-pole-expeditions.com (accessed 2 April 2003).

Professional Association of Dive Instructors (2003) http://www.padi.com (accessed 3 April 2003).

Quicksilver Cruises (2003) http://www.quicksilvercruises.com (accessed 2 April 2003).

Salani Surf Resort (2003) http://www.surfsamoa.com (accessed 3 April 2003).

Sa'moana Resort (2003) http://www.samoanaresort.com (accessed 3 April 2003).

Savaii Surfaris Operations (2003) http://www.atolltravel.com/savaii-operation.htm (accessed 3 April 2003).

Selkirk Tangiers Helicopter Skiing (2003) http://www.selkirk-tangiers.com (accessed 3 April 2003).

Smith Diving (2003) http://www.smithdiving.com/ice (accessed 4 April 2003).

Surf Travel Company (2003) http://www.surftravel.com.au (accessed 3 April 2003).

Tavarua Island Resort (2003) http://www.fiji-islands.com/taveuni-island.html (accessed 3 April 2003).

Tununiq Travel and Adventure (2003) http://www.tununiq.com (accessed 3 April 2003).

Ultimate Descents (2003) http://www.udnepal.com (accessed 31 March 2003).

Victory Adventures Diving Expedition (2003) http://www.victory-cruises.com/Antarctic-ice-diving (accessed 4 April 2003).

Whitney and Smith Expeditions (2003) http://www.legendaryex.com/tours/wilderness_adventures.html (accessed 2 April 2003).

World Expeditionary Association (2003) WEXAS: the independent travellers club. http://www.wexas.com (accessed 2 April 2003).

World Expeditions (2003) http://www.worldexpeditions.com.au (accessed 2 April 2003).

Yak and Yeti (2003) http://www.yak-yeti.com (accessed 4 April 2003).

5 Tourism Trespasses on the Himalayan Heritage: the Hermit Village, Malana

Tej Vir Singh[1], Purnima Chauhan[2] and Shalini Singh[3]

[1]Centre for Tourism Research and Development, A-965/6 Indira Nagar, Lucknow – 226016, India; [2]Government of Himachal Pradesh, Block-1, Set-4, Type-V, Richmond Hill, Shimla – 175001, India; [3]Department of Recreation and Leisure Studies, Brock University, 500 Glenridge Avenue, St Catharines, Ontario, Canada L2S 3A1

Introduction

Tourism forever seeks greener pastures to grow and expand. It uniquely celebrates 'differences' in places and peoples to create novel experiences. However, when it takes on new peripheries, they rarely remain the same and often undergo striking changes in their physical character and cultural ethos. Tragedy further heightens when it all happens in the most highly sensitive and fragile environments such as remote mountain areas, secluded coastlands, verdant wetlands and vulnerable tribal habitats. The damage caused by undesirable development is in most cases irreversible (Cohen, 1978; Mathieson and Wall, 1982; Gasparovic, 1984; Pizam and Milman, 1986; de Kadt, 1992; Harrison and Price, 1996; Brown, 1998; Singh, 1999; Urry, 2000). It has been reported that even the most seemingly innocuous forms of tourism development can interfere with the integrity of ecosystems (Bosselman, 1978). These are, perhaps, regions of 'no-tourism' or those which are too good for tourism. A question often asked but seldom answered candidly is whether tourism has any relevance in such ecospheres of vulnerabilities, or it is there merely to satisfy the curiosity and thirst for novelty of its consumers. These are admittedly precious patrimonies and should be passed on to posterity,

untainted and unharmed. Nevertheless, believers in new tourism, including the new moral tourism or alternative tourism have faith in good practices of tourism – a gentler and kinder form of tourism that should protect the natural and social capital of the industry with moral commitments to the future generation (Krippendorf, 1984, 1987; Poon, 1986; McCool and Moisey, 2001; Fennell and Dowling, 2003). However, not all these dreams have come true, for proverbially man kills the things he loves. Many attempts at responsible ecotourism have turned into mere 'greenwashing' exercises, leaving behind ruined paradises and lost El Dorados (Cohen, 1987; Smith and Eadington, 1992; Cater, 1994; Ashton, 1999). Critics, however, hold that good practices in tourism are made possible with the proactive involvement of the local community that participates in the business throughout its development and thereafter. Tourism becomes uncontrollable as the community slackens its efforts, withdraws or grows less vigilant (Murphy, 1985; Scheyvens, 2002, 2003; Singh *et al.*, 2003; Sofield, 2003)

Himalayan Heritage Under Threat

This chapter is an effort to examine the presence of tourism in Himalaya's fascinating Kulu Valley and to study its consequences in transforming the landscape and heritage resources. The valley was chosen for this study because for centuries it had remained virtually a closed ecosystem, giving it a singular insularity and unique monadic character. Considered as the end of human habitation (*Kulanthapitha*), it developed as a kind of spiritual laboratory where Hindu gods and goddesses, savants and sages, found an appropriate niche for noble pursuits. Interestingly, it evolved an institution of village gods in this part of the Himalayas – gods that were not just stone statues but who were friends, philosophers and guides to the valley residents (Sharma, 1990), who assemble once a year in celebration of *Dussehra* in Kulu to discuss the valley's socioeconomic and ecological problems. The green valley was a self-reliant and resilient agro-pastoral mountain community, known for its naturereverence and live spirit of conservation. It is surrounded by the most spectacular Himalayan scenery, which abounds in myths and mythologies and tribal traditions. Kulu dwellers are a handsome and hospitable people with a fondness for the picturesque; their vernacular settlements, scattered amidst green forests and fields, are objects of delight. They sing and dance in jollity – a happy human race. The valley still has some untouched virgin ecosystems where tourism could not find easy access.

The Kulu Valley held great promise for tourism development with its blend of agriculture and forestry. A meticulously prepared development plan was made for the valley, with Manali as a major destination in the upper Beas Basin, in the late 1970s. In the short time span of its growth, Manali appeared boldly on the world tourist map, but tourism quickly trampled on the Himalayan heritage. Manali had many more visitors than it could handle; agricultural land regressed, pastoral sights dimmed, outsiders pushed aside the locals, and soon Manali was overbuilt (Singh, 1989; Gardner *et al.*, 2002). It is a sad narrative of development where the forces of unsustainability overpowered an adequately planned scenario by perpetuating rampant consumerism.

Manali is gradually shedding its shades of green and its typical bucolic character. Instead of dispersing tourism activity to other beauty spots in the valley (Naggar, Jagatsukh, Katrain, Raison), Manali grew into a disastrous tourist monolith threatening the green environment (Chauhan, 2001). The worst spectacle was to witness an ethical and law-abiding society falling prey to the evil that tourism so spontaneously breeds. Known as the granary of Himachal Pradesh, famous for its fruits and orchards, it will soon be lost in a smoky haze. Cannabis and opium are gradually gaining the status of cash crops in the Kulu Valley. The Malana, Parvati and Banjar Valleys in the district of Kulu and the Chuhar Valley of neighbouring Mandi are gradually becoming the narcotic hubs of the region. Aping foreign tourists, the Kulu teenagers are turning into drug addicts by consuming cannabis, hashish and heroin (Pushkarna, 2003). To stem this tide of drug-taking, a special Customs Preventive Station was established in Kulu in August 2002. They reported that the Narcotic Control Bureau, with the help of police, has destroyed many cultivated fields of cannabis, arrested 115 foreign tourists involved in the business, and recovered 750 kg of opium, hashish and 'brown sugar' (heroin) in the past 2 years; but the evil still exists (Deol, 2003). Drug business is rampant in the Valley of Gods and soon it will destroy its prized culture and primordial values – a Himalayan tragedy. The sudden exposure of the valley to outside visitors has wrought more evil than can be recorded here. Recently the outsiders have found their way to culturally sacrosanct places that are forbidden for tourist visitation, and where even a Kuluvian has to seek permission from the village chief. These remote cultures still live in the past and follow ancient practices. They are indeed anthropological microcosms, xenophobic to the outside world, who live their own cocooned existence with unfamiliar lifestyles and strange, bewildering rites and rituals.

Malana: the Hermit Village

Sequestered Malana in the upper reaches of the Kulu Valley is one such living human museum that of late has become the object of the tourists' gaze. If Malana has been protecting and preserving its little mountain culture throughout the ages, this has mainly been for two important reasons; difficult physical access and a robust community attitude towards outsiders. It is indeed worth examining whether the recent tourism invasion in the Valley has had any influence on the native Malanis, who can barely keep their body and soul together in that harsh, marginal environment which offers few lifestyle choices.

Inexorable geographical forces isolate Malana from the rest of the world. Perched high (2520 m) on a precipitous gorge, it is enclaved by formidable physical barriers where over 1000 tribal people have created their own niche in that harsh environment. The village is situated on the Malana torrent that joins the Parvati river at Jari. Malana is 13 km north of Jari, and can be reached through Naggar (14 km) via the Chandrakhani Pass (3750 m); beyond is a narrow steep slope. The ascent is not easy but inhibiting and often threatening enough to deter any new visitor. Those who are experienced mountain climbers will be more confident of this adventure. Winters are long and cold, blocking all the passages to Malana with snow. Only a steeply narrow goat track leads to snowbound Malana. Except for the Malanis themselves, few travellers would dare to take this dangerous path where rock-falls and landslips are common. Loaded pack ponies cannot reach Malana by any of the paths. Travellers have to be on foot. Solitary Malana survives in utter wilderness. The nearest village to Malana is about 6 hours hard journey time away in difficult terrain through the gorge.

Malana is handicapped by extreme meteorological conditions, which only allow the raising of one crop a year – that of poor quality buckwheat; herding, forestry and gathering herbs are other activities that bring some marginal gains. The villagers have to supplement their food supplies by bartering *ghee* (clarified butter), wool and honey for rice, maize and rock-salt. They are poorer than other highlanders of the Valley. Despite these cruelties of the environment, an average Malani is self-respecting and holds his head high. He is proud of his heritage, highly conservative and deeply religious. They have one supreme god, Jamlu, to whom the whole village is apotheosized. All the land is owned by Jamlu (Dilaram, 1996) and Malanis consider themselves as tenants of the god (Rosser, 1955). They are god-fearing people who believe that Jamlu is omniscient and omnipresent. There is much more to Malana cosmogony than can be narrated here.

A Vigilant Community

Malanis are an indologist's enigma. Strange as it may seem, that a beautiful glen close to Parvati should house a community with such a distinct culture, outlook, beliefs and customs, and yet no one knows about their lineage; who they are; where they come from; and when they came to this part of the Himalaya. Even stranger is the fact that they themselves know very little about their origins.[1] However, legend has it that they can trace their ancestry to Alexander the Great who invaded India in the 4th century BC, when these war-like people stayed back and settled down in Malana (Thakur, 1997). Whether or not they are of Greek origin or mongrels of ancient Kirats or Kinnars, they certainly look quite different from their neighbouring highlanders. Living there for centuries, they have perfectly identified themselves with their ecosystems and have evolved a most interesting way of life that points to the 'theory of possibilism', based on self-defence, self-dependence, self-reliance and self-governance. Their physical isolation, to a large extent, is responsible for their Dionysian attitude of self-centredness, secretiveness and group solidarity (Sachar, 1992). The inhospitality of the milieu and perhaps the apathy of neighbouring communities, as well as the disinterestedness of local government, have made them inward-looking and suspicious in nature. Rosser (1955) a British anthropologist, who studied this community in the early 1950s, also supports this view:

> I stress this severe physical isolation of Malana because it is of great importance when considering the social organization of Malanis and it is indeed the first striking impression that a visitor has on reaching the village . . . One result of this isolation has been more or less ignored by the government and is rarely visited by government officials from Kulu.
>
> (1955: 78)

Surprisingly even today the police stay away from the village, perhaps for different reasons. No one is allowed to interfere with the community ethos. The people enjoy their 'primitiveness', respect their remoteness, and jealously guard their insularity. As Rosser comments:

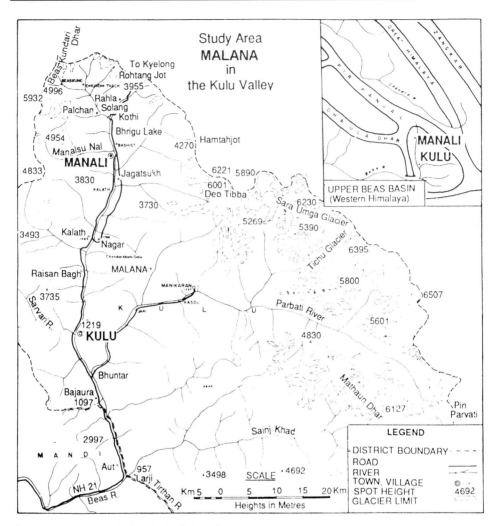

Fig. 5.1. Location map: Malana in the Kulu Valley.

Malana is essentially a hermit village. It has developed an almost fantastical sense of difference, of village cohesion and of intense group loyalty. All who do not 'belong' are treated with virulent suspicion and even contempt. No matter how open and friendly one is to them, this suspicion can only be allayed, rarely dispelled completely.

(1955: 88)

Space Organization

One of the remarkable features of the Malana community is its gift for communal space orga-

nization, admirably expressed in its settlement design. Being a caste-ridden endogamous society, it has taken care to maintain the sense of unity and neighbourhood and yet distanced diverse habitation areas to avoid possible conflict or clannish confrontation. Thus, the village territory is zoned into three units. The *Dhara Behr* is designed for *Kanets*, higher in the caste hierarchy and also in the majority. The *Sara Behr* area is for members of other castes. *Lohars* (blacksmiths) are further distanced from *Sara Behr* as they are considered outsiders, both psychologically and socially. In between the two *Behrs* is the central area known as

Fig. 5.2. *Harcha.* The central area of the Malana settlement where villagers meet for periodic ceremonies and social gatherings. Located on a higher platform surrounded by mamla grass is the lower house where the Village Council meets.

Harcha (meeting place), where three guest houses stand on a raised stone platform, surrounded by velvety mamla grass. *Harcha* guesthouses are meant for visitors who are allowed to stay with prior permission. *Harcha*, indeed, is the 'territorial hub' of the village that serves other social needs such as village fairs and ceremonial gatherings, especially during the winter, when heavy snow covers the village. At a distance from the village there is a place for camping where occasionally special-interest tourists can stay.

Malana is out-of-bounds territory for outsiders and is a well-guarded settlement. Visitors are forbidden to touch either the people or any other possession; wood, stone, crops or houses inside the village. One can see signboards both in English and Hindi with clear warnings for tourists: 'Don't touch anything. Touching of this sacred place will cost you fine of Rs1000'. Violation of these rules could lead to a fine, as stated above, or imprisonment in a closed room protected by 12 locked doors. Malanis strictly adhere to community codes of conduct laid down by the Village Council. Mixing with visitors is an offence and is strictly

discouraged. In the past, people desirous of visiting Malana had to seek permission from Jamlu for entry and once allowed in were fed at the god's expense. This practice was found to be impractical and was therefore abolished, although admittance to the village has to be sought.

Malana, over the years, has developed a perfect community system rooted in value-based expressions, both overt (tangible) and covert (intangible) that together protect the aspect of cohesiveness against extraneous devaluing forces and sustain the positive communal entity. This is what Pearce and Moscardo (1996) elaborate in 'social representations theory' in their book *Tourism– Community Relationships*. While their settlement patterns are vernacular (timber bonded with slate, shingled roof), their costumes and dress style are not much different from other Himachali tribal people. Their dialect is indeed distinct and rather unintelligible to anyone except other Malanis. It is a confusing mix of *Sanskrit*, *Bhatti* and *Kinnauri*. Linguists, however, believe that phonetically the words have some similarity in sound to the Greek language.

Fig. 5.3. Malana youth. With no development options, the young boys and girls of the village are overwhelmed with the burden of life; yet they can still smile.

Kanashi is the name of their language, which is thought to be one of the smallest languages in the world, having its own grammar, syntax and vocabulary. Only *Kanashi* is spoken in Malana and no Kulu villager understands it. This further isolates a Malani from the Kuluvian and fosters the 'sense of belonging' that binds the village as one community (Rosser, 1955).

While the deification of village gods is a common feature of communities in the Western Himalayas, Jamlu is surely a superior god – most powerful and all-pervasive as a presiding deity of Malana. He is the great integrating force of Malana society; he guides, counsels, commands, chastises, and supervises their day-to-day activities. He is the moving spirit of the village, although no temple stands in his name in the entire Kulu Valley. He lives in folklore, myths and miracles[2] so that people feel his presence and refrain from unworthy personal indulgences and unethical activities. He reigns supreme, and no one can challenge his authority. Of the 360 village gods that assemble in Kulu's *Devta Darbar*, in *Dussehra*,

he alone owes no allegiance to Lord Raghunathjee; perhaps he is conscious of his dignity as an indigenous pre-Aryan god. He is the supremo of the famous Village Council and is responsible for administration and judiciary. Before discussing the functions and attributes of the Village Council that raises Malana to the status of a living republic, it would be instructive to provide a short description of the composition and functions of this unique democratic system of self-government at village level. Malana, in this respect, stands alone, independent and autonomous as a tourist curiosity.

The Little Living World Republic

Malana is known far and wide for the effective and meaningful existence of the Village Council and its formation as a political and judicial organization. Malanis have tactfully used religion to make this system forceful and implementable. Again, it is the 'Village of Jamlu', the presiding deity who does it all for the village welfare. In his worship, the unity and solidarity of the village is conspicuously and elaborately expressed, and thus he is the sole source of power in all spheres – political, judicial and religious. He controls them by using his powerful influence. Invested with unlimited powers, the omnipotent Jamlu chooses democratic methods in administration. He has delegated his authority to the executive of the Village Council, composed of 11 members, three of them holding hereditary office and eight elected in keeping with democratic principles. The three high offices are collectively known as *Mundie* (leaders) and reserve more specific functions to perform, although they are equally ranked. By virtue of their office, the one known as *Karmisht* is considered god's manager who looks after god's treasury and supervises management of the lands owned by Jamlu. He presents all the accounts before the Village Council for inspection. Most Malanis are illiterate and *Karmisht* is no exception. Nevertheless, the person so appointed is carefully chosen, making sure that he has a good memory. Since a *Karmisht* holds important responsibilities for the village finance and land management, he acts as a chairperson to the council.[3] The other two senior positions are equally important in the working of the Village Council. The *Pujari* (priest) and the *Gur* (oracle) perform important functions and are held in high esteem by the villagers, as they interpret and communicate Jamlu's will. On important social or religious occasions, community gatherings, or in some matters of dispute or differences of opinion in following the old rites and traditions, or some calamity that might plague the villagers, their judgement as 'the voice of Jamlu', is anxiously sought.[4] On such occasions, *Gur* goes into a trance, as though possessed, to capture the spirit of Jamlu, and becomes a vehicle for communication between the god and the villagers. This is a bizarre and often frightening sight when *Gur* with his long unruly hair, shakes his head and swings violently with the rising beat of the drums. He looks ferocious and resembles a supernatural entity. When such a divine ecstasy reaches its acme, the *Gur* answers to the devotees' questions or problems. Jamlu's judgements are final and unquestionable.

The remaining eight elders, *Jestha*, of the council are elected through a democratic process, based on grouping known as *Chug*; four belong to *Dhara Behr* and four to *Sara Behr.* The Village Council meets periodically in *Harcha,* the raised platform at the village Centre; the elders sit on the platform, while the adult males assemble on the green patch of ground. All the adult villagers are required to attend the meeting. Absentees are fined. All matters that need deliberation are discussed before the executive and general house. Frequent consultations between the *Mundie* and *Jestha* are held before a decision is taken. An appeal, if preferred against their decision, lies with the god who speaks through his *Gur.* Harcourt (1871) in his gazetteer commends the excellent working of the Village Council. He writes:

> For settling disputes other than marital, the Malanis have an unmatched form of participatory court, a concept that was first introduced in the world by Greeks, and is also the only one of its kind in the country. It is divided into a lower and a higher court with *Kander* who looks after the god's property, the *Pujari* of the temple and the *Gur,* the voice of god, holding highest positions. It was for long custom in Malana to settle all disputes before a local tribunal . . .
>
> (1871: 75)

Harcourt confirms that all decisions made have to be unanimous. Otherwise, it goes through some peculiar tribal custom of cutting open the thighs and injecting two sheep of equal weight with a poisonous herb, *zaharmora.* Each sheep represents one party; the plaintiff and the defendant. The sheep that dies first is said to belong to the guilty party.

This indeed is an experience, witnessing a traditional society living up to its high democratic standards in these modern times when ethical principles are often easily compromised for personal gratification. A tour operator returning from Malana reported that he witnessed the entire Village Council dissolving for a re-elections as one of the elders was found at fault unbecoming of his high office or too officious to be kept there. Similarly village members who ignore verdicts of the Council are ostracized or excommunicated to live in exile. Nobody has ever gone to the Kulu courts for rescue or redress (Parthi, 1974)

A question that comes to mind is, can

Malana's timelessness resist the fast pace of post-modernity or the homogenizing process of globalization, where distances in time and space are coming closer? Access and beauty are incompatible. If Malana has survived as an anthropologist's delight, it is because of the fact that it has remained a kind of '*terra incognita*'. Only the Spartans, explorers or serious researchers have had the courage and will to reach this savage environment of beauty and mystery. It is for this reason that the Malana milieu still needs to be rediscovered to find out the ground realities of life. The intrepid Collin Rosser reported on Malana some half-a-century ago. After him, we don't come across any other authentic report on this forbidden habitat except for a few travelogues and mythical accounts in the journalistic literature. Lured by the Malana mystery, Vivek Mohan (1998), a Shimla-based film maker, prepared a documentary that provides an authentic visual record of the life of these strange highlanders.

In the 1950s about 500 people lived in Malana frugally on scarce land resources. For most of their needs they bartered to survive. Nobody knows how many times they multiplied in number after that. One wants to know what destiny they met when the barter system broke down.

The Trespass

There is something infectious about tourists. Wherever they move they influence the host societies with their style of living, culture of affluence and behaviour. Third-World scholars have fairly documented these impacts, good and bad, and found, as already stated, that tourism ought to be developed with more care and caution, particularly in fragile areas. We have seen how the green pastoral Kulu Valley has come under its influence. The evil that tourism has wrought in this critical environment will, assuredly, penetrate into nearby regions of sensitivity. Malana seems to be its first target. The symbol of modern development has already made its appearance in the establishment of the Malana hydro-electric project that will facilitate access to the remote villages in this area. Since last year, roadwork has started to service the nearby hydro-electric dam. This has

already reduced the walking time to Malana from 8 to 2 hours. There is a proposal for a second barrage, just downhill from the village, which would motivate tourists to unravel the Malana mystery (McDonald, 2003).

Malanis, having lived for so long in isolation, do not like the idea of being linked with the road, so abruptly and so closely, for fear of the likely damage to their age-old culture which they prize so much. Some of them know the cost of development, while many have witnessed the tragedy of Manali resort. They do not want to repeat these mistakes. They also know that they cannot halt this process of development, even if they wish to, for it will provide them with much-needed comforts. But all this should come about at a slower pace.

Paradoxically, many of the intrusive visitors are drug-peddlers who have found their way to Malana to collect cannabis. Malana, due to its unique microclimate, is famous for the wild growth of this plant. Autumn is the harvest season, when outsiders and visitors reach Malana for what they call the 'rubbing', to obtain resin (tetrahydrocannabinols) from the cannabis plants. Locally they call it *maal*; tourists pronounce it 'cream'. Malana cream is considered to be the highest quality to be found anywhere in the world. Sold at an exorbitant price in foreign markets (US$870 per kilogram), in Malana it can be bought for US$130 per kilogram (Deol, 2003). One report says that in Amsterdam 1 gram retails for €12.50. Marijuana is openly sold in 'coffee shops' around the city. The only restriction being how many coffee shops there can be in a given area. It is being branded under various names such as 'Malana Cream', 'Malana AK-47' and 'Parvati Cream'. Malana Cream can be obtained in Israel, France, Germany, Italy and the Netherlands. On average a villager can earn US$4350–6522 per year from the drug trade. This new economy has given the villagers a taste for comfortable living. They can have their house repaired, buy better tools for tilling the land, put some money in Jamlu's treasury and save some amount for a rainy day. However, they also feel that this cannot sustain them for much longer, as the rains are getting scantier and weather warmer every year. Last year's 'cream' harvest was only half that of 2001 (McDonald, 2003). Many culture-

Fig. 5.4. Cannabis grows wild all over the high Himalaya. Malana marijuana is of high quality and foreign visitors travel from far afield to take part in the 'rubbing'.

conscious villagers attributed this to the wrath of the god Jamlu, who evidently has not appreciated the new trends in village society.

There are a few questions to which the Village Council has to address itself before the structure of this unique Himalayan society crumbles. Have the people of Malana been led astray by the lust for money? The culture of cannabis has been with them ever since they came to settle there, as the plant grows wild all along the Himalayan ranges. They have also seen the *sannyasin* and anchorites using this herb for spiritual transcendentalism. Some of them find cannabis a source of physical vitality, but certainly they had never seen the unpleasant sight of foreigners mixing with their people under the influence of drugs. Quite a few visitors go to Malana just for the 'rubbing' simply to share in the act. A good number of Nepalese were seen rubbing cannabis on hire. Admirers of Malana's culture ask in dismay – is this the new barter system? or is god Jamlu sleeping? Where has the *Gur* gone? About 22 years ago the last *Gur* passed away and he has not been replaced yet. Is this the onset of cultural decadence in this unfound tribal civilization that has set up a model of democratic governance for the world to emulate?

The trespass is complete, with access reaching nearer to Malana; the new cannabis trade has further perfected it as a tourist pleasure-dome. These modern drifters, drug traffickers and unguarded trekkers have passed the 'limit', and soon they will consume the uniqueness of this place.

Beyond Trespass

Given a sustainable development of tourism, Malana would perhaps perform better in tourism dispersal than Manali, where growth has been largely centripetal. Surprisingly, the trek-starting points of Naggar, Manikaran and Bhuntar have developed accommodation facilities to serve the Malana clientele. Even Malana itself now has several guest-houses with basic rooms and an outside toilet. They normally charge US$2.20–3.20 per night (see McDonald, 2003).

Thus tourism has come to Malana! It is for the people of this wonderful village to use it as an economic opportunity for the well-being of their society and the conservation and preservation of its cultural assets. Malanis, by tradition, have always been excellent managers of their socio-cultural and ecological resources.

Inherent in their personality is human resource skill that will go a long way in setting up another example in tourism entrepreneurship. Hopefully the all-pervasive Jamlu will see some good in tourism and endow them with fresh vision and strength to accept this challenge, where tourism becomes a welcome partner of their unique culture and not an unwanted trespasser.

Conclusion

Tourism thrives on 'differences' in places and peoples. In search of new peripheries, it often embarks upon fragile environments and fragile communities of tender ecologies that attract the tourists' gaze. Since such ecosystems have a poor level of tolerance, tourism can harm these environments, if sustainable development processes are not taken care of. An experiment conducted in the Himalayas' most fascinating agro-pastoral Kulu Valley brought home the truth that only meticulously planned, sustainably developed and consistently monitored tourism can create desirable results. As it happened, tourism moved to forbidden areas of unspoilt ecosystems rather than targeting potentially more resilient areas. Malana, a remote tribal village on the Parvati river, was taken over. The highly efficient village administration that had earned a name for being one of the smallest existing world republics, lost its intrinsic character, probably for ever.

The evil that tourism brought to the Kulu Valley has recently reached the remote village of Malana as more and more inquisitive visitors want to experience this little Himalayan culture. Malana, by virtue of its microclimate, produces abundant wild cannabis, which has earned a name for itself in the world market of narcotics and can command an incredibly high price in international markets. Now more tourists than ever come to Malana not only to experience novelty, but also for this heady drug, demand for which is increasing. The recent Malana hydro-electricity project that has constructed an approach passage has made it easier to reach the highly perched precipitous abode of Malana. Tourism now finds it easy to trespass on the Himalayan heritage.

The time has now come when this vestige of culture should be saved or protected from decay and destruction. Tourism dynamics has an important role to play here. Malana has everything that a good tourism destination is often made of: the extraordinary land features, green cover with forested slopes, Malana river torrent with a profusion of white waters, high-altitude fauna including unique species of pheasant, musk deer and cold-water fish; easy, medium and hard trek routes to wondrous Himalayan landscapes in the north and north-east, power availability and, above all, the unique human distinctiveness of Jamlu's village with all its myths and miracles. The people of Malana as a human resource have no equal; a society that has learnt to live in perfect discipline, adhering to a specific code of conduct, will gradually mould itself to a benign tourism culture. Malana presents a great opportunity for developing what has been called 'deep eco-tourism' or 'indigenous tourism'. The problem is, who should be the stakeholders in this momentous enterprise – the capitalists from Delhi or Shimla, the Ministry of Tourism, Himachal Pradesh, local government, the NGOs or the expatriates who together unmade good tourism in Manali. While answers to these questions may not be easy, it is important that the vigilant community of Malana should have a strong voice in shaping a new tourism that sits well with their cultural ethos and timeless traditions. Any maker of this kind of indigenous tourism has the role of a leader, needing a spark of genius, who can create a successful tourist destination through local insight and entrepreneurship (Ritchie and Crouch, 2003), besides building confidence among the villagers and specially the *Mundie* who have been keeping aloof from the mundane world. Once involved in the tourism business, they will pick up the tricks of the trade. It is hoped that they will present a model of righteous tourism in this part of the Himalaya, as broadly outlined by Singh and Singh (2001) for the higher regions of Garhwal in Uttaranchal. This concept, named Bhotia Tourism, is largely based on United Nations' guidelines provided for the economic development of vulnerable groups of indigenous and tribal communities (UNO, 1992). It is holistic in approach and cares for the biophysical diversity and cultural authenticity of the destination, without causing major deviations from the local lifestyle. While it is true that no model repeats itself exactly over the Himalayas because of the complexity of its ecosystems and cultural uniqueness, it would certainly be helpful in designing a framework for soft development techniques. Since indigenous people have, through the ages, evolved the art of co-existence with Nature's challenges, it is suggested that they put this knowledge to further use, while discovering yet another option for subsistence. The most important issue in this development process is that tourism should not become the sole mainstay of the people.

For the present, one must think seriously how to divert the community of the Malanis from the cancerous drug trade, which is 1000 times more lucrative than traditional agro-pastoral pursuits. This consumptive drug-tourism is Himalaya's dystopia, and has to be curbed or stopped in order to make any fresh headway. Some efforts in this direction have already been made by local politicians and the Narcotic Control Bureau, by involving UN agencies for finding a suitable alternative to this menace.

There exists a strong lobby in the valley that advocates the legalization of cannabis cultivation, as the plant has many uses. For example, it has amazing medicinal properties, is used for making rope, shoes, clothing, paper, lighting oil, and is an important source of protein. They argue that before the establishment of the Narcotic Drugs and Psychotropic Act, the cultivation of cannabis was legal. One of the most convincing arguments that they put forward is that the Central Government has granted limited licenses to narcotic cultivation in three states (Rajasthan, Madhya Pradesh and Uttar Pradesh) of India to meet the requirements of the pharmaceutical industry. Himachal Pradesh should also be added to this list as the state has ample potential to meet the needs of the pharmaceutical industry, which is growing by 15% annually. If this happens, would the Malanis be legally permitted to serve their famous home-grown 'cream' in their guest houses?

Notes

1. According to some popular anecdotes, it is believed that people from the neighbouring valleys migrated here many centuries ago, as represented in eight distinct clans residing in the village today. In Malana, this is common knowledge that has been passed on down the centuries through word of mouth. Nevertheless, it is admirable that the people of Malana were able to preserve this blend of mountain culture against invading modernity (Chauhan, 2003).

2. Young (1916) in his article 'Malana and the Akbar–Jamlu legend' narrates the story of a miracle that says Akbar's tax-gatherers charged two pieces from a pious man in Delhi, who was given this petty amount from Jamlu's treasury in Malana. Akbar having come to know of this fact, and having being struck with leprosy, sent his men to Malana with the coin and his statue in gold and images of horses and elephants in silver. Thereupon, Jamlu was pleased and the emperor was completely cured of the deadly disease. Every year this incident is re-enacted at Malana and the images are brought out from Jamlu's treasure house.

3. Interestingly, the first *Karmisht* was a female named Sunni Bhatoli (Sharma, 1988).

4. The method of drawing the Council's attention to a dispute is fixed and formalized. The man with the grievance goes to the platform and there lights a fire in a special fireplace for this purpose. Here he sits until one of the members of the Council happens to pass. On seeing the fire burning it is the duty of the Council member to find out what the matter is and then either call an immediate meeting of the Council or arrange for one in a day or so (Rosser, 1955).

References

Ashton, R.E., Jr (1999) Working for a successful story: the case of Punta Sal National Park. In: Singh, T.V. and Singh, S. (eds) *Tourism Development in Critical Environments.* Cognizant Communication Corporation, New York, pp. 87–111.

Bosselman, F.P. (1978) *In the Wake of the Tourist: Managing Special Places in Eight Countries.* The Conservation Foundation, Washington, DC.

Brown, F. (1998) *Tourism Reassessed: Blight or Blessing?* Butterworth-Heinemann, Oxford, UK.

Cater, E. (1994) Ecotourism in the Third World: problems and prospects of sustainability. In: Cater, E. and Lowman, G. (eds) *Ecotourism: a Sustainable Option?* John Wiley & Sons, Chichester, UK, pp. 69–86.

Chauhan, P. (2001) Towards more sustainable tourism development: the case of Kullu Valley in the Himalayas. *Geographer,* (special issue) 48(1), 44–58.

Chauhan, P. (2003) The world's oldest democracy: Malana. *Monal* (a quarterly newsletter of H.P. Tourism, Shimla) 36, 7–8.

Cohen, E. (1978) The impact of tourism on the physical environment. *Annals of Tourism Research* 5(2), 215–237.

Cohen, E. (1987) Alternative tourism: a critique. *Tourism Recreation Research* 12(2), 13–18.

Deol, R. (2003) High in the valley. *Deccan Herald News Sunday*, May 25.

Dilaram, S. (1996) *Kullu: Himalayan Abode of the Divine*. Indus Publishing, New Delhi, India.

Fennell, D.A. and Dowling, R.K. (eds) (2003) *Ecotourism Policy and Planning*. CAB International, Wallingford, UK.

Gasparovic, F. (1984) The development of tourism and the environment on the Adriatic coast of Yugoslavia. *UNEP Industry and Environment* 7(1), 25–27.

Gardner, J., Sinclair, J., Berkes, F. and Singh, R.B. (2002) Accelerated tourism development and its impacts in Kulu-Manali, HP, India. *Tourism Recreation Research* 27(3), 9–20.

Harcourt, A.F.P. (1871) *The Himalayan Districts of Kooloo, Lahoul and Spiti* (reprinted 1982). Vivek Publishing Company, New Delhi, India.

Harrison, D. and Price, M. (1996) Fragile environments, fragile communities? An introduction. In: Price, M. (ed.) *People and Tourism in Fragile Environments*. John Wiley & Sons, Chichester, UK, pp. 1–18.

de Kadt, E. (1992) Making the alternative sustainable: lessons from development for tourism. In: Smith, V.L. and Eadington, W.R (eds) *Tourism Alternatives*. University of Pennsylvania Press, Philadelphia, pp. 45–87.

Krippendorf, J. (1984) The capital of tourism is in danger. In: Brugger, E.A., Furrer, G., Messerli, B. and Messerli, P. (eds) *Transformation of Swiss Mountain Regions*. Verlag Paul Haupt, Bern, Switzerland, pp. 427–450.

Krippendorf, J. (1987) *The Holiday Makers: Understanding the Impacts of Leisure and Travel*. Butterworth-Heinemann, Oxford, UK.

Mathieson, A. and Wall, G. (1982) *Tourism: Economic, Physical and Social Impacts*. John Wiley & Sons, New York.

McCool, S.F. and Moisey, N. (2001) Introduction: pathways and pitfalls in search of sustainable tourism. In: McCool, S.F. and Moisey, N. (eds) *Tourism Recreation and Sustainability: Linking Culture and the Environment*. CAB International, Wallingford, UK, pp. 1–16.

McDonald, A. (2003) Holy smoke: the mysteries of Malana. *Outlook Traveller (India)* 3(7), 90–94.

Mohan, V. (1998) *In Search of Malana*. A documentary film. Shimla, India.

Murphy, P.E (1985) *Tourism: a Community Approach*. Methuen, London.

Parthi, L.C. (1974) *Kulut Desh Ki Kahani* (Hindi). Neel Kamal, Kulu.

Pearce, P. and Moscardo, G. (1996) *Tourism Community Relationships*. Pergamon, Oxford.

Pizam, A. and Milman, A. (1986) The social impact of tourism. *Tourism Recreation Research* 9(1), 29–32.

Poon, A. (1986) Comparative strategies for a new tourism. In: Cooper, C. (eds) *Progress in Tourism, Recreation and Hospitality Management*, Vol. 1. Belhaven, London, pp. 91–102.

Pushkarna, V. (2003) Lost in the smoky haze. *The Week (India)*, July 13, 16–18.

Ritchie, J.R.B. and Crouch, G.I. (2003) *The Competitive Destination: a Sustainable Tourism Perspective*. CAB International, Wallingford, UK.

Rosser, C. (1955) A hermit village in Kulu. In: Srinivas, M.N. (ed.) *India's Villages*. Asia Publishing House, New Delhi, India, pp. 77–89.

Sachar, S.N. (1992) A flourishing village republic. *The Tribune, Saturday Plus*, December.

Scheyvens, R. (2002) *Tourism for Development: Empowering Communities*. Prentice-Hall, Harlow, UK.

Scheyvens, R. (2003) Local involvement in managing tourism. In: Singh, S., Timothy, D. and Dowling, R.K. (eds) *Tourism in Destination Communities*. CAB International, Wallingford, UK, pp. 229–252.

Sharma, B.R. (1990) The institution of the village gods in the Western Himalayas. In: Rustomjee, N.K. and Ramble, C. (eds) *Himalayan Environment and Culture*. Indus Publishing Company, New Delhi, India, pp. 131–140.

Sharma, N.K. (1988) *Malana: Puratan Sanskriti ka Pratik* (Hindi). Bhavana Prakashan, Delhi, India.

Singh, S., Timothy, D. and Dowling, R.K. (eds) (2003) *Tourism in Destination Communities*. CAB International, Wallingford, UK.

Singh, T.V (1989) *The Kulu Valley: Impacts of Tourism in the Mountain Areas*. Himalayan Books, New Delhi, India.

Singh, T.V. (1999) Keep the sharks out of the mountains. *Our Planet (UNEP, Nairobi)* 10(1), 22–23.

Singh, T.V and Singh, S. (2001) Initiating ecotourism in a peripheral Himalayan community: case of Bhotiyas of Garhwal. *Geographer* 48(1), 58–73.

Smith, V.L. and Eadington, W.B. (eds) (1992) *Tourism Alternatives: Potentials and Problems of Development of Tourism*. University of Pennsylavania Press, Philadelphia, USA.

Sofield, T. (2003) *Empowerment for Sustainable Tourism Development*. Pergamon, New York.

Thakur, M.R. (1997) *Myths, Rituals and Beliefs in Himachal Pradesh*. Indus Publishing Company, New Delhi, India.

UNO (1992) *Report of the United Nations Technical Meeting on the International Year for the World's Indigenous Peoples*, 9-11, March 1992, p. 18.

Urry, J. (2000) *Consuming Places*. Routledge, London.

Young, G.M. (1916) Malana and the Akbar–Jamlu legend. *Journal of Punjab Historical Society* 4(2), 98–112.

6 Thanatourism in the Early 21st Century: Moral Panics, Ulterior Motives and Alterior Desires

A.V. Seaton[1] and J.J. Lennon[2]

[1]*Luton Business School, Department of Tourism and Leisure, University of Luton, Putteridge Bury, Hitchin Road, Luton, Bedfordshire LU2 8LE, UK;* [2]*Moffat Centre for Travel and Tourism Business Development, Glasgow Caledonian University, Cowcaddens Road, Glasgow G4 0BA, UK*

Thanatourism (dark tourism) entered academic discourse in 1996 as a generic term for travel associated with death, atrocity or disaster (Foley and Lennon, 1996; Seaton, 1996). These had not previously featured as elements in the typologies periodically published in the academic literature of tourism motivation, but within 7 years they had stimulated significant academic attention, and had even merited an encyclopaedia entry in which thanatourism/ dark tourism was elaborated to comprise visits to battlefields, murder and atrocity locations, places where the famous died, graveyards and internment sites, memorials, and events and exhibitions featuring relics and reconstructions of death (Seaton, 2000a). This rapid acceptance of dark tourism/thanatourism as a distinct, motivational field is rather akin to astronomers agreeing to recognize the existence of a new planet in a solar system which was thought to have been pretty comprehensively mapped and delineated.

Equally striking has been the increasing weight of coverage from the mass media in news, guide-books and travel features. Indeed, the subject seems occasionally to have been ratcheted up, from the status of myth to metamyth, by sectors of the popular press, seeking to depict it, not just as a genre of travel motivation and attraction, but as a social pathology sufficiently new and threatening to create moral panic.

This chapter sketches out an overview of thanatourism's progress in the UK and USA including its academic development, the moral panic that has surrounded it in the media, the debate about its motivations, its political and ideological effects and its future, including the yet-to-be-resolved question as to whether it can properly be categorized as a single entity.

Dark tourism or thanatourism (the two terms have been used interchangeably, but the latter will be adopted in this chapter as a neutral term without any emotive connotations) were first named and described in a special issue of the *International Journal of Heritage Studies* (IJHS) 7 years ago. The issue included an overview of the phenomenon and the ethical issues it provoked (Foley and Lennon, 1996), a historical account of its development, and a typology of its main forms (Seaton, 1996), as well as three case studies: the *Titanic* (Deuchar, 1996), the JFK Museum (Foley and Lennon, 1996) and the Maginot Line (Smart, 1996). This issue was followed by a monograph-length study by Dann (1998) which provided a post-modernistically playful inventory of dark tourism's main forms, and its motivations, among which the writer identified: a regressive, childish desire for encounters with phantoms; a desire for novelty, derived from boredom with conventional tourism; nostalgia; an implicit enjoyment in the severities of retributional justice; a desire to celebrate crime and deviance, not permitted within the confines of everyday life; and because, allegedly, 'an awareness of death is very much linked to being a tourist', though this last idea was not developed in any detail. In 2000, Lennon and Foley published a book-length account of dark tourism which developed the ideas they had first introduced in the 1996 special issue of *IJHS*, with more case studies.

In addition to these overviews, academic work has over the last 7 years focused on a number of the tourism forms that are subsumed within the specific kinds of thanatourism. There have been several studies of battlefield tourism (Lloyd, 1998; Henderson, 1997, 2000; Smith, 1996, 1998; Seaton, 2000b; Iles, 2003), Holocaust tourism (Lennon and Foley, 2000; Tunbridge and Ashworth, 1996), cemetery and internment sites (Seaton, 2002), slavery heritage (Dann and Seaton, 2001), celebrity death sites (Alderman, 2002), and prisons and penal colonies as visitor attractions (Strange and Kempa, 2003; Ashworth, Chapter 8, this volume).

Alongside this academic output, there has been a notable weight of popular media coverage promoting thanatourism. Dann (2003) has catalogued some of the dimensions of this TV and print coverage of murder settings, battlefields and celebrity death sites including those of Versace, Elvis Presley and Princess Diana. In 2002 the *British Airways Magazine* (Calder, 2002) included a long article on how world trouble-spots and battlefields had metamorphosed into tourist attractions, including American Civil War sites, first packaged by Thomas Cook as tours in the 19th century; the USS *Arizona* memorial in Hawaii where a ship sunk at Pearl Harbour in 1941 can still be seen by tourists through a transparent viewing platform, leaking oil on the sea bed; the Museum of Genocide in Cambodia, formerly the torture camp of the Khmer Rouge; and in Vietnam the shady woodlands around Cu Chi where tourists may

> sample what life was like for the Vietcong who fought the world's mightiest war machine. The tunnels are an underground metropolis

> burrowed by communists to wage guerilla warfare.
>
> (Calder, 2002)

The same article also named Guantanamo Bay, Cuba and Panmunjon (in the middle of the demilitarized zone between North and South Korea) as two of the world's hotspots for afficionados of destinations that were 'on the edge'. In December 2002, Lonely Planet Guides developed their own thanatourism section with a website category called, *Fatal Attractions*, which lists the following:

- Torajan funerals – Indonesia
- Voodoo – New Orleans
- Day of the Dead – Mexico
- Wakes – Ireland
- Anzac Day – Turkey
- Varanasi's burning ghats – India
- Sky burials – Tibet
- Dying to get home.

Thanatourism as Moral Panic: Past and Present

In Britain the media have done more than merely report thanatourism. They have periodically constructed a metanarrative of moral panic around it, through sensational exposés of dubiously verified stories. In 1997 the English tabloid newspaper, the *Star*, having spent several days covering the mass shooting of schoolchildren by a gun fanatic in the Scottish town of Dunblane, ran a front-page story alleging tourism exploitation of serial murder sites there and in other places:

> Britain's vilest man is to run a ghoulish tour of Dunblane and Hungerford. Money grabbing Alex Chappel plans to make a killing out (of) gun monsters Michael Ryan and Thomas Hamilton's rampages. The sicko firm has even called his coach firm The Dennis Nilson Tour Company after the notorious gay mass murderer.

> And he promised guided tours of Britain's blood-soaked murder sites – including the Dunblane tour. Chappel, 22, is hopes [sic] to lure punters with tours of Nilson's Cranley Gardens blood-bath home and Gloucester's infamous Cromwell St, home of Fred and Rosemary West.

He even offers a 25% discount to pensioners and children and a 10% deduction to 'anyone with a proven conviction for murder'

(*Star* newspaper, 1996).

Nothing more was heard of this enterprise, although the paper could have pursued the issue of murder tourism further by coverage of the Jack the Ripper Tours and Kray Twins Gangland tours which did actually exist for London tourists. Five years later it was claimed that another infamous murder had attracted voyeuristic tourists. In 2002 a week after the arrest of Ian Huntley and his girlfriend Maxine Carr for the murder of Holly Wells and Jessica Chapman, two 10-year-olds from a small Cambridgeshire village called Soham, the *Daily Telegraph* warned:

> Soham has . . . become a day trip destination for some visitors attracted by its association with a heinous crime. The streets have been jammed with traffic over the Bank Holiday weekend. Coaches taking tourists to visit nearby Ely Cathedral or the sights of Cambridge have made detours to the fenland town. A couple were seen sitting in deckchairs in the churchyard of St. Andrews eating fish and chips.
>
> (O'Neill, 2002)

The same story recounted how a 16-year-old girl asserted that Soham had become a 'tourist attraction'. Once again, there was little follow-up on the story, and no hard evidence about the scale or duration of Soham's status as a tourist destination.

Later that year a more documented case re-reactivated moral panic about thanatourism. This was an exhibition of cadavers, called *Body Worlds* in the Atlantis Gallery, Brick Lane, in London's East End which had been staged by a German academic with the gothic-sounding name of Professor Gunther von Hagens. In 9 months it attracted 720,000 visitors. On one day alone 4112 people each paid £10 to see dissected and preserved human bodies in a variety of poses (Gibbons, 2003). Before it opened, interest had been fuelled by a torrent of moral outcry in the media, predicting police interventions to arrest the academic impressario. On the day, things passed off peacefully and the exhibition did not just attract spectators, but also future exhibits, with 60 visitors volunteering to donate their bodies (although no dates, it seems, were set for their delivery). A few months previously the professor had conducted the first public autopsy in the same gallery for 170 years. A *Guardian* critic writing about both events concluded, 'Gore means more as macabre shows pull in the crowds'.

Coverage by academics and the mass media has thus given thanatourism an increasing profile on the novelty tourism agenda. Yet in reality it is not as novel as the news coverage suggests. Death and violence displays have historically been a common sight for travellers: in the memorials, relics and images of martyred saints offered to pilgrims at mediaeval, religious shrines (Sumption, 1975; Finucane, 1977); in a variety of commercial travelling shows, fairground exhibitions and cabinets of curiosities found throughout Europe from the 16th century onwards (Altick, 1977); and in an incalculable number of battlefields, museums, internment sites, and disaster locations inventoried in guide-books from the time that modern popular tourism first started to take off in the 18th century. What is newer is the scale of public debate about the ethics of such displays, and even this debate was comprehensively trailered over a century ago by a case that still resonates today, that of Madame Tussaud.

Madame Tussaud was the first individual to have to confront ethical criticism for commercial displays of violence. She had started her career, in the late 18th century, making death masks of political celebrities, guillotined during the French Revolution. The history of her wax modelling was thus inflected from the start with an emphasis on representing the dead and victims of violence, rather than celebrating the living. Tussaud moved from France to England in 1802 and took her exhibitions as a travelling show round Britain. In 1835 she settled in permanent premises in Baker Street, London, where she expanded her products for the new market to include, not just English royal and political celebrities but notorious criminals and reconstructions of their crimes and punishments, exhibited in what came to be known as the Chamber of Horrors, a title coined by the satirical magazine, *Punch* in 1846, not by Tussaud herself.

The period during which Madame Tussaud operated from Baker Street was one of unprecedented expansion in cheap, popular newspapers, and by mid-century this 'penny press', comprising not just newspapers, but specialist magazines like the *Police Budget*, which stimulated an appetitite for details of crime and "orrible murder', which had previously been served by broadsheets sold in the street. Public interest in murder and criminal displays was thus, like modern thanatourism, fanned by the mass media. One famous double murder, committed by James B. Rush around 1850, led to an expanded Chamber of Horrors (Chapman, 1984).

The pursuit of verisimilitude extended, not just to wax modelling of criminals and their victims, but to showing relics. From its early beginnings, Madame Tussaud's had bought up artefacts associated with historical events (e.g. Napoleon's coach was exhibited after Waterloo). During the Victorian era the organization acquired effects associated with famous murders. One of Tussaud's most sensational exhibitions was the reconstruction of the Hampstead Murders of 1890, in which a Mrs Pearcy killed her husband's mistress, Mrs Hogg, and her baby. Publicity for the event stressed the authenticity of the artefacts on show:

> All the articles contained in the kitchen have been removed from No. 2, Priory Street, and are placed in exact relative position as found by the police when they entered the premises.
> (Chapman, 1984: 98)

The exhibition included the pram in which the murderess had transported the dismembered remains of her victims, the table against which Mrs Hogg was leaning when the blow was struck, and the window supposed to have been smashed by Mrs. Hogg in her death struggles. 30,000 people blocked the streets when the exhibition opened.

Despite the popular success of the Chamber of Horrors, it attracted criticism from a cadre of liberal, middle-class opinion formers, committed to evolving notions of rational amusement, useful knowledge and high moral seriousness that anticipates that collectivity of attitudes which has become known as 'political correctness' in our own time. Dickens, an inveterate moralist, marvelled that people could stand eating a pork pie in the Chamber of Horrors, despite himself having a developed an interest in murder, police work and the macabre. Thackeray deplored Madame Tussaud's habit of privileging violent crime as a subject of display:

> Should such indecent additions continue to be made to this exhibition the 'horrors' of the collection will surely predominate. It is painful to reflect that although there are noble and worthy characters really deserving of being immortalised in wax, these would have no chance in the scale of the thrice-dyed villains.
> (Chapman 1984: 65)

Madame Tussaud's reacted to the attack in much the same way as promoters of thanatourism attractions have done ever since, by denying its freak show connotations, and stressing its moralizing and educational features. A poster of 1864 announced:

> The proprietors assure the public that so far from the exhibition of the likenesses of criminals creating a desire to imitate them, experience teaches that it has a direct tendency to the contrary.
> (Chapman, 1984: 67)

To tone down the sensational character of the Chamber of Horrors an attempt was even made to rename it the 'Chamber of Comparative Physiognomy', but the original name has survived to this day.

Madame Tussaud's is a protypical instance of the tensions produced by attractions that, on the one hand, appeal to large audiences through displays of death and disaster, but then have to run the gauntlet of evangelically minded critics deploring the alleged exploitation of the murkier side of human nature. This tension has not gone away. In 1996 Madame Tussaud's was relaunched and, as part of its facelift, commissioned an English academic, David Canter, Professor of Psychology at Liverpool University, to produce a scientific report on the appeal of horror. Canter, whose track record included research on criminal psychology, since extended to several TV series on serial killers and 'murder mapping', produced a study which was thought to be too qualified and complicated for public consumption. Instead the organization published an edited synopsis of the main results, called, 'Horror: continuing attraction and common reaction'. It is interesting to wonder why it was produced, and to whom it was addressed. Attractions do not usually interrogate or deconstruct the basis of their appeal to visitors. It can be seen as an instance of the perennial defensive need for thanatourism attractions, however popular in audience terms, to justify their existence to opinion-forming minorities, to circumvent criticism in a PC age. Canter's study included a discussion of the motives that make people seek out displays of horror, and implicitly located them within the sphere of normal, rather than pathological, behaviour. The report suggested that displays of horror and violence could have a positive role and serve a cathartic function, which actually strengthened and promoted social norms, rather than glamourizing deviant behaviour.

> Overall then, confronting horrific behaviour is a good thing, when it is in moderation and in the right context. It enables us not only to put horrible and inhumane actions into context, but allows us to rationalise our fears and insecurities. But perhaps, most importantly of all, it is in recognizing horror that we re-affirm the basic rules of good and evil.
>
> (Canter, 1996: 22)

Madame Tussaud's and the continuing success of the Chamber of Horrors thus highlights the gap between what many people actually like, as reflected in their practices, and what 'civilizing' opinion formers, who influence the public agenda, suggest should be the case. This in turn means that there may also be a gap between what attractions publicly *claim to be offering* to appease public opinion, and what constitutes the true basis of their appeal to their audiences. This was commented on by Maurice Davies of the Museums Association during the debate about the *Body Worlds* exhibition of cadavers in 2002 discussed earlier. He accepted that even museums may derive their real appeal from the bizarre and macabre, not from the supposedly high cultural purposes they overtly promote in their catalogues:

> There is a fine tradition in this country of museums pretending to be above this sort of thing. But part of their origins are in the cabinet of curiosities of weird and freakish things assembled by rich people. Certainly in the 18th and 19th centuries there was much less distance between them and the fairground.
>
> (Gibbons, 2003: 12)

Many historical exhibitions, he concluded, masquerading as culture, draw their secret appeal from 'morbid thrill of looking at a corpse', inadmissable as the truth may be.

The truth may be less inadmissible outside the UK and USA. In some European countries, political correctness does not exert the same controlling hegemony over public display. The limits of the acceptable and the proscribed in public presentations of violence are, like those in sexual display, culturally determined. A recently established museum in Hungary, the Budapest Police Museum, exemplifies this cultural relativism in the determination of thanatouristic boundaries. Housed in a single-storey building in a back-street, the Museum's remit is to narrate the history of the Budapest Police Force. It is divided into two sections. To the left of the entrance is a room which focuses on the police, and to the right, a room which concentrates on crimes and victims. There is no programme or catalogue that prepares the visitor for what s/he is about to see.

The police room features a broadly sequential history of the Budapest Police exhibiting a range of guns, uniforms and photographic portraits of former chiefs of police, arrayed in order from the mid-19th century. These portraits are exhibited on the wall in lines, and in some cases look not unlike those harsh, wild-eyed, diagnostic 'mug-shots' featured in eugenics texts 100 years ago to exemplify the physiognomy of imbeciles, psychopaths and recidivists. Among them one is surprised to see the name Imre Nagy, famous as the martyred premier of the 1956 uprising, who was Budapest police chief in 1946.

Much more disturbing is the crime room, which offers a no-holds-barred series of tableaux depicting crimes, most of which are murder and atrocity, many with sexual motives. On a central stage is a reconstructed murder scene with model corpse and policemen looking for clues (Fig. 6.1). Framed on the walls are forensic photos of mutilated bodies, severed penises and gashed heads, as well as cabinets of murder relics, doll's houses with dead children

Fig. 6.1. Budapest Police Museum: reconstruction of murder scene showing victim lying on the floor and police looking for clues.

in them, a model well with bodies piled at the bottom, and an 18th-century painting of a child murder. Most numerous of all are photographs and newspaper reports of murders which leave nothing to the imagination, except the identity of the victims, who are all uniformly disguised with a white strip across their eyes to prevent recognition. The combination of documentary realism and melodramatic theatricality make the museum seem more like a Dadaist installation by Damien Hirst than a state attraction, and one that would be surely declared off-limits for children in Britain or America. Yet the museum is staffed by two pleasant, fresh-faced girls who greet the visitor from a kiosk in the lobby, without any indication that the exhibition holds anything morally questionable or subversive. The museum is an object lesson in the relativism of thanatouristic value judgements.

Thanatourism Motivations

Thanatourism and 'the other'

The discourses surrounding thanatourism in the UK apparently suggest a gap between the popular tastes and enjoyments of mass audiences, and that of more liberally 'educated', opinion-forming minorities (including academics and media critics) who have influence on the articulation of social norms and public agendas. How credible is this apparent schism? An alternative possibility is that thanatourism fascinates everyone, opinion-forming minorities included, and that this fascination is not a sectional pathology, but a universal condition that some are prepared to admit, while others are not. Death and violence may be seen as major kinds of *Other*, experiences at the opposite extreme to the world of everyday living, and travel to have encounters with them – at disaster sites, memorials, battlefields – may be just another kind of journey into this alterior territory that has frequently been seen as a principal motive for travel. The difference is that most academic discussion of 'the other' in tourism has articulated it as encounters with different, living cultures, rather than identifying death and violence as target 'others'. Alterior journeys into the realms of death and violence may have two distinct origins. The first is an inadmissable *schadenfreude*, that secret pleasure in witnessing the misfortunes of others that, for example, sends people rubbernecking to car- and air-crash sites, and also primes the media's desire for pictures when disasters strike. The existence of *schadenfreude*, as a general psychological tendency, has been infrequently explored in social science research agendas, though the experiments of Stanley Milgram famously demonstrated ordinary people's capacity to inflict pain on others under conditions that seemed to be legitimated by authority figures (Blass, 1992). Literary commentators, however, have occasionally ventured bolder insights into human nature than social scientists, whose model of human behaviour has generally been a liberal, rational one (particularly that of their own). The French epigammatist, De Rochefoucaud wrote: 'In the misfortune of our best friends we often find something that is not displeasing'.

Another writer, the novelist, Ian McEwen, writing on the day after 11 September 2001, went close to owning up to voyeuristic *schadenfreude* in analysing his compulsive TV viewing of the collapse of the Twin Towers:

> Our set in the corner is mostly unwatched. Now my son and I surfed – hungrily, ghoulishly – between CNN, CBC and BBC24. As soon as an expert was called in to pronounce on the politics or the symbolism, we moved on. We only wanted to know what was happening. Numbed, and in a state of sickened wonderment, we wanted only information, new developments – not opinion, analysis or noble sentiments; not yet. We had to know: was it two planes or three that hit the Twin Towers? Was the White House now under attack? Where was the plane the airforce was supposed to be tracking? An information junkie inside me was silently instructing the cameras: go round that tower and show me the aeroplane again; get down in the street; take me on the roof.
>
> (McEwen, 2001)

And if McEwen compulsively viewed images of the Twin Towers, visitors to New York were equally drawn to Ground Zero. A few weeks after the outrage, public demand forced the building of a viewing platform by civic authorities from which the wreckage could be safely observed. The significance of the attack on the World Trade Center was the mythic dimensions of its horror. Viewers across the world and

sightseers on the spot were witnesses to one of the most spectacular 'others' in modern times, a disaster that connected to almost all the cultural terrors established in the mythology of the techno-age: the plane crash, the mass murder, the collapsing skyscraper, the fanatical terrorist, the mass grave.

Yet *schadenfreude* may be only one aspect of the alterior fascination with representations of violence and death. Another may be what was, in the past, called thanatopsis, the contemplation of death. Since death is the fate of all, interest in, and meditation on it, was seen as a normal, even a moral requirement. The 18th-century biographer, James Boswell, justified his attendance at public hangings on the basis of the lessons it taught him about his own fate:

> Therefore it is that I feel an irresistible impulse to be present at every execution, as I there behold the various effects of the near approach of death, according to the various tempers of the unhappy sufferers, and by studying them I learn to quiet and fortify my own mind.
>
> (Boswell and Pottle, 1951: 345)

In modern times there are few spaces for this kind of preparatory contemplation. The world of personal, everyday life is dominated by discourses of fitness and health, and dwelling on death is seen as morbid or pathological. However, the media and tourism offer opportunities for legitimate, vicarious contact with death, and through it, imaginative meditation upon mortality. It may be this that makes Dann, following van Gennep and Graburn, assert that, 'death is very much linked to the tourist' (Dann, 1998: 32). In our times thanatopsis may happen on holiday through visits to war or disaster sites, churches, cemeteries and memorials, and the places where famous individuals or collectivities have died.

But all of this is speculation. There has been little significant research into either the motives of the customers, or the purveyors of thanatourism. Academic and mass media coverage has tended to imply ulterior motives and morbid undercurrents, underpinning both the habits of dark tourists, and, even more, the commercial practices of its entrepreneurs. Both sets of commentators have generally affected a tone of ironic distance or ethical disquiet in their fascinated analyses, to preserve them from being seen as proponents of a controversial form. It remains to be seen whether research will ultimately locate thanatourism as normal behaviour, or a darker kind of practice.

A rare instance of a benign view of thanatourism by the mass media was a report by Robert Ryan, a *Sunday Times* journalist, covering a newly constituted tour offered by the 'Original Berlin Walks in English', entitled *Infamous Third Reich Sites*. The tour comprised a subway ride to the Mohrenstrasse along what was once a square called Wilhelm Platz. The guided walk took in what was left of Goebbels Propaganda Ministry, the Reichs Kulturkammer (the Ministry of Culture), and the Reich Air Ministry. What most interested Ryan was not so much the tour's content, as the kind of people choosing to make it. His conclusion was that they were not closet fascists or Nazi sympathizers:

> no tattooed skinheads, holocaust deniers or David Irving fans but a brace of lecturers, a history teacher, a couple of dentists, three backpackers and, curiously, Uli and Gertrude, two East Germans from Potsdam, who were keen to correct the school curriculum that insisted that Hitler and the West were simply adjacent stops on the U-bahn of fascism.
> (Ryan, 2002)

If thanatouristic motives among the general population are little understood, even less is known about how they may vary sectionally among different social groups. A surprising suggestion in the Canter study for Madame Tussaud's was the alleged difference between men and women in their responses to death and violence. Canter asserted that women claimed to enjoy the Chamber of Horrors more than men did, and were more appreciative of scenes of prisoners being tortured. Canter also adduced as evidence of this general disposition to enjoy vicarious encounters with violence the facts that a large number of women were 'avid readers of *True Life Crime*', that 17 out of the top 20 crime writers were women, and that a number of women's societies and groups invited forensic speakers like himself to talk about gory crimes (Canter, 1996: 14). Though

probably different in kind from the appeal of Madame Tussaud's, the Princess Diana Memorial at Althorp is known to be mainly a women's trip, with most visitors being women aged over 40. In 2001 it was one of the few attractions, in an otherwise poor season for UK tourism, to increase its visitors by 11%.

There is some historical evidence for the Canter suggestion. Over 200 years ago James Boswell reported that women made up most of the audiences at public hangings, and during the French Revolution it was women who, reputedly, took up ringside seats to watch the heads roll. Women were also, as Jane Austen satirized in *Northanger Abbey*, the earliest enthusiasts for gothic horror fiction, a precursor of, and influence on, modern horror films and exhibitions. Again it remains for research to reveal what gendered differences in thanatouristic consumption and appreciation exist.

A fascination with violence and the darker aspects of human behaviour also extends to children. This was unexpectedly hinted at in a study carried out in Cambridge over 30 years ago. In 1966 Liam Hudson, then Director of the Research Unit on Intellectual Development at King's College Cambridge, conducted research into academic excellence among schoolboys. He focused on two types of high-achieving boys whom he called 'divergers' and 'convergers'. Divergers were those whose ability was arts-oriented, and characterized by creative, lateral thinking. Convergers were more science-oriented with orientations that were logical rather than lateral. One of the tests administered to the two groups was a creativity game in which the boys had to propose as many uses as they could for various everyday objects – a brick, a barrel, a blanket, a tin of boot polish, a paper clip etc. To the researcher's surprise, there was spontaneous evidence of violent and morbid responses from both groups, with the 'convergers' – those seen as the most level-headed and rational – often making the most ghoulish suggestions e.g. 'for wrapping up a dead wife so as blood does not stain car seats' (blanket), 'to put spikes round the inside and put someone in and roll the barrel along the ground' (barrel) (Hudson, 1966: 58–61, 89–90). It is evident from the most casual inspection of their visitors that attractions such as the Chamber of Horrors, the London Dungeon and funfairs with violent sideshows (ghost train rides, arcade war games) are popular with children. Children have always enjoyed books and stories with violent themes. In the past, fairy stories, more macabre than those that would be acceptable today, were enjoyed by children (Bettelheim, 1977). Yet no research defines the nature of children's responses at thanatouristic sites. One possibility is that those most popular with children, like the London Dungeon (which has been so successful it has been replicated in Edinburgh and other cities), need to incorporate an element of stylized, humorous burlesque that avoids the stark, documentary representations of the Budapest Museum, described earlier. But even this has yet to be proven. It may be that it is not children who are squeamish, but the parents who are squeamish on their behalf.

There is clearly need for a much fuller exploration of motivations for thanatourism in both general and micro-populations.

Modernity-seeking and thanatourism

In his well-known book, *The Tourist*, MacCannell argued that tourism motivation is essentially linked to the desire for encounters with modernity.

> As a tourist, the individual may step out into the universal drama of modernity. As a tourist, the individual may attempt to grasp the division of labour as a phenomenon *sui generis* and become a moral witness of its masterpieces of virtue and viciousness.
> (MacCannell, 1976,: 7)

Modernity is overwhelmingly, though not exclusively, articulated through the agenda-setting efforts of the mass media. Tourism goals thus become increasingly influenced by media representations, since topographic specificity is a common feature of media content, and this specificity tends to promote the meaning and significance of destinations in ways that attract or deter people from visiting them. This process is particularly likely to impact upon thanatourism, since the media, particularly at the popular level, routinely seek to maximize content featuring disaster, crime and social pathology, all of which are often identified and coded primarily through their geographical locations. As a result, if the tourist, *pace* MacCannell, really is seeking to engage with the 'drama of modernity', and witness 'its masterpieces of virtue and viciousness', this may increasingly become chasing down the places of murder, violence and martyrdom.

Several disasters and violent events have stimulated thanatourism that can be seen as journeys to international news locations. In the late 1990s, the locations of terrorist bombings in Northern Ireland were reported to be attracting tourists. The London paper, *The Evening Standard* in a story captioned 'War junkies flock to Ulster', reported that:

> Rich Americans and Europeans are flocking to Ulster for war tours – holidays spent visiting the hot spots of years of urban terrorism. Operators in the US call it the ABC tour – the sites of ambushes, bombings and churchyards where the dead are buried . . .

Many Americans are sympathetic to the Republican cause and look upon the IRA as heroic freedom fighters. Now Sinn Fein is handing out its own maps to tourists — maps that show the best anti-British murals, the site of British Army barracks, Catholic 'martyr graves' and notorious ambush sites. Sinn Fein's bookshop has IRA key chains, T-shirts emblazoned with heavily armed female guerillas and anti-British literature. Joe Mcdermott, from Boston, who recently returned with two friends from a visit, said: 'It is life on the edge, isn't it. I mean it's relatively safe but you get that marvellous sense of danger in the air' (Anon., 1999: 42).

Another more recent instance of news-induced thanatourism is Waco in Texas. This was a reclusive, religious community (described predictably, as a 'sect' in the media), that was immolated after a week-long siege by the FBI. Opinion differs as to whether the group chose to perish in the fire as a religious protest, or whether it was the result of a blundering overreaction by the FBI. In 2003 the site, presided over by a caretaker called Doyle, was attracting sightseers:

> From the front road Carmel is easy to miss. The tourists pull up cautiously, not sure if this is the place, or not. At the gate they find a

man dressed in black, and hurling abuse at Doyle – a weekly routine. He calls himself the Watchman. His placard reads, 'The Cover-Up Church', a reference to the conspiracy theory, propagated on the Internet, that Doyle is a government agent covering up for FBI atrocities.

(Hicklin, 2003: 16)

But modernity-seeking may also be the chasing down of 'old news'. It seems that it is possible to get nostalgic about great acts of social pathology that created headlines in the past. An interesting English work that frames a whole city as a historical, thanatourist news park is Martin Fido's *Murder Guide to London* (1985). The author, who started life as an English literature academic, brings to startling fruition an ironic proposal made by the early-19th-century writer, De Quincey, in his famous essay, 'Murder considered as one of the fine arts'. De Quincy argued that murder and violence could be judged by aesthetic criteria, rather than moral ones, and that appreciation of them could be as much a form of consumer discrimination as other kinds of taste. The golden age of British murder trials was, Fido argues, 1830–1966, and his purpose is to take the visitor on a trip through its main highlights. In his book he brings to the task of murder appraisal the model-building propensity of the trained academic, devising a typology of six murder variables which can be used to determine the relative claim of a murder to be considered 'a classic': Was the body mutilated? Was there a murder hunt? Was it a middle-class murder? Were there many victims? Was sex involved? Was the victim famous? He critically re-examines a number of famous murders, including those exhibited in the Chamber of Horrors, against this exacting grid of variables, concluding that Jack the Ripper scores as a classic on all counts except the celebrity of the victims. In contrast the Kray Twins, two notorious East End gangland thugs, fail to achieve classic status, being dismissed as mere criminals, whose gangland 'executions' met none of the main criteria of murder excellence. Fido's book supplies detailed London maps that allow the scholar of homicide to undertake his/her own fieldwork.

Thanatourism has been questioned, as we have seen earlier, by critics deploring the commercial exploitation of crime or disaster. What this discussion of thanatourism, as contact with modernity through the visitation of places featured in violent news agendas, suggests, is that there need be no commercial tourism organizations pulling the strings behind consumer practices. People seek out the 'black spots' reported in the media without the encouragement of commercial organizations, and they may even do it in the face of strong moral censure. The task of tourism planners and local authorities may be to meet or manage this unsought demand, as in the case of the provision of a viewing platform at Ground Zero after the 11 September attacks. In more extreme cases management may involve the destruction of the site itself, a phenomenon seen in the UK when local authorities in Gloucester demolished the house in Cromwell Street of the serial killer, Fred West, to stop the flow of sightseers.

Thanatourism, Ideology and the State

Apart from ethical and motivational questions raised about the consumption of thanatourism, there are often political issues relating to its production and effects. Public representations of man-made horror and violence invariably construct for the viewer judgemental positions in which some are seen as victims and others as offenders; some as heroes, others as oppressors; some as innocent, others as guilty. In the same way that atrocity stories have been used to engineer public support for a war, through demonization of the enemy, so attractions based on the horrific have been, and continue to be, used to inculcate support for states, regimes and other groups, and conversely, to subvert their opponents. Some thanatourism sites, particularly museums and certain heritage sites, may be particularly effective in inculcating ideological perspectives, since their audiences may see them primarily as entertainment, rather than vehicles of social engineering, and unconsciously respond to the contrasted categories of good/evil on show.

These ideological effects can be seen in thanatourism sites of the past and present. The Tower of London, one of London's principal attractions for several centuries after it lost its primary function as a state prison, became a spectacular exhibition promoting anti-Catholicism and patriotic Protestantism. Chamberlain's *History of London* (1770) (which devoted much space to tourist attractions such as the British Museum and other sights of London), inventoried items exhibited in the Tower in the centuries after the attempted Armada invasion of 1588, testifying to Spanish splendour and barbarism. The exhibition was intended to deliciously chill the spectators with counterfactual fantasies of what would have happened had the Spaniards won the war. Among the horrors on display were whips for flaying the population, Spanish spadas poisoned at the point that brought certain death at a touch, Spanish cravats (engines of torture, made of iron, and put on board to lock together the feet, arms and heads of English heretics), and an axe for delivering four head wounds at once with a pistol in the handle. Most of all there were thumbscrews:

> . . . of which there were several chests full on board the Spanish Fleet. The use they were intended for is said to have been to extort confession from the English people where their money was hid, had that cruel people prevailed. Certain it is, that after defeat, the whole conversation of the court turned upon the discovery made by the Spanish prisoners of the racks, the wheels, and the whips of wire, with which they were to scourge the English of every rank and age, and of both sexes.
> (Chamberlain, 1770: 98)

Later the Tower and its gory exhibits evolved to incorporate an additional ideological narrative, that of the development of parliamentary democracy and the triumph over the absolutism of monarchs who had used it as a place for the torture and execution of personal enemies or opponents. By the 19th century both narratives were consumed and adopted in burlesque enactments by American tourists:

> Visitors liked to lay their heads on the block, 'once wet with the blood of brave men and fair women' or to try screwing up their thumbs 'in a little trinket contrived for that operation', and to shudder at 'the Scavenger's Daughter', a torture device designed to compress its victim's head, hands and feet simultaneously.
> (Lockwood, 1981: 95)

Westminster Abbey, another major London heritage attraction, may be seen as a thanatourism site with implicit ideological effects. Probably the most awesome and spectacular collection of memorials, effigies, and tombs in Britain, the Abbey designates not just which people have distinguished themselves as great national figures, but also connotes what categories of achievement most centrally reflect Britain's national culture to the world. The roll-call of the dead commemorated in its monuments implicitly elevates achievements in military, scientific, political, and literary and artistic endeavour as pluralistic cornerstones of human worth in British society.

Strongly focused, nationalistic, thanatourism displays, celebrating an imperial past, are today less common in western Europe, where new museums and attractions with military themes tend to emphasize peace and reconciliation rather than patriotic pride. In some European countries, however, they are still seen as mechanisms of socialization into the grand narratives of national history. The Military Museum of Istanbul was, in the late 1990s, described frankly by General Cevet Bir as an agency for inculcating pride in their country among the population, especially military recruits. English programme notes to its historical sections enthusiastically laud the glories of Yavuz Sultan Selim (1466–1520) and the days of the Ottoman Empire:

> The conquest of Constantinople was the beginning of the new ages in the world history while, on the other hand, was the most important event that made the Ottoman take off to get started [sic] . . . All these conquests and victories brought the Empire to a very strong position in both military and economical aspects that really made the western countries get afraid of the Ottomans.

The Turkish museum includes a room dedicated to the great national unifier of the 1920s, Kemal Attaturk, which displays, among other personal relics, his pyjamas, silk underwear, and his polecat-hide knee covers. The story of Turkish military achievements is narrated right up to the present day, with tributes to Turkish leaders in NATO – including Cevet Bir. The most disturbing part of the contemporary narrative (visited by one of the authors in

June 2000) was a room with the chilling title, 'Internal Security Operations', consisting of atrocity photos of the activities of the Kurdish 'terrorist' group PKK – mutilated civilians, children and old people. However, if some of the museum's exhibits start to make visiting British visitors feel judgemental about the dominant, state militarism on display, this feeling is quickly dispelled by exhibits on the First World War. These force the visitor to consider oppositional readings of events that have been sacralized in British imperial records. For those brought up on Anzac and English military mythology, this account of Gallipoli and the Dardanelles provides an uncomfortable, alternative reading:

> The Dardanelles war is [sic] the peerless war to the history of heroism. It is possible to see a mother or a father who lost his son, or a son who lost his family in each Turkish village in Canakkale during the war. You see a spin piece which belongs to one of these unknown heroes, or a French bullet which martyred him, and they are now in the golden page of history and pieces of the motherland and in our hearts.

The broken English adds to the force of the epigraph.

All this is to recognize that thanatourism sites and practices often involve ideological issues and impacts affecting all heritage sites. By celebrating some individuals and groups, and ignoring or stigmatizing others, thanatourism inherently brings into question relationships between four distinct stakeholding groups: those promoting or constructing thanatourism sites; those consuming them as visitors; those living near or around them; and those who belong to the subject groups and individuals featured at the sites. This four-way interaction has been conceived as a force field that may vary through time as each respective group increases or wanes in social power, and has a critical effect on the fate of heritage attractions (Seaton, 2001). An exemplary example of this moving force field are two of the battlefields of the Anglo–Zulu War in Natal, Isandlwana and Rorke's Drift, which were initially controlled by imperialists, the British, who commemorated their dead in memorials that diversely celebrated heroism and patriotic mission. Now in post-Mandela South Africa, the

monuments are allowed to continue, partly because the battlefields appeal to the country's main international visitors, people from the UK. But alongside the older imperial memorials (Fig. 6.2) are more modern ones to the Zulu (Fig. 6.3), and near each site is a Zulu Cultural Centre to provide a counterbalancing narrative to military ones, dominated for so long by the British Empire. But there continues to be a tension, because at both of these battlefield sites there are local black African communities living nearby who every day watch white Europeans, many in conducted parties, touring grounds that have been the contested sites of an historical oppression that was forged by the ancestors of those making the tours (even though at Isandlwana it was the British who were temporarily defeated).

Thanatourism: One Thing or Many?

Thanatourism has so far been discussed as if it were a homogeneous, discrete entity, an assumption that is not surprising since it is a singular noun. However this generic naming conceals motivational variations that may often exist both between *different kinds of* thanatouristic practices, and also *within* single ones.

Thanatourism was originally defined as five major kinds of travel: to witness enactments of death; to see the sites of mass or individual deaths; to visit internment sites and memorials; to view the material evidence or symbolic representations of death (e.g. in museums, exhibitions); for re-enactments or simulation of death (Seaton, 1996). These five types comprise a wide range of different practices that may be difficult to assign to common motivational categories. Visiting a historic battlefield that one's relatives or ancestors have died on is clearly qualitatively different from seeking out the house where a serial killer lived. Attending a torture museum in the Netherlands is different from a pilgrimage by a devout Catholic to the religious shrine of St Francis in Assisi, or even to a modern secular shrine like the one described by a friend to the writer Alan Bennett, who recorded it in his diary.

> 17 July, 1990: Supper with Don Sriegowski and his wife Barbara, and with David and

Fig. 6.2. British imperial memorial at Isandlwana, Natal.

Maureen Vaisey. They have recently visited Poland, where they were taken to see the church of the murdered priest Father Popieluszko, which is in the process of being turned into a shrine. Here in the church is the car in which the young priest was driven to his death; here are the clothes he was wearing when he was murdered; and around the walls, as it were the stations of his particular cross, are scenes leading up to his murder. At Christmas the crib is placed in the boot of the car, the Christ-child curled up in the same position as Father Popieluszko was curled up as he was driven to the reservoir to be murdered. Day by day the devout bring in further relics. David, who began life as a medieval historian, is excited by all this, as it shows how medieval cults must have started: the accumulation of relics, the elevation of the martyr's life to the status of myth, until finally comes the sanctification, as in due course it will come for Father Popieluszko.

(Bennett, 1994: 190)

Many thanatourism sites and visits may be categorized within a long-standing tradition of religious pilgrimage, and also within an evolving, modern, secular category whose pilgrims desire to pay homage to dead celebrities made famous by the media, particularly those from the world of the arts and show business. The mass media have largely usurped the function of the church as institutions with the power to sacralize people and places as targets of devotional travel. The cultural critic Christopher Frayling recounts how one of his students, interested in heavy-metal rock music and the notorious cult, black magician, Aleister Crowley, explicitly recognized the similarities between historical and contemporary forms of pilgrimage :

> She . . . made connections between the special powers associated with saintly relics of the Middle Ages and the more secular attractions of rock music relics today – Elvis Presley's

Fig. 6.3. Zulu memorial at Isandlwana, Natal.

Graceland, the lampost near to Chippenham
where Eddie Cochrane met his death . . .
(Frayling, 1995: 16)

Just as important as the motivational differences to be found *between* different kinds of
thanatourism are those that may exist *within* a
single form. There may be widely different
motives in visiting the same thanatourism site.
This can be seen in the apparently narrow and
specialized practice of visiting churchyards and
cemeteries.

Celebrity chasing may be one motive for
visits. Père Lachaise Cemetery retains its pre-
eminence as one of the top visitor attractions in
Paris because of such celebrated occupants as
Edith Piaf, Yves Montand, Colette, Chopin,
Oscar Wilde and Jim Morrison. On a smaller
scale, St Enodoc churchyard in Cornwall,
always a picturesque tourist attraction, is now a
pilgrimage spot for those celebrating the
memory of the former English poet laureate,
Sir John Betjeman. In the last 20 years there

has been a marked increase in the promotion
of cemetery and graveyard visiting, with the
proliferation of guides to internment sites in
Paris, London, New York and many other destinations (Seaton, 2002), as well as websites
(e.g. http://www.politicalgraveyard.com and
http://www.findagrave.com), which direct the
star-struck to the last resting places of the
famous (Spano, 2002). Though mainly produced by publishing companies and media
organizations, guides have also been produced
by regional tourism organizations. In 1991 the
local authorities in Brighton commissioned a
booklet on its cemeteries, which directed the
visitor to St Nicholas churchyard to see the
graves of Sake Deen Mohammed, the man
who introduced Turkish baths into England,
and John Howard, the penal reformer. In
Brighton's Borough Cemetery the main
celebrity grave is that of Henry Solomon, Chief
Constable of Brighton, who was murdered in
the police station by John Lawrence on 13
March 1844 (Dale, 1991).

Visiting internment sites may thus be pilgrimages to pay tribute to significant others, public or personal. However, visits may derive from less specific impulses, embedded in cultural conditioning or personal idiosyncrasy. Graveyards and cemeteries occupy a special position for travellers socialized within literary and cultural traditions of romanticism and the gothic where their appeals may be various: to pleasurable feelings of melancholy; manageable feelings of nameless dread; or a comforting sense of the immemorial continuity of life and death. Interrment sites have always had a particular resonance with writers and artists. Hollis describes Harold Acton's dismay at Evelyn Waugh's curious behaviour, on holiday in 1952, in the catacombs in Sicily.

> When Evelyn was to visit Italy he wrote to suggest that Harold (Acton) should accompany him on a trip round the country. Harold agreed, but was somewhat perturbed by Evelyn's growing eccentricities. Thus they visited the Capucin catacomb near Palermo where the remains of the dead friars are permanently preserved. Evelyn remained in contemplation of the mummies an inordinately long time and at last emerged, pronouncing on them the verdict that their smell was 'delicious'. It had, he claimed, completely cured the lameness from which he had been suffering and he at once threw away the stick without whose aid he had up till then been walking.
>
> (Hollis, 1976: 109)

Italy was, and still is, famed for its interrment sites, and Sicily is particularly notable. Four years after Waugh's visit to the Catacombs of Palermo, the young artist Bruce Lacey, travelling on an Abbey Minor scholarship after he left the Royal College of Art, discovered the variety of gothic interrment sites that were the legacy of Italian Catholicism. These included: the embalmed form of Pope Pius X in Rome with gold lacquered face and hands; St Claire's body in Assisi; the Cimitero dei Cappuccini underneath a church near the Via Barbarini in Rome which comprised galleries stacked from wall to ceilings with the symetrically arranged bones of 4000 monks from the 16th to the 19th century. Even the light fittings and shades were made of bones.

But the high spot was, as for Waugh, the catacombs near Palermo, which Lacey knew about before leaving England from seeing pictures of them in a Victorian holiday album (Anon., 1956).

D.H. Lawrence's delight in the Etruscan tombs of Italy in 1927, 4 years before he died, was quite different from the Catholic, gothic fascinations of Waugh and Lacey, a celebration not of death, but of life.

> From the jewelled splendour of these dark tombs we came forth into the brightness of an April day and the blue sky broken by hurrying clouds: the fields through which we walked were gay with red poppies: our guide unlocked the door leading to another tomb and we would descend again to behold the joyous scenes with which the Etruscans, of such a distant world, chose to adorn the homes of their dead.
>
> (Quoted in de Sola Pinto, 1972: 18)

Over the past century, churchyards and cemeteries have also come to be visited for their architectural significance. This tendency developed in the early 20th century with the publication of works on funerary architecture and design such as Ferrari's *La Tomba nell'arte Italiana*, Esdaile's work on church monumental sculpture (Esdaile, 1927, 1946), and Lawrence Weaver's influential, *Memorials and Monuments*, which was published in 1915, as a critique of what he saw as the poor standards of design of Boer War monuments. This evolving focus on the monument as an aesthetic object in its own right, rather than primarily as an instrumental marker to the person interred, shifted the value from personal record to design history. So too did the practice of brass rubbing, which had its origins in antiquarian research, but later became a hobby of such widespread interest for its own sake, that it had to be stopped because of the damage it did to the brass effigies and monuments being rubbed. Brass rubbing still continues, but the rubbing is done from replicas supplied at, or close to, important brass monuments, like those available to the public near Holy Trinity Church, Stratford-upon-Avon, where Shakespeare is buried. Both the enthusiasts of monumental architecture and brass rubbing expanded the interest in internment sites as objects of sightseeing.

Another motivation for visiting church-yards and cemeteries, and one which has grown exponentially in the last 20 years, is as part of a genealogical quest for family history and ethnic roots. In the USA and UK, interest in these has resulted in the proliferation of web-sites offering census data, church and cemetery guides, and membership of groups like the Association for Gravestone Studies in the USA which has its own journal, *Markers*.

Finally, cemeteries and churchyards may be visited simply as havens of peace and tran-quillity. The wave of cemeteries built from the late 18th century in Britain and the USA were conceived as picturesque retreats for the living, as well as resting places for the dead (Etlin, 1984). This tradition continues in the way that Brighton promoted its cemetery heritage in the 1990s:

> The Extra-Mural Cemetery is one of the most delightful spots in the whole of Brighton. The site was and is ideal; a gentle gradient between two fairly steep banks, which were in 1851 folds in the downs..The cemetery is one of the most pleasant and quiet places in Brighton in which to take a walk.
>
> (Dale, 1991: 8–9)

In short, there may be no general thana-tourism motive or set of motives. Instead dif-ferent kinds of visit may take place for different reasons, and, as the churchyard/cemetery dis-cussion suggests, visitors to the same site may be there for a range of purposes.

Scanning the Future

What is the future for thanatourism? A tourism consultant charged with the task of performing an environmental scan on the factors likely to affect it over the next 10 years might consider several dimensions: the technological, socio-cultural, political and economic.

Technological trends, particularly those in information technology, all favour increasing public awareness of thanatourism as a field of attraction. The ever increasing expansion of the broadcast media through terrestrial, cable and satellite programming is likely to promote existing thanatourism sites, and create new ones through the publicity of death and disas-

ters that some viewers will want to trace back to their geographical locations. Thanatourism practices diffuse within an information loop activated, initially, by the mass media, but one which is then often elaborated and deepened through interactive reinforcement mechanisms via websites, chat-rooms and email targeting. This technological circuit will affect the supply of potential thanatouristic travel as it affects other consumer practices.

The social-cultural environment also offers conditions of expansion. Despite the moral panic that has surrounded thanatourism in some quarters, public tastes and institutional practices suggest that there is a growing accep-tance and enjoyment of in-your-face realism, involving shock and horror. Crime, death and disaster have always been a staple ingredient of tabloid press journalism, but in the last decade they have made ever increasing inroads into mainstream broadcasting, and, even more so, on cable and satellite channels. During the writ-ing of this chapter the authors kept an inven-tory of TV programmes that went out on prime time, autumn schedules for 3 days in October 2002 on four UK channels. Table 6.1 shows the results. Later in the same week came pro-grammes on the death of Marilyn Monroe; a docu-soap on fire fighting; a biography of the hippy, celebrity killer, Charles Manson; and a programme on an 8000-year-old mutilated body billed as, *Tales of the Living Dead*.

The subjects of this programming – war, murder, natural disaster, celebrity death – cor-respond so closely to those involved in thana-tourism that it may be time to create a complementary TV category called 'thana-viewing'. It seems that gothic voyeurism and *schadenfreude* are now part of the socio-cultural zeitgeist. Thanatourism has so far been seen as a discrete phenomenon, but it should more properly be placed within much broader social-cultural developments in broadcasting, video-gaming, fiction, comics etc. Interestingly, none of the channels directly promote their implicit sensationalist agenda, and in two cases (the History and Discovery channels) their overt remit is to serve an educational/cultural func-tion, very much as museums claim when stag-ing macabre exhibitions.

Finally, *politics and economics* will con-tinue to be parameters of thanatourism in the

Table 6.1. Inventory of TV programmes on four UK channels during October 2002.

	UK Horizons	Discovery	History Channel	BBC 2
7 October 2003	Forensic Files – blood trails (9.00–9.30) Scenes of Crime – notorious 20th century crimes (9.30–10.00) Mind of a Murderer (10.00–11.05)	Battlefield – the Midway (5.00–6.00) Venom One – injuries and deaths caused by snakes (9.30–10.30) Storm Force: terrifying tales involving avalanches (9.30–10.30)		
8 October 2003	Crimes of the 20th Century – Assassinations (9.00–10.00)	World's Deepest Gold Mine – one of the most dangerous environments (9.30–10.30) Murder Trail – hunt for Hillside Stranglers (11.30–12.30)	Secrets of War – Fascist Italy (8.00–9.00) Third Reich in Colour (9.00–10.00) Death Row Diaries – Sing Sing prison (10.00–11.00)	War Walks – Arras 1940 (7.30–8.00) Ancient Apocalypse: Death on the Nile – collapse of Egyptian civilization (9.00–9.50) Witness – buried alive in Japanese earthquake (9.50–10.00)
9 October 2003	Killer Instinct – poisonous snakes (6.00–7.00) Blues and Twos – following London helicopter medical team (8.00–8. 30) Haunted London (9.00–10.00) Scariest Places on Earth – haunted house in Missouri (10.00–10.55)	Battlefield- Stalingrad (5.00–6.00) Time Team – Roman skeleton is unearthed in York (7.00–8.00) Great Battles – Agincourt (8.00–8.30) The Lost Children of Roman Ashkelo – infanticide in Greece and Rome (9.30–10.30) Black Museum – murderers caught by their handwriting (10.30–11.00) Most Evil Men and Women in History – Caligula (11.00–11.30)	Secrets of War – Fascist Italy (8.00–9.00) Third Reich in Colour (9.00–10.00) Gary Gilmore – notorious double murderer (10.00–11.00)	

form of shaping what places and attractions will become public sites of mourning, remembrance and consumer interest, and how they will be presented. Politics has, as we have seen, historically driven the development of museums and exhibitions, not just to commemorate dead victims, but to mobilize populations to support living regimes. The power to perpetuate the memory of one's dead has always been unequally distributed (Tunbridge and Ashworth, 1996). There is, for instance, no necessary connection between the extent of societal extermination, and the memorials recording it, as is proven by the many and growing Jewish Holocaust memorials, and the relative absence of memorials to gypsies and homosexuals. This has been the subject of recent evaluation and analysis through a Czech case study, which provides clear evidence of 'selective interpretation' and clear political agendas in what is and what is not interpreted (Lennon and Smith, 2004). The sites examined provide a context for the emergent Czech Republic to examine its recent past and consider the problem of examining who participated in the atrocities and who participated in the violence and oppression of these peoples.

Paradoxically, although broad environmental conditions look favourable for thanatourism development, not all its specific forms will necessarily expand. It is unlikely, for example, that battlefield sites, as they have previously existed, will be greatly added to in the future. The military era that produced the kind of battlegrounds visited by tourists is now ending, due to the changed nature of military engagement. No longer do armies face each other, person to person, across a specified land space, and contest to be victors. The modern pattern is for massive, technologically advanced forces with a monopoly of air power, to strafe to destruction less well-equipped armies on the ground, or, alternatively, for protracted civil and guerilla wars. The old kind of battlefield, with its forms of human engagement, and acts of personal heroism, may become as obsolete as jousting tournaments and battering ram attacks on castle walls. In retrospect, it may be seen that the high-water mark for personalized combat and conventional land battles ended in the latter part of the 20th century. The result is that, though there will probably be little or no increase in sacralized battlefield sites, the importance of the existing ones will increase as part of nostalgia for a bygone era, before the diabolical advances of scientific warfare turned the winners of war into impersonal, button-pressing masters of guided weapon systems, and the losers into missile fodder to be incinerated or liquidized. Some visitors to the First World War battlefields France and Belgium in the 1990s said that their particular interest in the First World War was that it harked back to a time where battle, however terrible, had a human scale, with opportunities for personal and collective bravery, rendered irrelevant by the destructive impersonality of modern weapons of mass destruction (Seaton, 2000b).[1]

It is also possible that the continued supply of picturesque cemeteries and churchyards is diminishing for visitors in the future. There has always been a nostalgic element in the visiting of old graveyards and cemeteries with their often curious, heterogeneous styles of epitaph, headstones and memorials. In modern times regulations governing materials, size and design and the trend within the funeral industry for more uniform, mass-produced products, will reduce the variety of church and cemetery architecture. Thirty years ago one writer argued that the high tide of church and cemetery craftsmanship was the mid-18th to the early 20th century, since when design has deteriorated − and with it picturesque appeals (Lindley, 1965). It would now be impossible to develop burial grounds with the laissez faire, gothic variety and ornamental exuberance of a Père Lachaise or Highgate, but for that reason they, and others like them, will increase their impact as monuments to a bygone era.

Conversely, the modern increase in the manufacture of celebrities by the media will continue to feed the impetus for people to make pilgrimages to places where they die or are commemorated. Graceland and Althorp are only the latest in a long line of shrines to secular saints. Similarly, media coverage of murder and disaster will continue undiminished, and will continue to produce a topography of violence that will attract a certain kind of visitor, as well as occasionally providing Madame Tussaud with a new subject for the Chamber of Horrors.

Conclusion

This chapter has attempted to provide a swift overview of developments in academic and public discourses about thanatourism/dark tourism over the last 7 or 8 years, and some of the controversies and problematics associated with it. Some cautions are in order by way of conclusion.

Firstly the extent of thanatourism as consumer practice is unknown, because its audiences have hardly ever been audited or profiled. The raised awareness of the subject created by academics and the mass media may merely reflect their fascination with it, not that it is an important tourism phenomenon in social practice, although the present writers believe that this is not the case. There is a need for research into consumer practices and motivations that has hardly even begun. Most of the literature on thanatourism to date has been supply-side comment and analysis, rather than consumer oriented.

Moreover, it may be that thanatourism is rarely either a principal motive for travel, or a major activity at a destination – except in the case of battlefield tours. Visiting a cemetery, attending a Holocaust site, or viewing a secular shrine may occupy a shortish span of a vacation trip that is mainly spent doing other things. There are not yet, as far as is known, significant numbers of people making trips entirely devoted to catastrophe sites, museums of disaster, and interrment grounds, but that is not to say that there never will be, or that the potential for such tours does not exist.

In short, we must concur with the authors of a recent assessment of slavery site tourism (Dann and Seaton, 2001), that there are more questions than answers in relation to thanatourism. Its extent and motivations, and above all the identities of its pursuants, have yet to be revealed.

Note

1. The PR agencies of modern military organizations tacitly recognize this need to construct a heroic dimension to operations driven by mechanized technology. The much mythologized 'rescue' of Private Jessica Lynch, a teenage US soldier, during the Iraq war, may be seen as an attempt to personalize a war that was won, in reality, by overwhelming technolog-

ical dominance. The details of the story changed over time from being constructed in the first film report, released by the military, as an action movie rescue of a helpless captive, injured and detained by the Iraqis, to something much more like the emergency airlift of a road accident victim, that was done without resistance by the Iraqi hospital authorities, who had been treating her and even offered to return her. The apparent loss of memory of Private Lynch after the event means that the real details of the story may never be completely known.

References

Alderman, D.H. (2002) Writing on the Graceland wall: on the importance of authorship in pilgrimage landscapes. *Tourism Recreation Research* 27(2), 27–35.

Altick, R.D. (1977) *The Shows of London*. Bellknap Press, London.

Anon. (1956) *Ark 14*. Royal College of Art, London, pp. 18–21.

Anon. (1999) War junkies flock to Ulster. *Evening Standard*, 24 September.

Bennett, A. (1994) *Writing Home*. Faber and Faber, London.

Bettelheim, B. (1977) *The Uses of Enchantmen: the Meaning and Importance of Fairy Tales*. Vintage, New York.

Blass, T. (1992) The social psychology of Stanley Milgram. In: Zanna M.P. (ed.) *Advances in Experimental Social Psychology*, Vol. 25. Academic Press, San Diego, pp. 277–328.

Boswell, J. and Pottle, F. (eds) (1951) *Boswell's London Journal*. Heinemann, London.

Calder, S. (2002) Bermuda shorts and battle dress. *British Airways High Life*, 40–45.

Canter, D. (1996) *Horror: Continuing Attraction and Common Reactions*. Madame Tussauds, London.

Chamberlain, H. (1770) *History and Survey of the Cities of London and Westminster*. London.

Chapman, P. (1984) *Madame Tussaud's Chamber of Horrors: Two Hundred Years of Crime*. Constable, London.

Dale, A. (1991) *Brighton Cemeteries*. Brighton Borough Council, UK.

Dann, G.M.S. (1998) *The Dark Side of Tourism*. Etudes et Rapports/Studies and Reports, Serie Sociology/Psychology/Philosophy/Anthropology, Vol. 14.

Dann, G.M.S. (2003) Children of the dark. In: Ashworth, G.J. and Hartmann, R. (eds) *Human Tragedy and Trauma Revisited: the Management of Atrocity Sites for Tourism*. Cognizant, New York.

Dann, G.M.S. and Seaton A.V. (2001) Introduction. In: Dann, G.M.S. and Seaton, A.V. (eds) *Slavery, Contested Heritage and Thanatourism.* Haworth Hospitality Press, New York, pp. 1–30.

Deuchar, S. (1996) Sense and sensitivity: appraising the Titanic. *International Journal of Heritage Mangement* 2(4), 212–221.

Esdaile, K.A. (1927) *English Monumental Sculpture Since the Renaissance.* SPCK, London.

Esdaile, K. A. (1946) *English Church Monuments 1510–1840.* Batsford, London.

Etlin, R.A. (1984) *The Architecture of Death.* MIT Press, Cambridge, Massachusetts.

Ferrari, G. (n.d.) *La tomba nell'arte Italiana.* Ulrico Hoepli, Milan, Italy.

Fido, M. (1985) *Murder Guide to London.* Weidenfeld and Nicholson, London.

Finucane, R.C. (1977) *Miracles and Pilgrims: Popular Beliefs in Medieval England.* St Martin's Press, London.

Foley, M. and Lennon, J.J. (1996) JFK and a fascination with assassination. *International Journal of Heritage Studies* 2(4), 210–216.

Frayling, C. (1995) *Strange Landscape: a Journey Through the Middle Ages.* BBC Books, London.

Gibbons, F. (2003) Galleries tap rich vein of public's lust for blood. *Guardian*, 9 January.

Henderson, J.C. (1997) Singapore's wartime heritage attractions. *Journal of Tourism Research* 8(2), 39–49.

Henderson, J.C. (2000) War as a tourist attraction: the case of Vietnam. *International Journal of Tourism Research* 2, 269–280.

Hicklin, A. (2003) Siege mentality. *Independent on Sunday*, 13 April.

Hollis, C. (1976) *Oxford in the Twenties.* Heinemann, London.

Hudson, L. (1966) *Contrary Imaginations: a Psychological Study of the English Schoolboy.* Methuen, London.

Iles, J.J. (2003) Memorial landscapes of the Western Front: spaces of commemoration, tourism and pilgrimage. PhD thesis, University of Surrey, Roehampton, UK.

Lennon, J.J. and Foley, M. (2000) *Dark Tourism: the Attraction of Death and Disaster.* Cassell, London.

Lennon, J.J. and Smith. H. (2004) A tale of two camps: contrasting approaches to interpretation and commemoration in the sites at Terezin and Lety, Czech Republic. *Journal of Tourism Recreation Research* (in press).

Lindley, K. (1965) *Of Graves and Epitaphs.* Hutchinson, London.

Lloyd, D.W. (1998) *Battlefield Tourism: Pilgrimage and the Commemoration of the Great War in Britain, Australia and Canada 1919–1939.* Berg, Oxford.

Lockwood, A. (1981) *Passionate Pilgrims: the American Traveller in Great Britain 1800–1914.* Cornwall Books, New York.

MacCannell, D. (1976) *The Tourist: a New Theory of the Leisure Class.* Macmillan, London.

McEwen, I. (2001) *Guardian G2*, 12 September, p. 2.

O'Neill, S. (2002) *Daily Telegraph*, 26 August.

Pinto, V. de Sola (1972) *The Complete Poems of D. H Lawrence*, Vol.2. Heinemann, London.

Ryan, R. (2002) Standing where Hitler fell. *Sunday Times, Travel*, 15 December, p. T3.

Seaton, A.V. (1996) Guided by the dark: from thanatopsis to thanatourism. *International Journal of Heritage Studies* 2(4), 234–244.

Seaton, A.V. (2000a) Thanatourism. In: Jafari, J. (ed.) *Encyclopaedia of Tourism.* Routledge, London, p. 578.

Seaton, A.V. (2000b) Another weekend away looking for dead bodies: battlefield tourism on the Somme and in Flanders. *Tourism Recreation Research* 25(3), 63–78.

Seaton, A.V. (2001) Sources of slavery – destinations of slavery: the silences and disclosures of slavery heritage in the UK and US. In: Dann, G.M.S. and Seaton, A.V. (eds) *Slavery, Contested Heritage and Thanatourism.* Haworth Hospitality Press, New York, pp. 107–131.

Seaton, A.V. (2002) Thanatourism's final frontiers? Visits to cemeteries, churchyards and funerary sites as sacred and secular pilgrimage. *Tourism Recreation Research* 27(2), 73–82.

Smart, N. (1996) The Maginot Line: an indestructible inheritance. *International Journal of Heritage Studies* 2.

Smith, V. (1996) War and its tourist attractions. In: Pizam, A. and Mansfield, Y. (eds) *Tourism, Crime and International Security Issues.* John Wiley & Sons, Chichester, UK, pp. 247–264.

Smith, V. (1998) War and tourism: an American ethnography. *Annals of Tourism Research* 25(1), 202–207.

Spano, S. (2002) Cemetery tourists find 'tomb with a view'. *Los Angeles Times*, 21 April.

Star Newspaper (1996) Front page story, 12 July.

Strange, C. and Kempa M. (2003) Shades of dark tourism: Alcatraz and Robben Island. *Annals of Tourism Research* 30(2), 386–405.

Sumption, J. (1975) *Pilgrimage: an Image of Medieval Religion.* Faber, London.

Tunbridge, J.E. and Ashworth, G.J. (1996) *Dissonant Heritage: the Management of the Past as a Resource in Conflict.* John Wiley & Sons, Chichester, UK.

Weaver, L. (1915) *Memorials and Monuments.* Country Life, London.

7 Tourism at Borders of Conflict and (De)militarized Zones

Dallen J. Timothy[1], Bruce Prideaux[2] and Samuel SeongSeop Kim[3]

[1]Department of Recreation Management and Tourism, PO Box 974703, Arizona State University, Tempe, AZ 85287-4703, USA; [2]School of Business, James Cook University, Cairns, QLD 4811, Australia; [3]Department of Hotel Management and Tourism, Sejong University, #98 Gunja-Dong, Kwangjin-Gu, 143-150 Seoul, Korea

At the beginning of the 21st century, tourists enjoy the privilege of being able to travel to almost any place on the globe, largely free of heavy government restriction, with only a handful of exceptions. As Timothy (1995b, 2001) observed, there are few borders travellers cannot cross. As a consequence the early 21st century can be described as a golden age of travel, where borders are not fixed barriers and where those who have the means can travel to almost any corner of the world. There are, of course, exceptions. Citizens of several countries have limited travel rights as a consequence of home government restrictions; other citizens lack the accumulated wealth necessary to finance travel; and there are still some borders that divide belligerent nations.

The freedom to travel has opened new opportunities for tourism exploration, and previously restricted places and boundaries now have become woven into the fabric of travel while others, which have lost their significance, fall from fame into neglect. Prior to the UK's return of Hong Kong to the People's Republic of China in 1997, the border between China and Hong Kong marked a clear point of separation between Western capitalism and Maoist communism, and still does to some degree. The border became a place of fascination for west-ern tourists visiting Hong Kong, where they could gaze into the lands of the adversary (Timothy, 1995a). Today, while still fortified and somewhat restrictive, the same border serves only an administrative purpose, ignored more than feared by those who are permitted to pass over it. The same can be said of Checkpoint Charlie, where limited numbers of western tourists were allowed to enter East Berlin from West Berlin during the communist era. Today the border between East and West Germany has ceased to exist, except in museum form, and the communist regulatory mechanisms of power and civil society that it represented have vanished, consigned to an era that is reported in textbooks and contemplated with a mix of fear and contempt by those who endured the philosophy that Checkpoint Charlie symbolized.

Despite being symbols of military conflict and political hostility, these borders were important tourist attractions during their zenith, and now, over a decade since its fall, remnants of the Berlin Wall still appeal to the curious nature of tourists. While the East–West Germany and Hong Kong–China borders have ceased functioning to separate nations, or sovereign polities, there are a handful of conflict-ridden borders that still divide contrasting regimes. Today such borders, as they have done for decades, attract considerable tourist attention. This chapter examines borders that continue to divide hostilely partitioned nations and which, as a consequence of this division, themselves become objects of the tourist gaze, creating their own tourism subsystems, heritage, and management issues. The *de facto* border dividing the island of Cyprus and its repercussions are examined briefly, followed by a more detailed account of the armistice frontier that divides the two Koreas.

Visiting Borders of Conflict and (De)militarized Zones

There is a small but growing literature on international boundaries as barriers to tourism. Observers have noted that borders function as obstacles to individual travel and destination development in both physical and psychological terms (Leimgruber, 1989; Smith, 1984; Timothy and Tosun, 2003). Physically, borders are difficult to cross when they are heavily fortified with barbed wire, guard towers, minefields, and walls. Additionally, strict boundary policies and restrictions can also be a real or physical barrier to travel, since they limit people's ability or willingness to cross. Strict exit and entry formalities and harsh visa and currency restrictions imposed by home and/or host country are examples of policies that create real obstacles to travel.

Differences in language and culture, economics and money, political systems, food and water hygiene, as well as potential visitors' perceptions and images of what lies on the other side of a border, create perceived or psychological barriers and add functional distance to cross-border destinations (Reynolds and McNulty, 1968; Smith, 1984; Timothy, 2001; Timothy and Tosun, 2003).

> Even between friendly nations, travellers sometimes view entry procedures as a disturbing nuisance, for they must present proof of citizenship and respond to a battery of questions from intimidating immigration and customs officers.
> (Timothy and Tosun, 2003: 413)

Similarly, in the words of Budd (1990: 15), 'for some people, [crossing the border] is merely annoying, but for others it can be frightening'.

Borders are often the locations of conflict, war and political unrest, for historically countries have jealously guarded every metre of national space. In fact, most wars in recent years have had borders and national territory at their roots. While decreasing slowly, several borders exist today that came into being as wartime ceasefire lines or lines of armistice, creating what in geopolitical terms are known as partitioned states (Waterman, 1987). The Germanies were a good recent example, and the best examples today are the lines that divide Cyprus and the Korean Peninsula. These borders partition divergent ideological systems, societies and economics, and as such have become significant tourist attractions despite their intended function to hinder the flow of travel (Timothy, 2000). They are tourist attractions because people have always been interested in 'otherness', and in this case it is reflected in the 'forbidden' or inaccessible. It is largely for this reason that nearly 100,000 Americans visit Cuba each year, despite the US government's prohibitions on travel there (Timothy, 2001, 2003). The old viewing platforms, from which tourists in West Berlin could gaze on East Berlin, are another good example of this phenomenon. In fact nostalgia for, and curiosity about, the former east–west divide in Germany has spurred the development of some 30 border museums along the corridor that once formed this infamous boundary (Blacksell, 1998; Borneman, 1998; Light, 2000).

Cyprus and the Green Line

Before the 1974 partitioning of Cyprus, tourism had reached significant levels across the island, especially in the north, and was one of the country's largest sources of foreign exchange earnings. Between 1960 and 1973, tourism to Cyprus grew from an initial 20,000 international arrivals to approximately 300,000. In 1973, the island's two main resort destinations, Kyrenia and Famagusta, on their own accounted for 65% of the entire island's bed capacity and hosted two-thirds of the island's international tourists. However, this success was interrupted in July 1974 when, in response to a coup against the country's leader by activists who desired unification with Greece,

Turkish forces entered the island and occupied the northern third of its territory. Once the intervention was complete, the Turkish military proclaimed a ceasefire in August 1974 and drew a ceasefire line lengthwise, bisecting the island into two sections. During the following year, roughly 185,000 Greek Cypriots moved southward, and approximately 45,000 Turkish Cypriots moved north into the Turkish occupied zone (Grundy-Warr, 1994).

Following the partition, the island's political landscape was altered dramatically. In the words of Grundy-Warr (1994: 79),

> an artificial line cut through the island like a cheese-wire, cutting off villages from their fields, splitting streams and underground water resources, truncating roads and power lines.

United Nations peacekeeping forces were given the gruelling task of demarcating a defensive zone between the Turkish ceasefire line and the Greek Cypriot front. This demilitarized zone, which varied in width, extended 180 km from the north-western portion of the island south-eastward to the coast just south of Famagusta (Fig. 7.1). This border, known as the Attila Line, or the Green Line, immediately became a considerable barrier to tourism. Most of the finest beaches, the two largest resort communities, over 80% of tourist accommodation, 96% of the hotel rooms under construction, more than 60% of the groundwater supply, Nicosia's international airport, and the island's best farmland were severed from the Greek Cypriot southerners and international visitors by the new heavily fortified boundary (Kammas, 1991; Timothy, 2001). This confrontation and partition had immediate effects on tourism. International arrivals dropped to 150,000 in 1974, and a mere 47,100 visitors trickled to the island in 1975. However, since the mid-1970s, tourism in the southern portion of the island (The Republic of Cyprus) has gained considerable strength and recovered completely. New resorts have been developed, and annual tourist numbers consistently reach into the millions. On the other hand, tourism in the north (The Turkish Republic of Northern Cyprus – recognized only by Turkey as a sovereign state) has only recently begun to show signs of recovery (Akis and Warner, 1994;

Ioannides and Apostolopoulos, 1999; Lockhart, 1993; Lockhart and Ashton, 1990; Mansfeld and Kliot, 1996; Sönmez and Apostolopoulos, 2000). North Cyprus' impediments to tourism development were threefold: (i) Turkey and its new satellite, Northern Cyprus, were seen as the aggressors in the conflict, so as is the case in any political altercation, tourists were reluctant to visit, fearing for their safety; (ii) because of the Turkish intervention, international economic sanctions were placed on the north, restricting tourist flows and foreign investments; and (iii) the Turkish authorities stressed an economy based on manufacturing and agriculture, rather than tourism and other service-based industries (Timothy, 2001).

The Republic of Cyprus has been able to build a highly developed economy within a relatively short period of time. The north, however, has improved but is still entirely dependent on the government of Turkey. International support for the south assisted in its recovery, while sanctions against the north have hampered its development efforts (Kliot and Mansfeld, 1997). International economic relief poured into the south following the events of 1974, enabling a rapid economic recovery. The north, on the other hand, has not pursued tourism as a major catalyst for growth, owing to the international boycott and its overdependence on the fragile Turkish market (Mansfeld and Kliot, 1996).

Following the 1974 event, the Greek and Turkish Cypriot governments instituted severe restrictions on travel between the two sides. Travellers who entered the island in the north were not permitted to enter the south. Tourists who entered the island in the south were allowed to visit the Turkish sector during the day on foot, but they were forbidden to spend the night or bring back items purchased in the north (Akis and Warner, 1994; Kliot and Mansfeld, 1994; Lockhart and Ashton, 1990; Timothy, 2001), and Cypriots themselves were generally not permitted to cross the border in either direction. Despite these limitations, the Attila Line became a recognized tourist attraction in Nicosia, because it epitomized the extant hostilities between the two parts of the island and separated two opposing sociocultural groups.

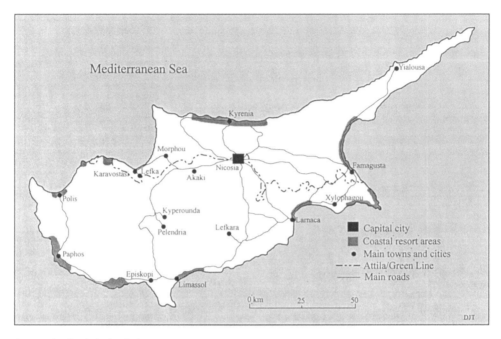

Fig 7.1. The divided island of Cyprus.

In April 2003, however, relations took a dramatic turn, when the government of the Turkish Republic of Northern Cyprus lifted its restrictions on travel to the south by its own citizens and travel to the north by Greek Cypriots. As a result of this change, two new border crossings were opened, allowing vehicular and pedestrian traffic to cross the 29-year-old 'Berlin Wall of Cyprus' (Theodoulou, 2003). Greek Cypriots are apparently now permitted to cross into the north on foot or by car, and Turkish Cypriots may make day excursions to the south on foot. However, non-Cypriot visitors are still restricted from entering the south from the north. As of late May 2003, 1 month after the restrictions were lifted, nearly 270,000 Greek Cypriots had crossed the border into the Turkish sector, and 111,000 Turkish Cypriots had visited the south. Estimates place the volume of cross-border travel at approximately 5000 people a day (Smith, 2003). Many people are undertaking visits to the homesteads they fled 29 years earlier, and many are searching for friends of the opposite ethnicity who they lost touch with in 1974. After all the years of being separated by a

concrete and barbed-wire barrier, Greek and Turkish Cypriots are suddenly mingling again and rushing to see their old homes and places of worship on the other side of the divide.

(Theodoulou, 2003: 6)

The Korean Peninsula

Following the 1953 ceasefire that halted hostilities between United Nations Forces and North Korean and Chinese forces in the Korean Peninsula, a demilitarized zone (DMZ) was established to separate the combatants. The DMZ continues to separate North and South Korea 50 years after the last major battles were fought, and tensions remain high, with some 1.17 million North Korean troops and 700,000 South Korean, US and UN troops deployed in the region on the edges of the DMZ (Korean National Defense, 2001). Following a relative easing of tensions in the 1990s, North Korea's October 2002 admission that it had an ongoing nuclear weapons programme, its withdrawal from the Nuclear Non-proliferation Agreement in December 2002, and accusations by the USA that the north possessed

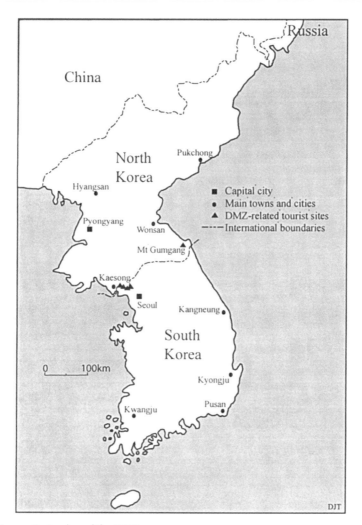

Fig. 7.2. The Korean Peninsula and the DMZ.

chemical and biological weapons greatly escalated tensions between North and South Korea.

The DMZ is an unusual area 4 kilometres in width, running 246 km from the east to the west coast of the Korean Peninsula following the tactical positions of the combatants as at the cessation of hostilities in 1953 (Fig. 7.2). While the DMZ is a demilitarized zone, its adjoining regions on both sides are heavily militarized, fortified and patrolled by combat forces authorized to use live ammunition if a threat is apparent. From both sides of the border casual observers are able to see various types of defensive zones, including a cleared

and fenced strip containing land mines that extends from coast to coast. Behind the obvious defensive barriers lie large fortifications camouflaged and hidden from casual observers.

Following the liberation of Korea from Japan at the conclusion of World War II, the country was partitioned at the 38th Parallel by the USA and USSR with little recognition of the wishes of the Korean people. The north became a region of Soviet control while the south came under the influence of the USA. As a consequence, the north adopted a Stalinist model of governance and economic organization, while the south adopted a capitalist system, although it took almost 40 years for representative democratic institutions to become firmly established.

The division of Korea into two nations, each following divergent economic and sociopolitical systems, has resulted in an impoverished north continuing to follow Stalinist-era central planning policies and a capitalist south that now has a well-developed economy and membership in the OECD. The DMZ has continued to be a zone of potential conflict long after the threat of a NATO–Warsaw Pact clash ceased in the early 1990s. Travellers have not failed to notice the profound implications of the DMZ, and a small-scale tourism sector has emerged to service the curiosity of visitors intent on viewing this symbol of ongoing conflict and the stark dividing line between complete sociopolitical seclusion and modern capitalism (Hall, 1990; Henderson, 2002; Pollack, 1996).

While the DMZ is a unique attraction on both sides, tourism activity within it is currently restricted to guided tours to very limited areas and overnight excursions to the nearby Mt Gumgang area in the DPRK. Except for a few sites in the vicinity of the Panmunjom Joint Security Area, the DMZ is off-limits to civilian visitors, and even South Korean nationals are barred from visiting Panmunjom unless given special clearance by the military authorities. Until diplomatic relations improve significantly there is little likelihood that citizens of either the DPRK or ROK, or from third nations, will be able to cross the border freely. Tourism in North Korea is extremely limited and tightly controlled; many tours in the north stop at the DMZ and Panmunjom armistice village (Hall, 1986a,b). DMZ tours are available from both the north and south, although it is not possible to cross from one side to the other except for visitors authorized to travel to Mt Gumgang by coach as part of an approved overnight tour. North Korean tours to the DMZ appear to run on a demand basis and are therefore less frequent than those originating in the south.

Several South Korean tour operators are authorized to conduct DMZ tours, the majority of which are day trips from Seoul. There are two primary itineraries available. First is a trip to the edge of the DMZ, which includes stops at a Korean War/DMZ museum, a lookout structure from which the North Korean city of Kaesong can be seen, one of several infiltration tunnels under the border that were dug by northern soldiers as a way to invade the south, and a small DMZ-themed entertainment and shopping area near the border adjacent to the Freedom Bridge. During this tour, visitors can see the barbed-wire fences and minefields that mark the demilitarized zone; North Korea's Gijeong-dong 'propaganda village', which is uninhabited except by soldiers; the world's largest flag (North Korean); and South Korea's Daesong-dong village, located inside the demilitarized zone and home to some 230 resident farmers, who receive preferential treatment by the South Korean government and must abide by strict curfews and rules of behaviour. The second common itinerary includes a visit to the UN forces headquarters at Camp Bonifas and the actual border line at Panmunjom armistice village. Participants on this tour can see North Korean soldiers and military installations up close, and the highlight is the chance to step into North Korea inside the conference room that straddles the divide. Costs for these tours are in the range of US$45–60, including lunch. Tour participants are required to observe exceedingly strict behavioural rules and meet stringent criteria. These include:

- Visitors must be over 10 years old.
- Visitors must carry their passports with them on the day of the tour.
- Visitors are not permitted to wear jeans, sandals, shorts or sports apparel.
- Visitors must not have shaggy or unkempt hair.
- Visitors must not touch any equipment, microphones or flags belonging to the North Korean side in the Panmunjom conference room.
- Visitors must not speak to, make any gesture toward, or in any way approach or respond to personnel from the other side.
- Visitors must not drink alcohol before the tour.
- Visitors must remain with the guide at all times (*Life in Korea*, 2003).

According to *Life in Korea* (2003), the UN Command guard forces have four primary duties: (i) to guard the Panmunjom Joint Security Area; (ii) to guard and support the Military Armistice Commission; (iii) to administrate over Daesong-dong Freedom Village; and (iv) to provide security for visitors to Panmunjom and conduct tours for them. This last responsibility is a curious phenomenon in tourism. One of the most fascinating aspects of South Korean DMZ tourism is the level of cooperation between the military authorities who control the zone adjoining the DMZ and the civilian tour companies, which are authorized to conduct tours. On the Panmunjom tours (tour type 2), visitors arrive at the border region in civilian coaches and then transfer to military vehicles driven by military personnel trained as guides. Because the sites visited fall within the South Korean/US/UN military area that would become a zone of combat if hostilities resumed, all movements (including tours) into and around the zone are tightly controlled and heavily guarded. Military guides, while escorting the tourist coaches and performing the same tasks as their civilian tour counterparts, are also armed and ready to engage in combat if necessary. Similarly, coaches visiting the DMZ region are escorted by military vehicles carrying armed soldiers. While this may seem excessive, military clashes have occurred in the past, and the open display of protective force is designed to prevent the reoccurrence of problems in the future. This becomes part of the tourist appeal in many cases.

The other component of DMZ-related tourism is the development of the Mt Gumgang region in North Korea, which possesses deep spiritual and religious meaning for all Koreans. One of the day-tours available during a visit to Mt Gumgang requires visitors, closely escorted by North Korean guides, to pass through several defensive zones that the PDRK has constructed to protect its border. The Hyundai Corporation-funded destination opened in 1998 and until recently required visitors to cross the border on overnight cruises along the east coast, dock, and undertake day trips into the scenic Gumgang Mountains during the day (Kim and Prideaux, 2003; Timothy, 2001). The project is a classic example of enclave tourism enforced with armed North Korean military guards and physical barriers allowing no opportunity for visitors to meet their northern counterparts. After attracting 212,000 visitors in 2001, demand fell to 59,000 visitors in 2002. Of the 448,000 visitors to Mt Gumgang

from 1998 to May 2002, only 1447 were non-Koreans. Arduous negotiations between the DPRK, ROK and Hyundai Corporation resulted in the opening of a road over the border and through the DMZ in February 2003 to allow visitors land access to Mt Gumgang. This move was hoped to re-ignite South Korean interest in visiting the area. This was a groundbreaking event for tourism, because it was the first time that regular trans-border traffic had been allowed since the 1950s.

If relations continue to improve, there is considerable potential to develop the DMZ as a major ecotourism zone (Lee, 2001). Remaining relatively untouched since the cessation of combat in 1953, the DMZ has become a refuge for wildlife and contains approximately one-third of the 2900 higher plant species, half of the mammal species, and about 20% of the 320 bird species found on the Korean Peninsula. Comprising 98,400 ha of land, the addition of the DMZ to the current total protected area of the DPRK (315,000 ha) and ROK (682,000 ha) (Westing, 2001) would expand both countries' protected areas by more than 7%. Likewise, there is considerable potential to develop heritage tourism in the DMZ, not only based on the wartime past, but also based on archaeological sites (e.g. Buddhist temple ruins, tombs and fortresses) and other cultural structures that are known to exist (Choi, 2001; Kirkbride, 1998; Lee, 2001).

Tourism to (De)militarized Zones and the Potential for Peace

According to the thinking of some researchers, tourism has the potential to exert a positive force on international relations, leading to a reduction in hostility and tension, and ultimately leading to some level of peace (Matthews, 1978; Var et al., 1989; Jafari, 1989; Matthews and Ritcher, 1991; Hobson and Ko, 1994; Richter, 1989, 1996). Several researchers (e.g. Butler and Mao, 1996; Kim and Crompton, 1990; Waterman, 1987; Yu, 1997; Zhang, 1993) have identified tourism as a factor in developing improved relations between partitioned countries such as the two Koreas and the two sides of Cyprus. This optimistic position has not always withstood rigorous testing, and some examples of tourism's limited ability to achieve peace have been identified by various authors (e.g. Anastasopoulous, 1992; Hall, 1991; Milman *et al.*, 1990; Pizam *et al.*, 1991). Kim and Prideaux (2003) noted that the First and Second World Wars occurred despite widespread travel between Germany, the UK and France in the pre-war years.

One approach to tourism development that has potential to create and sustain more peaceful relations is cross-border cooperation between neighbouring states. This form of collaboration in vital areas of tourism (e.g. conservation, flow of people, marketing, human resource issues, and transportation) may be a useful tool in enhancing the peace-building benefits that tourism may possess (Kliot, 1996; Fineberg, 1993; Saba, 1999; Timothy, 1999, 2002).

Even in situations where hostility is strong between neighbours, cooperation in matters of tourism might help build friendship and understanding. Traditionally, international boundaries and their protectionist roles have created competitive relationships between adjacent nations where neighbours offer similar goods and services, thereby creating competitive, sometimes unhealthy, market environments. While goodwill and peace can be critical outcomes of cross-border cooperation, they do not automatically follow. None the less, early signs from Europe, Asia and North America show that multinational cooperation can begin to break down competitive situations and advance symbiotic, complementary relationships, so that entire regions benefit from the growth of tourism and neighbours do not have to work in competition for a limited demand (Timothy, 2002).

Sönmez and Apostolopoulos (2000) argued for the potential peace dividend of cooperation between northern and southern Cyprus. They suggested several ways in which north–south relations might be healed through tourism cooperation: (i) setting policies to facilitate free tourist migration between sides; (ii) removing restrictions on contact between Turkish and Greek Cypriots; (iii) building free trade agreements; (iv) enacting cooperative marketing/promotion efforts; and (v) encouraging contact between peoples. Such efforts

are now in embryonic form, but there appears to be some potential for reconciliation on the island through cross-border cooperation and more open-door policies that allow more tourist contact between the two sides (Smith, 2003). There have also been some nascent efforts between the Turkish and Greek sectors of the islands to collaborate in the area of heritage tourism and conservation. In the mid-1980s, for instance, mayors and other city leaders from both sides of Nicosia collaborated to formulate the Nicosia Master Plan, which included goals to preserve the city's built heritage and to draw businesses and residents back to the decaying central city near the Green Line (Fig. 7.3). This theretofore unprecedented partnership between the two opposing sides faced many political and technical challenges (Rossides, 1995), but the plan did come to fruition, and both sides have been quite successful in adhering to it with a solid commitment to its long-term success (Kliot and Mansfeld, 1997).

To explore the opportunity for tourism to promote peace, Kim and Prideaux (2003) examined the opportunities the Mt Gumgang project created to promote peace between North and South Korea and found that tourism was a by-product of a political process implemented by both sides to promote dialogue outside of the UN process involving the Military Armistice Commission. According to Kim and Prideaux, Butler and Mao's (1996) postulate that travel between politically divided states is able to assist in reducing tensions and promote greater political understanding may have some peace-building potential in the future. Because travel to Mt Gumgang is strictly controlled and allows no open contact between residents and tourists, however, it is not possible for Butler and Mao's (1996) four stages of normalization of tourist contact to develop. Conversely, Kim and Prideaux (2003) found that in the Korean context Yu's (1997) thesis of *low politics activity* and *high politics activity*, where high politics activity is defined as sensitive political, economic and military issues dealt with at heads-of-government level, while low politics activity describes activities at the local level between ordinary people, more adequately described the conditions operating between North and South Korea.

Fig. 7.3. The Green Line in Nicosia/Lefkosa, Cyprus (Photo courtesy of Rolf Palmberg).

Symbolically the DMZ divides the Korean people into two opposing nations that share common ethnic heritages, cultures, and histories. Both nations regard the issue of reunification as a central political objective, although the method of achieving unification varies considerably and lies at the heart of the ongoing conflict. For the north, unification is a political objective that is to be achieved by force, while for the south, reunification is viewed as a process to be achieved by diplomacy aided by growing economic and social engagement. The belligerence of the north versus the more measured approach of the south can be more clearly understood by examining the way in which the two Koreas interpret the meaning of the word 'peace' (Kim and Prideaux, 2003). North Korea continues to follow an orthodox communist perspective that sanctions the exercise of military force to achieve political objectives, including territorial expansion, after which the absence of war, and of adversaries,

will allow a period of peace to prevail. The south has adopted a less adversarial position relying on deterrence backed by the military support of the USA and, in recent years, a more proactive political approach termed the Sunshine Policy, introduced by President Daejung Kim. The Sunshine Policy was developed by President Kim as a mechanism for drawing the north and south closer together without sacrificing the south's ability to deter aggression from the north and yet assure the north of its lack of intention to employ measures to achieve a forced unification (Go, 2002). A further aim of the policy was to expand south–north exchanges as a means of developing peaceful, mutually rewarding, and constructive dialogue and exchanges as a prelude for ultimate voluntary national unification. Tourism, based on the investment of South Korean capital in North Korea has been adopted by both countries as a policy instrument to improve political relations on the eventual road to reunification.

Initial tourism investment has been focused on the Mt Gumgang area which adjoins the DMZ on the east coast of the Korean Peninsula and possesses significant spiritual and religious meanings for all Koreans. In a recent analysis of the implications of the Mt Gumgang project for peace on the Korean Peninsula, Kim and Prideaux (2003) observed that the project has become a tool for achieving rapprochement, not the cause of rapprochement, and as a consequence tourism has not been the central factor in achieving improved relations between the two nations. Instead, tourism is a by-product of the quest for better relations. This interpretation varies from the thesis advanced by some observers that this tourism enterprise can be a central driver in promoting peace between the north and south (Lee, 1999).

Discussion and Conclusion

The form of tourism described in this chapter is closely connected to atrocity tourism and war tourism. In reality, the Turkish intervention on Cyprus and the Korean War resulted in many atrocities among all peoples involved, and conditions of war are responsible for the existence of both borders. Tourists' curiosity about forbidden places and boundaries that mark the front lines between opposing socio-economic and political systems comes to bear notably in the two examples discussed here. The relationships between war/atrocity and tourism could fruitfully be examined further in the context of international boundaries, since these are very commonly the roots of, and laboratories for, binational conflict.

In addition to experiences of morbidity, stepping into a forbidden country, or being able to say one has visited a place that is off-limits to many people around the world may also be another motivation for visiting borders of conflict and demilitarization. Such an experience will allow one to boast of adventures off the beaten tourist path to places virtually untouched by the outside world (Timothy, 1998). This may change, however, as international relations between hostile neighbours improve, especially to the point where partitioned states are reunited. Germany is proba-

bly the best example of this. While remnants of the 'iron curtain' are still important heritage attractions, the abolition of the wall and the disparities it represented has reduced the intrigue factor of visiting East Germany and looking at what is left of this infamous boundary. There is presently talk of the unification of Cyprus and Korea, and tourism is in both cases seen as a catalyst for helping to accomplish this goal.

The two borders highlighted here may face a similar fate to that of the Germanies. Urry's (1995) study, in *Consuming Places*, argued that 'the collapse of many spatial boundaries does not mean that the significance of space decreases'. He goes on to argue that 'as spatial barriers diminish so we become more sensitized to what different places in the world actually contain'. The borders that separate the Korean and Cypriot peoples have yet to collapse and thus continue to divide peoples who share much in common. The continued existence of the Attila Line and the DMZ has prevented tourists from discovering much of the manifold beauties of Northern Cyprus and North Korea and, as Urry suggests, the opening or abolition of these borders will sensitize tourists to the north in much the same way as the collapse of the Warsaw Pact and the Berlin Wall opened up Eastern Europe to the outside world and global tourism during the 1990s.

Despite what happens eventually to Cyprus and Korea, it is likely that there will always be conflict between neighbours, for power struggles are inherent in every culture and society. As a result, as history has so often revealed, there will continue to be wars, divisions and ceasefires, and there is little doubt that new armistice lines and frontiers of (de)militarization will continue to fascinate and intrigue amid the tourist gaze.

References

Akis, S. and Warner, J. (1994) A descriptive analysis of North Cyprus tourism. *Tourism Management* 15, 379–388.

Anastasopoulous, P.G. (1992) Tourism and attitude change: Greek tourists visiting Turkey. *Annals of Tourism Research* 19, 629–642.

Blacksell, M. (1998) Redrawing the political map. In: Pinder, D. (ed.) *The New Europe: Economy,*

Society and Environment. John Wiley & Sons, Chichester, pp. 23–42.

Borneman, J. (1998) Grenzregime (border regime): the Wall and its aftermath. In: Wilson, T.M. and Donnan, H. (eds) *Border Identities: Nation and State at International Frontiers*. Cambridge University Press, Cambridge, pp. 162–190.

Budd, J. (1990) Mexico's border towns to be focus of new tourism imperative. *Travel Weekly* 49, 15.

Butler, R.W. and Mao, B. (1996) Conceptual and theoretical implications of tourism between partitioned states. *Asia Pacific Journal of Tourism Research* 1(1), 25–34.

Choi, Y.H. (2001) The historic significance of the DMZ. In: Kim, C.H. (ed.) *The Korean DMZ: Reverting Beyond Division*. Sowha, Seoul, pp. 57–78.

Fineberg, A. (1993) *Regional Cooperation in the Tourism Industry*. Israel/Palestine Center for Research and Information, Jerusalem.

Go, Y. (2002) Evaluation of Mt. Gumgang tour business. In: *Proceedings of Academic Forum of Mt. Gumgang Tour Project and Inter-Korea Economic Cooperation*. Hyundai Economy Institute, Seoul.

Grundy-Warr, C. (1994) Peacekeeping lessons from divided Cyprus. In: Grundy-Warr, C. (ed.) *World Boundaries, Vol. 3: Eurasia*. Routledge, London, pp. 71–88.

Hall, D.R. (1986a) North Korea opens to tourism: a last resort. *Inside Asia* 9(4), 21–23.

Hall, D.R. (1986b) North of the divide. *Geographical Magazine* 58(11), 590–592.

Hall, D.R. (1990) Stalinism and tourism: a study of Albania and North Korea. *Annals of Tourism Research* 17, 36–54.

Hall, D.R. (1991) Introduction. In: Hall, D.R. (ed.) *Tourism and Economic Development in Eastern Europe and the Soviet Union*. Belhaven Press, London, pp. 3–28.

Henderson, J. (2002) Tourism and politics in the Korean Peninsula. *Journal of Tourism Studies* 13(2), 16–27.

Hobson, J.S.P. and Ko, G. (1994) Tourism and politics: the implications of the change in sovereignty on the future development of Hong Kong's tourism industry. *Journal of Travel Research* 32(4), 2–8.

Ioannides, D. and Apostolopoulos, Y. (1999) Political instability, war, and tourism in Cyprus: effects, management, and prospects for recovery. *Journal of Travel Research* 38(1), 51–56.

Jafari, J. (1989) Tourism and peace. *Annals of Tourism Research* 16, 439–444.

Kammas, M. (1991) Tourism development in Cyprus. *Cyprus Review* 3(2), 7–26.

Kim, S. and Prideaux, B. (2003) Tourism, peace, politics and ideology: impacts of the Mt.Gumgang Tour project in the Korean Peninsula. *Tourism Management*, 24(6): 675–685.

Kim, Y. and Crompton, J.L. (1990) Role of tourism in unifying the two Koreas. *Annals of Tourism Research* 17(3), 353–366.

Kirkbride, W.A. (1998) *Panmunjom: Facts About the Korean DMZ*, 5th edn. Hollym International, Elizabeth, New Jersey.

Kliot, N. (1996) Turning desert to bloom: Israeli–Jordanian peace proposals for the Jordan Rift Valley. *Journal of Borderlands Studies* 11(1), 1–24.

Kliot, N. and Mansfeld, Y. (1994) The dual landscape of a portioned city: Nicosia. In: Gallusser, W.A. (ed.) *Political Boundaries and Coexistence*. Peter Lang, Bern, pp. 151–161.

Kliot, N. and Mansfeld, Y. (1997) The political landscape of partition: the case of Cyprus. *Political Geography* 16(6), 495–521.

Korean National Defense (2001) *2000 White Paper of National Defense*. Korean National Defense, Seoul.

Lee, J. (1999) Impacts of Mt. Gumgang tour on reconciliation between two Koreas. *Unification Economy* January, 55–71.

Lee, J.H. (2001) International legal issues in the peaceful utilization of the Korean DMZ. In: Kim, C.H. (ed.) *The Korean DMZ: Reverting Beyond Division*. Sowha, Seoul, pp. 127–155.

Leimgruber, W. (1989) The perception of boundaries: barriers or invitation to interaction. *Regio Basiliensis* 22, 192–201.

Life in Korea (2003) Joint security area (Panmunjeom). *Life in Korea* website at http://www.lifeinkorea.com/drs/tours/list.cfm (accessed 2003).

Light, D. (2000) Gazing on communism: heritage tourism and post-communist identities in Germany, Hungary and Romania. *Tourism Geographies* 2(2), 157–176.

Lockhart, D.G. (1993) Tourism and politics: the example of Cyprus. In: Lockhart, D.G., Drakakis-Smith, D. and Schembri, J. (eds) *The Development Process in Small Island States*, Routledge, London, pp. 228–246.

Lockhart, D.G. and Ashton, S. (1990) Tourism to Northern Cyprus. *Geography* 75(2), 163–167.

Mansfeld, Y. and Kliot, N. (1996) The tourism industry in the partitioned island of Cyprus. In: Pizam, A. and Mansfeld, Y. (eds) *Tourism, Crime and International Security Issues*. John Wiley & Sons, Chichester, pp. 187–202.

Matthews, H.G. (1978) *International Tourism: a Political and Social Analysis*. Schenkman, Cambridge, Massachusetts.

Matthews, H.G., and Ritcher, L.K. (1991) Political science and tourism. *Annals of Tourism Research* 18, 120–135.

Milman, A., Reichel, A. and Pizam, A. (1990) The impact of tourism on ethnic attitudes: the Israeli–Egyptian case. *Journal of Travel Research* 29(1), 45–49.

Pizam, A., Milman, A. and Jafari, J. (1991) Influence of tourism on attitudes: US students visiting the USSR. *Tourism Management* 12, 47–54.

Pollack, A. (1996) At the DMZ, another invasion: tourists. *New York Times* 10 April, A10.

Reynolds, D.R. and McNulty, M.L. (1968) On the analysis of political boundaries as barriers: a perceptual approach. *East Lakes Geographer* 4, 21–38.

Richter, L.K. (1989) *The Politics of Tourism in Asia*. University of Hawaii Press, Honolulu.

Richter, L.K. (1996) The political dimensions of tourism. In: Ritchie, J.R.B. and Goeldner, C.R. (eds) *Travel, Tourism and Hospitality Research: a Handbook for Managers and Researchers*. John Wiley & Sons, New York.

Rossides, N. (1995) The conservation of the cultural heritage in Cyprus: a planner's perspective. *Regional Development Dialogue* 16(1), 110–125.

Saba, R.P. (1999) From peace to partnership: challenges of integration and development along the Peru–Ecuador border. *Journal of Borderlands Studies* 14(2), 1–22.

Smith, H. (2003) Open-door policy seeks to mend Cyprus. *Boston Globe* 25 May, A6.

Smith, S.L.J. (1984) A method for estimating the distance equivalence of international boundaries. *Journal of Travel Research* 22(3), 37–39.

Sönmez, S.F and Apostolopoulos, Y. (2000) Conflict resolution through tourism cooperation? The case of the partitioned island-state of Cyprus. *Journal of Travel and Tourism Marketing* 9(4), 35–48.

Theodoulou, M. (2003) Cracks in Cyprus's 'Berlin Wall'. *Christian Science Monitor* 7 May, 6.

Timothy, D.J. (1995a) International boundaries: new frontiers for tourism research. *Progress in Tourism and Hospitality Research* 1(2), 141–152.

Timothy, D.J. (1995b) Political boundaries and tourism: borders as tourist attractions. *Tourism Management* 16, 525–532.

Timothy, D.J. (1998) Collecting places: geodetic lines in tourist space. *Journal of Travel and Tourism Marketing* 7(4), 123–129.

Timothy, D.J. (1999) Cross–border partnership in tourism research management: international parks along the US–Canada border. *Journal of Sustainable Tourism* 7(3/4), 182–205.

Timothy, D.J. (2000) Borderlands: an unlikely tourist destination? *Boundary and Security Bulletin* 8(1), 57–65.

Timothy, D.J. (2001) *Tourism and Political Boundaries*. Routledge, London.

Timothy, D.J. (2002) Tourism in borderlands: competition, complementarity, and cross-frontier cooperation. In: Krakover, S. and Gradus, Y. (eds) *Tourism in Frontier Areas*. Lexington Books, Lanham, Maryland, pp. 233–258.

Timothy, D.J. (2003) Border regions as tourist destinations. In: Wall, G. (ed.) *Tourism: People, Places and Products*. Department of Geography, University of Waterloo, Waterloo, pp. 81–100.

Timothy, D.J. and Tosun, C. (2003) Tourists' perceptions of the Canada–USA border as a barrier to tourism at the International Peace Garden. *Tourism Management* 24, 411–421.

Urry, J. (1995) *Consuming Places*. Routledge, London.

Var, T., Brayle, R. and Korsay, M. (1989) Tourism and world peace: the case of Turkey. *Annals of Tourism Research* 16, 282–286.

Waterman, S. (1987) Partitioned states. *Political Geography Quarterly* 6(2), 151–171.

Westing, A.H. (2001) A Korean DMZ park for peace and nature: towards a code of conduct. In: Kim, C.H. (ed.) *The Korean DMZ: Reverting Beyond Division*. Sowha, Seoul, pp. 157–191.

Yu, L. (1997) Travel between politically divided China and Taiwan. *Asia Pacific Journal of Tourism Research* 2(1), 19–30.

Zhang, G. (1993) Tourism across the Taiwan Straits. *Tourism Management* 14, 228–231.

8 Tourism and the Heritage of Atrocity: Managing the Heritage of South African Apartheid for Entertainment

Gregory J. Ashworth

Heritage Management and Urban Tourism, Department of Planning, Faculty of Spatial Science, University of Groningen, Post Box 800, 9700 AV Groningen, The Netherlands

Combining the Uncombinable: Enjoying the Uncomfortable

The focus of this book is on tourism's persistent search for novelty, which has come to include an ever widening search for tourism products and experiences to satisfy a restless and fickle market. As part of this search, the extremes in human experience are being utilized for the tourist who attains gratification either as a participant or a spectator, with the line between the two being frequently blurred. Atrocities contain many elements of such extremes, which can be used to create marketable products from human cruelty and trauma. Using the heritage of atrocity (which is, after all, the deliberate infliction of suffering on people by other people) in tourism, a discretionary activity pursued for entertainment, seems an inherently improbable combination of phenomena. Indeed the relating of these two human activities may be viewed as at the very least bizarre, and probably also as distasteful, for atrocity heritage introduces a tone of seriousness into entertainment, while tourism threatens to trivialize the serious.

However, the exploitation of the heritage of the suffering of others for pleasure through the development of tourism products and experiences is not particularly new and is now rela-tively commonplace in tourism in some form or other.

The enormous range of events, sites and historic associations that attract tourists include many that commemorate or recall unpleasant or traumatic occurrences from the past. The justification for this chapter is that the use of such heritage poses distinctive issues and requires careful management based upon an understanding of the phenomenon.

Approaches

Although many elements of atrocity have a mass appeal, such tourism can be classified within the broad category of 'special interest', which is an amalgam of many quite different interests. From the viewpoint of the commodified site or event, atrocity tourism overlaps with many such spe-cialized 'adjectival tourisms' as 'war tourism', 'battlefield tourism', 'disaster tourism' and even 'killing-fields tourism' or 'hot-spots tourism' (i.e. visits to currently or recently well publicized places of conflict). Secondly, it can be incorpo-rated into a categorization that relates to the dis-position of the tourist or the sort of satisfaction obtained from the experience. Atrocity heritage tourism can be considered as one more narrowly defined aspect of the 'dark tourism' of Lennon and Foley (2000) and the 'thanatourism' of Dann and Seaton (2003). These encompass many motives (Dann, 2004), from a pilgrimage of penance and repentance for an assumed complicity (a 'mea culpa tourism'), through a quest for identity ('roots tourism'), a less personally engaged search for knowledge, understanding and enlightenment ('edutourism'), a social mission to shape more desirable or responsible futures ('lest we forget' or 'never-again tourism'), to much darker and less socially acceptable emotions where gratification is obtained from violence and suffering, becoming in its extreme form a 'sado-masochistic pornographic tourism'. Finally, the much broader field of heritage interpretation has long had to confront the difficulty of managing the large quantity of the remembered and memorialized human past that involves atrocity (Uzzel, 1989). Tourism is not the only, and rarely even the most important, market for the consumption of interpretations of such a 'dissonant heritage' (Tunbridge and Ashworth, 1996) from a history that may hurt, confuse or marginalize someone in some way.

The Selected Cases

The long sad chronicle of human history provides no shortage of cruelty from which cases could be selected and the possible range of atrocity sites is as wide as human creativity. The past is so full of acts of collective physical violence imposed on others by governments, ideologies and social groups that it is possible to interpret not only every battlefield and war museum but also every castle, ruler's palace, cathedral, merchant's house, country house, plantation or factory as an atrocity site. However, the possibility for successful commodification for tourism can be limited by a requirement that the event itself has four main characteristics.

First, there must be *a human perpetrator and a human victim* so that people, as tourists, can identify, or are identified by others, with people as perpetrators or victims.

Secondly, *the perpetrator must be engaged in a conscious, deliberate action and the victims must be innocent*, thus not contributing significantly to their own condition, for it is the knowing consciousness of the perpe-

trator in an intentional act that renders it an atrocity.

Thirdly, *atrocity implies an extraordinary seriousness*, whether of scale, however difficult that may be to quantify, or unusualness that is out of the ordinary for it is this bizarreness which draws the attention of the observer to the event that transforms routine cruelty into atrocity.

Fourthly, *an atrocity is an event that is known and remembered* which requires knowledge and memorability. A secret, unknown or forgotten atrocity can only be potentially usable. This memorability stems not only from the inherent nature and circumstances of the event, but also from the way in which knowledge of it is promoted and subsequently used. There is a need for the event to capture the imagination of others at the time and later. This would seem to suggest that recentness is an advantage, not only because of the surviving human memory of those directly involved, but also because of the efficiency of modern global information distribution techniques.

Three episodes in modern history seem to fulfil these requirements: of which two have been studied in this way and thus can serve as precedents for a focus here upon the third. The Holocaust of the Jewish people in Europe from 1933 to 1945, as a culmination of a much longer persecution, and the pursuit of the Atlantic slave trade from the 16th to the 19th centuries, have both the necessary multimillion scale and multi-century longevity. Both are memorialized through many specific sites, occurrences and individuals, and both have powerful contemporary implications for personal and group identities and for political nation and state building. Both are currently used in part for tourism although tourism was not, and remains not, the main motive for heritage interpretations in either case. Finally both were world-scale, long-term, systematic, top-down impositions of injustice and oppression from one large group of perpetrators upon another equally large group of victims. Identification is thus so widespread in practice that it may be extended to include all humanity in one way or another. We are thus all involved whether as tourists or not.

The third such episode which is studied here builds upon these two precedents, the first of which has now a large academic literature (see Ashworth and Hartmann, 2004) and the second of which has recently been comprehensively introduced by Dann and Seaton (2003). It is the imposition in South Africa of the ideology of racial separation, known as 'apartheid' from 1948 to 1994. As in the other episodes, it was only the culmination of a much longer period of racial discrimination which was not confined to this period or to that country; it is reflected in the memorialization of many specific sites, events and personalities; it has a contemporary significance for social identities and nation building; it involves a wider world as legatee of victimization or perpetration; and finally, and most relevant in this context, it is now beginning, somewhat hesitantly, to be used for tourism.

The noticeable differences are in the timing, as the ending of the apartheid system is much more recent than the abolition of slavery or the ending of the Jewish Holocaust. Secondly, and most significantly, is the continuing presence of both victims and perpetrators in the same country. The victims were neither eliminated nor physically expelled in a diaspora and the perpetrators are neither physically distant nor could they be demonized into a mythical, conveniently now non-existent, caricature of 'slave trader' or 'Nazi'. Furthermore this coexistence is not just a tolerated spatial coincidence; it has become a necessity to be maintained as economically and politically central to the creation of the new 'rainbow nation' of the explicitly multiracial South Africa. This adds a further dimension of complexity to an already inherently complex problem.

The Motives

Motives of tourists

An explanation of why tourists are attracted to the heritage of atrocity is necessary for understanding how such heritage is actually used by tourists and how it should be managed. Tourists are people and thus the uncomfortable question arises, 'Why are people attracted by atrocity?' This attraction may be condemned as a strange and aberrant social behaviour, betraying personal deviancy from the norms of the socially acceptable and from a balanced individual psy-

chological disposition. If atrocity heritage tourists are antisocial 'weirdoes' and psychically disturbed 'ghouls', then such heritage must be at least carefully managed and probably actively discouraged. However the alternative to this deviance hypothesis is that an interest in atrocity is an aspect of quite normal behaviour or, at worst, only a more open or exaggerated form of normal intrinsic character traits of people. If that is so, then we are all actual or potential atrocity tourists and the elements that favour the commodification of such sites, events and associations for tourism are easy to appreciate.

Four main arguments, each of which places atrocity within a much more familiar and generally unexceptional context, can be made.

The curiosity argument

The unusual or the unique is interesting to people and thus to tourists. Therefore the reason why tourists are attracted to atrocity comes at least in part from the same curiosity that motivates people to notice and remember occurrences that are out of the ordinary. The unique and unusual evokes and satisfies human curiosity: the tourist is not strange in this respect, only perhaps less inhibited in this exercise by the constraints of daily life. Curiosity about the atypical motivates 'disaster tourism', where accidents and natural calamities attract spectators, souvenir hunters and popular media attention. On a more organized, and socially acceptable level, some spectator sports, and even traditional circus activities, owe their popularity to the entertainment value of the perceived possibility of a personal disaster overtaking the performers. Atrocity, being a unique, non-everyday event, has a similar entertainment value.

The identity arguments

The explanation for an increasing interest in atrocity heritage may be the same as for heritage as a whole, and heritage tourism is just an expression of this interest while on holiday. All heritage tourism is arguably a form of 'roots' tourism, as the tourist seeks self-understanding and self-identity through heritage wherever it might be located. As much history has been unpleasant for many, it is not surprising that such a search almost inevitably reveals past atrocity with which the searcher can identify, most usually as a victim. The motives for such a self-identifying visitor may be instruction in personal or family history, or may have the spiritual and reflective characteristics of a pilgrimage to 'pay respects' to others with whom the visitor feels a personal link.

Equally, the increasing differentiation and fragmentation of the tourism market has been matched by attempts to increase the specificity of the tourist destination. Heritage has long been a major instrument for the transmission of this distinctiveness, answering the question, 'What happened here that makes this place different?' As with personal identities, atrocity heritage is an especially powerful instrument for differentiating places. It can transform an otherwise unprepossessing 'anywhere' into a very notable, recognizable and promotable 'somewhere'. Places may welcome such powerful indelible marking as 'putting them on the map' but, equally, if it is an undesirable map, may attempt to escape from such ill repute. A place such as Sharpeville may find its notoriety a disadvantage, and even townships such as Soweto, that have figured prominently in world news bulletins over many decades, may find the persistent evocation of association with violence, lawlessness and conflict a major disadvantage in attracting not only visitors but economic activities, investment and residents.

The horror argument

The idea that some people are attracted by horrific occurrences may appear a less acceptable argument than those advanced above. It may seem repugnant and morally unacceptable for people to be entertained by the accounts of the suffering of others. However, horror tourism is not new. From Roman gladiatorial spectacles to Madame Tussaud's 'Chamber of Horrors', suffering and death have been used as public entertainment. The link between portrayals of violence and amusement may be only an extreme form of a more general and socially acceptable attraction to the dramatic. The deliberate evocation of a mix of the emotions of fascination and fear through a voyeuristic contact with horror is a staple product of not just many tourism sites and trails but much of

literature, folk stories, art, and more recently film and television production. The relating to tourists of the heritage of atrocity is thus as entertaining as any of these media and for precisely the same reasons and with the same moral loading. Furthermore, if the tourism experience is essentially an emotional occurrence which contrasts with the experience of daily reality and offers a temporary escape from it, then the tourist is posing the question, 'What extraordinary feelings can I experience at this site or facility?' Sites of atrocity would seem particularly apposite because there are simply more and rawer emotions to experience.

The empathy argument

This could just be a more acceptable way of expressing a fascination with horror, as the distinction between an acceptable empathetic identification and an unacceptable voyeurism is vague and difficult to draw or to express through interpretation. Empathy relies upon the capacity of heritage consumers to identify themselves with the atrocity narrative being related, which is much easier to obtain with named and personified individuals – in this case overwhelmingly Mandela – than with large abstract groups. This identification is more usually assumed to be with the portrayed victims: it could equally, however, be with the perpetrators. If tourists engage in fantasy (Dann, 1981), then is a visitor to an atrocity becoming, in fantasy, a victim, a perpetrator or both?

None of these arguments are, of course, exclusive. Conscious political homage or atonement of largely sympathetic liberal markets in Europe and North America, meritorious self-education and a search for exemplars applicable elsewhere may combine with a curiosity about places made notorious by their repetition in news bulletins, with a frisson of excitement through exposure to previous violence and present perceived criminality, and obsessive interest in the exercise of human cruelty.

Motives of producers

The creators, custodians, interpreters and managers of atrocity heritage not only may have, but are very likely to have, quite different motives and objectives than the visitors. The explicit intentions of many of the managers and interpreters of sites and museums of atrocity heritage is frequently and openly expressed to be didactic. From the viewpoint of governments, the principal function of heritage is the legitimation of dominant ideologies and jurisdictions, and thus a revolutionary change in the ideology of the state will be reflected in a radical change in public heritage which is adjusted to concur with new power relations, popular aspirations and values. A new past needs to be explicitly created to reflect and support the new present, whilst the old becomes at best irrelevant and at worst contradictory. However, the simple argument for change is modified in South Africa by two constraints. First, realization of a new heritage agenda costs time and money and there is a shortage of both. Secondly, a simple and definitive shift from the old to the new would threaten the stability of the transition. The new democratic government is publicly committed to a multiracial and multi-ethnic consensus. This raises the sensitive issues of establishing the trappings of the new state legitimacy while assuaging the minorities, including those who were committed to the old. In simple terms, if the new South Africa wishes to continue to involve its white, coloured and Asian minorities in its economic, social and political life, which is its clearly stated policy, then it cannot either demonize them or write them out of the script of the country's founding mythology. It needs at least their passive consent, if not active embracing, of the official heritage narrative. The 'rainbow nation' therefore may well have to accommodate separate heritages within the public domain, however uncomfortable or even contradictory these may be.

In addition, past atrocity is often used not only to stimulate empathy with past victims but to make any future repetition of such events in comparable circumstances less likely. Further, many interpretations attempt to draw lessons from the past that are considered to be relevant for the present and the future. Heritage managers have agendas which may be broadly and vaguely philanthropic, anti-racist, anti-militarist and multi-ethnic. The significant point is just that the motives and messages of the heritage

producers may not be the same as those of the consumers.

Motives of residents

Finally, although the motives of the visitors and of the official producers may well be very mixed, so also may be the reactions of the local population. Residents and participants in the events commemorated may be gratified by outside interest or might be expected to resent the voyeuristic intrusion of 'poverty tourists' of another race and income. However, local entrepreneurs, tour operators, guides, shebeen owners and those claiming to have been active in the resistance are prominent among the operators of such tours. This, together with a lack of overtly expressed hostility to tourists, suggests at the very least that locals welcome the income more than they resent the intrusion.

The Nature and Location of the Product

The narratives

The heritage of resistance to apartheid is communicated through two very commonly encountered heritage narratives. These can be labelled 'the progress thesis' and 'the freedom struggle'. The '*progress thesis*' presents information in such a way that the historical chronicle of events is reduced to an inevitable sequence of improvement from bad to better in a straight and unswerving line. This is the 'road to freedom' or equally could be the 'road' to prosperity, enlightenment, civilization or any other such description of the completed present. This is the dominant narrative of museums and of 'national histories' worldwide. It is not only chronologically simple, it is easy to comprehend and avoids the complications of contradictory or competing ideas. It is also remarkably satisfying not only for the producer of such heritage narrative, as a self-justification, but also for the consumer, who has the satisfaction of knowing that he is the epitome of progress, standing upon the pinnacle of achievement and is thus more fortunate than previous generations who have further to travel or have not yet embarked upon such a journey.

Fig. 8.1. 'Liberty Square', Kiptown, Soweto. An undistinguished space now dedicated to Walter Sisulu and the 'freedom charter'.

The *'freedom struggle'*, a term that encapsulates both goal and process, has similar attributes of simplicity and inevitability as the progress thesis, but within the context of struggle. The dichotomy between the conditions of freedom and oppression, and the actors as freedom fighter and oppressor, admits of only two homogeneous categories. This is unifying, both within the group and in relation to the external and necessarily demonized enemy outside. The nature of the 'struggle' introduces the elements of drama and heroism and is strengthened by the ferocity and determination of fighting against odds. It thus produces heroes, as role models and foci of identification, and critical events – 'turning points' – around which the narrative can be constructed. Small wonder that almost every existing sovereign state has created for itself a founding mythology derived from the history of an ultimately successful freedom struggle.

The locations

The location of apartheid heritage has three characteristics. First, every 'homeland' and township is a monument to the apartheid system. Indeed the whole spatial relationships of areas and districts, of work, service and residential functions and of the transport systems that bound them together is a product of the attempt to establish racially separate development and thus a visible omnipresent heritage of that era and ideology. Secondly, the recentness of the attempt to create a heritage of apartheid and its insertion into an already existing panoply of British and Afrikaner heritages has almost inevitably resulted in a piecemeal scatter of sites and collections. Thirdly, much of the heritage does not easily lend itself to the architecturally impressive or the historically dramatic. Much of the history of the anti-apartheid movement was acted out by poor people in the townships amongst the mundane and ordinary structures and environments of the poor. The homes of its heroes and the sites of its events are by their nature unimpressive and commonplace, especially compared with the imposing public buildings and grandiloquent monumental statuary of the previous regime. Events such as the Sharpeville shootings of 1960 or the Soweto school uprising of 1976 may have been dramatic and memorable. but the settings in which they took place are not.

Buildings and sites

Although sacralized sites are often linked with buildings, as structures become imbued with the spirit of the historical events that occurred in and around them, there are, however, also sites which are just locations in space with no other distinguishing physical attributes.

The Regina Mundi Catholic church at Rockville, Soweto, for example, is the site in and around which political gatherings occurred in evasion of the Congregating Act. It was the so-called 'Soweto parliament' which attracted meetings of more than 6000 dissidents and was the site of the funeral of the victims of the 1976 school uprising. It is also a physical monument as a building, accommodating diverse relics, from the 'black Madonna' statue, to the bullet holes in the walls. The Morris Isaacson School in Mpathi Street, Soweto, is visually unremarkable but is sacralized as the place where the 1976 school protests against the introduction of Afrikaans as a medium of instruction are reputed to have begun. The nearby Vilakazi Street memorial mural commemorates the subsequent protest march and violent police reaction to it that focused upon that street. Indeed, Vilakazi Street, composed of quite ordinary small houses in Orlando West, has received the epithet, 'Home of the great' as former residence of two Nobel prize winners (Mandela and Tutu). The Hector Peterson Memorial in the Soweto cemetery is a commemorative sculpted object rather than a specific site marker, linking an individual with the other 300 similar victims of this episode. Typical of the otherwise characterless space is the recently named 'Freedom Square' in Kiptown, Soweto. It is just an empty, as yet totally unmarked, space between residential districts used now, as previously, for access, some informal trading, socializing and meeting. Its heritage significance is the link with the so-called 'freedom charter' declared here by the ANC spokesman Walter Sisulu.

The museums

Cape Town's District Six Museum was opened as a housed collection in an already preserved Baptist chapel in 1994, although it can be argued that District Six itself had since the 1980s been a monument, in the sense of a sacralized empty space. The concept of 'salted earth', upon which developers were reluctant to build, represented in itself 'space on which meanings could be inscribed in the imagination' (McEachern, 2001: 127). The 'meanings' so inscribed are those of forced removal and survival, after the designation of the district as 'white' in 1966, a theme later transferred to the museum located on the edge of the district and significantly opposite the forbidding and infamous Caledon Road police station. As on Robben Island, ex-residents of the area are used as interpreters, with such 'autoethnography' being expressed both verbally through guides and also visually and in writing through the personal accounts that dominate the exhibits. The museum is basically a reconstruction of a remembered past with the historical map in a process of continuous construction from the recollections of individuals, assuming a significance larger than the empty space of the reality outside (Pratt, 1994). The political message is that of the 'rainbow nation' as past reality rather than only future aspiration. It is demonstrated to have existed prior to the deportations but was disrupted by its antithesis, the apartheid state. It may be that the District Six community is a romanticized image of racial and social harmony that has taken on the significance of a myth. If so, or if such communities are largely created by the opposition evoked by threats to their existence, then apartheid effectively created District Six as an idea. It now stands as representative of many such disrupted communities throughout South Africa, some commemorated in a similar way, such as Pageview, Johannesburg (de Kleuver, 1999), and many that are not.

The Winnie Mandela House, Orlando West, Soweto, is the least architecturally impressive of the museums, being a small otherwise unremarkable township house, but its very small size and unpretentious ordinariness endow it with a quality of domestic cosiness. The content is similarly commonplace, composed of the utensils, accumulated souvenirs and cuttings of the Mandelas. The visitor has the feeling of a chance visit to a neighbour. This is, of course, both the content of its message of the struggle of ordinary people (like the visitor) against an oppressive and powerful state, and its effective means of conveying it. It was for a long time privately owned by Mandela's ex-wife but is now in the hands of the Soweto Heritage Trust, and remains without much information, visitor management or facilities.

The Apartheid Museum in Johannesburg, opened in 2001 as a private museum, contrasts sharply in every respect with the Winnie Mandela House. It is large, purpose-built, architecturally notable, and filled with carefully selected artefacts and exhibits. The visitor is professionally managed and guided from the outset, and the exhibits are thoughtfully arranged and interpreted. The building design is deliberately stark, with sharply contrasting shapes and materials, 'bringing to mind images of detention, oppression, division' (visitor brochure), reminiscent of Daniel Libeskind's Jewish Life museum in Berlin. The interpretative theme is deliberately universal rather than particular to the South African experience and is clearly designed to appeal to all racial groups in South Africa as well as to foreign visitors. It didactically relates a narrative of injustice and resistance that avoids a stereotypical white versus black confrontation. It also does not ignore the existing heritage narratives familiar to whites, as for example the mythology of the Trekboers, but includes and builds upon it as part of the wider story. It stresses the wide moral dichotomies of 'tragedy and heroism; tyranny and freedom; chaos and peace', which are intended to refer to all forms of racial inequality. It provides an experiential metaphor of the 'road to freedom' in the journey of the visitor from the racially segregated entry to the final triumph of the exit in 1994. Its location is also distinctive and not irrelevant to the intended message. If the message of the Winnie Mandela House is inseparable from its location in Soweto, the location of the Apartheid Museum on the outskirts of Johannesburg is also significant. It is sited next to the Gold Reef City historical theme and amusement park, inside a gated compound surrounded by an extensive car park. The promotional literature significantly points out that the museum is only 15 minutes from the international airport and 20 minutes from Sandton (the largest and dominantly white residential and commercial edge

city of the Johannesburg urban region): no information on access from Johannesburg or using public transport is given. Its intended market of tourists, educational groups and suburban residents with access by car and coach is not dissimilar to that of its Gold Reef neighbour, although its heritage message is much more serious, eschewing the more casual and entertainment-oriented history of its neighbour.

Although neither so extensive nor so well known as the above examples, many other local museums attempt to narrate aspects of the apartheid experience (Berning and Dominy, 1992). Both the Natal Museum, Pietermaritzburg, and the KwaMuhle Museum, Durban, relate the daily life of the township and thus contain an implicit message of continuous grinding inconvenience, if not hardship, stemming from the local consequences of the imposition of apartheid (Goudie et al., 1999). The Bo-Kaap Museum, Cape Town, similarly houses largely domestic artefacts and records relating to the long-standing dominantly Malay community of Bo-Kaap. Its political message is muted and its relationship to the anti-apartheid struggle indirect (Murphy, 1997). Like the District Six Museum, it concentrates on evoking the image of a lively and harmonious past community which is in the process of disappearing: it is thus in this sense typical of many such museums in South Africa and beyond. The very existence of such racially defined communities is itself a memorial to segregation. However, unlike District Six, far from being disrupted by the Group Areas Act of the apartheid regime, the ethnicity of this otherwise centrally located and attractive residential location was preserved from a gentrification which would, at least in part, have been white. The disappearance of the traditional community can thus be attributed to the removal of such residential restrictions.

The prisons

Prisons, penal colonies and detention centres are frequently used as powerful symbols of a heritage narrative based upon struggle, not least because they convey particularly evocative heritage experiences with which the visitor can empathize (see Tunbridge's (2004) comparative study of the heritage of penal colonies). The Robben Island prison complex is in many

Fig. 8.2. Exercise yard, Robben Island high-security prison.

respects the centrepiece of the whole resistance-to-apartheid heritage system and is the main and sometimes only such experience of visitors to South Africa, and as such it has generated a substantial literature since 1994 (see Smith, 1997). It owes its success (indicated by the 300,000+ annual visitors) in part to its ease of association with a single individual, Nelson Mandela, imprisoned here for 18 years, and in part to its fortuitous location in Table Bay, 11 km from Cape Town. The island is only accessible by official inclusive boat tours from the Victoria and Alfred waterfront (via the purpose-built quayside Nelson Mandela Reception Centre), which allows a strongly directed visitor tour management. Graham *et al.* (2001: 244–248) recognize three perspectives on Robben Island that have an uneasy relationship with each other, namely the '*political*', the '*tourist-commercial*' and the '*environmental*'.

The *political* use as the centrepiece of the resistance to apartheid narrative and flagship site of the new national identity is the most obvious. It was declared a National Monument and Museum in 1997 and applied to UNESCO for World Heritage inscription in 1998. The interpretation contains a simple explicit ideology of injustice. The interpretation is strongly personalized by both the ex-detainee interpreters and by the focus upon the experience of a single familiar individual. The oppression is related as largely devoid of perpetrators: the oppressor is the 'system' as instrument of an abstract idea. The Afrikaner guards are seen to an extent as ignorant innocents in the process of education by the inmates and as co-residents and thus co-victims.

The '*tourist-commercial*' dimension is enhanced by the island's location near Cape Town and by its effective incorporation into the Victoria and Alfred waterfront development, which is a major centre for recreational shopping and entertainment for residents and tourists alike. The use of a heritage site by tourists creates potential tension if only through the existence of multiple markets at the same time and place. This becomes problematic if the behaviour and expectations of the different groups conflict. One aspect of this is that from a standpoint of the tourism industry, heritage products are consumed very rapidly and rarely lead to repeat visits. There is thus the need to both constantly diversify and extend the product itself as well as to lengthen the tourist stay by the provision of other attractions and facilities and preferably overnight accommodation.

Fig. 8.3. The pile of stones, Robben Island. The impromptu prisoners' memorial in the quarry.

Widening the heritage product range to include heritages other than that of the anti-apartheid struggle is certainly possible. The island has a long history of use as detention centre for political dissidents long before those of the anti-apartheid struggle, and also has a heritage related to its use as a quarantine station, leper colony and war-time base. These additional strands could widen and complement the core message or dilute it and distract from it. Even more distracting would be the use of the '*environmental*' perspective whereby non-heritage tourism products, such as the nature/wildlife components (notably penguins), or even picnic facilities and outdoor recreation would be added to the visitor package. More controversial still would be proposals for hotel, and even casino, development which would be anathema to many who would regard this as a devaluation of the political and ideological message (Worden, 1996, 1997). This potential conflict between the political didactic intentions that are currently dominant and the tourism entertainment and natural environmental themes is likely to become more significant if commercial success is to be maintained and the immediacy and novelty of the anti-apartheid victory heritage and its living participants as both visitors,

presenters and principal exhibit, recedes into the past.

The success of Robben Island has prompted the development of other similar prison museums but none are comparable in features or visitor numbers. The Drakenstein Open Prison where Mandela spent the 14 months from December 1988, immediately prior to his release, lacks the drama of the sparseness of the site and setting of Robben Island.

The nomenclature

The renaming of places and streets is an obvious, visible, cheap and easily executed form of reinterpreting public heritage. Some of the most high-profile architects of the apartheid state, such as Malan or Verwoerd, have largely disappeared from at least officially used place names. Notably, however, the historic figures associated with the founding of the Afrikaner state, the white politicians of the succeeding Union and the capitalist adventurers have generally not been so treated. The names as well as the public statuary of Kruger, Smuts, Rhodes and the like have not been replaced by figures from the resistance struggle. Indeed some, such as Oppenheimer of the Anglo-American Corporation, are commemorated as local benefactors in places like Soweto.

Although few existing place names have been changed, the opportunity to add a new nomenclature has been taken when needed. The cities of Pretoria (named after a leading 'voortrekker') and Port Elizabeth (after a British governor's wife) remain, but the new urban regions of which they are to be a constituent part are Tswane and Mandela Urban Regions respectively. Most notably the country itself remains South Africa and not, as some would prefer as a clear statement of new beginning, Azania.

Non-place-specific heritage

Much heritage, including that of resistance to apartheid, is not place-specific, but could be located almost anywhere. This is the case with the many buildings, streets, and organizations named after individuals associated with the 'freedom struggle' and most usually to Mandela. This personification of the struggle around a single named individual is epitomized by the planned 65-m high statue of Mandela in Port Elizabeth, an attention that, it is reported (Campbell and Beresford, 2002), concerns and embarrasses the subject of this personality-cult adulation. However the point is that this, and other such, is not intended to commemorate any specific link with the site or the city.

Apartheid Tourism

The heritage of the resistance to apartheid has been developed rapidly as a tourism product especially on foreign markets since 1994. Attractions such as Robben Island or District Six Museum are now firmly on the tourism circuit of Cape Town, and the many memorials in Soweto in particular form a part of the burgeoning 'township tours' of Gauteng and elsewhere. The steady growth of 'township tourism' has widened the market with an increasingly professional packaging of 'authentic' 'meet the people' walkabouts, sanitized

'shebeen visits' and private caterers offering authentic lunches 'at home'. This has removed some of the attraction of pioneering adventure into a potentially dangerous area. It is reminiscent of other former 'hot-spot tourism' in Northern Ireland, Lebanon, the former Yugoslavia and elsewhere; 'township tours' are similar to the 'ghetto tourism' that is commercially successful in for example Harlem, New York or Watts, Los Angeles.

However, although apartheid heritage is developing into a significant tourism product line, two caveats need mentioning.

First, apartheid heritage is dominantly an add-on to other tourism products in South Africa and the two main categories of products on offer to tourists to South Africa have changed little since the demise of the apartheid government. The 'South African experience' as marketed externally is still composed principally of a combination of wildlife (especially the 'big six' animals but including more broadly African natural landscapes, reservations and parks) and secondly, what could be termed 'vernacular tribalism', that is the 'traditional' performances, customs, craftwork and cultures of the indigenous black African tribes. The sites most visited by western tourists (Robben Island, District Six Museum, the Apartheid Museum Johannesburg) are those that fit most easily into networks of the more traditional tourism sites (in the cases mentioned above, the Victoria and Alfred Waterfront, Downtown Cape Town and 'Gold Reef City').

Secondly, even in the specifically heritage tourism market, apartheid heritage is a relatively minor addition to a more established set of heritage products. The two most notable of these are the interlinked narratives of the founding of the Afrikaner state and society and the British imperial saga. These dominate in museums, monuments, markers and place names. The battlefields of the South African and Zulu wars, the Voortrekker monument outside Pretoria and the public buildings and statuary of the VOC and the Union are still the most visited heritage sites.

This marginal nature of apartheid heritage is not dissimilar to most Holocaust tourism in Europe, in which the Kazimierz ghetto is linked to baroque Krakow or Buchenwald to Dresden. One major difference, however, is that apartheid tourism has not attracted a substantial specialized and personally involved pilgrimage tourism in the same way as Holocaust tours. This may be in part because there is just not enough apartheid heritage, at least as yet, to in itself justify the long travelling distances involved from the main European and North American tourism generating markets, while the neighbouring African markets which might associate with the experience are simply too poor to generate much tourism. However the main explanation of this difference is again in the critical distinction about the location of victims. In South Africa, the direct victims and those who associate most strongly with them are still in the same country and indeed often in the same sites. They are therefore excursionists (school parties are prominent in many of the museums mentioned) or at most domestic tourists. Diasporic tourism, so important in the Israeli and US markets for Jewish heritage in particular, and even the beginnings of such tourism from the USA to slavery sites in West Africa (Dann and Seaton, 2003) has no real parallel in apartheid tourism.

A glance at the major guide-books (*Insight, Footprint, Lonely Planet*) directed at foreign visitors demonstrates this ambivalent situation. All mention the major museums and sites referred to above but usually with smaller entries than those for Gold Reef City, Sun City, Cape Castle or the Voortrekker Monument. Townships are described in historical sections but only Soweto is recommended as a place to visit as part of an organized tour. Indeed all the guide-books contain stern warnings discouraging individual visits to townships on grounds of personal safety.

The Management Issues

The management of sites of atrocity for tourism is rendered more difficult but more necessary by some inherent characteristics and contexts of such sites.

First, as with almost all heritage, there is an almost inevitable multiple use in which tourism is only one, and frequently not the most important, function. Atrocity heritage has important functions for political legitimation, social cohesion and individual 'settlement of memory'. The recentness and central importance of the apartheid experience enhances its importance in South African nation building. It is managed by authorities in furtherance of these goals, which may not concur with the objectives of tourism development. A further complication is that the strength of the individual and collective emotions evoked and conveyed by such sites imposes constraints and responsibilities on their management for tourism. Such management may operate thorough initial market segmentation, selection and targeting, on-site interpretation and marking, to physical or social constraints on visitor access, circulation or behaviour. However the motives of visitors remain varied and turnstiles do not operate policies that discriminate between acceptable and unacceptable visitors on the grounds of their motivation.

Secondly, the new heritage is being created within the context of the old. There are three main policy options. The heritage of resistance to apartheid as a new national narrative can *replace*, *accommodate* or *coexist with* the previously dominant heritage narratives. First, replacement of the old heritage of 'Boer, Briton and Bantu' by the new dominant heritage of the 'freedom struggle' disinherits the white minority whose continued commitment to the state is essential. It would also discard the main existing heritage tourism assets. Secondly, accommodation would not eradicate the past as narrated nor ignore its sites and relics but modify it and incorporate it into the new dominant interpretation. Some Anglo-Boer war memorials have been modified to include the roles and sacrifices of nonwhite participants (Tunbridge, 1999). New place names have appeared on the map for new provinces and metropolitan regions rather than as a renaming of existing places. The 16 December 'Day of the Vow' sacred to Afrikaner Trek mythology has been retained but renamed the 'Day of the Nation'. The two potentially highly divisive centenaries in 2002 (the 350th anniversary of the landing of Van Riebeeck at the Cape and the 400th anniversary of the incorporation of his employer, the Dutch East Indies Company) were mutedly commemorated as largely unspecified historical occurrences. Thirdly, in this spectrum of approaches, the new can be added to a largely un-reconstituted old in what could either be termed the 'core-plus model' or in 'the parallel heritages model'. The former uses the new heritage as the integrating national core with which all groups identify as a common base which is then enhanced by various optional add-ons, which could be existing regional, social or ethnic heritages. The latter merely adds the new heritage to an existing, tolerated pool of different heritages with which different groups identify. Both raise questions about whether the heritage of resistance to apartheid would be equally acceptable as such a national core and whether other heritages would comfortably coexist or contradict and conflict with such a core. It should be noted here that much of the 'old' heritage is now in private (Voortrekker Monument, Pretoria; Taal Monument, Paarl) or corporate (Victoria and Alfred Waterfront; Kimberley Mining Museum and Kimberley Club) hands which removes it, probably intentionally, from direct state influence and which renders much of the discussion about national policy largely irrelevant.

Thirdly, the issue is more complex than a simple confrontation between a black heritage of victimization and a white heritage of repression. The minority non-white heritage (Coloured, Malay, Indian) suffers a degree of ambiguity in its relation to resistance heritage concerning its ambivalent role as either co-victim of apartheid or collaborator in its imposition. Also, the previous white minority regime did not 'disregard' (Timothy and Boyd, 2003: 261; Gawe and Meli, 1990), or 'exclude' (Stone and Mackenzie, 1990) black African heritage; it reduced it to a 'tribal vernacular' which was and still is prominently narrated and promoted to tourists. Colourful, tribally distinctive, crafts, customs and performances reinforce group identities, and also remain a highly saleable tourism product on overseas markets. The heritage of resistance to apartheid is, however, non-tribal in its affiliations, political aspirations and goals of national identity.

Finally, the above discussion raises the more general issue of the wider impacts of heritage atrocity tourism upon the societies of both hosts and guests. The objectives of most atrocity heritage producers are unambiguously altruistic and humanitarian. However, whether

visitors accept their pedagogic moralizing messages, and even whether they are actually received at all, and whether the later behaviour of visitors is thereby altered to the benefit of their home societies, remains unknown. The experience of atrocity tourism may have impacts upon the individual tourist and the tourist's home society. Atrocity tourism may anaesthetize rather than sensitize visitors, making horror and suffering more normal or acceptable, rather than shocking and unacceptable. It may be psychologically undesirable and even destabilizing for susceptible individuals and the publication of especially horrific events may even lead to their repetition. There is also an argument that promoting the visiting of atrocity sites may legitimate the atrocity or those who committed the atrocities and thus encourage more in the future. Finally, tourists may be repelled rather than attracted by atrocity if they feel that they themselves could become victims of continuing terror, inconvenienced by the results of atrocity, or merely because they find its recent memory distasteful.

The heritage of apartheid, its systematic imposition of suffering and of the ultimately successful resistance to it, is central to the founding narrative of the new state, the reconciliation of its 'rainbow' constituents, and the way that the state projects itself to nationals and visitors alike. It will be enhanced and expanded as the state develops and will play an increasingly significant role in extending the heritage tourism products on offer. However, its very importance in all these fields adds to the complexity of its management. The future, not only of a nascent tourism industry earning much needed foreign exchange but of South Africa itself, and especially of its unique multiracial and multi-ethnic experiment in nation building, may depend upon the successful management of this past.

Acknowledgement

I am grateful for the comments of John Tunbridge of Carleton University, whose knowledge of South Africa is longer and often deeper than mine.

References

Ashworth, G.J. and Hartmann, R. (eds) (2004) *Horror and Human Tragedy Revisited: The Management of Sites of Atrocity for Tourism.* Cognizant, New York.

Berning, G. and Dominy, G. (1992) The presentation of the industrial heritage in South African museums: a critique. *South African Museums Bulletin* 19, 1–14.

Campbell, D. and Beresford, D. (2002) Mandela: a giant among men. *Guardian Weekly* December 26, 2.

Dann, G.M.S. (1981) Tourist motivation: an appraisal. *Annals of Tourism Research* 8, 187–219.

Dann, G.M.S. (2004) Children of the dark. In: Ashworth, G.J. and Hartmann, R. (eds) *Horror and Human Tragedy Revisited: The Management of Sites of Atrocity for Tourism.* Cognizant, New York.

Dann, G.M.S and Seaton, A.V. (eds) (2003) *Slavery, Contested Heritage and Thanatourism.* Haworth Press, New York.

Gawe, S. and Meli, F. (1990) The missing past in South Africa. In: Stone, P. and Mackenzie, R. (eds) *The Excluded Past: Archaeology in Education.* Unwin Hyman, London, pp. 98–108.

Goudie, S.C., Khan, F. and Kilian, D. (1999) Transforming tourism: black empowerment, heritage and identity beyond apartheid. *South African Geographical Journal* 81(1), 22–31.

Graham, B.J., Ashworth, G.J. and Tunbridge, J.E. (2001) *A Geography of Heritage: Power, Culture, Economy.* Arnold, London, pp. 244–248.

Kleuver, J. de (1999) De dood van Pageview. *Geografie* 4/8.

Lennon, J.J. and Foley, M. (2000) *Dark Tourism: in the Footsteps of Death and Disaster.* Cassell, London.

McEachern, C. (2001) Mapping the memories: politics, place and identity in the District Six museum. In: Zegeye, A. (ed.) *Social Identities in the New South Africa.* Kwela Books, Cape Town, pp. 223–247.

Murphy, D. (1997) *South from the Limpopo.* Murray, London.

Pratt, M.L. (1994) Women, literature and national brotherhood. *Nineteenth Century Contexts: An Interdisciplinary Journal* 18, 29–45.

Smith, C. (1997) *Robben Island.* Struik, Cape Town.

Stone, P. and Mackenzie, R. (eds) (1990) *The Excluded Past: Archaeology in Education.* Unwin Hyman, London.

Timothy, D.J. and Boyd, S.W. (2003) *Heritage Tourism.* Harlow, Prentice Hall.

Tunbridge, J.E (1999) Pietermaritzburg, South Africa: trials and traumas of conservation. *Built Environment* 25(3), 222–235.

Tunbridge, J.E. (2004) Penal colonies as tourism sites. In: Ashworth, G.J. and Hartmann, R. (eds) *Horror and Human Tragedy Revisited: The Management of Sites of Atrocity for Tourism.* Cognizant, New York.

Tunbridge, J.E. and Ashworth, G.J. (1996) *Dissonant Heritage: The Management of the Past as a Resource in Conflict.* Wiley, London.

Uzzel, D. (1989) *Heritage Interpretation.* Belhaven, London.

Worden, N. (1996) Contesting heritage at the Cape Town waterfront. *International Journal of Heritage Studies* 2, 59–75.

Worden, N. (1997) Contesting heritage in a South African city: Cape Town. In: Shaw, B.J. and Jones, R. (eds) *Contested Urban Heritage: Voices from the Periphery.* Ashgate, Aldershot, pp. 31–61.

9 Deep Ecotourism: Seeking Theoretical and Practical Reverence

David A. Fennell

Department of Recreation and Leisure Studies, Brock University, St Catharines, Ontario, Canada L2S 3A1

Introduction

In being presented with the opportunity to write this chapter, it was suggested that I infuse a deep and focused view of the moral underpinnings that are missing in our current attempts to construct a responsible ecotourism industry. In my efforts to conform to this perspective I have thus been forced, by my own will, to take a less frequently travelled road, especially in terms of the conventional way in which we regard ecotourism. The word 'deep', at least in environmental terms, makes reference to a perspective which has garnered relatively little support in the broader socio-economic arena. To some, ecocentric perspectives such as deep ecology are suitable only as heuristic devices which might provide a foundation from which to stretch our interpretations as regards responsible human–environment relationships. As perhaps the most ecocentric form of tourism, it is not inapt to ask some very pointed questions about ecotourism's roles and responsibilities within environmentalism. Because ecotourism is not always able to live up to its reputation as an ecologically and socially responsible form of tourism, the argument carried forward in this chapter is that we must look deeper in our attempts to understand why it is not, and how it can be.

The Well-travelled Road

One of the most oft-quoted claims in the tourism literature is that ecotourism is the fastest growing segment of the world's largest industry. During the 1990s, ecotourism – or variations on this theme – represented upwards of 20–40% of the global travel market (Hawkins, cited in Giannecchini, 1993; The Ecotourism Society, cited in Western, 1993). The reported growth of the sector is particularly amazing given that other researchers have found that ecotourism represented only 1.5–2.5% of all tourism in the late 1980s (Whelan, 1991, cited in Page and Dowling, 2002), even allowing for the fact that ecotourism grew tremendously during this time (let us view the mid-1980s as a reasonable take-off point for ecotourism, despite the fact that it was operationalized in name and practice well before this time). The latter figures, above, appear to be more realistic, as corroborated by the WTO (2002), who suggest that ecotourism constitutes only 2–4% of global tourism. The significance of these smaller percentages should not be dismissed, especially given the universal interest in such a small market of specialized tourists, as evident in the recent designation of 2002 as the International Year of Ecotourism (Cater, 2002).

The issue surrounding the magnitude of ecotourism is one that is very much tied to

© CAB International 2004. *New Horizons in Tourism: Strange Experiences and Stranger Practices* (ed. T.V. Singh)

definitions and classifications. It is only too clear in the year 2004 that we have been overwhelmed by too many definitions of ecotourism, and thus the inability to correctly categorize and understand ecotourists. For example, the author has noted in past research (Fennell, 2000a) that definitions have provided grounds for a great deal of misinterpretation regarding what is and what is not ecotourism, as outlined below:

- Responsible travel that conserves the environment and sustains the well-being of local people (The Ecotourism Society, cited in Western, 1993).
- Responsible travel to natural areas that conserves the environment and improves the welfare of local people (South Carolina Nature-Based Tourism Association).

The first of these is an ecotourism definition, while the second is a definition of nature-based tourism (which we know to encompass activities such as ecotourism, hunting, fishing, cycling, boat tours, and so on). Let us, for example, use fishing to demonstrate why definitions of ecotourism that are relatively weak or middle-of-the-road are at times incapable of separating ecotourism from other forms of tourism that are a lot more consumptive in orientation. Using the definitions stated above, which, in general, are almost identical, we can suggest that:

1. Fishing can be responsible (e.g. regulations/catch limits).
2. It can conserve the environment (e.g. as certain hunting organizations conserve habitat for duck hunting).
3. It can contribute to or improve the welfare of local people (e.g. soliciting the use of an aboriginal guide).

As such, the misinterpretation on the part of ecotourists and service providers alike, as well as the inherent mismanagement of the industry that follows, is not difficult to imagine. Given the foregoing approach to definition, it is also not surprising that ecotourists themselves have come in all shapes and sizes – perhaps demonstrating why there have been such inflated figures given in the past on the magnitude of the ecotourism industry. As such, the question

regarding who is an ecotourist and who is not has become an important one, and one that research has yet to fully embrace. The same applies from the intra-group perspective, where research has only just begun to examine the socio-psychological, setting and activity differences that exist between various types of ecotourists, despite the early work of Laarman and Durst (1987) and Lindberg (1991). The link between definition and tourist type is demonstrated in the work of Page and Dowling (2002) who observe that the smaller percentages adhere to a strict definition of ecotourism, while those which are larger include activities which encompass the entire hard–soft path spectrum of ecotourism, and perhaps those which border on mass tourism (see Weaver, 2001, for a good discussion of these linkages).

Ecotourism in partnership with mass tourism is an intriguing proposition. Indeed this relationship has already begun to evolve. It is based on the belief that the tenets of ecotourism might go a long way towards better informing the mass tourist, and that we might bring more advocates into the realm of ecotourism. There is not much of an argument against attempts to educate tourists as much as possible about environmental issues, flora and fauna, and so on. But there is an argument against how we might effectively cater to these sizeable groups without disrupting delicate ecological and social systems. I am reminded of the old adage that if ecotourism is to become successful in an economic sense, it will have undermined and destroyed everything it had initially set out to achieve: namely, low numbers, responsible development and virtuous behaviour. Unfortunately, in places like Mekong, the concept of ecotourism has been used by developers, in association with willing government officials, as a catalyst for the development of mass tourism facilities in regions which are not necessarily able to absorb the social and ecological effects of these enterprises (Cater, 2002). In such cases the magnitude of the mass tourism engine puts it at direct odds with the principles of ecotourism. Ecotourism development should remain scale-dependent, and therefore any changes which might be appropriate in mass tourism might best be accomplished through the philosophies of sustainable tourism. Sustainable tourism and ecotourism are not one and the same. Unfortunately this is not universally understood.

A further constraint to the development of a responsible ecotourism industry is that we still have not been able to distil common approaches to ecotourism, across sectors. This point is made abundantly clear at tourism conferences and workshops where fundamental differences between what operators, government, local people, and tourists want are obvious. Operators, for example, are often wary of government officials (regulators), as well as academics, the latter of which are dismissed as having no practical value to add to the industry. Issues of territory, cross-over, understanding, shared knowledge and intent have been mired down in a stew of confusion, with an unwillingness to adapt, and to find and use the appropriate expertise. This is especially troublesome for ecotourism, which must balance the competing aspects of conservation and profit, with the latter often taking precedence. This appears to be the case in South Africa, where ecotourism is tempered by a primary focus on community economic development (i.e. ecotourism is designed almost solely as a vehicle for economic development). In a recent visit to the country, it was explained that 'ecotourism begins and ends with economic development'. Such a perspective is not difficult to appreciate given the degree of poverty in the region and the ease with which communities succumb to the promise of prosperity. The consequence of this stance, however, is that just about any form of outdoor activity (e.g. fishing and rural-based farm stays) bringing money to such communities is viewed as ecotourism. The danger of the economic hinge here is described by Saul (2001), who notes that the well-being of a society should never be decided solely on the basis of economics. Although important, it is dangerous.

Unfortunately an overarching focus on the economics of tourism from the industry side has tended to spill over into the realm of tourism research. The main side-effect of this is that it has tempered the values and methods – the worldview – that tourism researchers bring to their work. The same can be said for ecotourism research, which has elected to go down the same path. If this is true, such an approach to research suggests that we are almost afraid to view ecotourism in any other context (e.g. from a human ecology standpoint), when in fact its nature begs for us to view it differently.

The Road Less Travelled

Upon being asked where he was from, the Greek philosopher Diogenes referred to himself as a 'citizen of the world'. That is, his thoughts and concerns were not solely confined to his current position, but transcended this to include the entire world. His perspectives on this topic led to the term *kosmopolites* (meaning world citizen), suggesting that each of us dwells in two realms: the place of our birth and the global community. In more contemporary times, one's sense of space, place, and scale have been considered in detail by the geographer J.K. Wright (1966), in one of his many geo-isms, as they have come to be known. Among these, Wright described the concepts of geopiety and georeligion. Geopiety refers to the emotional bond or awareness (piety) that people have towards space (geo), the latter of which is so central to the discipline of geography. In referencing the work of Tuan (1976), Singh *et al.* (2003) note that geopiety is a religious concept that combines ecology and territoriality through attitude, beliefs and values. Indeed, Tuan notes that feelings of belonging transcend both culture and religion. And, as Singh *et al.* (2003) observe, 'it is the 'rootedness' of values arising from such soulful attachments to place that creates communities' (2003: 8). From the spatial context, geopiety appears to be more closely linked with one's local environment, and the territorial aspects which go along with this association. In a wider context, geopiety is a microcosm of georeligion, which refers to one's emotions about the earth in general. Typically, emotions associated with the concepts of geopiety and georeligion include love, reverence, affection, pity and compassion.

From Diogenes and Wright we have come to understand some of the basic spiritual and philosophical principles which are so vital to the stewardship of the planet today. The local–cosmopolitan perspective of Diogenes accentuates the importance of acting locally, but thinking globally, which is an underlying theme in environmentalism. And from Wright, the love and compassion for place, at multiple scales, underscores the importance of valuing the places where we live, work and play. For tourism, the interplay between place and emotion is critical if tourists are to be able to transfer their love of place beyond the scope of generating revenue in those destinations which receive tourists. This means that the same love that we supposedly have for our own houses, streets and communities can and perhaps should be transferable to the places we visit as tourists.

Perhaps in a less spatially oriented fashion, the same 'geopietic' argument has held true in our regard for plants, animals and natural areas for years. In the English-speaking world this 'nature–piety' has its roots in England where the worship of nature corresponded with the collapse of Christianity during the 1720s (Clark, 1969). As Clark suggests, however, faith was not completely eliminated at this time, but was to enter Western Europe *through* nature. In the beginning it would come from the minor poets, provincial painters, and gardeners, but later would take hold in the writings and art of some of the most famous minds of the time. Foremost in this regard was Rousseau, who was successful in inspiring people to look at the landscape in a romantic and existential fashion. For example, mountains were valued spiritually and recreationally as more than just a nuisance to communication and development. Perhaps even more significant, though, was his perspectives on what was to become existential philosophy, about the same time that David Hume had written on the topic. As described by Clark, Rousseau, when immersed in the natural world,

> lost all consciousness of an independent self, all painful memories of the past or anxieties about the future, everything accept the sense of being.
>
> (1969: 274–275)

Existence was thus a function of a series of events that were perceived through the senses; events which were tied to the natural world first and later to people. The idea that virtue was intricately tied to the natural world ('natural man') stood in stark contrast to the rest of industrialized Europe. Rousseau's philosophy could not have been more unconventional.

Rousseau was followed by others, including Coleridge and Wordsworth, the latter of which wrote that the new religion was one that was anti-hierarchical, values-based, instinctual and moral (Clark, 1969). It included the English painters Turner and Constable, and it prompted others to seek these out in attempting to discover different truths from religion. These perspectives gained a larger following in the early 1830s when the American, Ralph Waldo Emerson, visited Western Europe, in an effort to shed his dissatisfaction with conventional religion and to overcome personal loss. During his stay Emerson met Wordsworth, Coleridge and Carlyle, all of whom influenced his views on perception and nature, leading Emerson to establish the American transcendentalist paradigm. This doctrine gave forceful expression to older ideas about the presence of divinity in the natural world. As outlined by Nash:

> The core of Transcendentalism was the belief that a correspondence or parallelism existed between the higher realm of spiritual truth and the lower one of material objects . . . Transcendentalists had a definite conception of man's place in a universe divided between object and essence. His physical existence rooted him to the material portion, like all natural objects, but his soul gave him the potential to transcend this condition. Using intuition or imagination (as distinct from rational understanding), man might penetrate to spiritual truths.
>
> (1982: 85)

Transcendentalists sought to reveal the direct relationship between the natural world and the good within humanity; a common theme that paralleled Rousseau's 'virtuous man'. However, while Emerson was content to write about his love of nature, Thoreau, and more particularly Muir (both of whom subscribed to the transcendentalist philosophy), were bound to live it. The evolution from sedentary scholar to scholarly activist can be seen quite clearly in these individuals at a time when American corporate development had intensified, and when there was a great need to pressure government for the establishment of

Table 9.1. Contrasting paradigms.

Dominant worldview	Deep ecology
Dominance over nature	Harmony with Nature
Natural environment as a resource for humans	All Nature has intrinsic worth/biospecies equality
Material/economic growth for growing human population	Elegantly simple material needs (material goals serving the larger goal of self-realization)
Belief in ample resource reserves	Earth 'supplies' limited
High technological progress and solutions	Appropriate technology; non-dominating science
Consumerism	Doing with enough/recycling
National/centralized community	Minority tradition/bioregion

Source: Devall and Sessions (1985).

parks and protected areas. The messages quite apparent in the preservationist movement were that as society continues to move towards the mechanistic and materialistic, there will always be those who will push hard in the opposite direction.

During the 1960s the push was championed by Rachel Carson. In her book *Silent Spring* (1962), Carson noted that the post-World War II era had created the market and need for a whole host of materials that were designed to keep pace with unprecedented levels of growth. Until *Silent Spring*, the effects of these materials (e.g. pesticides) were largely unknown. Carson thus provided solid evidence that human actions can have irreversible implications, the likes of which were inconceivable at the time. From World War II we learned that technology and science could alter the course of history. Carson demonstrated that the same could hold true at the smallest of scales. This knowledge – the understanding of what we were allowed to do to each other in the name of science and corporate advancement – provided a foundation for the development of quite extreme ecocentric frameworks designed to provide an expanded view of human consciousness. One of the most prevailing of these is the 'deep ecology' movement, first described by Naess (1973), which in turn was based on attempts to provide a deeper understanding of the work of Carson and Aldo Leopold. The essence of deep ecology (Devall and Sessions, 1985), is to probe beyond the limited information afforded to us through sci-

ence, into the realm of the religious and philosophical. These authors note that deep ecology is a representation of basic intuitions and experiences of the individual in the context of a broader holistic ecological consciousness. In this regard, deep ecology is the antithesis of the dominant worldview of today (Table 9.1).

What resonates through the deep ecology philosophy is the importance of ethics, harmony and equity. As such, it is intricately tied to the basic assumptions surrounding human behaviour (i.e. good versus bad), the reasons for these behaviours, their effects, and how we may institute change. A book that had a similar message during the same time, and of particular importance to our discussion here, was Taylor's (1986) *Respect for Nature: a Theory of Environmental Ethics*. Taylor's work provided a theoretical argument for the importance of respecting the natural world, at a time when environmental ethics began to emerge. He defined environmental ethics as that which is 'concerned with the moral relations that hold between humans and the natural world' (1986: 3). Our duties, obligations and responsibilities, regarding the natural world, Taylor observes, must be governed by ethical principles. Taylor noted, as other ethicists have, the importance of following an ethical ideal or ethical spirit. That is, in order to realize the vision of a 'best possible world'; stakeholder groups must be motivated to provide the needed willpower to implement shared measures for the benefit of all. This is particularly relevant to tourism studies where there are virtually no

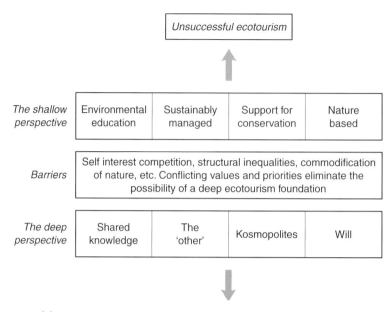

Fig. 9.1. Unsuccessful ecotourism.

underlying ethical principles – in a theoretical context – which might act in guiding a comprehensive vision for the importance of human values in tourism decision making. The same can be said for ecotourism.

Converging Roads

The foregoing discussion on lack of vision, human values, and the ethical spirit in ecotourism is especially troubling, given ecotourism's responsible status. Although there is mounting consensus regarding what ecotourism is (i.e. tourism that includes environmental education, a nature base, conservation, and which is sustainably managed) the sheer number of definitions detracts from our ability to find clarity for all stakeholders in time and space. In an attempt to link the foregoing discussion into a 'way forward', it is suggested that these shallow descriptors that we use to define ecotourism, but which mask its underlying essence, need to stem from a foundation of core values or qualities which could be used as fundamental, underlying 'essentials' for the creation of an ethical, efficient and future-focused ecotourism industry (Figs 9.1 and 9.2). The

suggestion is that unless we have these fundamental values in place, it is unlikely that the concepts that we have historically used to define ecotourism will be helpful. The premise driving this framework is the notion that ecotourism has grown without a basic ontological foundation that might be helpful in putting all stakeholder groups on equal footing. Each of the proposed core values has some connection to social and ecological reverence.

Figure 9.1 illustrates that ecotourism will be *unsuccessful* if there is a relatively strict adherence to the fundamental defining aspects of ecotourism alone. Although these shallow descriptors, as noted above and in the figure, tell us how we may differentiate ecotourism from other types of tourism, they are not rooted in any philosophical domain. Consequently, the barrier between shallow ecotourism and deep ecotourism perspectives is created because of self-interest and unhealthy competition (Saul, 2001), and because of the political and economic forces in place which have prevented ecotourism from realizing its potential to, for example, protect habitats, conserve biodiversity and prevent poverty. These disparities and dysfunctions, it is argued, will continue unless we provide meaning at a

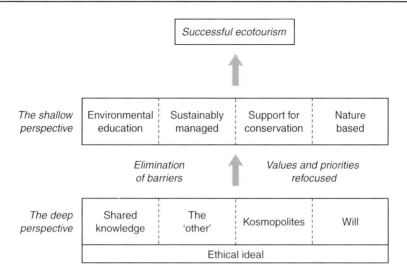

Fig. 9.2. Successful ecotourism

deeper level, and in a collective fashion. Figure 9.1 also illustrates that because of the barriers that exist, there is a relatively weak relationship between the four central defining aspects of ecotourism (as shown by the solid lines). The corollary to this is that ecotourism is unsuccessful even at the most shallow or rudimentary of levels because of this disjointedness and lack of a fundamental core. Without a philosophical basis, the barriers in place are so firmly ingrained that they are insurmountable.

In contrast, Fig. 9.2 illustrates that these constraints may be eliminated through the incorporation of a series of core values that will dictate the development of definitions, policies, practices and procedures for the entire ecotourism industry (*shared knowledge, the 'other', kosmopolites and will*). These core values strengthen the moral fabric of the industry, but also serve to strengthen the mechanisms that we use to define ecotourism at the shallow level. Processes and policies for environmental education, for example, are more effective because they emerge from the same core values which underscore the entire ecotourism industry. This can also be seen through the overlapping bonds that exist between the four defining aspects of the shallow perspective (the dashed lines between each). The deep perspective is essential if we

are to have the opportunity to achieve a successful ecotourism operation (at the individual level) or industry (at broader levels). Underlying these is the importance of an ethical foundation which provides the basis for ecotourism. This implies that the use of normative ethics such as deontology, teleology and justice will be useful in delineating best practice and relevant research. The four core values for a deep ecotourism foundation are elaborated upon below.

Shared knowledge

In arguing for 'knowing' over 'understanding', Saul (2001) observed that there is actually very little that people understand collectively. The problem with this is that we do not really understand most of what we know, and therefore, an understanding does not necessarily help us use our knowledge. Shared knowledge, he suggests

> is a manifestation of our collective consciousness, and its value lies in the citizenry and in their expression of their shared knowledge through their collective conscious.

(2001: 32)

When shared knowledge is taken away, we have a reduced capacity to solve problems. Knowledge has thus become a key tool for the private sector and a determinant of economic growth for governments – two key stakeholder groups in the ecotourism field. As Beijerse (1999) illustrates, this macro-level focus on knowledge management has implications at all scales, including those such as service providers at the micro-level. Cooper (2002), notes that the emerging study of knowledge management entails

> a process by which information is transformed into capabilities for effective action and used to reduce the uncertainty of decision making.
> (2002: 375)

The intention is to allow entities, like organizations, to act as intelligently as possible, as well as to realize the best value of its knowledge assets (Wiig, 1997). While this provides the organization with a competitive advantage, success must be based on financial, social and ecological criteria. This is especially important for ecotourism, which is often lauded as a tool for community development, conservation and education. In practice, however, it can deviate little from other forms of tourism which are concerned more with profit than social and ecological responsibility (Page and Dowling, 2002). Ecotourism thus falls short of its goals because of an inability to find common ground amongst a number of competing stakeholder groups, including conservationists, developers, aboriginal people, local people and tourists. The reason for this is competing agendas, different core values, and a lack of connectedness. If such groups are not integrated in their manner of developing policies and guidelines, there is little chance of making intelligent decisions to the benefit of all. Shared knowledge may thus provide a foundation for the development of ethically based norms and core values both within and between organizations. A good representation of the importance of this mindset is in the work of Edginton *et al.* (1980), who have compiled a list of professional responsibilities that guides must adhere to in working towards the best interests of participants (adapted for our purposes here). Some of these include:

- *Placing the need of the participant first.* Ensuring that the whole organization is devoted to meeting this goal.
- *Commitment to the ideals of ecotourism.* The entrepreneur should be consistent with the philosophical tenets and most up-to-date approaches of the industry.
- *Acquisition of adequate and appropriate knowledge before engaging in professional activities.* The service provider should have sufficient education or experience to carry out the responsibilities of the job.
- *Continuous upgrading of professional knowledge, skill and ability.* The programmer must be motivated to pursue learning and advancement, and to keep abreast of current trends and concerns.
- *Operating ethically and equitably.* Responsibility to be honest, forthright and direct in his or her relationship with the client, and to avoid being coerced, bribed or have one's integrity compromised.
- *Self-regulation.* It is the responsibility of the profession to establish performance guidelines and standards. Operators must regulate their behaviour accordingly.
- *Contributing to the development of the profession and other professionals.* The professional ecotourism operator must endeavour, unselfishly, to share knowledge, skills and abilities for the betterment of the field.

The denial of shared knowledge, therefore, creates barriers that limit the implementation of common sense and maximize territoriality and insularity.

The 'other'

Kant made reference to the notion that too much reliance on one's *sensus privatus* (or 'one's own sense') contributes, not surprisingly, to the loss of our sense of the 'other'. This might be interpreted to mean our fellow man, but can also include every other thing on the planet that we use for our instrumental ends. Kant suggested that this insularity is one of the only general symptoms of insanity, which is the 'loss of common sense and the logical stubbornness in insisting on one's own sense' (Kant, cited in Saul, 2001). This pattern of thought has also been highlighted by Frankel (1985), who argued that

> success, like happiness, cannot be pursued; it must ensue, and it only does so as the unintended side-effect of one's personal dedication to a cause greater than oneself or as the by-product of one's surrender to a person other than oneself.
>
> (1985: 17)

The choice to work in the ecotourism field therefore must be hinged on the notion that one's involvement represents a tangible benefit that goes beyond the sphere of the individual. Sustaining oneself financially is obviously of great importance, but working for the benefit of the environment, local people and the good of the industry must also be valued. This might first be recognized in knowing the value of giving something back (to nature or a community) and sharing resources in an equitable fashion.

The concept of the 'other' might also be extended to include the inherent or intrinsic worth of other beings and the development of respectful relationships that are based on equity. This may be acknowledged through programmes and operations which strive to limit stress and pressure on plants, animals and other stakeholder groups involved in the ecotourism industry. For example, although arguments have been made to suggest that forms of consumptive outdoor recreation such as fishing can be classed as ecotourism (see Holland *et al.*, 1998), the rationale for such decisions is often linked to instrumental ends. Fennell (2000b) argued that any type of conventional fishing could not be viewed as ecotourism, because of our failure to recognize some key factors in differentiating ecotourism from other forms of tourism. That is, while there was disagreement with the variables used by Holland *et al.* to define ecotourism, there was also the belief that some very crucial aspects of human–animal relations had not been considered. These included the intention to entrap the animal (which is not the same as the intentions of ecotourists which should be geared towards minimum disturbance and impact in all cases);

the pain and stress which results from catching the animal; consumptiveness (catch-and-release practices still may be viewed as consumptive along a continuum); and values, such that ecotourists have a different set of values related to sport and the intrinsic/extrinsic motivations surrounding participation in these activities. The author noted that despite the angler's best intentions to minimize stress on the animal, one can only do so up to a point – after which he or she must cease to pursue and capture the animal. The argument follows that the treatment of animals cannot be based on an acknowledgement of healthy populations (i.e. it is fine to catch or hunt animals because of the healthy state of the population as a whole), but rather that respect must be shown to the individuals comprising these populations. The use of weak definitions or principles behind ecotourism thus opens the door for a great deal of misrepresentation and the prospect of any number of different activities (probably including hunting) that place human needs over the basic requirements of other species.

Beyond the importance of relationships that limit ecological and sociological stress, ecotourism would thrive when there is an opportunity to develop an affective or emotional bond with the 'other'. This might only occur when nature is on equal footing with people, and when people can experience nature in conditions which are as natural or ecologically authentic as possible, whether these conditions be within an urban park or an international peace park. This may provide a reasonable explanation why zoos and aquaria might not be considered by some as acceptable forms of ecotourism supply.

Kosmopolites

As suggested by Diogenes, although we are born to a place and time, each of us remains a citizen of the world. The responsibility that comes with this sensitivity to scale should not be taken lightly regarding the implications of our actions in our immediate space and beyond. It follows that within these nested scales, stakeholder groups must continue to maintain a value set that is broadly socio-ecological in its orientation. This is particularly

true of the service provider, who must incorporate social responsibility and ecological well-
being alongside commercial success. For
example, in an application of the business and
moral development literature to ecotourism,
Malloy and Fennell (1998) noted that ecotourism businesses could be of three kinds:
market (pre-conventional), *utilitarian* (conventional), and *socio-ecological* (post-conven-
tional). The business literature confirms that
most organizations in operation today are ruled
by market values, meaning that such groups are
internally oriented, they stick to rules only to
avoid punishment, follow rules only if these
reflect their best interests, and feel that ethics
are only useful if they are good for business.
Conversely, the utilitarian business views ethical business practice as good for all stakeholders; they tend to be externally oriented, attempt
to fulfil the duties of the social system, and promote ethical standards. The status least represented in the realm of business is the
socio-ecological organization, which maintains
a cosmopolitan view of business, will not
exploit for profit, and values profit on the basis
of ecologically just behaviour alone. This latter
perspective advocates the notion that businesses must adhere to a triple bottom line in
their accounting and basis for success.
Operating otherwise suggests that we have lost
the ability to see outside of ourselves, and to
envision ourselves within a broader context.

Following from the observation of
Dostoevski, who wrote that 'man is a being
who can get used to anything', it strikes me that
we in the 21st century have got quite used to
viewing just about everything, including
tourism, in terms of its economic worth. The
unfortunate consequence of this might be that
the regard we have for wealth and power completely blinds our ability to value other things.
Coupled with this is the fact that we have
become rather used to viewing bigger (i.e. the
scale of commerce) as better. In fact this push
for bigger can undermine our ability to establish scale-sensitive, reputable and innovative
programmes that are distinctive. Better, not
necessarily bigger, programmes provide the
ability to value benefit as something more than
just an economic concept. This focus on an
optimal business scale (in much the same way
we have reduced the size of developments to fit

the scale of the community) can have both local
and regional benefits.

Will

Nietzsche observed that 'He who has a *why* to
live can bear with almost any *how*'. In our
struggles to find meaning in and from ecotourism we must not lose sight of '*why*' ecotourism can be so important as a vehicle for
sustainable development. To this end, those
who are responsible for the planning and management of ecotourism must have the will to
articulate core values to all involved stakeholders. The fact is, however, that we continue to
bear with almost any '*how*' in the philosophy
and practice of ecotourism which thus makes it
indistinguishable from the many other forms of
tourism that are less future-focused and less
concerned with social and ecological integrity.
Just any *how* (in reference to the tremendous
array of different ways in which to operational-
ize ecotourism) continues to be a central issue
and one that continues to constrain ecotourism's potential.

Acknowledging that ecotourism is a
process and not an end, much like sustainability, allows us to continually strive towards the
realization of some future desired state. With
this view in place, and being mindful of placing
too much stock in idealism, we might hope to
transcend the belief that ecotourism by nature
and intent is unachievable – as some
researchers and service providers are wont to
do. We must have the willingness in ecotourism
to look at old problems in a different light in
attempts to make more informed resolutions.
This further entails the will to make decisions
which are based on the best interests of as
many people as possible, including an elimination of the moral knowledge gap which acts as
a barrier to effective administrative and man-
agerial thought and action. Closely tied to this
agenda is the need to stimulate freedom within
organizations to make ethical decisions. This
freedom is often repressed as we continue to be
tied up in systems of thought which are almost
exclusively tied to commerce. This lack of freedom is linked in turn to fear: fear that what we
have paid for is not what we may experience;
fear that each seat on the bus has not been

filled; fear of telling the boss about mistakes that have been made; fear of other service providers and their share of the market; fear about looking beyond one's level of education or training; and fear about sharing better programme techniques with other service providers in making for a better ecotourism industry. It is only the right thing to do if we are thinking beyond ourselves.

Conclusion

It has been said that one of the biggest issues constraining the development of the eco-tourism industry is the inability to turn princi-ples into practice (as it is for sustainable tourism). We do seem to know what ecotourism is, so it then becomes more a matter of how it is operationalized rather than how it is philoso-phized. However, even armed with this 'knowl-edge', I have serious doubts that we will be able to achieve a successful ecotourism industry until we put in place a common pool of core values which allow us to articulate what it is that eco-tourism must be. The examples used in this paper include shared knowledge, the 'other', *kosmopolites,* and will, as well as an underly-ing ethical spirit that ties these core values together. To this I would add that we wrongly elevate ecotourism as the solution to many of our touristic problems. Critics write that eco-tourism can never exist in its purist form. For that matter, neither can humanity. In my esti-mation we have not given ecotourism a chance because we have not come close to infusing a philosophy of ecology (an 'ecosophy' in Naess' terms) to help instil meaning across sectors. Failing to do so implies that the prefix 'eco' (from the Greek word *oikos,* meaning home) is insignificant.

In all likelihood Rousseau would suggest that humanity's interest and involvement in ecotourism is simply a manifestation of the need to seek virtue. Such behaviour would seem natural to Rousseau in an effort to escape the shame that is tied to living in societies which are overly industrialized. Unfortunately, and in general, we might suggest that people have lost the love and passion for place; lost (or never had) geopiety, which is so important in inspir-ing creativity, imagination and reverence. In

losing our sense of ecological place in this vastly changing world, as we have, it is almost as though we have become exotic varieties in our own lands and are incapable of seeing our-selves *through* nature. For the author, love and passion for place is intricately tied to the forests, rivers and lakes of Ontario's Pre-cambrian Shield. Misty lakes, the echo of voices, rustic cabins, canoes on silent lakes, and impatient waters over time-worn rocks are the images of wilderness that cannot be replicated, duplicated or fabricated by any means. These are the timeless places of my youth and some of my earliest memories, forged by grandpar-ents and parents who found it essential that identities be intricately tied to the natural world. These places are the same ones that my chil-dren are beginning to explore and revere, con-tinuing a cycle that, for us, has been essential in defining the family unit. Our cottage is a component part of a broader ecological com-munity that we claim to be ours – as it has claimed us.

Given the magnitude of travel in space and time, and the inauthenticity that is often a com-ponent part, it is indeed unfortunate that the spaces we visit as travellers are so overwhelm-ingly tied to extrinsic motivation and com-merce, as to be divorced from the inner (consciousness) and outer (the world of experi-ence) journeys that can be so essential in travel (Graburn, 2002). Ecotourism can be viewed as a vehicle for individuals to reaffirm or redis-cover their roles and responsibilities in the nat-ural world. If this is true, ecotourism then becomes an outlet to allow the individual to return to nature for enlightenment and bal-ance. After all, we are creatures that continu-ally seek a homeostatic state, or equilibrium, both psychologically and physiologically. This is as true in our own bodies as it is in our com-munities and nations. It is also why individuals like Rousseau, Emerson and Carson have been able to pull us back from the precipice. And we are quite willing to be pulled back periodically because we know somewhere deep inside that our course of action might not be the best road to travel. It then becomes a struggle, both inter-nally and collectively, to mediate between what is right and uncomfortable and wrong and com-fortable. Of course it does not have to be so cut and dried. But if we are to move towards a deeper level in ecotourism, we must move beyond the reluctance to incorporate core values which are essential in providing a solid foundation. In doing so we will need to be open to an examination of how geopiety, georeligion, naturepiety, or other philosophical perspectives, might inspire us to establish a spirit of ecotourism which is based on principled values and ethics.

References

Beijerse, R.P. (1999) Questions in knowledge management: defining and conceptualising a phenomenon. *Journal of Knowledge Management* 3(2), 94–109.

Carson, R. (1962) *Silent Spring*. Houghton Mifflin, Boston, Massachusetts.

Cater, E. (2002) Ecotourism: the wheel keeps turning. Paper presented at the Tourism and the Natural Environment Symposium, Eastbourne, UK, 23–25 October.

Clark, K. (1969) *Civilization*. Harper and Row, New York.

Cooper, C. (2002) Knowledge management and research commercialisation agendas. *Current Issues in Tourism* 5(2), 375–377.

Devall, B. and Sessions, G. (1985) *Deep Ecology: Living as if Nature Mattered*. Peregrine Smith, Salt Lake City, Utah.

Edginton, C., Compton, D. and Hanson, C. (1980) *Recreation and Leisure Programming: a Guide for the Professional*. Saunders, Philadelphia, Pennsylvania.

Fennell, D.A. (2000a) What's in a name? Conceptualising natural resource-based tourism. *Tourism Recreation Research* 25(1), 97–100.

Fennell, D.A. (2000b) Ecotourism on trial: the case of billfish angling as ecotourism. *Journal of Sustainable Tourism* 8(4), 341–345.

Frankel, V. (1985) *Man's Search for Meaning*. Washington Square Press, New York.

Giannecchini, J. (1993) Ecotourism: new partners, new relationships. *Conservation Biology* 7(2), 429–432.

Graburn, N. (2002) The ethnographic tourist. In: Dann, G. (ed.) *The Tourist as a Metaphor of the Social World*. CAB International, Wallingford, UK, pp. 61–76.

Holland, S., Diton, R. and Graefe, A. (1998) An ecotourism perspective on billfish fisheries. *Journal of Sustainable Tourism* 6(2), 97–116.

Laarman, J. and Durst, P. (1987) Nature travel and tropical forests. *FPEI Working Paper Series*, Southeastern Center for Forest Economics Research, North Carolina State University.

Lindberg, K. (1991) *Policies for Maximising Nature Tourism's Ecological and Economic Benefits*. World Resources Institute, Washington, DC.

Malloy, D.C. and Fennell, D.A. (1998) Ecotourism and ethics: moral development and organisational cultures. *Journal of Travel Research* 26(4), 47–56.

Naess, A. (1973) The shallow and the deep, long-range ecology movement. *Inquiry* 16, 95–100.

Nash, R. (1982) *Wilderness and the American Mind*. Yale University Press, New Haven, Connecticut.

Page, S. and Dowling, R.K. (2002) *Ecotourism*. Pearson Education, London.

Saul, J.R. (2001) *On Equilibrium*. Penguin Books, Toronto.

Singh, S., Timothy, D. and Dowling, R. (2003) Tourism and destination communities. In: Singh, S., Timothy D. and Dowling, R. (eds) *Tourism in Destination Communities*. CAB International, Wallingford, UK, pp. 3–18.

Taylor, P.W. (1986) *Respect for Nature: a Theory of Environmental Ethics*. Princeton University Press, Princeton, New Jersey.

Tuan, Y.-F. (1976) Geopiety: a theme in man's attachment to nature and to place. In: Lowenthal, D. and Bowden, M. (eds) *Geographies of the Mind: Essays in Historical Geosophy*. Oxford University Press, New York, pp. 11–39.

Weaver, D.B. (2001) Ecotourism in the context of other tourism types. In: Weaver, D.B. (ed.) *The Encyclopedia of Ecotourism*. CAB International, Wallingford, UK, pp. 73–83.

Western, D. (1993) Defining ecotourism. In: Lindberg, K. and Hawkins, D. (eds) *Ecotourism: a Guide for Planners and Managers*. The Ecotourism Society, North Bennington, Vermont, pp. 7–11.

Whelan, T. (ed.) (1991) *Nature Tourism*. Earthscan Publications, London.

Wiig, K.M. (1997) Knowledge management: an introduction and perspective. *Journal of Knowledge Management* 1(1), 6–14.

Wright, J.K. (1966) *Human Nature in Geography: Fourteen Papers*, 1925–1965. Harvard University Press, Cambridge, Massachusetts.

WTO (2002) *International Year of Ecotourism launched in New York* (on line) http://www.world-tourism.org/newsroom/Releases/more_releases/january2002/launch (accessed 1 April 2003).

10 Against the Wind – Impermanence in Wilderness: the Tasmanian Experience

Trevor H.B. Sofield

Tourism Program, University of Tasmania, Locked Bag 1-340G, Launceston 7250, Tasmania, Australia

Introduction

Isolated in the wilderness of one of the most isolated destinations in the world is a tourism product and a tourism experience constructed around a binary paradox – the impermanence of humans and nature's individual component organisms, on the one hand, and the durability of humankind and nature, on the other. A philosophical underpinning for this touristic experience is that only through an understanding of the impermanence of individual organisms can harmony between the opposite, that is, man and nature as enduring realities, be realized. In other words, individual humans live and die, trees live and die, but humanity continues, forests endure and mountains simply get geologically older as the millennia pass. The transience of humans in the enduring landscapes of the planet constitutes the basis of the experience.

This numinous conundrum is presented to walkers on 4-day and 6-day treks in two contrasting locations, the 'Overland Track' of 80 km in the mountainous inland World Heritage-listed wilderness of Cradle Mountain–Lake St Clair National Park, and the rugged coastal wilderness of the Bay of Fires walk of 20 km, both in Tasmania, the island province of Australia. The 'roaring forties', the global winds which circle the earth above the southern oceans, slam into Tasmania after 12,000 km of unimpeded passage across the Indian Ocean. They buffet the central highlands and the east coast with gale force winds for more than 80 days of the year. Whatever the season, walkers will find themselves battling the elements, the winds a powerful force to contend with. Place and space are created for humans as part of (yet apart from) the natural world as they are guided over the mountains and coastline: natural space becomes humanized place as trekkers seek to break out of attachment to place (of residence wherein lies security) and embrace the freedom of the wilderness (Tuan, 1977).

The majority of the guides are university graduates, educated not only in the geology and biology of the fragile environments through which they journey but also able to converse as 'philosophers' with their guests, and each evening in the wilderness they engage in *haute cuisine* and prepare fine meals for their guests. Personally trained by the owner, award-winning architect Ken Latona, to understand and implement his philosophy, the guides manage small group tours in ways which ensure that the trekkers have less impact on the environment than so-called 'freedom walkers'. Latona's attitude influences all aspects of the operation, from hut design and development to selection and training of staff. His philosophical framework is the edifice through which his application of architectural knowledge is

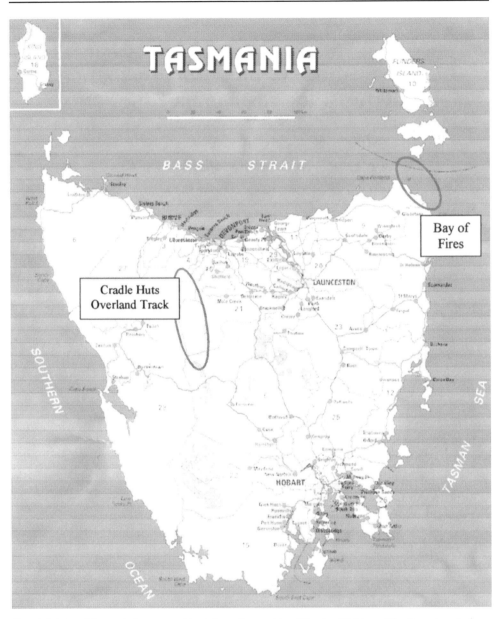

Fig. 10.1. Map of Tasmania (courtesy of the Information and Land Service Division of the Department of Primary Industries, Water and Environment, Government of Tasmania).

interpreted and configured, made manifest in the deliberately designed impermanence of his structures. He deals with spatial dimensions that range from the physical to the abstract, from the physicality of natural phenomena and tangible built environments to the intangibility of nostalgia for a rural, romantic, pristine world that no longer exists in the suburban jungles inhabited by most people. Like the essence of the wind, felt but unseen, intangible social, cultural and mental or psychological spaces are created for and experienced by his guests; abstract spaces temporarily inhabited despite their lack of physical bulk and presence, spaces that are as present and real in the wilderness experience as the wind in one's hair, the rain on one's face or the rock that stubs one's toe. Those who enter Latona's Tasmanian wilderness experience are likely to leave with new meaning to the concept of sustainability, and to the ideal of 'putting people into the natural environment'.

It is contended here that an understanding of this tourism product must soar beyond the realms of physical space to explore abstract space, along the lines explored by the French philosopher Henri Lefebvre, who in his 1974 book *The Production of Space* (translated from the French in 1991) identified

> the domain of abstract space with the built environment, a set of social behaviours, an ensemble of cognitive relations, scientific and technical procedures, and ideologically coded knowledge.
>
> (Dimendberg, 1997: 17)

Lefebvre (1991) conceptualized social space as a concrete universal of three terms (*spatial practice*, *representations of space*, and *spaces of representations*), of three levels (*perceived*, *conceived*, *lived*) and of three forms (*absolute*, *historical*, *abstract*). A key feature of abstract space is its mediated character, and Latona is engaged in active mediation on multi-levels, interpenetrating natural space with social space.

In subjecting this Tasmanian wilderness experience to close scrutiny there are four major spatial constructs to contend with – the *bio-geological space* of the wilderness itself and the way it is interpreted through the medium of guides; the *physical space* of architectural forms which provide shelter (the built environment) as transient humans navigate the ancient bio-geological space; the *social space* of visitors and guides engaged in small group relationships; and the *mental or psychological spaces* that visitors construct from the thoughts that crowd in upon them as they physically traverse the other three spaces. In constructing and integrating these spaces holistically and translating his thinking about sustainability into operational processes, Latona is more than an architect of built havens in which his trekkers can seek rest at the end of the day; he is the architect of an experience that reaches into all

of Lefebvre's different spaces. As Lefebvre (1991: 88) himself noted:

> The hyper-complexity of social space (embraces) individual entities and peculiarities, relatively fixed points, movements and flows and waves – some interpenetrating, others in conflict, and so on.

For analytical purposes the spaces identified above are discussed separately; but in fact, like the Holy Trinity of the Christian religion, they cannot be separated; each one is meaningless without the others. This chapter begins with a brief description of the nature of the trekking experience before exploring the biological and geological features of the Tasmanian wilderness and the other spaces Latona has constructed in natural space.

It is acknowledged that the focus of Lefebvre's approach to spatiality is founded in a Marxist analysis of society and production and that he goes close to writing the natural environment out of the equation by arguing that all that is left are 'fragments of nature, settled and socialized for various reasons of environment, location and resources', in other words a 'populated natural space' (Smith, 1997: 57). But it is argued that the broader scope of his theories have application that is valid for an analysis of the spaces which tourism creates for its visitors, in much the same way that Urry (2000) has taken Foucault's theory of 'the clinical gaze' and re-interpreted it as 'the tourist gaze'. This chapter is not intended to take such an ambitious path as Urry's, but it follows the same academic 'mining' of a theoretical framework for a lode than can prove invaluable in aiding our understanding of tourism phenomena.

The Nature of the Trek Through Nature

The wilderness experiences of the Overland Track and the Bay of Fires are soundly based in the principles of ecologically sustainable tourism, and Latona's guided tours are designed to foster in his guests love and stewardship of the Tasmanian wilderness and all wild, natural places. The company's philosophy of respect for place is demonstrated through minimal-impact track and hut practices. The

Fig. 10.2. The Lodge sits inconspicuously below the skyline, almost swallowed by the coastal bushland, Bay of Fires.

huts are designed to be ecologically sustainable, with self-contained, non-polluting services and waste management practices. Both trails are seasonal, operated for only 6 months of the year. The Overland Track can experience heavy snowfalls even in summer. It is impassable for most of the winter when the 'roaring forties' hold the highlands in their icy, blustery grip. The Bay of Fires trail experiences inclement weather in winter also. Trekkers are restricted to a maximum of ten in any one group, and they are accompanied at all times by two guides. Depending upon the terrain, 9–12 km is the average length of each day's walk. Stops are frequent and in fine weather side trips to additional points of interest (such as scaling Tasmania's highest peak, Mt Ossa) can be undertaken. The guides share their knowledge of the flora, fauna, geology and history of the parks, and their interpretation is presented in the context of ecological sustainability.

Guests must carry their own backpacks, complete with changes of clothes, cold/wet weather protective clothing in case of sudden temperature changes, their own toiletries and towel (but not soap: the lodges are provided with a phosphorus-free, biodegradable liquid soap for ablutions); a groundsheet and sleeping bag. This latter is a safety requirement: with guides carrying a tent between huts, walkers

would be safe if they were required to make an emergency camp. Laundry is minimized by making guests responsible for their own bedding. No laundry is done on-site. Accommodation is twin-share in unheated bedrooms (thus saving fuel and energy consumption), in isolated austere huts, along the lines of a monastery rather than a luxury hotel (the design features are detailed below). The cuisine is a feature of the trek; fresh bread is baked by the guides for breakfast each morning, supplemented with cereals and fresh fruit. Three-course meals served with Tasmanian fine wines are standard evening meals (food is flown in by helicopter on a regular basis).

Operational aspects cover conservation of fuel and energy; recycling; composting toilets that have no drainage, thus limiting pollution (wastes are flown out by helicopter); waste minimization, e.g. by using bulk sugar, coffee and similar foods rather than individual packets, and biodegradable products wherever possible; and water conservation – in short many features which limit the possible adverse impacts of the operations on the fragile environments and which enhance in practical ways the principles of sustainability. All grey water is treated (kitchen and bathroom systems are separated, grease arresters and biological filters are used) before disposal in clean form to absorption trenches.

Fig. 10.3. All supplies are helicoptered in, and wastes helicoptered out, negating the necessity for a service road and the environmental impact it would cause.

The philosophical approach to sustainability is perhaps most clearly apparent in the conservation of water. Rainwater is collected off the roof in two relatively small tanks and guests are advised that supply is limited and that water must be used sparingly. There is no bath. Showers are linked to a 10-litre container which each guest must fill by hand-pump prior to taking a shower. The water is then gravity-fed through a small gas heater and a low-pressure shower rose and this allows for a 2-minute shower per person per day. Handbasins are small and supplied with cold water only. No water is used for irrigation, landscaping, toilets or laundry, although guests can handwash one or two items per day in the cold-water basins using the biodegradable soap. For the privilege of carrying their own gear, hand-pumping their own 2-minute shower and sleeping in their own unwashed bedding in unheated bedrooms in un-insulated isolated, impermanent huts without electricity, television, telephones, hair dryers or any other electronic convenience, guests pay up to US$300 per day.

While the natural beauty of the landscapes through which the visitors pass each day provides the spiritual foundation of the wilderness experience, the success of the treks relies heavily on the guides, both as an ecologically sustainable operation and for their role in interpretation, safety and education (http://twin share.crctourism.com.au/CaseStudies/).

It is not intended to project Latona as the 'great innovator' but rather to present his 'product' as being more unified and holistic from start to finish than many others who purport to offer a similar experience in such fragile environments. There are other architects who have similar approaches to design, melding their constructions into their surroundings both environmentally and culturally. But they tend to be involved only in the design/construction element and to have little or no control over the total product/experience, and certainly not down to determining what sort of multi-skilling and 'outlook on life' a guide should have. There are ecotourism operators in Australia and other countries who practice an ecocentric approach similar to that exhibited in the treks constructed by Latona but they rarely extend into the same fine detail across every aspect of the operations spectrum as in the case of the Cradle Huts and Bay of Fires experiences. Latona does not pretend to provide a *total* wilderness immersion experience, as is possible in many places, where there are no huts to overnight in, where one carries one's own one-person tent, plastic bags for personal bodily wastes, all one's food, even 'living off the land' to some extent – but then he is not attempting a minimalist survival approach; it is deliberately differentiated. Relatively few other ecotour operators provide the all-encompassing experience that is offered and articulated by its creator here, where the social spaces have been deliberately constructed to create a particular blend of experiential familiarization with 'wilderness', grounded in temporality and transitory-ness combined with a deeply considered application of principles of sustainability.

Bio-geological space

The *Tasmanian Wilderness World Heritage Area* is one of the largest nature reserves in Australia, incorporating about 20% of the land area of the island of Tasmania, and covering 1.38 million ha. The boundaries of the conservation area extend from sea level (the wild and isolated south-west coast of Tasmania whose beaches are pounded by surf driven by the roaring forties, to Tasmania's highest peaks (Mt Ossa is 1617 m or 4945 ft). Landscapes include extensive glaciated valleys, deep river gorges, moorlands and heathlands, swamps and wetlands, and some of the most extensive tracts of cool temperate rainforests in the world. The area was inscribed on the World Heritage List in 1982, and extended in 1989, because of its outstanding natural features which include fragile alpine habitats, extensive rivers and cave systems, rare and endemic plants and animals, and old-growth remnant forests whose antecedents date back to the ancient mega-continent of Gondwanaland. Its isolation and rugged terrain has allowed several animals that are either extinct or threatened on the mainland of Australia to thrive, such as the carnivorous marsupials, the Tasmanian devil, and the spotted-tailed and eastern quolls. Platypus and echidna are abundant. Bird species number more than 180 and include the endemic green rosella and the rare orange-bellied parrot. Other noteworthy fauna include the moss froglet and the Tasmanian tree frog, the Tasmanian cave spider, and the burrowing crayfish. Rocks from every geological period are represented in the area and water-soluble layers of dolomite and limestone have resulted in the formation of some of the deepest and longest cave systems in Australia (http://www.dpiwe.tas.gov.au/inter.nsf/).

Located within the WHA is the Overland Track, 80 km long, which traverses Cradle Mountain–Lake St Clair National Park, a reserve of 161,000 ha making up the north-ernmost section of the Wilderness reserve. In the north is a high treeless plateau with deep glacial lakes and tarns, and the ridge on which Cradle Mountain rises to 1525 m (4758 ft). Tasmania's highest mountain, Mt Ossa can be climbed from the central section of the park, an area dominated by alpine heathland. The track then follows the Mersey River valley before climbing to Du Cane Gap and descending along the Narcissus River to the northern shores of Lake St Clair, the deepest lake in Australia at 215 m (670 ft). It is this 6-day walk which constitutes the basis for Latona's alpine wilderness experience (Cradle Huts) (http://www.cradlehuts.com.au/hutfrme.html).

The Bay of Fires wilderness trek, by contrast, is a coastal experience which takes the traveller along the beaches, fringing sand dunes, wetlands and eucalyptus forests of Mount William National Park. The park is located in the north-east of Tasmania and the bay is near the southern boundary of the park. It was named by the French explorer, Captain Tobias Furneaux, in 1773. Sailing along the coast he saw a string of Aborigines' fires along the beaches. At that time the whole north-east coast of Tasmania was well populated and the nomadic Aborigines traditionally moved to the coast during winter to feast on shellfish, shearwaters (mutton birds) and seals. Numerous Aboriginal middens are evident along the beaches and sandhills of the Park. Middens are of particular archaeological interest because they are evidence of ancient Aboriginal camps. They consist largely of huge piles of shells, interspersed with the bones of birds and animals and occasional flints, spearheads, etc., many of the remains blackened after having been roasted on open fires (Berndt and Berndt, 1964).

While the park does not have world heritage status, it is rich in flora and fauna. It is the main sanctuary for the Forester kangaroo, and has abundant populations of wallabies, wom-

Fig. 10.4. The huts are subsumed by the landscape of the central highlands of Tasmania, the eucalyptus trees and mountains towering above them, Cradle Huts Overland Track.

Fig. 10.5. The 'roaring forties' waft mists across the rugged highlands along the Overland Track.

bats, Tasmanian devils, possums, platypus and echidna and more than 100 species of birds. The extensive coastal heaths favour various species of honey-eaters, wrens, finches, parrots, cockatoos and kookaburras. Seals, penguins and seabirds such as gulls, terns, gannets, albatrosses, oystercatchers, sea eagles and the migratory shearwaters are prolific along the sea shore. The penultimate day of this tour involves kayaking along the Anson's River which is fringed with pristine forests and also has plentiful wildlife.

Geologically the park is dominated by granite dating back 380 million years. Huge granite boulders line many of the beaches and are covered in bright orange lichen. Over millennia granite quartz has weathered and disintegrated to form glistening white sand, and this combined with the huge orange-coloured boulders make the beaches scenically some of the most attractive in Australia (http://www.dpiwe.tas.gov.au/inter.nsf/).

The interpretation of these natural spaces by guides automatically transforms them into cultural and social spaces, their biological and geological features mediated by the values inherent in the knowledge base of science and history.

Physical space: architecture applied to wilderness

Most architects design for permanence, with the buildings they construct intended to stand as statements of their creativity and as enduring monuments to their vision. This is of course an ancient human trait, with the pyramids of Egypt, the Taj Mahal of India and the Great Wall of China standing as mute testimony over millennia to their designers' genius. It is evident in the resorts and hotels that the tourism industry has constructed globally, whether it be the Peninsula Hotel in Hong Kong, the Hideaway Resort in Tahiti, or the Club Med villas in Mauritius. Mountain summits, cliff tops and similar vantage points are favoured by thousands of resorts around the world.

But Ken Latona's approach is markedly different. The accommodation space that visitors occupy during their encounter with Tasmania's alpine and coastal wilderness is designed to meld into the landscape. The lodges do not dominate the skyline but are hidden in folds in the hills, carefully sited in order to be invisible from surrounding vantage points so that only pristine countryside may be seen. They 'tread lightly' upon the ancient land. They required no excavation, are lightweight, easy to dismantle and take away so that within 12 months of their going the footprint of the space they occupied would again be taken over by the surrounding bush. They provide a degree of comfort yet are impermanent. They provide simultaneously shelter from the elements yet exposure to the elements. They are there only to provide a safe haven for the walkers rather than a means of isolating guests in luxurious artificiality divorced from the natural environment. There is a deliberate blurring between the inside and the outside: windows have no blinds or curtains so that the guest is in touch with the moon and the stars in the night sky and the sun at dawn. Latona believes that:

> nomadic instincts still lie dormant within us and the guided walks offer a remote connection with these ancestral roots which is subtly acknowledged in the layout and austerity of his lodges.
>
> (Spence, 2000: 43)

Cradle Huts

For the five Cradle Mountain cabins constructed along the Overland Track the planning and construction amongst complex land forms posed an exacting challenge. An individual environmental impact assessment was undertaken for each hut site before development was approved. The evaluation process took 3 years and approval was granted by the Tasmanian Ministerial Council for the World Heritage Area (quoted in http://www.cradlehuts.com.au/hutfrme.html). The fragility of the varied alpine environments made it imperative to use low-impact construction techniques. Soil types varied from site to site, including glacial moraine ridges composed of peat whose slow decomposition in high altitudes means that the peat can be up to 1000 years old. Other sites had a high water table so that any excavation or in-ground construction could impede groundwater flows. Yet others had mature trees besides other vegetation that dictated the exact siting of a hut. Standard practice in the southern hemisphere is for buildings to face north or north-east for best passive thermal qualities but in this case the environmental impact assessment weighted natural elements over human comfort, and only two of the five lodges face north (http://twinshare.crc-tourism.com.au/CaseStudies/).

Each construction site was therefore restricted to a clearly delineated area and construction staff were required to ensure they did not move equipment outside that area, created no disturbance to the surrounding vegetation, and observed minimal impact techniques, including waste control. No mature trees were cut down and the positioning of each hut avoided any disruption to the hydrology of the area. All materials were flown in by helicopter, thus avoiding the need to bulldoze an access road (which inevitably would have been environmentally damaging). Portable generators and petrol compressors were used to provide power during construction. Plantation softwood timber (used for framing, and external and internal cladding) and Oregon frames (for the roof and floor to provide structural stability) are the main construction materials, with roofs of corrugated iron. Each hut has five twin-share bedrooms, plus a room for three guides. Each hut has a kitchen/dining space and a heated common amenities area which comprises two shower cubicles, two composting toilets, and hanging space for wet clothing. Each hut also has a helipad constructed from timber, essential for the twice-per-season delivery of supplies, and emergency access (http://twinshare.crc-tourism.com.au/CaseStudies/).

The huts have not been designed for thermal efficiency. At first sight this would appear to be inconsistent with energy conservation since any heating would be quickly dissipated, resulting in inordinate fuel consumption. But the company's philosophy is that the huts are to provide a safe refuge for walkers, rather than a means of isolating guests from the outside environment, so heating is limited. Energy conservation remains an important aspect of the huts' operations and liquid petroleum gas (LPG) is used for cooking, hot water and some space heating. Solar panels provide a limited source for water heating (consistent cloud cover restricts their efficiency). Other heating is supplied by coal and firewood (sourced from plantations, not from the surrounding forests) in slow combustion stoves for the amenities area, but not the bedrooms. Due to the consistently cold climate, neither refrigeration nor air conditioning is required. Windows are used for natural lighting, particularly in the living area. Artificial lighting is provided by gas lamps and solar power, as well as candles. Solar panels power the ventilation systems of the two com-

posting toilets in each hut (http://twinshare. crctourism.com.au/CaseStudies/).

Bay of Fires Lodge

The Bay of Fires facility was constructed several years after the Cradle Huts and drew on the experience of the earlier construction effort. Rather than scattering a number of lodges across the site, Latona chose to centralize facilities in two parallel, offset pavilions joined by a central walkway open to the sky, positioned below the summit of a steep ridge and screened for the most part by a canopy of casuarina trees (Spence, 2002). According to Spence:

> The theme of light, linear pavilions with curved or skillion roofs, sometimes linked by outdoor spines, has been a fertile field of exploration in recent Australian architecture; and is especially fruitful for inserting buildings into sensitive rural sites with minimal cut-and-fill and for encouraging cross-ventilation and winter sun penetration.
>
> (2002: 42)

One pavilion houses communal spaces, a long kitchen, and staff quarters. The other pavilion consists of five twin bedrooms and a small library. Uncurtained glass louvre windows constitute the external walls of the bedrooms which retain the simplicity of a camp site or a monastery rather than a hotel, in keeping with the infusion of nomadic roaming that underlies the wilderness experience. This spirit is further enhanced by the siting of the communal eating space along the centre of one pavilion as a porch which opens out on to a secluded clearing among the casuarinas. The inner wall of the porch has ovens, sinks and cooking benches, while barbecues and fires are lit in the evenings in the outdoor space. Guests can chose to sit on the ground, on rocks under the trees, or in chairs on the porch to eat their meals, and this space constitutes the social focus of the building. In effect it is an abstracted campsite and its firm linkage to the earth anchors the building to the way of life of the first wanderers to this area, the Tasmanian Aborigines. Conceptually it creates a social bond between the first nomads and today's ephemeral nomads escaping temporarily from their urban lifestyles (http://www.bayoffires.com.au/firefrme.html).

Instead of the usual penchant for buildings to dominate the landscape with 180° views over beaches and bays, this building peers into the bush with only the eastern end facing the wider scenic prospect. In stark and deliberate contrast to the rugged irregularity of the surrounding terrain the uncompromising linearity of the building frames only a distant view of the sea through the long gash of the central walkway. As Spence (2002: 42) notes:

> This severely abstract slot of outdoor space is the backbone of the project: providing a link to the cosmos it emerges from the journey taken by walkers up the ridge through the park, connecting up with another winding track

at the far end of the walkway which leads down to a secluded beach. There is an elevated porch at the eastern end of the central walkway,

> a dramatic climax of the communal area, commanding a view out along the coastline that the walkers have just traversed . . . the skillion roof hinged up to acknowledge and frame the view in a more formal manner (so that) from the beach below, the building, mouth open, seems to be in animated conversation with the landscape.
>
> (Spence, 2002: 46)

As with the Cradle Huts, all materials were flown into the site by helicopter and the same stringent environmental standards were applied during construction. Timber is the main material, and many of the uprights, posts and studs are left exposed rather than lined, an abstract reflection of the vertical forms of the surrounding forest tree trunks. Operational standards for waste disposal and energy are also similar. Composting toilets are utilized and black water channelled into an evaporation chamber in the bush. Grey water is biologically filtered before being released into an absorption trench. Solar panels generate power for lighting, while cooking, refrigeration and water heating are powered by LPG. Water is provided through rainfall collected off the roofs and fed into tanks which are in a compact service area that limits the footprint of the building.

The lodge is supported by a campsite at Forrester Beach (the first night's stop-over). Nestled in a protected dune swale behind a white sand beach, it is a temporary seasonal structure. Twin-share rooms with timber floors,

canvas roofs and full kitchen facilities are complemented by private wash areas and composting toilets which provide comfort that minimizes impacts on the environment. The warmer temperatures of the coastal trail mean that, unlike the huts of the Overland Track, heating is not an issue. LPG and solar panels are the main sources of energy.

Social spaces

The architectural forms of Cradle Huts and the Bay of Fires pavilions create physical spaces that interact intimately with their environments, blending not dominating, giving not taking, adding to not subtracting from their surrounding habitats. As an outcome of human artistic and scientific endeavour they are also representative of social space – what Lefebvre has termed 'Perceived Space/Spatial Practice' which is defined as:

> the process of producing the material form of social spatiality, and thus presented as both a medium and outcome of human activity, behaviour and experience. From an analytical standpoint, the spatial practice of a society is revealed through the deciphering of its space.
>
> (1991: 31)

In this context the construction of Latona's wilderness lodges may be interpreted as the outcome of social activity or spatial practice.

But these lodges also constitute Lefebvre's 'Conceived Space/Representations of Space'. These spaces are defined as:

> conceptualized space, the space of scientists, planners, urbanists, technocrat subdividers, as a certain type of artist with a scientific bent – all of whom identify what is lived and what is perceived with what is conceived. This conceived space is also tied into the relations of production and, especially, to the order or design that they impose. Such order is constituted via control over knowledge, signs, and codes: over the means of deciphering spatial practice and hence over the production of spatial knowledge.
>
> (Lefebvre, 1991: 38–39)

Latona's wilderness experience is thus a combination of contrived physical spaces designed around quite specific mental spaces located in natural spaces. The experience constitutes what Soja (1996: 39) has termed: 'a primary space of utopian thought, spaces of the purely creative imagination'. It is in this second space that the visionary elements of Latona's architectural creativity and the touristic journey he creates for his visitors are manifested, the ephemerality of the wind and the impermanence of individual components of nature taking precedence over monumental materialism. The relationship between inside and outside, constitutive of much architectural signification, is also a representation of space (Dimendberg, 1999: 21). This second space overlaps with Lefebvre's first space but is immediately distinguishable by its explanatory concentration on conceived rather than perceived space and its implicit assumption that spatial knowledge is primarily produced through discursively devised representations of space, through the spatial workings of the human mind.

As people move into and through the physical spaces of wilderness and architectural design and use them in a variety of ways, interacting and developing relationships between and with one another, and incorporating the mental constructs of conceived space, the space becomes 'Lived Space/Spaces of Representation', Lefebvre's third space. Tuan (1977, 1988) has theorized this transition as natural place which has become humanized space – 'that is, a locality that has been transformed to place from space through human presence and nurturing' (Hubbard *et al.*, 2002: 38). Tuan examined the intricacies of human interaction with the environment, arguing that:

> the world consists of a mosaic of special places whose uniqueness can only be understood from the perspective of the individuals who give them meaning.
>
> (Tuan 1977 cited in Hubbard *et al.*, 2002: 129)

In other words, the subjective or affective links between people and space results in place/identity, which Tuan termed 'topophilia' (Tuan, 1977).

These lived spaces are seen by Lefebvre both as distinct from his other two spaces and as encompassing them. Spaces of representa-

tion embody 'complex symbolisms, sometimes coded, sometimes not' (Lefebvre, 1991: 39). According to Soja (1996: 46):

> all social relations become real and concrete, a part of our lived social existence, only when they are spatially 'inscribed' – that is, concretely represented – in the social production of social space.

For Lefebvre (1991), spaces of representation shape our subjective experience and our imagination. There is a similar

> trialectics of spatiality, where each mode of thinking about space, each 'field' of human spatiality – the physical, the mental, the social – should be seen as simultaneously real and imagined, concrete and abstract, material and metaphorical.
>
> (Soja, 1996: 49)

Latona's Overland Track and the Bay of Fires ecotourism venture provide a wilderness experience that corresponds to the

> absolute and relative locations of things and activities, sites and situations; in patterns of distribution, designs, and the differentiation of a multitude of materialized phenomena across spaces and places; in concrete and mappable geographies of (different) lifeworlds, ranging from the emotional and behavioural space 'bubbles' which invisibly surround the bodies (of participants – visitors and guides alike) to the complex spatial organization of social practices that shape (their) 'action spaces'.
>
> (Soja, 1996: 43)

Lefebvre's third space is found in the bio-geological formations of valleys and hilltops, in the built environment of the lodges, and in the conceptual environment of world heritage national parks where the economy and geopolitics of government instrumentalities and interest groups compete and clash and occasionally cooperate. Spaces of representation contain all other real and imagined spaces simultaneously.

The defining qualities of Latona's wilderness walks reflect the binary division of the centre and the periphery that characterizes Lefebvre's and Soja's descriptions of conventional spatiality. The guests are from centres, sophisticated   urban/suburban/cities/towns/

built steel-and-concrete environments. The wilderness experience transports them physically to the edge, to the simplicity of the periphery; from the 'all-mod-cons' cocoon of home to the austerity of the contrived primitive campsite; from air-conditioned restaurant to bush barbecue; and thus from the concrete lived of 'modern human' to the abstract imagined of 'ancient nomad'. This last element foregrounds another duality inherent in this geographical binary division:

> that of the lived, the reality, the day-to-day living, the material as representative of where they have come from, and on the other hand the conceived, the spiritual, the ideal and the idealistic, the romantic Other, the abstract.
>
> (Soja, 1996: 30)

The juxtaposition of guides and resident managers as cooks and fellow diners around the same campfires and tables in the wilderness as the guests, and the guests as porters of their own basic requirements, de-differentiates the served/servant stereotype of the hospitality industry and extends the construction of social space that envelops the Overland Track and the Bay of Fires experience. In Lefebvre's terms it is not just the duality of 'the representations of space' and the 'spaces of representation' but the trialectics of 'perceived space' being incorporated as well so that the physical, social and psychological factors combine holistically in a multi-dimensional spatiality to provide a wilderness experience that transcends the normal.

Conclusion

Lefebvre's unitary spatial theory provides a tool for overcoming the current fragmentation that divides the study of space between disciplines such as geography, architecture, sociology and philosophy; and Latona, in his own small way, has contributed to that integration. A special interstitial space has been created where eco-tourism and ecological sustainability take on a reality that is paradoxical; paradoxical because the reality of the periphery is not the reality of visitors who live and dwell in the centre and for whom these 4- or 6-day treks are but an ephemeral interlude, and whose architecturally designed shelters for those few days also echo

that impermanence. New values, new meanings, new signifiers, transform wilderness into a new kind of space for the traveller. In effect uninhabited landscape has become culture in the sense that Guarrasi (2001: 226) suggests:

> We strive to discover and describe natural phenomena and in doing so we inscribe an artificial 'order', that of 'culture' as a signifying system within which every material object is associated with a mental representation: every signifier with a corresponding signified. All manifestations of human spatiality are thus both material and mental objects . . . And if we hold the above to be true then space and culture become indistinguishable.

Guarrasi argues that humans have demonstrated

> a capacity for crafting ever new spatialities which allow us to introduce endless new orders to the world around us . . . (and that) . . . landscape is but one of the multiplicity of metalinguistics acts which allow us to resignify the world.
>
> (2001: 227)

Thus, in a fundamental way 'wilderness' does not exist until we label it. The very concept of 'wilderness' is a cultural term applied to a particular imagining of nature, we draw a boundary around it, we invest it with a range of meanings, we manage it – and in the very act of managing it, it loses aspects of its 'naturalness' and becomes an artifice, a cultural construct. We give it 'a new reality (and) this kind of re-imagining (is) an essential process of tourism' (Horne, 1992: 21). This enculturation is especially apparent when we consider the way in which some peoples empower landscape with spirituality and transform space into sacred place, as with Australia's Aborigines (Berndt and Berndt, 1964), or Tibetans who transform many of their mountain tops from geographical space into sacred place sites (Bishop, 1989). Tuan (1977, 1990) coined the terms 'geopiety' and 'topophilia' to describe the intense relationship between humans and geographical entities such as woods, streams and hills that is exemplified in the social context of sacred landscapes.

The wilderness experience presented in these two treks is also paradoxical in the sense that while a framework of deep ecotourism and environmental sustainability is constructed in a comprehensive way, there is tension between the biocentric and anthropocentric. As Hendee *et al.* (1990) note, the biocentric approach emphasizes the maintenance or enhancement of natural systems, if necessary at the expense of recreational and other human uses. They contend that the goal of the biocentric philosophy is to permit natural ecological processes to operate as freely as possible without human intervention, because wilderness values for society ultimately depend on the retention of 'naturalness'. By contrast the anthropocentric position accepts, encourages and facilitates programmes to alter the physical and biological environment in order to produce desired 'improvements' with the character of the wilderness changed to reflect the desires of humans and contemporary standards of 'comfort in nature'. In the case of Latona he is redefining the landscapes of wilderness for his guests and the principles of biocentricity are applied to govern the overall experience. But the intervention of human agency through the provision of fabricated shelters in the bushland coupled with the incongruity of fine dining deep in the wilderness constitute a degree of lost naturalness and are decidedly anthropocentric. Yet one may make the case that the elements of anthropocentricity are peripheral and so subordinated to the natural that this form of ecotourism is promoting ecological and social responsibility. As Dowling and Fennell (2003: 5) state:

> Achieving the goal of environmental conservation includes . . . avoiding all actions that are environmentally irreversible . . . promoting appropriate environmental uses and activities, and cooperating in establishing and attaining environmentally acceptable tourism.

In this context one could argue that all 'invasions' of wilderness inevitably introduce degrees of anthropocentricity. The moment *Homo sapiens* move into space it becomes endowed with a range of characteristics physically, socially, culturally or psychologically (Cohen, 1988): it is transformed from 'u-topia' (ideal space or literally, non-space) into humanized space (Bishop, 1989; Tuan, 1977). Spaces and places are inexorably created by the mere presence of the agency of humans in the environment, as Lefebvre contends. No matter how hard humans try to absorb and be absorbed into the landscape with minimal impact they are always apart: as if on a trampoline, they may bounce up and down and penetrate deeper into 'Nature' the higher and harder they bounce, but there is always the membrane of the trampoline separating the modern human from the wilderness, a social bubble or cocoon encasing the travellers that are 'in' the wilderness, surrounded by the wilderness, yet not 'of' the wilderness. They walk a physical route located in space and time: geographical markers along the route fix a particular event or occurrence in space and time so that the landscape 'talks' to them. Thus the human intellect organizes the journey as a narrative and leaves the physical dimensions of the route to embark on explorations of the mind and spirit. Tuan (1977, 1988, 1990) captures this in his explorations of the ways that people feel and think about place and space and how such sentiments are affected by time. They are attached to home, neighbourhood, and nation – place – wherein lies their sense of identity and security; but they long for the freedom of space. Whether he is considering cultural attachments to space, transient time in experiential space, sacred/spiritual versus 'biased' space, or mythical space and place, Tuan's analysis echoes Lefebvre's contention that all space is socially constructed. Hence the geographical physicality of the journey might remain anchored in the landscape but the imaginative quality varies for each participant as the route is socially structured and sanctioned by them as if in a pilgrimage (Graburn, 1989), a search for inner self and authenticity (MacCannell, 1999), or a temporary escape from the mundane (Tuan, 1988; Urry, 2000). The Cradle Huts highland trek and the Bay of Fires coastal hike encompass all of these elements and privilege the traveller in reaching out to that elusive 'wilderness' of a prehistoric past.

The last words are left to a visitor whose sentiments are typical of those who have entered these special spaces:

> I don't want to leave. I want to settle in for a week or two, if only to watch the sun on the water and prolong the enjoyment . . . If you

want to escape this has to be the ultimate . . .
We're quiet and a little deflated now that the
time has come to leave. We're returning to jobs,
husbands, kids, the real world. This journey has
been a joy, a kind of reprieve from our ordinary
lives, in a pristine wilderness with great people
and great food. We all begin plotting our return.
(Cerentha Harris, a visitor from Sydney,
11 March 2002)

Acknowledgement

For all the photographs: courtesy Ken Latona,
owner/operator of Bay of Fires.

References

Berndt, R.M. and Berndt, C.H. (1964) *The World of
the First Australians.* Ure Smith, Sydney.
Bishop, P. (1989) *The Myth of Shangri-La.* Athlone
Press, London.
Cohen, E. (1988) Traditions in the qualitative sociol-
ogy of tourism. *Annals of Tourism Research*
15(1), 29–46.
Dimendberg, E. (1997) Henri Lefebvre on abstract
space. In: Light, A. and Smith, J.M. (eds) *The
Production of Public Space.* Rowman and
Littlefield, New York, pp. 17–47.
Dowling, R. and Fennell, D. (2003) The context of
ecotourism policy and planning. In: Fennell, D.
and Dowling, R. (eds) *Ecotourism Policy and
Planning.* CAB International, Wallingford, UK,
pp.1–20.
Graburn, N. (1989) Tourism: the sacred journey. In:
Smith, V. (ed.) *Hosts and Guests: The
Anthropology of Tourism,* 2nd edn. University
of Pennsylvania Press, Philadelphia, pp.
21–36.
Guarrasi, V. (2001) Paradoxes of modern and post-
modern geography: heterotopia of landscape
and cartographic logic. In: Minca, C. (ed.)
Postmodern Geography: Theory and Praxis.
Blackwell Publishers, Oxford, pp. 226–237.
Hendee, J.C., Stankey, G.H. and Lucas, R. (1990)
Wilderness Management, 2nd edn. North
America Press, Golden, Colorado.
Horne, D. (1992) *The Intelligent Tourist.* Harper-
Collins, Sydney.

Hubbard, P., Kitchin, R., Bartley, B. and Fuller, D.
(2002) *Thinking Geography: Space, Theory
and Contemporary Human Geography.*
Continuum, London.
Lefebvre, H. (1991) *The Production of Space.*
Translated by Donald Nicholson Smith from the
original in French, 1974. Blackwell, Oxford.
MacCannell, Dean (1999) *The Tourist: a New
Theory of the Leisure Class,* 2nd edn.
Macmillan, London.
Smith, N. (1997) Antinomies of space and nature in
Henri Lefebvre's "The Production of Space".
In: Light, A. and Smith, J.M. (eds) *The
Production of Public Space.* Rowman and
Littlefield, New York, pp. 49–69.
Soja, E. (1996) *Postmodern Geographies: the
Reassertion of Space in Critical Social
Theory.* Verso, London.
Spence, R. (2002) Sublime camping: Ken Latona's
bush lodge at the Bay of Fires. *Architecture
Australia* July/August, pp. 40–47.
Tuan, Y.-F. (1977) *Space and Place: the Perspective
of Experience.* University of Minnesota Press,
Minneapolis.
Tuan, Y.-F. (1988) *Escapism.* Johns Hopkins
University Press, Baltimore, Maryland.
Tuan, Y.-F. (1990) *Topophilia: A Study of
Environmental Perceptions, Attitudes, and
Values.* Columbia University Press, New York.
Urry, J. (2000) *The Tourist Gaze. Leisure and
Travel in Contemporary Societies,* 2nd edn.
Sage, London.

Websites

http://www.bayoffires.com.au/firefrme.html [Bay of
Fires Walk home page] accessed November
2002.
http: // www. cradlehuts. com. au / hutfrme. html
[Cradle Huts Walk home page] accessed
November 2002.
http: // twinshare.crctourism.com.au/ CaseStudies/
[Cooperative Research Centre for Sustainable
Tourism: Case Studies: Cradle Huts Walk,
Tasmania] accessed November 2002.
http://www.dpiwe.tas.gov.au/inter.nsf/ [Tasmanian
Department of Primary Industries, Water and
Environment (DPIWE): 1. Cradle Mountain-
Lake St Clair National Park – Highlights. 2. Mt
Williams National Park – Highlights] accessed
November 2002.

11 Health Tourism in the Kyrgyz Republic: the Soviet Salt Mine Experience

Peter Schofield

Management Research Institute, University of Salford, M6 6PU, UK

Introduction

Tourism plays a vital role in contributing to people's well-being (Aho, 2001) as it breaks the monotony of work-a-day life and provides space to recreate and re-vitalize. Health tourism, in its various guises, ensures physical, mental and social well-being, as illustrated elsewhere in this volume. Seen historically, visits to spas were motivated largely by health considerations. There is evidence from the Neolithic period that water sources were used across Europe for various rituals and, by the medieval period, the belief in the efficacy of mineral waters and thermal springs for medicinal purposes was widespread. By the 18th century and throughout the 19th, 'taking the waters' was a fashionable leisure pursuit among the upper classes of Europe (Burkart and Medlik, 1981). Today, around 20 million people in Europe (including Russia) visit traditional spas (ESPA, 2000) and the market continues to grow worldwide in line with the increasing interest in healthy living and preventive medicine. This chapter examines the contemporary health tourism market with specific reference to salt mines, their idiosyncratic microclimates and the practice of 'subterranotherapy'. Within this context, the case of 'Salt World', an unusual health resort at Chon Tuz in Kyrgyzstan's Naryn region, is discussed with specific reference to the visitor experience of place, the

Republic's traditional health tourism product, and its prospects for future development.

Health Tourism in the Kyrgyz Republic

In 1991 the Kyrgyz Republic, a small Central Asian state (198,500 km^2) gained independence from the USSR and has since made significant progress in its development of a free market economy and democratic society, thereby differentiating itself from its powerful neighbours: China, Kazakhstan, Uzbekistan and Tajikistan (Fig. 11.1). The Akaev government's chosen development path has followed a Swiss model because of its political, economic and social aspirations and its topographic similarities with the European country – 94% of the Kyrgyz Republic is mountainous. The strategic potential of tourism has been recognized and it has become a focus for state policy because of the opportunities it provides for the pursuit of economic and political goals, including the development of a national identity and international recognition for the state. Prior to 1991, much of Kyrgyzstan was off-limits to international visitors because of Soviet military activity and weapons development and testing. As a result, consumer awareness of the destination in the world's major tourist generating areas is poor and the present image tends to be indistinguishable from other Central Asian countries (Schofield, 2004).

Fig. 11.1. Map of Kyrgyzstan in central Asia.

During the Soviet occupation of Kyrgyzstan, and despite the country's 'backyard' status, particularly with respect to its servicing of the USSR's military–industrial complex, it was a major domestic tourism destination largely due to its outstanding natural beauty. The tourism demand was mainly health- and sports-oriented, with sanatoria developing at hot springs and lakes. Foremost among these resort areas was, and still is, the perimeter of Lake Ysyk-Kol situated in the Alatau mountain ranges that form the northern arm of the Tian Shan, in the north of Kyrgyzstan. Ironically the lake was also home to a military research complex near Karakol at its eastern end, where the activities included the testing of high-precision torpedoes, and this, together with the mining of uranium, has left a significant legacy of health problems (*Economist*, 1994). There has been some contraction of health and sports tourism in the post-colonial period because of the reduction in the size of the domestic market. Since 1991, tourism activity has developed along the route of the Great Silk Road, the focus of World Tourism Organization promotion in Central Asia, in an attempt to stimulate economic development across the region (WTO, 2001). 'Health and sports tourism' has nevertheless retained its position as the most important market segment in terms of visitor numbers. Furthermore, the Akaev government's vision for the further development of tourism in

Kyrgyzstan, as outlined in the 'Development of the Tourism Sector of the Kyrgyz Republic Until 2010' (KSATS, 2001), has identified the 'health and recreational tourism' segment as one of the country's four main product-markets, together with 'cultural tourism', 'adventure tourism and mountaineering' and 'ecological tourism'.

Tourism is playing a strategic role both politically at national level in terms of creating opportunities for developing a coherent image for the Republic, and economically at regional level through the enhancement of development opportunities in remote areas (KSATS, 2001). Kyrgyzstan is the poorest of the emerging Central Asian states (Anderson, 1999) with external debt of US$1.5 billion (*Europe-East*, 2002). This results from a number of factors including its largely unproductive high ground, its underdeveloped hydroelectric power capability and its seriously unbalanced and overspecialized industrial base. Social and economic indicators categorize the state as a low to middle-income developing country with over half of the national output and employment coming from agriculture, despite the relatively small area of fertile land (UNICEF/WHO, 1992). Not surprisingly, a recent United Nations report estimated that 50% of the Kyrgyz population were living at or below the poverty line (60% were earning less than US$40 per month) with all the attendant health problems (UNDP, 1999). Tourism is therefore a key sector in Kyrgyzstan's economic development strategy, particularly with regard to enhancing regional development in some of the most underdeveloped areas of the Republic, such as the central Naryn region (KSATS, 2001). Within this framework, the development of health tourism offers some potential because of the available resources including the extant sanatoria, albeit outdated and in urgent need of renovation, the country's spa culture, and the benefits it could provide for the well-being of the Kyrgyz people.

Developments in the Health Tourism Sector

Health tourism centres on the notion of promoting, stabilizing or restoring physical, mental and social well-being while using health service facilities outside the tourists' permanent place of residence or work (Kaspar, 1996). Mueller and Kaufman (2001) subdivide health tourism into 'illness prevention tourism' and 'spa/convalescence tourism', the former being further divisible into 'individual health services' and 'wellness tourism'. Health tourism, centred on the use of spas for both illness prevention and convalescence, has long been an important feature of Kyrgyz leisure. It is therefore not surprising that this sector of the country's tourism industry is currently holding its own in the marketplace given the growing consumer interest in healthier lifestyles and alternative medicine (including more holistic, natural remedies). The demand also reflects consumer interest in combining health and tourism, including a substantial domestic demand resulting from its tradition of visiting spas and environmental health problems.

Nevertheless, it is clear that in Europe and North America, traditional mineral spa resorts are facing increasing competition from their more modern health and fitness counterparts which could be a significant threat to this sector in Kyrgyzstan in view of the limited resources available for product augmentation. Given these recent developments in health-care provision, the term 'spa' is now being applied more liberally to describe places that use natural health-giving elements and provide hospitality to guests without using natural mineral springs. A wide range of treatments is now

available, including hydrotherapy, thalassotherapy, therapeutic massage, mud treatments, herbal wraps, Kneipp[1] and watsu[2] (Smith and Jenner, 2000). In addition to the growth in health-care spas, many three- to five-star hotels now provide comprehensive 'wellness' benefits that include general health information, individual care and relaxation programmes as distinct from 'cures' (Mueller and Kaufman, 2001). In a European context, the 'spa, health and fitness' market is considered to be one of the fastest growing areas of the tourism industry up to 2010 (EU High Level Group on Tourism and Employment, 1998).

In the USA, health tourism (the outgrowth of the 1980s health club craze), especially the combination of holiday-taking and spa usage, is still in its infancy with only 2.5 million annual visits to spas (1% of the population represented) compared with 2.6 million (5%) in Italy, 10 million (12%) in Germany and 142 million (115%) in Japan (Strategy Group, 1996). Unlike Germany and Japan, the USA does not have a spa culture, nevertheless, demand is increasing as the population ages (particularly the baby boomers that make up almost one-third of the country's inhabitants). This has resulted from a greater health consciousness and a growing interest in health-care products together with the changing image of health tourism both in general and because of a deliberate strategy by spa operators to attract more tourists. The spa industry is now working more closely with the tourism sector to market its products more effectively and gain wider acceptance among tourists of all ages. In addition to the traditional affluent, middle-aged, female consumer, new markets have emerged such as a younger, less affluent segment, a 40+ male segment and a corporate segment; the majority of spa-goers are now working professionals aged between 30 and 55 (Loverseed, 1998). Government interest has also been stimulated because of the growing acceptance of spa treatments among the medical profession and the fact that payment is made privately rather than from public coffers, an important consideration from the perspective of overall health-care expenditure.

The US market, motivated mainly by the need for relaxation, is generally becoming more leisure and beauty-oriented and less concerned with the medicinal efficacy of health-care treatments (Smith and Jenner, 2000). The trend in Europe is less clear as yet, although growth in both the 'recreational health' and 'serious health' segments is evident. Europe has a stronger tradition of medical and preventive health with a steady demand for such treatment underpinned by government subsidization despite cutbacks in recent years. Nevertheless, there is some consensus that the main growth in the market will come from spas that emphasize relaxation, fitness, stress-reduction and beauty. Research by Mueller and Kaufman (2001) has shown that a clear demarcation should be made between 'wellness' and 'cure' concepts so that the distinct requirements of the two guest segments can be managed more appropriately. They also argue that the quality of provision is a key issue because of high consumer expectations and international competition in the health tourism market.

Perhaps one of the most unusual aspects of health tourism provision, though nevertheless consistent with the trends, is the demand for subterranotherapy – the treatment of predominantly respiratory ailments in salt mines because of the healing properties of their microclimates (Gama International, 2001). Whilst the focus of the chapter is on the role of salt mines in health tourism with specific reference to subterranotherapy at Salt World at Chon Tuz in Kyrgyzstan's Naryn region, it is worth considering the wider importance of salt and its interest for recreational tourists generally. This provides a useful context for examining both the reuse of salt mines to provide meaningful health and cultural tourism experiences and the potential for the development of the Salt World resort.

The Attraction of the Salt Mines: Tour or Cure?

There is an abundance of salt on the earth, much of which is found in the oceans that cover approximately two-thirds of the planet. This natural source is being degraded by waste disposal that pollutes the water with heavy metals such as lead, arsenic, mercury and cadmium. As a result, the quality of sea salt is being reduced and the majority of producers (89%) are chem-

ically refining it. This removes impurities – important minerals and trace elements – leaving sodium chloride, the consumption of which results in the development of oedema, or excess fluid in the body tissues, which is also the cause of cellulite. For every gram of sodium chloride the body cannot dispose of, the body uses 23 times the amount of cell water to neutralize the salt. If the amount of sodium chloride is still excessive, the body recrystallizes the salt by using available animal proteins to produce uric acid in order to get rid of it. Uric acid cannot be disposed of; it binds with the sodium chloride to form new crystals that are deposited in the bones and joints causing arthritis, kidney and gall bladder stones, and gout (Anon., 2003a).

As a result of modern processes and a growing concern for personal health, public interest in rock salt (granular masses of halite) and its commercial value has increased in recent years. Rock salt lies beneath the surface of many parts of the globe in beds laid down hundreds of millions of years ago, when ancient oceans evaporated. The beds were subsequently buried beneath sediments as mountains eroded and in many cases, they were disturbed by tectonic activity. Natural crystal salt therefore consists of elements that existed in the primal ocean from where all life originated and from which our bodies have been built. In its pure form, it contains 84 natural elements that are needed by the human body (Salt Institute, 2003).

Salt has also been an important element of economic and political life throughout history. As such, it has spawned many legends, folk tales and fables. At various times it has been used as currency and as a major revenue source through trade and taxation; it has even been the cause of warfare. Today, the USA is the world's largest producer, with extensive deposits in Michigan, Ohio, Kansas, Louisiana, Texas, New York and New Mexico. Canada also produces significant amounts of salt from mines in Nova Scotia, Saskatchewan and Ontario. China, Germany, India, Mexico, Australia, France, Brazil and the UK are also major producers of rock salt (US Geological Survey, 2002). The significance of salt is reflected in numerous place names across the globe from As-Salt in Jordan to Salzburg in Austria (Salt Institute, 2003). Chon Tuz in the Kyrgyz Republic also takes its name from the salt that is mined there, '*tuz*' being the Turkish name for salt.

Rock salt is therefore an intrinsically attractive concept to base a visitor attraction on because it is an essential element for life on earth. More than this, the lure of mines or, more specifically, the prospect of descending deep beneath the surface of the earth is a significant pull factor for tourists. Moreover, the idea of being 'sent to the salt mines' carries foreboding connotations in the western psyche because of the associative cognitive network[3] with Siberia. The motivation to visit salt mines has probably less to do with an interest in salt *per se* and more to do with a darker impetus and/or the exciting experience of descending beneath the earth's surface and the unusual and sometimes spectacular subterranean world that is discovered there. However, it is probably the combined effect of a number of factors that gives salt mining its touristic appeal and, as a result, many salt mines are important visitor attractions, some having visitor centres or museums to satisfy financial and/or educational objectives. Examples of established salt mine attractions include the four salt mines in Salzburg, Austria, and the salt mine at Berchtesgaden in Bavaria, near Hitler's retreat, which are all major tourist attractions receiving hundreds of thousands of visitors per annum. New attractions include a salt museum opened in Hutchinson, Kansas, in 2003 (Salt Institute, 2003). Visitors will be taken more than 200 m below ground into salt reserves discovered in 1887. In addition to historic relics associated directly with the mining of salt, a number of other treasures and oddities that have been preserved in the salt mine warehouse's ideal conditions for generations, will be displayed. For example, the original film negative for *The Wizard of Oz* and a collection of New York newspapers dating from the time of President Lincoln's assassination (Anon., 2003b).

Perhaps the best known international salt mine attraction is the Wieliczka mine near Krakow in southern Poland (Halsall, 1998), which receives up to a million visitors each year now that commercial mining activity has been phased out in favour of tourism (Salmon, 1993). The mine consists of approximately 200 km of underground passages with 2040 galleries on nine levels down to 327 m beneath

the surface. Wieliczka is one of the oldest European working salt mines that are open for tourists. According to legend, salt was first extracted here in the 13th century, although there is documentary evidence dating from 1044 that refers to the mine (Anon., 2003c). For hundreds of years, the miners creatively carved sculptures from the Miocene rock salt, including statues, chambers and even churches that have gained worldwide artistic and cultural renown (Taylor, 1993). According to Raloff (1996: 1) 'few who emerge from the mine describe the effect of these carvings as anything less than awesome and breathtakingly beautiful'. The largest of the chapels, the Chapel of the Blessed Kinga (named after a Hungarian princess who married the sovereign of Krakow in the middle ages), is over 50 m long with a volume of 10,000 m³. The Chapel's floor tiles, vaulted ceiling, walls (decorated with scenes from the bible) and numerous sculptures are all made from salt. Even the chandeliers that light the chamber have been made from crystalline salt. There is also an underground museum in the mine and special purpose chambers such as a sanatorium for people suffering from respiratory ailments. Given the mine's historical and artistic importance, it is not surprising that it achieved UNESCO World Heritage Site status in 1978 in recognition of its 'outstanding universal value to mankind' (Salmon, 1993: 1). The mine was also one of the first eight entries on the UN Inventory of Endangered World Cultural Heritage Sites because many of its sculpted features were being eroded by water.

Professor Mieczyslaw Skulimowski's research on subterranotherapy was instrumental in the reinstitution of a health spa in the salt mine at Wieliczka in 1958 (the spa had originally been in operation between 1826 and 1846 although the salt's curative properties had been identified as early as the 16th century). Skulimowski's work provided the requisite scientific credibility for the unorthodox therapy for respiratory ailments based on the microclimate of the Wieliczka mine; its bacteriological purity, constant temperature (around 54°F), humidity (40–45%) and large quantities of certain elements, notably sodium chloride, magnesium, manganese and calcium, were the key factors. Subterranotherapy for asthma, chronic bronchitis, throat and larynx ailments is

Fig. 11.2. Salt World: the restaurant, chalets and recreation area.

now available in a number of salt mines throughout the world because there is evidence that a 14-day visit to an underground spa (8 h per day), assuming it satisfies the requisite conditions, results in the total elimination of bacterial flora in the nose and throat cavities. It is therefore considered to be a viable alternative to pharmaceutical treatment. Subterranotherapy is even recommended for cardiovascular disease, metabolic dysfunction, skin diseases and allergies (Gama International, 2001). Clearly there are a variety of motivations for visiting salt mines and a range of experiences on offer but, arguably, subterranotherapy is the most unusual and intriguing. The Wieliczka mine, like other salt mines around the world, is responding to the increasing demand for alternative medicine and in the process, creating an alternative health tourism experience.

The 'Salt World' Experience

'Salt World' is an interesting health tourism attraction because it is a subterranotherapy centre but, more than that, it is an unusual one by either subterranotherapy norms or compared with international health tourism standards. It is situated approximately 5 km from Cholpen in the Naryn region, a remote and sparsely populated area of central Kyrgyzstan. The resort (Fig. 11.2) is based on a Soviet salt mine that began extraction in the early 1980s, although there is evidence that salt had been mined at the site at least 100 years earlier. At the height of its operation in the late 1980s, salt was extracted at two levels in the mine. The lower level of the mine is still in operation with 500,000 t of salt remaining – a relatively small-scale operation compared with many of its European and North American counterparts. The upper level, a series of passageways and chambers hewn from the rock salt and stretching for over 1000 m, has been reused for subterranotherapy because of the mine's favourable microclimate relating to its bacterial make-up, relative humidity and the presence of 18 elements from the periodic table in the ionic rock salt. In 1998 a hospital was built at Cholpen and patients were transported to and from the mine by bus, but it closed shortly afterwards and in 1999 Salt World was created at Chon Tuz.

The sign at the entrance to the resort reads, 'Health is everyone's goal. Salt World gives you good health' and this simple truth sets the scene for the no-frills visitor experience in this unassuming place. What it lacks in sophistication and style, it makes up for in authentic-

Fig. 11.3. The main passageway into the subterranotherapy spa.

ity and intrigue. Using a variation of the Wieliczka formula, guests are offered a 16-day package at the resort including treatment, food and accommodation for US$180 or US$300 depending on the standard of the chalets situated at ground level and whether single or a shared accommodation is required belowground in the mine. This tariff compares very favourably with health tourism products elsewhere, particularly with spa programmes, although the facilities at Chon Tuz are basic and, in that sense, the price and product elements of the marketing mix are consistent.

At ground level in the resort, the 'standard' (shared) accommodation takes the form of wooden chalets that are simply furnished with two single beds, easy chairs, a refrigerator and a kettle, with shared toilet and shower facilities. The superior accommodation is furnished with one single bed, a television and a video cassette recorder. The restaurant serves traditional Kyrgyz fare such as *laghman* (noodle dishes), *jarkop* (braised meat and vegetables) and *hoshan* (fried and steamed dumplings) with strong tea, although the ubiquitous vodka is notably absent from the site, as are other alcoholic beverages in keeping with the Salt World promise of 'good health' noted earlier. Below ground, the subterranotherapy spa has little in

the way of creature comforts (Fig. 11.3). It has retained many of the utilitarian features of the working salt mine it once was and, in that sense, it reflects the national picture with respect to the government's inability to resource its embryonic tourism industry. It also symbolizes the Republic's struggle to graft its own identity on to a pervasive Soviet legacy. The mine's roughly hewn walls, unsophisticated shoring and generally unfinished appearance contrast starkly with the artistic beauty of the Wieliczka mine's fixtures and fittings; Salt World's chandeliers, which hang incongruously throughout the mine are, at best, a pathetic parody of its Polish counterpart. Generally, it has an untidy and unfinished appearance but, despite this, its distinctive charm and noncommercial innocence are refreshing.

During the 1980s, many excavations in the mine uncovered relics of archaeological significance that, together with numerous other treasures from elsewhere in Kyrgyzstan, were taken to Moscow and St Petersburg to be displayed as museum pieces. The remains of bear, camel, porcupine and bird, preserved by the salt, in the walls of the mine, are interesting but in need of further excavation and interpretation, as are all other artefacts and themes in Salt World. One of the most interesting discoveries, from the writer's perspective as a general interest tourist, was the subterranean accommodation consisting of a number of beds in open 'rooms' branching directly from the main passageway. Clearly, the 'core' benefit of the Salt World experience, the subterranotherapy, has taken precedence over a wide range of product augmentation, service and security considerations. The subterranean recreational facilities include a table tennis room, a television lounge, a library and even a disco bar, complete with a DJ, all housed in the underground chambers of the mine. Generally speaking, the 'technical' aspects of service are only weakly developed, as they are in the Republic generally – the legacy of Soviet occupation. However, what the Kyrgyz lack in technical service know-how, they make up for in 'functional' service strength; they have a well earned reputation for being the friendliest of the newly independent Central Asian countries, a warm welcome and excellent hospitality being their characteristic traits.

Promotion, like that of the tourism industry elsewhere in Kyrgyzstan, is poor with word-of-mouth from former patients or 'guests' and recommendation by medical practitioners being the main lines of communication. Traditional brochures and leaflets are notably absent because of both the lack of technical know-how and the prohibitive cost of production. Place is perhaps the weakest element; the resort is resource-based because of the location of the salt. It is therefore remote from major population centres and access to the site is limited because of the difficult terrain and weak tourism transport infrastructure; there are no major road or rail connections. Furthermore, there is no established distribution system either through tour operators or electronically in the form of an Internet presence.

The process of subterranotherapy provides a unique experience for the guests. They spend the first 2 days in the subterranotherapy spa in the mine, but the first 2 nights sleeping in the wooden chalets on the surface to facilitate their adjustment to the mine's microclimate; the next 14 nights are spent in the mine and guests surface during the day to participate in sports, for example, football and basketball, or to go walking in the hills. For mild bronchial complaints, one 16-day course of treatment is held to be sufficient to remove the offending

bacterial flora; a lengthier remedy of three courses over 3 successive years is required for more serious cases of asthma. The majority of the resort's visitors are motivated by the specific purpose of improving their health. Most of the guests are domestic health tourists although the resort does attract some visitors from Kyrgyzstan's nearest neighbours: Kazakhstan, Uzbekistan and Tajikistan. It is a small-scale operation with at best, a few hundred visitors per year. Occasionally the resort is patronized by travellers passing through the region, in which case, chalet accommodation and refreshment are the main reasons for the visit. A tour of the salt mine may feature in their activities at some stage, but this would normally be a secondary consideration.

The health tourist experience of Chon Tuz could perhaps be summarized as a 'three-S' model: clearly not 'sun, sand and sea', but 'salt, sport and subterranotherapy'. However, this would imply a homogeneity of experience that is unlikely to exist in reality (Ryan, 2002), even in this somewhat controlled environment. The tourist experience, though based on the therapy and centred on the mine, is multi-dimensional and more complex than first impressions would indicate. Aho (2001) distinguishes between four essential core touristic experiences: getting *emotionally effected* (an emotional impression felt), *informed* (some new intellectual impression or learning), *practised* (increase in some capability) and *transformed* (permanent change in the state of mind or body or way of life). While Salt World undoubtedly focuses on a physical transformation as the core experience, it presents guests with the opportunity to gain both practice experiences in relation to certain sports, albeit to a limited extent, and to become informed about the practice and process of subterranotherapy. Emotional experiences, which are usually present, to some extent, in all touristic experiences, are likely to result from spending 2 weeks with other guests in such unusual circumstances. The experience, whilst individual, is also collective and as such, it has a social dimension; at very least, they share both a common motivation for and a collective experience of the therapy. Before entering the mine, it was tempting to think of 'seclusion' being one of the three 'S's, but on seeing the

Fig. 11.4. Communal television-watching.

facilities and the guest interaction, 'socialization' would be more appropriate. The quality of social interaction is a key issue in tourist experience normally (Baum, 2002), but under these particular circumstances, its significance will doubtless increase. Consequently, Salt World guests are likely to have the four core experiences in various degrees simultaneously.

Salt World's subterranotherapy is a special experience outside of normal routines and it is likely that the guests have a diminished awareness of the passage of time resulting from their spatial and temporal displacement. Notwithstanding the fact that time is a relative concept and different cultures and individuals within cultural groups have varying perspectives on daily routines, it is holidays that normally provide an opportunity to escape a mechanistic interpretation of time and aptly demonstrate its subjectivity because tourists' sense of time is shaped by their experience of activities, including social contacts, meal times, entertainment and event schedules. It is notable that the writer, as a general interest visitor, was given a tour of the mine and its subterranotherapy unit at midnight; none of the guests, many of whom were young teenagers, were sleeping, and many were watching television together (Fig. 11.4). The resort's temporal framework could be described

as partially regulated by set meal times, but otherwise the guests enjoy the relative freedom from normal diurnal constraints. The overall experience of Salt World for both the general recreation visitor and the recipient of subterranotherapy could probably be described as memorable, interesting and serendipitous because of the unusual nature of the resort and the surprising recreational facilities and sights that are available in the mine. The surprise results not from the nature of the facilities, but because of their location; although it is perfectly logical for such facilities to redefine this subterranean space because they provide the necessary recreation for the guests, they are nevertheless unexpected and at the same time comforting – the familiar in an unfamiliar place.

Stuck Between Rock Salt and a Hard Place?

Salt World could generally be described as a 'health resort', although it does not fit neatly into the normal classification consisting of 'destination spas', 'resort spas' and 'day spas' because of the limited range of health-care facilities, therapies and medical consultation opportunities that are available. Nevertheless, given the favourable international health tourism trends and the country's tradition of spa tourism, there is considerable scope for developing the resort's subterranotherapy programme with supporting health-care treatments to enhance the visitor experience. Following the recommendations of Mueller and Kaufman (2001), Salt World should continue to focus on the 'cure' concept within a health tourism framework. In the short term, however, it is likely that the overall quality of the visitor experience will prevent the resort from competing in an international market other than in a Central Asian context.

The resort is an interesting case because of its unusual character and its symbolism of the country's struggle to both forge a post-colonial identity from its Kyrgyz and Soviet cultures and create a viable tourism product whilst overcoming significant constraints. Salt World is also a microcosm of the Republic's transitional status because although the economy still gains much of its momentum from its mining activity, the government is attempting to become more export-oriented and tourism is beginning to play an increasingly important and strategic role in this transformation because of its invisible export potential. The reuse of the salt mine reflects this reorientation, but the prospects for the development of Salt World's facilities in line with both international market trends (particularly those in North America) and consumer expectations, in terms of product and service norms, are uncertain, as are those for any real and significant growth in the Republic's health tourism sector generally. The motivation for health tourism with respect to modern spa use in European and North American markets is increasingly recreational rather than medicinal. This indicates that substantial investment in and reorientation of outmoded resorts may be necessary to establish a competitive foothold in this market.

Despite its primarily agricultural base, Kyrgyzstan has an abundance of rare minerals such as gold, caesium, mercury and antimony, but the importance of mining is not widely known, even less so in the case of salt. The attraction therefore represents an important part of the state's cultural heritage that could potentially be augmented through the appropriate interpretation of the mine's history both chronologically and thematically, including the presentation of mining artefacts, methods, human interest stories together with the archaeological specimens and other relevant features of interest. Emphasis on the site's heritage is not only needed because of its cultural significance, it would also provide additional advantages with respect to establishing linkages with other cultural tourism products in the region, such as the 'Shepherd's Life' experience that focuses on the traditional Kyrgyz pastoral nomadic lifestyle before collectivization. In that way, the resort is likely to attract more cultural tourists. The 'Shepherd's Life' has been presented for tourist consumption through the 'Helvetas Agro' project, a joint venture between the Kyrgyz and Swiss governments featuring authentic cultural heritage and hospitality. Common themes of nature, health, tradition, culture, authenticity and sustainability could be developed further to package these and other attractions in the region, which are becoming increasingly popular with international tourists.

It is likely that any developments in either cultural or health tourism will be constrained by *inter alia* the lack of investment capital, poor infrastructure, an uneducated and unskilled workforce and poor standards of service quality and hygiene, not forgetting the growing doubts about the country's political stability. Moreover, attractions in the Naryn region particularly, but in Kyrgyzstan generally, especially the secondary attractions and associated facilities, are not widely known or visited because of the country's weak international image, low budget for promotional expenditure, unfamiliar language and competition from more established destinations. However, there is a spa culture in Kyrgyzstan and the surrounding former Soviet Central Asian countries. As such, there is a significant market potential for the development of health tourism from both domestic and regional tourism perspectives, but without significant improvements in the quality of the product and the way in which it is marketed, perhaps the Republic's ambitions in this area should be taken with a 'pinch of salt'!

Notes

1. Therapy based on immersion in clear, cold water (named after Sebastian Kneipp, a priest in the Dominican monastery in Bud Worishofen).

2. Watsu is derived from *Water* Shiatsu – gentle movement and acupressure in warm water performed by a trained therapist.

3. Cognitive psychologists have for many years held that knowledge consists of nodes that are connected through a network of associations (see Anderson, 1983; Halford *et al.*, 1998).

References

Aho, S.K. (2001) Towards a general theory of touristic experiences: modelling experience process in tourism. *Tourism Review* 56(3/4), pp. 33–37.

Anderson, J. (1999) *Kyrgyzstan: an Island of Democracy in Central Asia*, Harwood Academic Publishers, Amsterdam.

Anderson, J.R. (1983) *The Architecture of Cognition*. Harvard University Press, Boston, Massachusetts.

Anon. (2003a) Arthritis, kidney and gall stones and cellulite caused by common salt. See http://www.profoundliving.org/the_salt_/salt_iii/salt_iii.html (accessed 9 May 2003).

Anon. (2003b) Lyons Salt Company. See http://www.bouwman.com/bouwman/trips/Kansas/salt-mine.html (accessed on 9 May 2003).

Anon. (2003c) The history of the mine. See http://www.salt-mine.com / english / historia _ t. html (accessed 12 May 2003).

Baum, T. (2002) Making or breaking the tourist experience: the role of human resource management. In: Ryan, C. (ed.) *The Tourist Experience*. Continuum, London, pp. 94–111.

Burkart, A.J. and Medlik, S. (1981) *Tourism: Past, Present and Future*, 2nd edn. Heinemann, London.

Economist (1994) Deadly secret: Kyrgyzstan. *Economist* 333(7892), 45–47.

ESPA (European Spas Association) (2000) Cited in *Travel and Tourism Analyst* 1, 41–59.

EU High Level Group on Tourism and Employment (1998) Cited in *Travel and Tourism Analyst* 1, 41.

Europe-East (2002) IMF concludes 2001 consultation with the Kyrgyz Republic. *Europe-East* 23 January, 317–318.

Gama International (2001) Come to the Wieliczka salt mine for health treatment. See http://www.naturalsaltcrystallamps.com / salt _ mine . html (accessed 12 May 2003).

Halford, G.S., Bain, J.D., Mayberry, M.T. and Andrews, G. (1998) Induction of rational schemas: common processes in reasoning and complex learning. *Cognitive Psychology* 35, 201–245.

Halsall, P. (1998) The salt mines of Wieliczka. See http://www.fordham.edu/halsall/mod/1850Wieliczka.html (accessed 8 May 2003).

Kaspar, C. (1996) Gesundheitstourismus im Trend. In: Kaspar, C. (ed.) *Jahrbuch der Schweizer Tourismuswirtschaft*. Institut fur Tourismus and Verkehrswirtschaft, St. Gallen, Switzerland, pp. 53–61.

KSATS (2001) *Development of the Tourism Sector of the Kyrgyz Republic Until 2010*. Kyrgyz State Agency of Tourism and Sport, Bishkek, Kyrgyzstan.

Loverseed, H. (1998) Health and spa tourism in North America. *Travel and Tourism Analyst* 1, 46–61.

Mueller, H. and Kaufman, E.L. (2001) Wellness tourism: market analysis of a special health tourism segment and implications for the hotel industry. *Journal of Vacation Marketing* 7(1), 5–17.

Raloff, J. (1996) Licking the problem of Poland's melting treasures. See http://www.sciencenews. org / sn _ arch / 4 _ 27 _ 96 / bobl. html (accessed 10 May 2003).

Ryan, C. (2002) Motives, behaviours, body and mind. In: Ryan C. (ed.) *The Tourist Experience*. Continuum, London, pp. 27–57.

Salmon, L. (1993) Air pollutant intrusion into the Wieliczka salt mine. See http://www.fp.thesalmons.org/lynn/saltmine.html (accessed 9 May 2003).

Salt Institute (2003) See http://www.saltinstitute.org/38.html (accessed 12 May 2003).

Schofield, P. (2004) Positioning the tourism product of an emerging industry: image, resources and politics in Kyrgyzstan. In: Hall. D. (ed.) *Tourism in Transition: Global Processes, Local Impacts*. CAB International, Wallingford, UK.

Smith, C. and Jenner, P. (2000) Health tourism in Europe. *Travel and Tourism Analyst* 1, 41–59.

Strategy Group (1996) The use of spas in selected countries. *Travel and Tourism Analyst* 1, 46–61.

Taylor, B. (1993) The salt mines of Wieliczka, 1850, modern history sourcebook. See http://www.showcaves.com/english/pl/mines/Wieliczka.html (accessed 12 May 2003).

UNDP (1999) *Kyrgyzstan: National Report on Human Development*. UNDP, Bishkek, Kyrgyzstan.

UNICEF/WHO (1992) The looming crisis and fresh opportunity: health in Kazakhstan, Kyrgyzstan, Tajikistan, Turkmenistan and Uzbekhistan. *UNICEF/World Health Organization*, New York. February–March.

US Geological Survey (2002) World salt production. See http://www.saltinstitute.org/36.html (accessed 12 May 2003).

WTO (2001) *Study on Visa Facilitation in the Silk Road Countries*. World Tourism Organization, Madrid.

12 Pro-poor Tourism: Benefiting the Poor

Dilys Roe[1], Harold Goodwin[2] and Caroline Ashley[3]

[1]International Institute for Environment and Development (IIED), 3 Endsleigh Street, London WC1H 0DD, UK; [2]International Centre for Responsible Tourism, University of Greenwich, UK; [3]Overseas Development Institute (ODI), 111 Westminster Bridge Road, London SE1 7JD, UK;

Poverty reduction and the role of tourism

Tackling poverty has long been a challenge faced by the international community. While, at a global level, poverty has decreased in the last 10 years, progress has been uneven and at the start of the second millennium, 20% of the global population exists on an income of less than US$1 per day and nearly 50% on less than US$2 per day (World Bank, 2000). But poverty is not just about lack of money. Poverty is also about hunger and lack of shelter, not having access to clean drinking water and sanitation, illness and illiteracy – and the inability to do anything about it.

At the United Nations Millennium Summit in September 2000, the international community reaffirmed its commitment to tackling poverty stating:

> We will spare no effort to free our fellow men, women and children from the abject and dehumanizing conditions of extreme poverty to which more than a billion of them are currently subjected.

The first of the eight Millennium Development Goals is thus to halve, between 1990 and 2015, the proportion of people whose income is less than US$1 per day and to halve the proportion of people who suffer from hunger. Together, the eight goals have been commonly accepted as a framework for measuring development progress (United Nations, 2000).

Contemporary thinking on poverty reduction emphasizes the complexity of the process and the need for strategies on a variety of complementary fronts and scales. Most would accept, however, that pro-poor growth (economic growth that benefits poor people) is the essential underpinning of long-term, sustainable poverty reduction (see for example McKay, 1997; Goudie and Ladd, 1999; Ravallion, 1997; World Bank, 2000).

As one of the world's largest, and growing, economic sectors, tourism can be a significant contributor to economic growth (and is critical in some countries).[1] However, the structure of the industry means that the economic potential of tourism is often not realized by developing countries: a significant proportion of the economic benefits of tourism are repatriated to the tourist-originating countries of the North and, of that which is retained, much is captured by richer groups, with a small proportion reaching the poor (and very little reaching the poorest of the poor). However, if it were possible to retain more of the profits of tourism within the host country, and to ensure that more of the benefits reach poor groups, there should be considerable potential for tourism-based poverty reduction. This is the basis of pro-poor tourism (PPT) – tourism that generates net benefits for the poor.

Table 12.1. Significance of international tourism to poor countries.

Country	Population below US$1 a day[a] (%)	Contribution of tourism industry to GDP[b] (%)	Growth in demand, year 2000[b] (%)
Mali	73		9.0
Nigeria	70	0.5	13.5
Central African Republic	66	1.2	10.8
Zambia	64	3.9	3.4
Madagascar	63	3.8	3.4
Niger	61	1.9	7.5
Burkina Faso	61	2.2	3.0
Sierra Leone	57	1.8	15.9
The Gambia	54	5.6	3.5
India	44	2.5	9.7
Lesotho	43	2.0	NA
Honduras	41	4.4	4.3
Ghana	39	5.5	34.0
Mozambique	38	NA	NA
Nepal	38	4.5	6.3

[a] World Bank (2001).
[b] WTTC (2001) growth in international tourism arrivals.
NA = not available.

This chapter reviews the impacts of tourism on the poor, outlines the concept of pro-poor tourism and reviews recent experience of implementing a variety of strategies aimed at making tourism more pro-poor.

Why Address Poverty Reduction Through Tourism?

While, like many other development sectors, tourism has a number of well-documented negative aspects, the rationale for 'pro-poor tourism' (PPT) is that the sector is exceedingly large, growing, and involves many countries and individuals in the South (the developing countries, most of which are below the equator). Tourism therefore already affects the livelihoods of many of the world's poor. Table 12.1 illustrates the significance of tourism to the 15 countries with the highest proportions of poor people.

Some argue that because foreign, private-sector interests drive tourism, it has limited potential to contribute to poverty reduction. Indeed, it can disadvantage the poor by causing displacement, increased local costs, loss of access to resources, and social and cultural disruption. An opposite view is that, where it is a viable option, tourism has better prospects for promoting pro-poor growth than many other sectors and that many of the supposed disadvantages of tourism are in fact common to most types of economic development in a globalizing world.

Tourism's pro-poor potential derives from the fact that:

- It is a diverse industry. This increases the scope for wide participation, including the participation of the informal sector.
- The customer comes to the product, providing considerable opportunities for linkages (e.g. souvenir selling).
- Tourism is highly dependent upon natural capital (e.g. wildlife, scenery) and culture. These are assets that some of the poor have, even if they have no financial resources.
- Tourism is labour-intensive (albeit less so than agriculture).
- Compared with other economic sectors, a higher proportion of tourism benefits (jobs, petty trade opportunities) go to women.

A further reason for focusing on tourism is that there is already a strong movement to make the industry more sustainable and more responsible. There is therefore great opportunity to expand this debate to take on board poverty reduction.

Impacts of Tourism on Poor People

Poverty reduction is about improving the quality of life for individual people. It entails more than increasing national GDP or other macro-economic indicators. So to understand the impact of tourism on poverty, we must look behind the national aggregates, to understand the impacts at the local level: on individuals, families and communities. Analysing tourism's impacts from the perspective of poor people[2] soon reveals that the impacts are positive and negative, direct and indirect, and generally a lot more varied than outsiders may assume. Understanding which of these impacts matter most to the poor is essential, if we are to enhance them in pro-poor ways.

Research on pro-poor tourism (Ashley *et al.*, 2001)[3] demonstrates that poor people identify many different types of impacts as important. These can be broadly divided into economic and non-economic impacts.

The main economic impacts include:

Job oppportunities: employment in the tourism sector, and opportunities for training are generally highly valued – even when regarded as 'menial' cleaning jobs by Westerners.

Small enterprise opportunities: these may be in enterprises that supply inputs (food, fuel, building materials) to tourism businesses, or that are small tourism businesses themselves (local guide services, craft and cultural enterprises).

Community collective income: this may come from lease fees, rentals, equity dividends paid by the tourism operation etc. Though funds are not always well used and are small per person, they are valued as one of the few sources of *community* income – to spend on shared investments (infrastructure, drought-coping, etc.).

Access to credit: this may be from a tourism support programme, from staff using their wages in a credit programme, or from community collective income.

Non-economic impacts may be less tangible but are just as important – and usually of significance to *more people* than the earnings:

Infrastructure: access to infrastructure developed for tourists; shared use (e.g. of roads, water), or extension of facilities during construction. This emerged as a priority issue in many PPT case studies even though it had not been an explicit pro-poor strategy of operators or government.

Health care: shared access to health facilities or programmes developed due to tourism, use of transport (e.g. lodge vehicle) and communications (e.g. radio) for medical emergencies.

Donations for community assets: for example schools, clinics, water pumps. Donated by tourists and/or collected by operators.

Participation or control: Consultation in planning processes and a voice in decision making can be very important for the poor who, by definition, are usually marginalized and voiceless. Where tenure or ownership rights lie with the poor, the control they gain over tourism operations is invaluable.

Social organization and institutional change: Change can be very negative, for example where conflicts arise over the spoils of tourism. Positive change can also occur through social mobilization, and incentives for community organization.

Natural resources: Lost access to land, water supplies, coast and forest can be the most damaging aspect of tourism for poor people, particularly as the poor are so heavily dependent on these natural resources for livelihoods. In some cases, tourism can have positive impacts on the resource base, for example by providing incentives for sustainable collective use.

Information: Increased access to information and communication emerged in several PPT case studies as a highly valued benefit of participating in tourism development. This is particularly important to more remote and marginalized communities.

Access to markets: tourism development can be seen as creating new opportunities, particularly in remote areas. Market information is valuable.

Exposure to risk: where livelihoods are dependent on tourism they are also vulnerable to industry downswings. This is a big problem for poor households, as they are usually more risk-averse than those who have a cushion of savings.

Exposure to exploitation: in some jobs, poor working conditions and pay can amount to exploitation. The more desperately the jobs are needed, the more the wages or conditions can be driven down.

Culture: in some cases cultural tourism is welcomed for valuing local culture. In others, however, it can bring problems of commercialization and negative influences such as drug use and prostitution.

Optimism and pride: where local people have a say in decisions and planning, optimism and pride are valued.

Physical security: actions to increase security for tourists can be of great benefit to locals.[4] Insecurity can arise from increased numbers of wild animals, and tourist behaviour (e.g. to elephants) that makes them aggressive.

Defining Pro-poor Tourism

PPT is not a specific tourism product or niche sector of the industry but an *approach to tourism development* that attempts to enhance the linkages between tourism businesses and poor people, in order to change the current distribution of benefits and increase tourism's contribution to poverty reduction. Benefits may be economic, but they may also be social, environmental or cultural. PPT can involve any type of company – a small lodge, an urban hotel, a tour operator, an infrastructure developer – and engages with many different types of stakeholders: staff, neighbouring communities, landholders, producers of food, fuel and other suppliers, operators of microtourism businesses, craftworkers, other users of tourism infrastructure (roads) and resources (water) etc.

While PPT overlaps with other approaches, including sustainable, responsible, community-based or ecotourism, the key distinctive feature is that PPT focuses on practical initiatives which can use tourism to benefit poor people and reduce poverty. There are many such initiatives which can be taken by different government agencies, NGOs and companies; whilst there are a number of general approaches and principles (discussed below), it is essential that all initiatives are developed to meet the requirements of particular groups in particular places. The current debate on *sustainable tourism* has focused largely on mass tourism destinations – only a minority of which occur in poor countries. Social issues are usually an add-on to environmental concerns and the poor people of the South are thus at the edge of the picture. Similarly, *ecotourism* initiatives usually benefit local people, but with a strong environmental angle (particularly in the eyes of international tourists). Integrated conservation and development approaches emphasize the need for broadly distributed local benefits (often cash) as incentives for conservation. In contrast, PPT aims to deliver net benefits to the poor as a goal in itself. *Community-based tourism* initiatives aim to increase local people's involvement in tourism and are one useful component of PPT, but efforts are also needed on marketing, employment opportunities, linkages with the established private sector, policy and regulation, and participation in decision making. Finally, *responsible tourism* initiatives by companies often increase benefit flows to local people (while also addressing environmental impacts). However, a PPT perspective is both wider, in that it pursues a broad range of poverty impacts and levels of intervention, and narrower, in that impacts on poverty are the key indicator.

Having highlighted the differences, it is important also to point out that many community-based, responsible, sustainable and ecotourism initiatives are good examples of 'PPT strategies' without being named as such, and indeed have pro-poor impacts. The difference is more one of perspective and of impact, in that a PPT focus prioritizes and highlights impacts on the poor.

Strategies for making tourism pro-poor should focus specifically on unlocking opportunities for the poor within tourism, rather than expanding the overall size of the sector. A wide range of actions is needed in order to increase benefits to the poor from tourism. Pro-poor tourism strategies can thus be broadly grouped into three types: *expanding economic benefits* for the poor; *addressing non-economic impacts*; and *developing pro-poor policies/ processes/partnerships* (see Box 12.1).

PPT Case Studies

A recent research project (2000–2001) funded by the UK Department for International Development (DFID) analysed six case studies of pro-poor tourism interventions and assessed their progress from a pro-poor perspective. They were selected to cover different continents and types of actors and strategies. Three operate in southern Africa: Wilderness Safaris' (WS) operation of two lodges in Maputaland, which are tripartite ventures with the Tribal Authority

and provincial government; the approach of the Government's Spatial Development Initiative and Community–Public–Private Partnership (CPPP) programme as implemented at Makuleke and Manyeleti in Northern Province; and the work of the Namibian Community-Based Tourism Association (NACOBTA), which was compared with the Uganda Community Tourism Association (UCOTA). The other three case studies were: donor-supported community-level tourism capacity building by the Netherlands Development Organization (SNV) in Nepal, linkages between a small private operator, Tropic Ecological Adventures, and community tourism enterprises in Ecuador, and the large EU-funded 'Heritage Tourism Programme' of the Government of St Lucia (in the Caribbean).

The case studies are summarized in the boxes below.

Box 12.1. Pro-poor tourism strategies.

I) *Strategies focused on economic benefits*

(i) **Expanding business opportunities for the poor:** small enterprises, particularly in the informal sector, often provide the greatest opportunities for the poor.

(ii) **Expanding employment opportunities for the poor:** unskilled jobs may be limited and low-paid by international standards, but are much sought after by the poor.

(iii) **Enhancing collective benefits:** collective community income from tourism can be a new source of income, and can spread benefits well beyond the direct earners.

I) *Strategies focused on non-economic impacts*

(i) **Capacity building, training and empowerment:** the poor often lack the skills and knowledge to take advantage of opportunities in tourism.

(ii) **Mitigating the environmental impact of tourism on the poor:** tourism can lead to displacement of the poor from their land and/or degradation of the natural resources on which the poor depend.

(iii) **Addressing social and cultural impact of tourism:** tourists' behaviour, such as photography and western habits, is often regarded as cultural intrusion. Sex tourism exploits women. Tourism can affect many other social issues, such as health care.

III) *Strategies focused on policy process reform*

(i) **Building a more supportive policy and planning framework:** many governments see tourism as a means to generate foreign exchange rather than to address poverty. The policy framework can inhibit progress in PPT; reform is often needed.

(ii) **Promoting participation:** the poor are often excluded from decision-making processes and institutions, making it very unlikely that their priorities will be reflected in decisions.

(iii) **Bringing the private sector into pro-poor partnerships:** locally driven tourism enterprises may require input to develop skills, marketing links, and commercial expertise.

Case Studies

Case study 1: Wilderness Safaris, Maputaland, South Africa

This is an example of a commercial company entering into a contractual relationship with a community and the state conservation agency to develop up-market tourist lodges. In addition, Wilderness Safaris (WS) is taking initiatives relating to local employment, local service provision and the development of complementary community-based initiatives.

WS is a large, well-established southern African tour operator that caters to the luxury end of the market. It has a number of lodges and camps across southern Africa and at a number of these it is involved in some form of partnership or revenue-sharing agreement with local communities. This case study looks at two lodges run by WS in Maputaland in the South African province of KwaZulu Natal – Rocktail Bay, which opened in 1992, and Ndumu, opened in 1995.

Ownership and management of the lodges is vested in two companies – a 'lodge-owning company' in which the conservation agency, a commercial bank and the community have stakes; and a 'lodge-operating company' in which the conservation agency, the community and WS are partners (although not equal). Despite this tripartite equity structure, the community has received little in the way of financial dividends so far, because neither lodge has yet returned a profit. Increased occupancy at the lodges is required to make them profitable, but this requires development of the destination as a whole and diversification of the product. It is noted that the support of the conservation authority is needed for further infrastructural and product development, but that the conservation agency seems reluctant to sanction this due to concerns about the likely impact on the conservation status of the area.

Progress has been mixed on the other elements of WS's PPT initiative. The local employment strategy has resulted in a high proportion of jobs going to local people. Considerable training and skills transfer has taken place and staff turnover is low. Local provision of services has occurred to a certain extent, with WS utilizing local security and taxi services, and joint planning and implementation of new complementary products has started, with cultural visits to a traditional healer (*Sangoma*). However, growth of local businesses associated with the lodges has been slow, and the case study notes 'untapped potential' for local supply of services and products. A consultant has been brought in to help WS work with the community to develop products, but it is felt that a third party is needed to organize, coordinate, develop and train for this, since these activities are outside the mandate, and capacity, of one private sector operator.

The case study illustrates three key challenges to such a private sector–community initiative:

- Success is somewhat *out of the control of the central actors*, being dependent on other players and on the health of tourism in the wider region
- The initiative needs to be *incorporated within a larger PPT programme* involving other stakeholders to maximize potential
- Many communities have *overly high expectations* of involvement in tourism – both in terms of the levels and rates of returns and also the roles and responsibilities of their private-sector partners.

Case study 2: Tropic Ecological Adventures, Ecuador

This case study illustrates how a small company, driven by motivated individuals, has gone well beyond normal business practice to support community tourism. It focuses on the role of Tropic Ecological Adventures in seeking to establish joint products with remote Amazonian communities, and in marketing other well-established community initiatives.

Tropic Ecological Adventures is a small for-profit company that was established with the spe-cific objective of demonstrating the 'viability of environmentally, socially and culturally responsible tourism' as an alternative, for particular communities, to oil extraction in the Ecuadorian Amazon. It operates tours to natural areas in Ecuador, including the Amazon, usually for small, high-paying groups. It has links with several communities, of which two are the focus of the case study: Tropic has worked with the Huaorani people to develop a joint initiative, bringing

(continued)

(Case study 2 continued)

tourists into the community for overnight stays and to experience the Huaorani culture and lifestyle. It was marketing the long-established Cofan initiative at Zabalo, although it has recently been forced to suspend these operations due to security issues in this area near the Colombian border.

Although Tropic found that its community-based programmes were less profitable and less marketable than some of its other activities, it has managed to successfully address this problem by coupling them with more mainstream packages such as visits to the Galapagos Islands. Unfortunately, however, a decline in tourism in the Ecuadorian Amazon in 1999 and 2000, following kidnappings and political upheaval, has heightened competition amongst tour operators and driven down prices, and this has undermined Tropic's impact-minimizing approach of bringing in small groups of high-paying tourists. A further

setback arose from the Civil Aviation Authority's decision to close down the airstrip at the Huaorani site (due to poor maintenance – a community responsibility). However, a new site has been identified and a business plan developed for which external support is being sought.

The case study highlights a number of key issues affecting PPT:

- The *importance of non-financial benefits* and the important role that a company like Tropic plays in *linking remote communities with the outside world*
- The *limitations of community-based programmes* (because of a lack of awareness of tourism in the community, as well as the need for external investment in infrastructure, marketing and training)
- The challenges of *achieving commercial viability*.

Case study 3: Community-Based Tourism Associations in Namibia and Uganda

This case study covers two broadly similar organizations in Namibia and Uganda. The Namibia Community-Based Tourism Association (NACOBTA) and the Uganda Community Tourism Association (UCOTA) are membership associations of community-based tourism initiatives.

NACOBTA and UCOTA aim to increase financial benefits to poor communities through the improvement and expansion of the niche, community-based, segment of the industry, and through wider integration of communities into the mainstream industry. Both organizations work simultaneously at three levels:

Local – providing support in the form of training, finance, technical assistance and marketing to individual community-based tourism enterprises;

Private sector – lobbying for private sector support and patronage of community-based enterprises and (NACOBTA only) facilitating the development of partnerships between the private sector and communities;

Policy – lobbying and advocacy for policy reforms that support community-based tourism, and providing a voice for marginalized groups.

It is perhaps at the micro-level that most progress has been made, with activities focusing around training, technical assistance and business advice, grants and loans for enterprise develop-

ment or improved marketing and other business advice. UCOTA is also involved with conservation and education activities. Many initiatives are now well-established and self-sufficient. However, it is noted, for NACOBTA particularly, that there is a limit to the organization's capacity to deliver the level and amount of training required to an increasing number of enterprises.

Building links with the private sector is seen as a slow but critical process. Whereas NACOBTA faced great difficulties with this at first, lacking credibility with the private sector, considerable progress has been made in this area with a number of avenues of contact now established. The case study identifies the need for business skills and a thorough understanding of the workings of the industry and 'corporate culture' in order to gain credibility with the private sector, or to negotiate effectively. Policy level work is similarly slow, and it is difficult to separate impacts that have come about as a result of NACOBTA/UCOTA interventions directly from those that have been part of a wider process of policy development.

Nevertheless, it is clear that the two organizations provide a role that others do not, and a momentum for change.

(continued)

(Case study 3 continued)

The case study highlights:
- The value of *membership organizations in providing a 'voice for the poor'* and in promoting PPT at all levels
- The *dependence of such organizations on external funding* and the implications this has for their long-term sustainability

- The huge *need for business skills* including marketing, strategic planning and general awareness of the tourism industry if member enterprises are to become self-supporting and able to compete with the private sector.

Case study 4: SNV-Nepal

The SNV-Nepal case study explores the approach of a development agency working with local communities through social mobilization, participatory planning and capacity-building in a very poor and remote area of Nepal. The study provides a valuable example of the 'import substitution' process – whereby the goods and services required by the tourism industry are to be produced and supplied locally rather than from Kathmandu.

The Dutch development agency SNV works through its District Partners Programme (DPP) with district and village development committees, NGOs and the private sector to 'benefit women and disadvantaged groups at village level'. Tourism development is one means of achieving that objective in the remote Humla District of north-west Nepal.

SNV's PPT strategy revolves around developing tourism initiatives that benefit poor and disempowered groups as opposed to the Kathmandu-based trekking agencies. The focus of the initiative is therefore at the local level – on specific enterprises and communities along a trekking trail – although SNV also engages at the policy level with the Nepal Tourism Board in Kathmandu. The emphasis of the PPT strategy is on social mobilization through the development of community-based organizations; business planning and training designed to enable the poor to develop micro-enterprises and to take up employment opportunities.

Since the tourism programme commenced in October 1999, the community-based organizations (CBOs) have developed micro-enterprise plans, of which 32 have been approved. Six further business plans have been prepared and venture capital fund loans approved. Kermi has also opened a community campsite and other communities are planning to follow suit. Community enterprise options for hot springs and village tours have also been studied and plans are under way to develop them. A Multiple-Use Visitors Centre is planned to provide a focal point for the local provision of tourism services – such as portering, mules, horses etc. – and produce (such as vegetables) to trekking agents and tourists. In addition to SME development, a number of other initiatives have been implemented including construction of toilets along the trekking trail, a US$2 per tourist trail maintenance tax and a tax on pack animal grazing in the community forest areas.

The case study highlights:
- The *value of a long-term approach to building participation of the poor*, given the extreme poverty in Humla and lack of capacity amongst the poor
- The *limited time* the landless, the poorest of the poor, have to participate in the CBOs
- The challenges of *breaking into the existing well-established and connected tourism elite.*

Case study 5: St Lucia Heritage Tourism Programme

This case study is an example of PPT that goes well beyond supporting community-based tourism. It describes a donor-funded government programme that operates at many levels – from micro to macro – and attempts not just to develop

a niche product, but to shift a country's whole tourism sector to a more sustainable footing. It is not a case of 'a pro-poor tourism initiative', but of a comprehensive national tourism initiative that has a strong pro-poor component.

(continued)

(Case study 5 continued)

The St Lucia HTP arose out of concerns about the sustainability and equity of tourism development in St Lucia. The programme attempts to develop concurrent and complementary initiatives in the fields of policy reform, capacity building, marketing, product development and public awareness in order to fulfil two key objectives:

- to facilitate a broader distribution of the benefits of the existing tourism sector (cruise ship passengers and stay-over visitors)
- to create a new complementary sub-sector, qualified as Heritage Tourism.

This is a 4-year initiative that has reached its third year. The case study notes that foundations have been laid for effective PPT through work at many levels, but in some ways the progress so far has been in awareness-raising rather than action on the ground.

The programme claims some success in 'making cracks in the fortress' of the existing industry through, for example, competing for clients on the cruise ship wharf, raising the profile of local operators, developing new attractive products and attracting tourists to inland initiatives. However, it recognizes that enterprise development by the poor will often be around communal assets, and for this a supportive policy framework that provides for collaborative management and for devolution of rights of use and exclusion is required. Lack of local capacity has also constrained the effectiveness of some interventions, but the case study also notes that capacity-building efforts bode well for the long-term sustainability of the programme. However, sustainable results will require more time than the funded time-frame of the project, and additional external assistance in training, institutional development and planning is likely to be needed.

At the policy level, the programme has made a number of specific recommendations – on incentives and on tour guides – but the case study highlights that far more attention is required at this level to foster political support and to develop a supportive policy framework. Marketing activities have also been limited, and the programme needs to build stronger links and develop a comprehensive marketing framework. Progress in attracting an entirely new clientele to 'heritage tourism' is not apparent.

The St Lucia HTP highlights:

- The importance of a good and *thorough knowledge of the industry*
- The challenge of attracting *beach and package tourists* away to cultural products
- The *slow pace* of a multi-level approach to deliver real change on the ground.

Case study 6: The South Africa SDI and Community–Public–Private Partnerships (CPPP) Programmes at Makuleke and Manyeleti (Northern Province, South Africa)

This case study looks at how pro-poor tourism can be built into the rural growth and investment strategies of the South African government and, in so doing, explores the tensions between promoting growth and achieving social objectives. It provides a detailed example of the use of 'planning gain' in influencing private investors. Planning gain occurs when planning permission or a license to operate has conditions attached to it for the provision of (for example) roads or a fresh water supply which benefits the poor.

The case study focuses on Manyeleti Game Reserve and Makuleke contractual park (bordering and inside Kruger National Park, respectively).

- Manyeleti Game Reserve is a focus of the Northern Province Government's commercialization programme and is heavily supported by the Phalaborwa SDI. Manyeleti is one of the first tourism investment packages to near fruition.
- The Makuleke project is a community-based initiative that has been supported by, *inter alia*, both the Spatial Development Initiative (SDI) and CPPP programmes, and is being used as a pilot project to guide the future work of the CPPP programme in the tourism sector. Makuleke is the first example of land inside a national park being returned to a community for use as a contractual park through restitution.

In both cases, a tender process to attract private-sector investment has been implemented with a strong use of planning gain – i.e. socio-economic criteria featured strongly in the evaluation of bids

(continued)

(continued)

– to encourage pro-poor commitments. Both the SDI and CPPP programmes are using lessons from Manyeleti and Makuleke for future investment preparation.

A number of tenders were received for Manyeleti Game Reserve – all of which included practical proposals on equity sharing, outsourcing, local employment and local service provision – and negotiations with the short-listed bidders are under way. At Makuleke, the newly formed Community Property Association (CPA) was assisted in the tendering process by the CPPP programme, and potential bidders were required to address a similar set of socio-economic issues in the tender document. However few bids were received, mainly due to the availability of other more commercially attractive investment opportunities within the Kruger Park, and not all met the basic conditions set down. However, agreement with a private investor proceeded and the Outpost camp – a 6-star, 36-bed lodge, opened in 2003. All jobs in the lodge go to local people while the Makuleke community earns 10% of turnover generated by the business, with a further 2% of turnover going into a bursary fund to train local residents. The CPA has subsequently also entered into a new agreement with Wilderness Safaris (a top eco-tourism operator in SADC) to develop a further four lodges. The deal signed with Wilderness Safaris is a significant boost and it is hoped this will stimulate further private sector investment into the region.

The case study highlights:
- It is easier to move away from existing models in which communities are 'recipients' of donated benefits from tourism, to community empowerment because they have a stake in an enterprise, if there are *secure land rights* in place.
- There is a *tension between pursuing pro-poor objectives and ensuring private investment*, which although not insurmountable, cannot be completely avoided, and must be addressed
- The *commercial attractiveness of the site is critical* both to the scale of financial benefits and to securing pro-poor commitments from the private sector.

The case studies highlight the diversity of actors involved in PPT strategies – including national and provincial government agencies, large and small commercial companies and domestic and international organizations. The case studies also illustrate a variety of types and levels of intervention ranging from top-down, government-led approaches to the micro-level work of enterprise support. One of the key issues, which comes out in the case studies, is the importance of facilitating and improving access for community tourism ventures to the mainstream industry, which is not always enthusiastic about engaging positively with these initiatives.

The market segments involved include wildlife, coastal, mountain, adventure and safari tourism. Though these may be seen as 'niche' segments in that they are not mass tourism destinations, in most cases they are the mainstream segments in the countries concerned: i.e. safari tourism is mainstream in South Africa. The target markets range from the luxury market to backpackers while the tourism products involved include accommodation, cultural activities, and tourism supplies. Three broad types of product can be distinguished:

1. *Development of cultural products* which are complementary to the core tourism product. These include trips to the traditional healer from Wilderness Safaris lodges, and black history tours and cultural performances in Namibia.

2. *Development of mainstream up-market products*, such as safari lodges, where the pro-poor component comes from the shared ownership of the venture, as in the SDI model and the tripartite equity structure of the WS lodges.

3. *Provision of inputs to the tourism industry* through developing supply linkages with poor producers. This is a strong focus in Nepal, where the aim is to substitute locally grown supplies for flown-in supplies, but is not a strong emphasis in the southern African cases.

The Contribution of Pro-poor Tourism to Poverty Reduction

Findings from the six PPT case studies show that for those in regular employment, earnings can often reach US$1000–4000 per worker per year. Such earnings are sufficient to bring the core group of earners (usually fewer than 20 in each enterprise) and their families above the poverty line. For example, in South Africa, at two Wilderness Safaris lodges each employee earns twice the average income of a rural homestead in the area. Furthermore, virtually all the case studies found that workers would not otherwise be employed because there are few other viable economic activities in the areas studied.

Casual and small business earnings per person are generally lower than earnings from regular employment, though case studies demonstrate very high variability: from a low of US$6–10 to a high in the thousands of dollars. However, there are far more people involved on a casual and small business basis[5] (4–10 times the number of employees, without taking into account the multiplier effects of re-spending of tourism earnings). In almost all the case studies, the importance of even small amounts of income was noted (see Box 12.2). An additional point to note is that although the numbers of actual earners may be limited, several case studies emphasize that the earnings of one person may support many more:

> This new enterprise already brings financial benefits to 48 people in terms of a monthly income that amounts to up to N$5000. These financial benefits have a more far-reaching impact than for just the direct income earners, as each earner supports on average 15 people. Thus the total financial benefits can be felt by as many as 720 people.
>
> (Nicanor, 2001)

Collective income is generally used for community investment, rather than being distributed to households. Although the actual sums per person may be small – usually the equivalent of only a few cents or dollars per person – they can be disproportionately important as they are a rare source of community funds. However, they can also be 'lost' through misappropriation and poor management.

> Money distributed by the Community Trust amounts to a very small amount per person if averaged across the village population, but is used to finance community development that would not otherwise take place.
>
> (Poultney and Spenceley, 2001: 20)

Box 12.2. Use of earnings by the poor.

Humla, Nepal
In most cases, the earnings make a significant difference to the welfare of households, enabling them in particular to buy shoes, cloth, ready made clothes, salt and flour from Tibet . . . Without these earnings, families would be more severely underfed and poorly clothed than they currently are.

(Saville, 2001:33)

Cofan community, Ecuador
[Income also] goes towards soap, toothpaste, aspirin, rice, sardines, pasta, and flour. Money earned is also used to buy clothes, more expensive items such as radios, and more commonly, gasoline to fuel many of the motor boats owned by community members for transportation purposes.

(Braman and Fundación Acción Amazonia, 2001:15)

Maputaland, South Africa
For the majority of employees at Rocktail and Ndumu, it is clear that a large number of immediate and wider family are being supported by their wages. Although the study areas are suitable for subsistence agriculture, and people are not starving, the wages could be used to finance additional activities such as house-building and clothes purchases.

(Poultney and Spenceley, 2001:23)

UCOTA members, Uganda
Women traditionally spend their income on their children's education, health care and clothes. Some is kept for emergencies.

(Williams, White and Spenceley, 2001:16)

In most cases, regular wage-earners are relatively skilled and well educated (for example, they may know how to drive or be able to communicate in English), though they are still classified as 'poor'. Sometimes jobs are only available to those who are 'connected' (e.g. in Humla, Nepal). The less skilled and the poorer people do, however, gain casual employment. For example, in Humla, porters and horsemen tend to be landless and amongst the poorest people. Craft earners are clearly well-skilled in one domain, but may lack other marketable skills. They are often women (for example, women account for 65% of staff employed at Wilderness Safaris' lodges in South Africa) and are frequently from poorer groups. Many of these people have few other income-generating opportunities.

In principle, collective income benefits the community as a whole. However, inequality in the distribution of collective income and in participation in community decision making is noted as a common – though not universal – problem. Where public investments are made (such as in schools, water) the case studies do not explore how access to the benefits varies between groups within the community.

Our case studies demonstrated that overall the impact of PPT strategies is positive. At the local level:

- Although many of those involved often remain poor, they are better off than before. In particular, they are less vulnerable to hunger, for example, and better able to meet their daily needs. The PPT enterprises are therefore very important to these people.
- Some households, with a member in regular employment, earn enough to move from 'poor' to fairly 'secure'.
- Benefits are spread unevenly but widely across poor households: earnings accrue directly to a few, but are used to support a larger number of relatives or are re-spent locally, generating multipliers. Collective income and other livelihood benefits generally affect many more in the population.
- In a few cases whole communities can actually be said to have 'escaped' poverty through the impact of the PPT.

The increase in livelihood security comes from a *combination* of several elements including: increased regular wage income; opportunities for small income to fill gaps; business opportunities beyond agriculture; better access to markets, infrastructure and information, and financial assets; and the presence of an outside 'friend'.

The scale of benefits can be small in absolute terms from an outside perspective. And they can be small in relative terms, if dwarfed by benefits to the non-poor. Nevertheless from the perspective of the poor, they can be very significant (see Box 12.3). Indeed, where benefits are small because the destination is remote and tourism is highly inequitable (as in Humla), the significance of benefits to the poor can be all the greater.

Nevertheless, it is probably true that the small size of the PPT initiatives to date has meant that pro-poor tourism still generates a minor dent in national poverty even when multiplier effects are taken into account. Pro-poor tourism is not a panacea but is one contribution to the reduction of poverty in rural areas Tourism has the advantage that it brings a new market to marginal rural areas, within direct access of poor rural producers.

Conclusions

We noted above that pro-poor tourism is not a panacea. It is also clear that several critical factors can constrain progress and need to be addressed including:

- *Access of the poor to the market*: physical location, economic elites, social constraints on poor producers.
- *Commercial viability*: product quality and price, marketing, strength of the broader destination.
- *Policy framework*: land tenure, regulatory context, planning process, government attitude and capacity.
- *Implementation challenges in the local context*: filling the skills gap, managing costs and expectations, maximizing collaboration across stakeholders.

Box 12.3. Small but significant benefits.

Benefits can be small, in absolute or relative terms, but still valued by the poor. For example, the remoteness of Humla makes benefits small in national terms, but significant to those involved (who should amount to about 40% of the local population in the area concerned):

> The contribution of tourism is small relative to the more accessible areas of the country (e.g. Annapurna region etc). However, if revenue from tourism could be better trapped in Humla, instead of being concentrated with outside trekking agencies, the potential for benefits to Humla people is great, especially in view of the lack of alternatives available to improve livelihoods for people of Humla.
>
> (Saville, 2001:1)

Substantial benefits accruing to the non-poor are not necessarily an argument against investment, if the scale of benefits to the poor can still be increased. As the evaluator of a Community Tourism Programme in Tanzania summarized it:

> Of course, this small project will hardly bring about much change in the underlying conditions, e.g. in the unequal distribution of foreign exchange earnings from tourism . . . [but] people participating in the programme are not so much interested to know whether the major share from the tourism business continues to go to the mainstream entrepreneurs; what they are interested in is the small share which they can earn themselves in order to improve their livelihood and that of their families.
>
> (Studienkreis für Tourismus und Entwicklung (1999) cited in Cattarinich 2001:62)

Table 12.2 summarizes the key issues and their implications.

It is clear that PPT is relatively untried and untested, and there is no blueprint. 'Best practice' cannot yet be established and key challenges remain to be addressed. Nevertheless, lessons on 'good practice' emerge:

1. PPT needs a diversity of actions, from micro- to macro-level, including product development, marketing, planning, policy and investment. It goes well beyond community tourism.

2. A driving force for PPT is useful, but other stakeholders, with broader mandates, are critical. PPT can be incorporated into tourism development strategies of government or business (with or without explicit pro-poor language). Broader policy frameworks and initiatives outside tourism, such as on land tenure, small enterprise and representative government, are also key.

3. Location matters: PPT works best where the wider destination is developing well.

4. The poverty impact may be greater in remote areas, though tourism itself may be on a limited scale.

5. PPT strategies often involve the development of new products, particularly based on local culture. These should be integrated with mainstream products if they are to find markets.

6. Ensuring commercial viability is a priority. This requires close attention to demand, product quality, marketing, investment in business skills, and inclusion of the private sector.

7. Economic measures should expand both regular jobs and casual earning opportunities, while tackling both demand (e.g. markets) and supply (e.g. products of the poor).

8. Non-financial benefits (e.g. increased participation, access to assets) can reduce vulnerability; more could be done to address these.

9. PPT is a long-term investment. Expectations must be managed and short-term benefits developed in the interim.

10. External funding may be required and justified to cover the substantial transaction costs of establishing partnerships, developing skills, and revising policies (not generally for direct subsidies to enterprises).

If the PPT focus is to develop further, continued efforts to test out strategies, learn from experience and share findings are needed. It is important to work and develop knowledge with four particular constituencies:

1. Those who manage, plan, or influence tourism operations in poor countries of the South.

2. Those who are developing and promoting the 'sustainable tourism' agenda internationally.

Table 12.2. Critical issues and implications for PPT.

Issues		Implications
Market access	Strength of existing economic elites	Breaking in is not easy. *Government intervention, marketing links, intensive communication, profit motives and realism are needed.*
	Location of poor people	Poor people – and hence PPT products – are often in remote areas with poor infrastructure. *Investment in infrastructure – particularly roads and communications – may be needed to ensure viability.*
Commercial sustainability	Attractiveness and quality of product	Unattractive products do not sell and will threaten the commercial viability of an enterprise. *Involving the private sector in product development should help ensure that initiatives are commercially realistic.*
	Marketing	Marketing is critical if PPT is to compete in the crowded tourist product market. *Government or private sector support may be needed to develop effective links and marketing strategies.*
	Cost–benefit	PPT can be expensive, especially when transaction costs are included. Costs may exceed the capacity of a company, community, or even government tourism department to cover, making *external (donor?) funding important.*
Policy framework	Land tenure	Secure land tenure is important for attracting PPT investment. *Land rights need to be clarified before tourism development goes ahead.*
	Government attitudes	Government attitudes can be the driving force or the stumbling block for PPT. *Commitment is critical* but is not enough, on its own.
Implementation issues	Skills and capacity gap	Capacity building is likely to be an essential part of any PPT initiative. *Some form of external facilitation may be required.*
	Communication and collaboration	PPT is most effective when different stakeholders work together. *Investment in communication is required.*
	Meeting expectations	Mismatched expectations and benefits can kill initiatives. It is important to *deliver short-term benefits* while long-term schemes are developing.

3. Those implementing poverty reduction approaches in areas with tourism potential.
4. Those who help form opinions about effective strategies for poverty reduction.

Pro-poor tourism can make a difference to the poor and can 'tilt' the sector towards the poor, even if only at the margin. Mainstreaming a focus on poverty across the tourism industry in the South would be a formidable challenge. But, given the importance of tourism in many very poor areas, it is surely worth rising to this challenge.

Acknowledgement

The chapter is based on the results of case study research funded by the UK Department for International Development in 2000–2001, published in Ashley *et al.* (2001).

Notes

1. The World Travel and Tourism Council has estimated that 'tourism and general travel' accounts for 11% of world GDP (WTTC, 2001); even the more

conservative estimates of 6–7% imply that the resource transfers involved in tourism may have significant potential for the developing world (Page, 1999). With a high income elasticity, tourism is growing rapidly at a global level (c. 4% p.a.) and is increasing its share of total GDP.

2. See, for example, case studies coordinated by the Pro-Poor Tourism Team at http://www.propoortourism.org.uk.

3. And see also case studies analysed by Ashley et al. (2001), including: Poultney and Spenceley (2001), Nicanor (2001), Saville (2001), Mahoney and van Zyl (2001), Renard (2001), Williams et al. (2001), Braman and Fundación Acción Amazonia (2001).

4. While not highlighted in the PPT case studies, this has emerged strongly in other work in Namibia and South Africa.

5. As micro-enterprises (commercial or community-based) and sole traders.

References

Ashley, C., Roe, D. and Goodwin, H. (2001) *Pro-Poor Tourism Strategies: Making Tourism Work for the Poor*. ODI, IIED and CRT, London.

Braman, S. and Fundación Acción Amazonia (2001) *Practical Strategies for Pro-Poor Tourism. Tropic Ecological Adventures – Ecuador*. PPT Discussion Paper No. 6. ODI, IIED and CRT, London.

Cattarinich, X. (2001) *Pro-Poor Tourism Initiatives in Developing Countries: Analysis of Secondary Case Studies*. PPT Discussion Paper No. 8, ODI, IIED and CRT, London.

Goudie, A. and Ladd, P. (1999) Economic growth, poverty and inequality. *Journal of International Development* 11, 177–195.

Mahoney, K. and van Zyl, J. (2001) *Practical Strategies for Pro-Poor Tourism: Case Studies of Makuleke and Manyeleti Tourism Initiatives: South Africa*. PPT Discussion Paper No. 2. ODI, IIED and CRT, London.

McKay, A. (1997) Poverty reduction through economic growth: some issues. *Journal of International Development* 9(4), 665–673.

Nicanor, N. (2001) *Practical Strategies for Pro-Poor Tourism: Nacobta, the Namibian Case Study*. PPT Discussion Paper No. 4. ODI, IIED and CRT, London.

Page, S. (1999) *Tourism and Development: the Evidence from Mauritius, South Africa and Zimbabwe*. ODI, London.

Poultney, C. and Spenceley, A. (2001) *Practical Strategies for Pro-Poor Tourism, Wilderness Safaris South Africa: Rocktail Bay and Ndumu Lodge*. PPT Discussion Paper No. 1. ODI, IIED and CRT, London.

Ravallion, M. (1997) Good and bad growth: the human development reports. *World Development* 25(5), 631–638.

Renard, Y. (2001) *Practical Strategies for Pro-Poor Tourism: a Case Study of the St. Lucia Heritage Tourism Programme*. PPT Discussion Paper No. 7. ODI, IIED and CRT, London.

Saville, N. (2001) *Practical Strategies for Pro-Poor Tourism: Case Study of Pro-Poor Tourism and SNV in Humla District, West Nepal*. PPT Discussion Paper No. 3. ODI, IIED and CRT, London.

Studienkreis für Tourismus und Entwicklung (1999) Evaluation of a winning project under the To Do scheme, awarded for Socially Responsible Tourism, www.studienkreis.org/eng/wettbeweerbe/todo/main_welt.html (accessed 5 May 2000).

United Nations (2000) *55/2. United Nations Millennium Declaration*, http://www.un.org/millennium/declaration/ares552e.htm (accessed 6 November 2003).

Williams, E., White, A. and Spenceley, A. (2001) *UCOTA: The Uganda Community Tourism Association: A Comparison with NACOBTA*. PPT Discussion Paper No. 5. ODI, IIED and CRT, London.

World Bank (2000) *Attacking Poverty: World Development Report 2000/01*. Oxford University Press, Oxford.

World Bank (2001) *World Development Indicators*. World Bank, Washington, DC.

WTTC (2001) *WTTC Economic Research: Country League Tables*. World Travel and Tourism Council, London.

13 Tourism for the Young-old and Old-old

Megan Cleaver Sellick[1] and Thomas E. Muller[2]

[1]Central Washington University, College of Business, 400 E. 8th Avenue, Ellensburg, WA 98926-7485, USA; [2]Griffith University, PO Box 905, Runaway Bay, QLD 4216, Australia

Novelty Tourism for the Young at Heart

The climb to the summit of Mt Kilimanjaro, a 5896-metre volcanic peak, is a non-technical climb, in that no crampons, ropes or ice axes are required. The mountain lies close to the equator, in Tanzania, thereby adding an element of exotic foreignness to its geographical location in East Africa. The porters who carry the climbers' gear up the mountain are from the Chagga tribe of Tanzania, and they add to the experience of 'mixing with the natives' and arouse curiosity in the travel setting. Between 2000 and 2002, about 15,000 people trudged up this mountain annually. Since the number of tourists who climbed Mt Kilimanjaro in 1988 was 10,764, it is clear that the hard-adventure of climbing such a mountain is a growing trend in novelty-seeking. There is an element of danger in the attempt to scale this volcano. Just 40% of climbers who attempt Kilimanjaro ever reach the summit and, each year, about ten people die trying.

Picture in your mind a group of climbers attempting Africa's highest peak, Mt Kilimanjaro. Create an image of the people enjoying this hard-adventure challenge, and then ask yourself, 'What age are they?' It is usual to associate the exertion required for mountain climbing with youth, therefore a group of young people will have most probably come to your mind. In fact, many of the climbers who attempt the adventure of scaling Mt Kilimanjaro are aged in their fifties, sixties, or older. Thus, the conundrum of novelty travel and older travellers becomes apparent. A novel travel activity, such as mountain climbing, is worthy of novelty tourism discussion in itself (which various chapters within this book provide), yet the involvement of an aged person creates a further element of curiosity. This latter dimension is this chapter's focus – novelty travel for senior travellers.

Let us now consider a soft-adventure activity, scuba diving. Contrary to popular belief, scuba diving is not a dangerous activity; in fact, statistically, it is quite safe. This activity does not require physical exertion, and it can be relaxing because the buoyancy of salt water neutralizes the pull of gravity underwater. Scuba diving can be mastered very quickly; the necessary equipment can be readily hired from the dive centre at the operational end of the product; and the best diving sites are in the tropical, warm waters of the Pacific – in locations like the Great Barrier Reef, the Hawaiian Islands, Micronesia, Melanesia, Polynesia, and Australian, New Zealand and US territories in the Equatorial or South Pacific. Yet, scuba diving is a largely untapped potential novelty tourism activity for the soft-adventure-prone senior traveller segment.

These two examples of novelty travel represent emerging trends among travelling seniors as well as opportunities for travel and tourism operators. One is an illustration of the attractiveness of hard-adventure – in the form of climbing Mt Kilimanjaro; the second is an example of soft-adventure tourism – namely scuba diving in the warm tropical regions of the globe. Both examples represent high-quality experiences, which are also authentic in that they cannot be faked or simulated. Both are good examples of curiosity-satisfying experiences that meet the desire for novelty, and give some idea of the potential for developing and marketing novelty tourism designed for senior travellers.

The thesis of this chapter challenges the stereotypes demonstrated above by addressing novelty-seeking as a motive for travel that transcends demographic characteristics, in particular age. Both novelty- and age-related travel are discussed with various examples provided to demonstrate the interwoven characteristics within the two travel segments. The aim of this chapter is to demonstrate that novelty tourism operators cannot ignore the senior traveller. There are six steps outlined to encourage and guide the development of travel and tourism services that explore the opportunities and meet the challenges of the senior traveller who is interested in novelty tourism.

The Era of the Senior Tourist

To clarify the definition of a 'senior', researchers commonly delineate seniors as those who are 50 years of age or older (Bartos, 1983; Cleaver, 2001; Lewis, 1996; Ostroff, 1989; Silvers, 1997). Similarly, the America Association of Retired Persons within the USA (the largest seniors' organization in the world), and their Australian equivalent, the National Seniors Association, define their membership by including only those 50 years or older.

The Centre for Strategic and International Studies (2000) describes global ageing as the challenge of the new millennium. The United Nations concurred, declaring 1999 the International Year of Older Persons. Most Western nations – and many developed nations in the East, such as Japan – face the challenge of a rapidly ageing population (United Nations, 1997). For most of human history, the elderly

have never represented more than 2–3% of the population. By 1985, the proportion of the elderly in the developed world had swelled to 13%, and the arrival of the 21st century brought this sobering statistic: two-thirds of all the elderly who have ever lived on this planet are still alive today. By the year 2025, the elderly will represent a very significant proportion of a nation's entire population (examples: 21% of Australians and New Zealanders, 24% of Americans and Canadians, and 26% of Japanese). These nations demonstrate a steadily growing proportion of people who are leading longer, healthier and more productive lives than was the case in the past.

The staggering change in the population age structures of developed countries – and the increase in the proportion of older citizens – herald an enormous opportunity. Seniors, long ignored by a youth-obsessed Western culture (Dychtwald, 1997), are capturing the attention of product manufacturers and service providers and are beginning to lose the title of 'invisible consumers' (Bartos, 1983). Even in the Far East, the stereotypical view is that age is venerated and respected, but efforts to maintain youth by keeping physically fit, eating healthily and seeking preventative medical care are becoming global and may reflect 'the adoption of an ageless society' (Barak et al., 2001).

Within the international tourism industry the 'era of the senior tourist' has well and truly arrived. The importance of this oft-forgotten group of travellers is swelling as seniors continue to travel, while the international tourism industry strives to recover from the knock-on effects of the events of 11 September 2001. The Wall Street Journal indicated that despite the recent massive downturn in tourism, 'seniors are a surprising bright spot for the travel industry' (Bhatia, 2003: W5).

By and large, this older segment of the population is still relatively healthy, mobile, mentally and physically active, and is projected to live longer than previous generations (Moschis et al., 1997). Also, senior tourists often have the financial resources to spend on tourism, since they commonly already own all the major consumer products they need. Thus, many seniors have the desire and financial means to travel for pleasure, curiosity, discovery, learning and, if sought, novelty.

Novelty Tourism

Novelty is a motive for travel and thus an important component of tourism management (Crompton, 1979; Dann, 1981). Much research of travel motivation has concentrated on the desire to experience novelty, whether it is a novel destination, novel activities and/or novel experiences (Cohen, 1972; Crompton, 1979; Oh *et al.*, 1995). Travel decisions are made by weighing travellers' conflicting needs for psychological security and novelty (Crotts, 1993), thus the degree of novelty motivation varies for each individual (Cohen, 1984). Tourists can be classified into four types: *organized mass tourist*, *individual mass tourist*, *explorer* and *drifter*. These four types of tourists can be differentiated by the amount of novelty they seek with their travel choices. An organized mass tourist seeks familiarity, therefore they are the least likely to be influenced by novelty in their travel decisions, while drifters are novelty-seekers (Cohen, 1972).

A population segment that is not often associated with novelty tourism is seniors. The stereotypical view of a tour-bus filled with aged citizens moving from one well-established destination to the next may be the polar opposite of the definition of 'novelty tourism'. A large sample (2730 respondents) of tourists to Alaska was segmented into organized mass tourists (approximately 54% of the sample); individualized mass tourists (20%); and explorers (26%; Snepenger, 1987). The average age of each novelty-seeking segment indicated an inverse relationship with age; that is, the older a person, the less novelty-seeking their segment membership. The use of age groups rather than actual ages may have magnified the differences between groups. For example, the average age group of organized mass tourists and individual mass tourists was 45–54 years and the average age group of the explorer group was 35–44 years. But if the older group actual average age was 46 years and the 'younger' explorer group average age was 43 years, this 'difference' takes on a new perspective, or perhaps disappears altogether.

More recently, Basala and Klenosky (2001) divided a sample of 325 respondents into three groups: *familiarity seekers*, *average travellers* and *novelty seekers*. No significant difference was found within the dispersion of senior respondents (measured in two groups: 55–65 years; and 66 years and older) across the three travel motive segments, indicating that age has no bearing on whether a person seeks familiarity or novelty when they travel. This finding supports what travel professionals have always understood, but are only now applying to the senior market: people's values are shaped by their life experiences; thus the experiences of one person's life, rather than their age, shape the way they live. Thus, a person who has enjoyed active travel throughout their life is not about to become more staid because the clock has ticked by and they now fit into a category that someone else has labelled 'old,' 'senior' or whatever politically correct title the industry currently uses to describe those who are most often seen as a less-important market. The idea of a service provider stopping a service based on the arrival of an American Association of Retired Persons card, or the like, is nonsensical. For example, the ageing of an avid hiker may change the length or the challenge of the hikes over time, but the hiker will continue to hike, just as the skier will continue to ski and the scuba diver will continue to scuba dive.

A comparable study of 150 Singaporean overseas travellers explored novelty-seeking behaviour (Keng and Cheng, 1999). Four clusters were explored: *culture dissimilarity seekers*, *destination novelty seekers*, *novelty seekers* and *familiarity seekers*. When age was considered, a significant difference was found between the four age groups (29 years and younger; 30–39 years; 40–49 years; and 50 years and older) and their membership within the four novelty classifications. Within the 50 years and older age group there were more familiarity seekers and culture dissimilarity seekers. While there were mature-aged respondents placed in both the destination novelty seekers and novelty seekers segments, there was no clear pattern indicating that older travellers were less likely to seek novelty. In fact, the age group with the highest proportion within familiarity seekers was the 30–39-year-olds. Similarly, three clusters, namely *sports seekers*, *novelty seekers* and *family/relaxation seekers* were uncovered in a sample of 1194 Japanese visitors to Canada and the

USA. The novelty-seekers had the largest proportion of the 50 to 59-year-old and the 60+
age groups (Cha *et al.*, 1995).

Issues of Age and Ageing

Issues of ageing can be divided into three inter-
related sources: *physiological*; *psychological*;
and *sociological*. The physiological changes
include appearance and physical mobility, which
are caused by a decline in internal organ functioning and in body systems, including the muscles and bones and cardiovascular, nervous,
immune and reproductive systems (Bee, 1992).
While physiological ageing describes the decline
occurring from the passage of life, psychological
development has a more positive connotation
(Perlmutter, 1988). Adulthood encompasses the
psychological desire for intimacy, generativity
(establishing and guiding the next generation),
and – in late life (65 years and older) – ego-
integrity, or the acceptance of oneself (Erikson,
1978). Finally, sociological aspects of ageing
acknowledge the importance of the external
social environment on the human ageing
process. The combination and interrelationship
of these three aspects of ageing – physiological,
psychological and sociological – each contribute
to 'successful ageing'.

While the combination of physiological,
psychological and sociological effects of ageing
determine how successfully a person ages, the
development of values and beliefs about ageing
begins with individuals' views of their own
ageing. This perspective revolves around a
socially defined view of ageing, reflecting the
commonly held beliefs of individuals. Age –
representing the number of years since birth –
was strongly associated within Western society
with certain activities and behaviours, i.e. a
person's actual age and the activities in their life
were closely related. 'School age', for example,
reflects the period children spend at school,
which chronologically develops towards university, or college, and then marriage, children,
grandchildren, etc. Each stage of life was associated with an age range that depicted a socially
accepted timeline of life (Erikson, 1978;
Levinson *et al.*, 1978). The lifestyle marketing
model (Silvers, 1997) labels *early adulthood* as
18–34 years, which encompasses moving out

of home, first job, first marriage, and the
birth of the first child. *Middle adulthood*
(35–49 years) includes life-stages such as the
empty nest, mid-life crises, divorce and career
change. *Late adulthood* (50 years and above)
includes life-stages such as empty nest, retirement and widowhood.

The recent relaxation in the time-defini-
tions of this 'social clock' (Neugarten, 1976)
demonstrate a move away from clearly defined
stages of life and the acceptance of a more fluid
cycle of life (Neugarten and Neugarten, 1986).
Activities such as returning to education later in
life or starting a second family at an older age
reflect the changing circumstances in people's
lives. This demonstrates that the definition of
what is socially acceptable evolves as individuals' circumstances change; in other words, individuals' subjective views of their personal
circumstances collectively drive society's view
of what is socially acceptable. As people's lives
deviate from the accepted timeline by missing
the key age milestones (e.g. unmarried at 30 or
still working at 70), greater numbers of personal deviations have led to greater societal
leniency in age life-stage markers.

The 'success' of a person's ageing can
only be evaluated by the individual against his
or her own criteria for successful ageing, whatever that may encompass. These personally
held meanings of age and ageing are developed
through interaction with the environment and
are actualized in the individual's behaviour
(Russell, 1981). The age of 50 may be more
widely acknowledged as a midpoint of the lifespan rather than an endpoint (Silvers, 1997),
therefore the view of 'old age' is changing. For
example, 'baby boomers' classify 79 years as
the age when they will consider themselves
'old,' while they considered their parents as
'old' at 50 years (Dychtwald, 1997). Subsequently, the gerontological literature has
warned against using age as a predictor of attitudes and behaviours of the elderly (Norman *et
al.*, 2001).

Of course, non-Western cultures are commonly thought to have varying levels of societal
respect dependent on age. For example, ori-
ental cultures have deeply ingrained connotations of wisdom, mastery, privilege and
precedence based on age (Muller and O'Cass,
2001). Thus, the societal views of age are

somewhat culturally specific. However, recent research is providing evidence that individuals in the USA, Europe, Asia (in particular, India, China and Korea) and Nigeria as a representation of African nations, all have similar perceptions about their age (Barak *et al.*, 2003).

A subjective view of age and its influence over behaviour invites consideration of the construct of cognitive age. Cognitive age divulges how old a person feels, irrespective of chronological age (Blau, 1956; George *et al.*, 1980; Wylie, 1974). A person's cognitive age could be quite independent of his or her actual age. As people grow older, in mid-life and beyond, the gap between cognitive age and chronological age tends to widen, with people reporting that they feel younger than their actual ages (Hubley and Hultsch, 1994; Kastenbaum *et al.*, 1972). Middle-aged adults place their self-perceived ages at between 5 and 15 years younger than their chronological ages and more than half of all adults aged over 60 feel between 16 and 17 years younger (Underhill and Cadwell, 1983).

The demarcation of actual age and cognitive age emphasizes the difference between the socially defined attitudes of age – and a more personal, or subjective, view. It has been argued that the subjective view of ageing more accurately represents a person's age than the chronological measurement of their years alive (Tornstram, 1989). Therefore, both in research and application, factors that an individual believes to be important should supersede the predetermined age-related issues of importance, since the personal and subjective factors dictate choices and behaviour (Neugarten, 1980; Wolfe, 1997). Travel and tourism marketers are wise to recognize the way in which senior vacationers view themselves. Seniors who are young-at-heart are usually in better health, seek fun and enjoyment in life, travel for physical stimulation and a sense of accomplishment, and have higher expectations of a vacation, which in turn makes them more prone to disappointment when travel does not satisfy their needs (Muller and O'Cass, 2001). These factors indicate that cognitively younger or 'young-at-heart' seniors are a prime market for novelty-tourism operators – although they are demanding customers – ensuring that this market must be thoroughly understood to

ensure the joint rewards of the senior traveller's satisfaction and the operator's success.

A New Perspective of Age

Two complementary changes within current society may encourage a new perspective of ageing. The longer lifespan and greater numbers of seniors who are educated, healthy and self-sufficient members of society, coupled with the fact that they view themselves not by chronological age but by cognitive age, may encourage rejection of the traditional view of life as an older person. Older people most often do not define themselves by their age, nor do they think of themselves as old (Kaufman, 1993). Moreover, contributions from older people within all facets of society will be required if countries are to maintain or improve their standards of living and economic security. This combination of a large number of seniors expecting greater integration in society than was afforded their predecessors and the economic and social pressures to harness a greater contribution from seniors may be a catalyst for a changed view of ageing, encompassing a less negative view of the later stages of life.

Positive ageing reflects an impetus to increase the quality of life of seniors by providing opportunities for participation, learning, recreation and cultural pursuits (Pfeffer and Green, 1997). Lloyd and Auld (2002: 43) found that:

> people who engage in social activities more frequently and who are more satisfied with the psychological benefits they derive from leisure, experience higher levels of perceived quality of life.

Thus, greater opportunities for older people to participate in society, including leisure outlets such as travel, must be provided (Edgar, 1991). The Australian Federal and State governments are encouraging such opportunities for seniors with the Seniors Card programme. Apart from providing discounts on goods and services, the card also represents the government and community's recognition of the social and economic contribution of seniors, and extends an invitation to seniors to participate in community life (Pfeffer and Green, 1997). Programmes such as this help society's values, beliefs and attitudes evolve to accommodate greater formal participation by older adults (Russell, 1981) and view seniors' general integration into society as a societal opportunity.

Societal views that classify seniors as non-contributing members of society require realignment with current-day actualities. Members of the senior boom are better educated, healthier, better housed and more self-sufficient than any previous generation (Edgar, 1991). Data on the self-rated health of seniors – measured by the Australian Bureau of Statistics as persons aged 65 years or older – indicated that 63% of men and 65% of women assessed their health as either good, very good or excellent (McLennan, 1999a). In addition, seniors spend approximately 45.2 hours per week on recreation and leisure, in comparison with younger people who average 29.5 hours a week (McLennan, 1999b). For example, within the year prior to June 1999, 42% of older men and 33% of older women participated in a sport or physical activity (Australian Bureau of Statistics, 1999). Better health and fitness and greater emphasis on recreation are just the tip of the iceberg in relation to the reinvention of the later stages of life. Thus, the seniors of today are the catalysts for a new perspective of ageing.

The travel industry, and in particular markets related to novelty travel, should not ignore the senior market, for physiological, psychological and sociological stereotypes do not fit this market, and instead, a large, financially secure market exists, waiting for astute marketing professionals to produce and promote travel opportunities to them. All types of travel offer a sense of purpose 'thereby enhancing sentiments of self-worth, self-identity and overall life satisfaction' (Dann, 2001: 11). Therefore, the profit potential of offering products to this age segment is coupled with the rewards of offering socially responsible products and services that benefit the physical and mental health of the senior traveller, and may also represent significant savings in the provision of health services to the older segments of society (Dann, 2001).

For example, the potential of educational scuba diving for older adults is almost entirely untapped. For one thing, there is an opportu-nity to sensitize the public to the plight of ecologically sensitive coral reefs and marine life. Thus, developing travel options to dive in waters designated as conservation areas, accompanied by biologists and naturalists, combines ecotourism with novelty. Also, educational scuba diving opens up the opportunity of exploring sites that have historical significance. The relatively shallow parts of the South Pacific are littered with the sunken navies of Imperial Japan, the USA, Australia and New Zealand. Many of these naval vessel graveyards are well within safe diving depths, hence the opportunity to visit them with historians and marine archaeologists serving as guides.

An enterprising tourism operator can increase the potential of this type of educational and novel travel by sponsoring the engineering and development of compressed-air tanks that not only contain oxygen-enriched air (nitrox) – which makes diving much less tiring – but that are much smaller, and therefore lighter, when worn by the diver out of the water. The size and weight to aim for would be those of oxygen bottles used by high-altitude mountain climbers in the Himalayas considering the strength and/or confidence issues that may be problematic to some senior travellers. This demonstrates the type of necessary changes required to provide products and services that fulfil the needs of senior tourists.

Taking the Right Approach with Senior Travellers: Best-practice Strategies

The proposed strategies and recommended tactics are adapted from a list of 11 strategies aimed at tourism operators interested in offering tourism products and services to the explorer and adventure segments of the post-World-War II baby boom generation in the CANZUS nations (Canada, Australia, New Zealand and the USA; Muller and Cleaver, 2000). Outlined and discussed below are a reduced number of steps (six in total), modified to the issues of senior travellers in general and novelty tourism, in particular. However, as the practitioner gains experience in both targeting the senior traveller market and developing novelty tourism products for this market, these steps will require refinement over time.

Step 1: Using lifestyle survey data

Practitioners would be wise to subscribe to a syndicated research service that conducts periodic lifestyle surveys in the population and supplies data on vacation travel. Such reports must provide breakdowns by age, preferably year of birth, as well as a selection of other demographic variables and lifestyle and vacation measures deemed most beneficial to the practitioner's clientele.

Much research focuses on traditional descriptions of senior travel behaviour, such as Blazey's (1992) identification of seniors' preference for passive and relaxing activities while travelling. The same study also identified lack of interest in travel as a key constraint to travel within the senior population aged 50 or older. Seniors use travel as a vehicle to learn about themselves, and about the world around them (Muller and Strickland, 1995). Muller (1995) identified both adult education and travel as areas of growth as the population ages, thus those activities which seek to combine the activities of travel and education have seen growth, and continue to grow and diversify to ensure coverage of those activities and destinations that the powerful and large older segments of the population demand. In Singapore the impending retirement boom represents a silver lining for the travel industry (Lum, 2002). Two types of travellers have been identified: *mainstream*, who visit the usual destinations, and the *adventurous*, who have usually been travelling for some time and are more likely to have higher education levels. These 'adventurous' Singaporean travellers may be a potential market segment for novelty travel products.

Japanese travel agencies are beginning to focus their marketing skills at seniors acknowledging that those within, or entering, retirement are eager to 'satisfy their intellectual curiosity' by travelling (*Japan Economic Newswire*, 2002). However, retirement is not a catalyst for travel (Blazey, 1992). Instead, travellers continue to travel, once they retire, while those who were not already travellers continue to refrain from travel. The movement away from work environment goals to a leisure context within retirement is a positive development with age, according to Atchley's (1972, 1989) continuity theory. The continuation of

motivation to achieve goals, regardless of a change in goals, is a key to successful ageing.

Commercial firms that track lifestyle patterns use established measures of values, activities, attitudes, interests and opinions, and later apply algorithms to identify individual consumers by lifestyle group membership. Segmentation within the tourism industry is not new, including segmentation of the older segments of the travel market. Segmentation requires identification of the segment; clear division between segments; reasons behind each segment's consumer choices and a means of reaching the segment (Mathur *et al.*, 1998). Segment membership will have an impact on consumption behaviour, including preferences for products and services, information needs, patronage motives, industry and advertising perspectives (Moschis, 1996). For example, SRI's VALS2 is a psychographic segmentation programme that was introduced in 1978 and revised in 1989. The programme segments American adults into eight distinctive value and lifestyle patterns based on respondents' self-orientation and resources (Hawkins *et al.*, 2001). A Japanese version of VALS is also now available (SRI International, 2001).

The new-age elderly (Schiffman and Sherman, 1991) are segmented based on a value-orientation approach that is argued to be superior to age-based segmentation (Mathur *et al.*, 1998). When segmenting seniors aged 55 years or older, the new-age elderly were distinguished by their state of mind, younger outlook, self-confidence and willingness to accept change (Mathur *et al.*, 1998). The new-age elderly may indicate a move towards an ageless market (Schiffman and Sherman, 1991) and offer promising marketing opportunities for the travel and tourism industry, including novelty travel products.

The concept of gerontographics (Moschis, 1996) is similar to psychographics or lifestyle segmentation, but focuses on the needs, attitudes, lifestyles and behaviour of older adults. Gerontographics identified four senior segments: *healthy indulgers* are settled within their careers, have high financial capabilities, enjoy life and have not experienced life events such as retirement and widowhood that are acknowledged to change a person's perspective; *healthy hermits* have experienced life events which have altered their self-concept and forced withdrawal from society; *ailing outgoers* maintain a positive self-image, despite their ailments, and aim to get the most out of life; and *frail recluses* have accepted old age and largely behave in a manner which they believe reflects their stage of life (Moschis, 1996).

The four older consumer segments described above allow marketers to design strategies to meet a segment's unique needs. Within the travel and tourism industry, healthy indulgers are the most financially secure segment and are most likely to be still coupled; therefore overseas travel, and perhaps cruises, for either short or extended time periods may be of interest to this segment. Ailing outgoers, on the other hand, are positive about life and are likely to be interested in travel, although they suffer from some ailments that may encourage them to stay closer to home when they choose travel destinations (Moschis, 1996). Both these segments may be lucrative for novelty travel operators to explore further.

It is far more cost-effective for the practitioner to subscribe to a lifestyle survey data service than to design and carry out lifestyle surveys in-house. Similarly, if data on very specific vacation habits, in particular novelty travel activities, are needed for marketing strategy, questions will need to be formulated to capture these and added (at relatively low cost) to an established omnibus lifestyle survey that serves many cost-sharing clients.

Step 2: Compiling travel profiles of the segments

Make sure to request from the syndicated data service specific reports that give detailed breakdowns by both lifestyle segment and vacation consumption behaviour. Use these data to compile a travel profile of each segment, paying attention to which variables reveal a tendency to experience (or an interest in) novelty travel.

Research within the senior market has recently heavily focused on travel motives (Backman *et al.*, 1999; Cleaver *et al.*, 1999) based on the assumption that recreational travel behaviour is related to need satisfaction

(Gilbert, 1991; Mill and Morrison, 1985; Pitts and Woodside, 1986). The motivation to travel often comes from long-term psychological needs and life plans and, with older age, needs such as self-actualization become increasingly important as a travel motivator (Cohen, 1989). The *hierarchy of needs* (Maslow, 1970) indicates that higher-order needs, such as self-esteem and self-actualization, become the focus for older people who have accomplished lower-order survival and relationship needs.

The *travel career ladder* (Pearce, 1988, 1993) details the motivation to travel and travel behaviour through a travel career based on Maslow's (1970) hierarchy of needs. The travel career model incorporates both internal and external motivations and records any changes in these as the travellers age. The travel career can be linked to age, since with growing travel experience one is also getting older. Lower-order need attainment (rest and relaxation, family travel needs) are usually the prime motivation in early adulthood. The reason for travel changes as the person gets older and higher-order need attainment become the goal, while travel constraints lessen. The only caveat is that higher-order travel needs are attained only by experienced travellers who have graduated from lower-order travel need accomplishment; therefore travel motives may be influenced by not only age, but travel experience as well.

Four major travel-motive segments are *discovery and self-enhancement*, *enthusiastic connectors*, *reluctant travellers* and *nostalgic travellers* (Cleaver, 2001). These travel-motives emerged from a large sample of Australian seniors and the labels capture the key travel motives of each group. For example, enthusiastic connectors tended to rate most motives for travel quite highly, indicating their overall enthusiasm for travel, but the highest-rated motives were those which enable relationships with others. Also, nostalgia is a travel motive shared by many senior travellers; the same is true of discovery (Cleaver Sellick, 2004). While novelty-seeking was not explicitly measured in this study, it appears that three of the four segments, reluctant travellers aside, demonstrate travel motives that could coincide with novelty tourism products. In particular, nostalgic excursions into a selective past may enhance senior travellers' quality of life, otherwise referred to as life satisfaction (Dann, 2001).

In another study of the Australian senior population, the travel behaviour of six predefined segments (conservatives, pioneers, Aussies, big spenders, indulgers and enthusiasts) were analysed (Horneman et al., 2002). Conservatives prefer reliable package tours that cover all the best tourist locations. They prefer to stay in resorts where everything is included and visit historic sites and return to familiar places. On the other hand, pioneers favour places where tourists rarely go, avoiding commercial sites. Pioneers are individual, inner-directed and are often committed environmentalists and conservationists. This segment coincides with the discovery and self-enhancement segment identified by Cleaver (2001) and the explorer and/or drifter novelty-seeking categories identified by Cohen (1972), and may offer the most appeal to novelty tourism operators.

Step 3: Generating product concepts

It is wise to tentatively select one or more lifestyle segments as a target market, and generate tourism product ideas that would probably appeal to the target market(s). The goal here is using a formal idea-generating process (such as brainstorming) to arrive at the concrete description of several new tourism products. Compiling behavioural data is a helpful exercise in achieving this goal.

Active or adventure travel is the fastest growing segment of the travel market (Morris, 1999). Furthermore, adventure is a travel motive for many seniors. Saga Holidays specialize in adventure travel for seniors (who must be aged over 50, although their travel partner may be aged over 40). Exotic locations and adventurous activities are aplenty, including Kenyan safari in hotels, lodges and tented camps, cycling tours of Vietnam, travel throughout the Nepalese jungle, as well as rafting in Borneo. Themed travel is also popular, such as 'Trailblazing in the Old West', where tourists live like a cowboy, horseback riding and target shooting (*Western Mail*, 2003).

This type of tourism is characterized by its ability to provide the tourist with relatively high levels of sensory stimulation, usually achieved by including physically challenging experiential components within the (typically short) touristic experience. The experience itself is physically bracing, 'adrenaline-driven', somewhat risky, with moments of exhilaration punctuated by many opportunities to assess and reassess what has just been done or accomplished. Examples are trips taken to participate in white-water rafting, horse riding or hiking in remote, often rugged, locations endowed with natural beauty, scuba diving or snorkelling, mountain-biking, backpacking and camping, photo safaris, helicopter skiing, hot-air ballooning, and so forth. Given that the degree of adventure offered and experienced varies widely, the industry distinguishes soft-adventure and hard-adventure tourism (Travel Industry Association of America, 1998a,b). At the more benign end of the adventure continuum are soft-adventure activities such as bird-watching; while at the other extreme is the hard-adventure category. One might include the scaling of Mt Everest as a paying client on a guided expedition, where the adventure tourist risks the very real possibility of death within this hard-adventure category. New Zealand tourism marketers have been especially innovative and astute in developing hard-adventure tourism products and promoting them internationally. New Zealand is attributed with the invention of bungee jumping, black-water rafting, and zorbing, demonstrating a model of innovative thinking for exploiting the potential of that country's vast supply and variety of natural tourism resources.

Alternatively, in *discovery travel*, the emphasis is much less on physical thrill and challenge than on mental stimulation and mind-broadening experiences. Key characteristics of this tourism category are that the trip, voyage or journey provides the traveller with opportunities for learning, discovery and personal growth. Typically, the travel experience is somewhat lengthier than in adventure travel and contains elements that offer self-enrichment via exposure to novel places, novel cultures, novel activities and a requirement for the traveller to immerse him/herself in the learning environment provided by the tourism product. Designed properly, this type of tourism allows the participant to contribute to the experience. Examples include educational expeditions to an archaeological site (even participating in an archaeological dig), visits to wineries, castles, manufacturing plants, wildlife sanctuaries or Neolithic worship sites, accompanied by experts; speciality cruises led by scientist-guides to observe a solar eclipse or a penguin hatchery in the Antarctic; educational retreats or study holidays to observe or learn from an artist; and trips to a radically different culture to observe and interact with the natives.

Step 4: Assessing resources and competitive strengths

An audit of touristic resources and strengths available to the organization (transport agreements, accommodation arrangements, knowledge of the destination, experience with the touristic theme or product type, etc.), including resources available through links with other elements within the industry or community, is required. For example, if the new tourism concept is a nature-oriented experience combined with learning, there is access to learning institutions that make available experts in a particular field of research or knowledge.

Pioneers in the development and marketing of educational travel experiences and discovery tourism products for active mature adults are ElderTreks in Canada (Muller and Strickland, 1995); U3A, University of the Third Age (Hort and Strickland, 1995); Australian and New Zealand College for Seniors (1999); and Elderhostel (1999) in the USA. This category of tourism product had its initial development in the tourism market of retirees and senior travellers who have more leisure time than the typically busy, working senior does. However, educational travel is expected to become even more important when CANZUS baby boomers (M. Cleaver Sellick and T.E. Muller, unpublished) become the bulk of the older age categories within their respective countries. Similarly, the potential for discovery travel in the 21st century is even greater, as ageing baby boomers approach and enter their retirement years and they switch emphasis from work to leisure. Correspondingly, economic goals will be replaced by a less materialistic, more self-fulfilling search for meaning in life (Muller, 1995).

ElderHostel (Goggin, 1999; Perkins, 2000) is an international concern that develops programmes based on travel research of the aged featuring a combination of leisure and learning through a travel experience. Elderhostel's initial offering of five programmes to 220 participants, in 1975, now incorporates 270,000 hostellers signing up for 10,000 programmes in 1999 (Elderhostel, 1999). Comparable to Elderhostel, Odyssey Ed-ventures (2003) pitches that 'travel is not merely meant as a pleasant diversion, but an opportunity to broaden your knowledge, increase understanding and enrich your life' and provide educational programmes for senior travellers.

An innovative tour company, Grandtravel, has utilized a team of teachers, psychologists and leisure counsellors to develop tour destination and activities which grandparents can enjoy with their grandchildren (Moldofsky, 2001). These intergenerational tours allow grandparents and their grandchildren to spend more time together and share experiences, as well as allowing seniors to develop by guiding younger generations. Furthermore, this novel aspect of travel can have positive effects on attitudes of one group toward another due to the positive social climate. Leitner's (1999a) research examined intergenerational travel by Jewish and Arab communities in Tel Aviv-Yafo in Israel which produced the added reward of greater inter-racial understanding, promoting peaceful relations and reducing prejudice. Alternately, nude recreation in the USA has begun to lose its stigma. Research indicates that 30% of participants are aged 55 years or older, and 25% visit with friends and family members, indicating intergenerational participation (Razzouk and Seitz, 2003).

Step 5: Testing the selected concepts

To test the selected concepts, ensure that several waves of focus-group interviews are conducted on individuals drawn from the intended target market. The syndicated research supplier can identify and recruit the participants for these focus groups. Refine the concepts following the focus-group interview findings, and put the tourism components together as a product to be marketed.

It is crucial to be aware of other variables beside travel motives that influence travel decisions, such as travel risk and constraints, and type of travel. Just because a senior is motivated by the need to learn and discover a new activity, such as fly-fishing, it does not automatically follow that a fly-fishing holiday will occur. There are a number of factors that prevent a person from acting on travel motives. The factors that may be barriers or constraints to older travellers include limitation in external resources, such as equipment, information and money; lack of time; fear of lack of approval by others; lack of abilities necessary to participate and the social network to encourage development of these new skills; and limitations due to physical well-being (McGuire, 1984). Often, seniors require unique physical infrastructure and service personnel, as well as specific itinerary preparation (Gay, 1999; Leitner, 1999b), support for both low-functioning travellers and their spouses (Leitner, 1999b); and health-insurance services (Grabowski, 1999) to enable travel to effectively take place. Indeed, when it comes to older, single travellers, older women in particular, the industry is 'insensitive to their specific requirements' (Stone and Nicol, 1999).

A major caveat to the potential of the senior market is that:

> physical enfeeblement does reduce activity participation among elderly, who may be highly spirited to travel but are incapacitated to do so.
> (Pearce and Singh, 1999: 3)

This may impede many travel and tourism operators from adequately exploring the potential of senior markets. However, the command that the senior market has is becoming evident by the growing demand for and availability of senior discounts as demonstrated by the 2003 edition of *Unbelievably Good Deals and Great Adventures That You Absolutely Can't Get Unless You're Over 50* and the growth of an online guide, www.seniordiscounts.com (SeniorDiscounts.com, 2001), that expanded from 25,000 listings to more than 115,000 in just 1 year (Engle, 2002). In fact, approximately half of all seniors receive a special deal when travelling (Shifflet and Bhatia, 1999).

A survey of 446 Elderhostel customers compared half of the customers who travelled internationally with the other half who experienced domestic travel (Szucs *et al.*, 2001). The domestic travellers were motivated by course topics, accommodation, programme dates, word of mouth and to escape the problems in their everyday lives; while the international travellers were motivated by the history and culture offered by the destination(s), as well as the desire to travel, travel safety, the ability to socialize with local people and the opportunity to visit an ancestral location.

When senior travellers to the USA from Japan, Germany and the UK were compared, Japanese travellers were more likely than their European counterparts to choose a tour package (Bai *et al.*, 2001). This difference can be aligned with the collectivism of the Japanese culture, showing that seniors do not become different travellers as they age, instead they are just as influenced by many factors, age being only one of them.

A traditional method of travel for seniors is motor coach tours, although only 32% of motor coach tour occupants are seniors (Baloglu and Shoemaker, 2001). Seniors' satisfaction with a coach tour is determined by the reliability of the tour company, its reputation, the safety precautions of the tour operator and an interesting tour guide. Also, the comfort of the bus, tour pace and frequent comfort stops were additional satisfaction factors. Travel based on novelty motives does not excuse or supersede these issues. A novelty tourism operator must ensure that basic issues, such as those listed above for a motor coach tour and the necessities for hotel comfort discussed below, are catered for within the novel travel experience. The satisfaction of seniors' needs extends to the travel experience as a whole, meaning that the novel travel activities themselves are not viewed in isolation.

A study within the USA found that the selection of a hotel by seniors was based on numerous factors, including recreation/entertainment, room conveniences, comfort and security, ambiance (including décor, landscaping and facilities), reputation, information aids, fitness amenities, simplicity (including simple check-in procedures), familiarity with the geographical area, and free continental breakfast. 'Little things' were also important to seniors, including handicapped-friendly rooms, non-smoking rooms, ground-floor rooms, twin-bedded rooms, picnic packs, consistency and value for money. Comfort and security, as well as reputation, were particularly important to female travellers (Gustin and Weaver, 1993).

Likewise, a study of Australian seniors (Ruys and Wei, 1998) identified five dimensions related to travel accommodation choice. *Safety factors* included a non-slip bathroom, well-lit public areas, anti-slip mats in the bathtub, safety bars in the bathroom, and seats in the lobby. *Convenience items* were tea- and coffee-making facilities within the room; temperature control, credit-card facilities, bedside lamps (bright), manoeuvrable door handles, spacious bathrooms, large-print guest information, low-pile carpet and luminous light switches. *Security factors*, such as emergency phone in lifts, extra security locks on doors and windows, alarm system in room and alarm indicator lamp were preferred. *Services*, such as a non-smoking room, glass of water with meals, standard and small portions for meals, a complimentary newspaper delivered to the room, complimentary breakfast, room service, a coffee shop in the hotel, a coin laundry and dietary menus were also preferred. *Comfort and recreation issues* included a firm mattress, comfortable chairs, extra pillows and large size beds, while a swimming pool and recreation room were unimportant.

An encouraging finding by Wuest *et al.* (2001) was that senior travellers and lodging managers generally agreed on the importance of hospitality services. However, differences arose in the specific services, such as dependability and accurate record keeping, both of which appear to be related to reducing the risk of transactions for the senior traveller.

Travel is usually a high-risk purchase because of the high price and large differences in product alternatives (Capella and Greco, 1987). Particularly in post-retirement, cost and security concerns become greater constraints to travel (Blazey, 1992). Of course, concern for safety is increasingly on the minds of all travellers in a world where a threat of terrorist attacks is always present. Surprisingly, Vantage Delux World Travel of Boston, who specialize in travel for seniors, recorded an upswing after the terrorist attacks in the USA on 11

September 2001 (usually referred to as 9/11), with many seniors eager to capitalize on the price cutting that the industry was forced to perform to kick-start a depressed travel market. Meanwhile, a similar-sized Boston travel agency whose clients were more likely to be non-seniors continued to struggle to meet economic forecasts despite price cutting. Elderhostel, as a non-profit company, was also able to pass on large savings to its customers; thus enrolment returned to pre-9/11 levels at the beginning of 2003 (Bhatia, 2003). Likewise, Grand Circles, another senior-friendly travel business, increased 30% in January 2002, compared to the pre-9/11 level less than 3 months earlier.

Countries such as Egypt, Turkey, Morocco, Zimbabwe, India/Nepal and Israel continue to be travel beacons for senior travellers. Seniors are usually less concerned with time constraints caused by extra security at airports and the like and many see these current scares pale in comparison to the Great Depression or two World Wars, therefore many have been able to return to 'life as usual' more quickly than younger generations. While seniors may be described as more intrepid, many choose to travel while they can; that is, they have the money, the ability, and do not want to miss out on chances to travel (Mohl, 2002).

The factors outlined above indicate the level of specification required to attract the senior market. The socio-cultural treatment of the senior market through the incorporation of these services offers seniors more options and choice in which to travel to the destinations they prefer and in the manner that they wish. This type of encouragement and open invitation to travel helps to overcome previous misconceptions of the aged and by the aged (Prakash, 1999).

Step 6: Developing the promotional plan

The next step is to develop a promotional plan. Consult data from the syndicated research supplier which identify the geographical dispersion of the targeted lifestyle group. Such data are particularly useful for direct marketing promotions (mailings to targeted households) and for assessments of media reach (radio and television stations, newspapers, outdoor advertising). In addition to this information, the mass-medium readership and listening profiles are available at the lifestyle segment level, so these can be requested for the senior bracket only. All these data are considered when evaluating and choosing the most cost-effective channels for getting the promotional message to the targeted senior novelty traveller.

Develop the promotional message for each chosen medium by reflecting the targeted values and lifestyle priorities. The lifestyle profiles given by the syndicated research service are a starting point. In addition, perusing tabular data on the designated senior segment's other behaviours related to travel and tourism (e.g. leisure activities, consumption related to health and fitness, sporting equipment purchases, family life-cycle status, purchases of luxury and non-essential items) will give a fuller portrait of the targeted segments. An advertising agency will need this information in order to design messages and promotional pieces that strike a resonant chord in the viewer or reader.

Travel service promotional materials should not rely entirely on glossy pictures of the destination; they must also be informational in order to satisfy the needs of the senior market. It is interesting to note that seekers of travel information tend to take longer and more expensive trips (Etzel and Wahlers, 1985), while experienced senior travellers and those who regularly travel overseas tend to seek out marketer-dominated (commercial travel) information sources. However, overall, seniors favoured general media sources, although level of risk aversion confounded the issue. Those who perceive high equipment risk, financial risk and physical risk most often seek professional advice (Cleaver, 2000). Seniors can be cynical and often require answers to many questions; therefore, they tend to read more than younger age segments and prefer to interact with people when making purchase decisions (Leventhal, 1997). Within Japan, travel consultants who are older have been hired to present and market travel products to senior travellers (*Japan Economic Newswire*, 2002). In addition, word-of-mouth is often reported as the most often-used source of travel information by seniors (Cleaver, 2000). For example, positive word of mouth was highlighted as a key way to convey information to and from motor coach tour clients (Hsu, 2000).

Given the growing importance and wealth of seniors, promotions should look to ensure that misrepresentations and negative stereotypes are avoided in order to ensure that senior consumers are reached.

> Such a positioning strategy is not likely to be effective in attracting the patronage of this segment, which is substantial in size and growing rapidly.
> (Peterson and McQuitty, 2001: 48)

The gradual evolution from a youth-oriented marketing strategy to a focus that includes and caters for senior travellers requires detailed knowledge of the senior market. Disinterest towards the older markets has ensured that marketing to them has rarely been done and, when it is attempted, it often misses the mark. The preoccupation with youth is partly mass-media-driven and often results in negative portrayals of older people. This can lead to misconceptions about older age groups (Dychtwald, 1997; Carrigan and Szmigin, 1999) and may engender a cost to society at large by indicating that seniors have predictable lives. This may also reinforce a negative self-image for many older people, perhaps creating a self-defined barrier to travel; that is, a potential senior traveller may either not consider the possibility of travel at all or may dismiss the more novel types of travel, based on the negative reinforcements offered as 'promotions' (Peterson and McQuitty, 2001).

While older people are portrayed relatively fairly in terms of proportion of society, they are portrayed less favourably than their younger counterparts (Peterson and McQuitty, 2001). This is an improvement from previous research that indicated that seniors are both negatively and infrequently portrayed (Gantz et al., 1980; Kobey, 1980). In an examination of travel information, in particular travel brochures of the major senior tour operators in the UK, Dann (2001) recorded only one picture including a disabled person, namely a man with a walking stick. This one picture was part of a collection of 1487 examined, representing 0.07%, thus vastly under-representing the proportion of seniors who are disabled in some way.

While seniors are often mistakenly considered a minority within the travel market, there are minorities within the senior travel market that do require particular attention of marketing mix variables to ensure that travel and tourism products and services are offered to suit their needs. While seniors with disabilities have been mentioned above, racial minorities and gay couples are two other minorities to be considered (Dann, 2001) and perhaps explored in terms of novel product offerings, including heritage tours for racial groups and social events sympathetic to older gay travellers as singles or couples. These groups should also be included in promotional materials in order to reach these markets.

Conclusion

Popular thought, both within the general population and the travel and tourism industry, dictates that older consumers are less important consumers. However, as people age they do not necessarily become less interested in consumption, and it is a mistake to ignore or alienate such a potentially lucrative market (Szmigin and Carrigan, 2001). It is essential to understand the consumption needs of the elderly market and how they will respond to various marketing activities for the purpose of new tourism product development, destination positioning and branding. The proper approach is to begin with a thorough understanding of the ageing process and the needs of the senior traveller. These needs must then be incorporated into the product development and marketing strategies to attract the senior travel segments. The aim should be to develop themes and tourism products that represent authentic, high-quality and enriching experiences – often in faraway lands – while maintaining the sustainability of the touristic activities.

The senior market is large, with high disposable income, but this comes at the cost of complexities, such as the heterogeneity of the market, generational differences and continual change (Moschis et al., 1997; Schlueter, 1998). The complexity arises from the fact that ageing is not a uniform process, and that cohorts of seniors are influenced by different environments, both in their formative years, as well as

during their advanced years (Moschis, 1992). The aged population is expected to continually evolve and reshape the process of ageing and the reality of life as a senior. For example, while young adults use material possessions to satisfy the needs of social belonging and status, seniors are less likely to use products to boost their status or to provide luxury. Instead, they seek products or services, such as travel, from companies that portray the purchase as a gateway to a 'being experience' (Goodhead, 1991; Wolfe, 1990). This rewards them emotionally and psychologically and contributes to personal growth.

Understanding today's seniors is paramount to ensure that the present and future needs of seniors are met. However, both new players and those with established relationships with the older segment of the marketplace will need to continually monitor their market in order to allow for the changes expected with the evolution of seniors' role in a society dominated by older ages. Less negative views of the senior market and less obsession with youth are expected outcomes of the shift towards older median ages in Western nations (Dytchwald, 1997).

Novelty tourism product developers wanting to tap the older traveller market in the 21st century cannot simply continue applying strategies based on outmoded perceptions of the older traveller as someone frail and retiring, who wants passive exposure to touristic elements. Such a gambit would almost certainly fail with the older traveller who is inviting novelty during the touristic encounter, who is looking to experience new horizons, and who is yearning for learning, personal growth, discovery, sensory stimulation and having fun in the twilight years of life.

References

Atchley, R.C. (1972) The Social Forces of Later Life. Wadsworth, Belmont, California.

Atchley, R.C. (1989) Continuity theory and the evolution of activity in later adulthood. In: Kelly, J.R. (ed.) Activity and Ageing: Staying Involved in Later Life. Sage, Newbury Park, California, pp. 5–24.

Australian Bureau of Statistics (1999) Older People, Australia: a Social Report, Cat. No. 4109.0. Australian Bureau of Statistics, Canberra.

Australian and New Zealand College for Seniors (1999) *Odyssey Magazine*, August, pp.1, 27.

Backman, K.F., Backman, S.J. and Silverberg, K.E. (1999) An investigation into the psychographics of senior nature-based travellers. *Tourism Recreation Research* 25(1),13–22.

Bai, B., Jang, S.S., Cai, L.A. and O'Leary, J.T. (2001) Determinants of travel mode choice of senior travellers to the United States. *Journal of Hospitality and Leisure Marketing* 8(3/4), 147–168.

Baloglu, S. and Shoemaker, S. (2001) Prediction of senior traveller's motorcoach use from demographic, psychological and psychographical characteristics. *Journal of Travel Research* 40(August), 12–18.

Barak, B., Mathur, A., Lee, K. and Zhang, Y. (2001) Perceptions of age-identity: a cross-cultural inner-age exploration. *Psychology and Marketing* 18(10), 1003–1029.

Barak, B., Mathur, A., Zhang, Y., Lee, K. and Erondu, E. (2003) Inner-age satisfaction in Africa and Asia: a cross-cultural exploration. *Asia Pacific Journal of Marketing and Logistics* 15(1/2), 3–26.

Bartos, R. (1983) Over 49: the invisible consumer. *Marketing Communications in a Changing Environment*. Harvard Business Review, Boston, Massachusetts.

Basala, S.L. and Klenosky, D.B. (2001) Travel-style preferences for visiting a novel destination: a conjoint investigation across the novelty–familiarity continuum. *Journal of Travel Research* 40(November), 172–182.

Bee, H. (1992) *The Journey of Adulthood*, 2nd edn. Macmillan, New York.

Bhatia, P. (2003) You only live once. *Wall Street Journal* 10 January, W5.

Blau, Z.S. (1956) Changes in status and age identification. *American Sociological Review* 21, 198–203.

Blazey, M.A. (1992) Travel and retirement status. *Annals of Tourism Research* 19(4), 771–783.

Capella, L.M. and Greco, A. (1987) Information sources of elderly for vacation decisions. *Annals of Tourism Research* 14(1), 148–151.

Carrigan, M. and Szmigin, I. (1999) The representation of older people in advertisements. *Journal of the Marketing Research Society* 41(3), 311–326.

Centre for Strategic and International Studies (2000) *Global Ageing: the Challenge of the New Millennium*. Centre for Strategic and International Studies and Watson Wyatt Worldwide, Washington, DC.

Cha, S., McCleary, K.W. and Uysal, M. (1995) Travel motivations of Japanese overseas travellers: a factor-cluster segmentation approach. *Journal of Travel Research* 34(1), 33.

Cleaver, M. (2000) Australian seniors' use of travel information: perceived usefulness of word-of-mouth, marketer-dominated, professional-advice and general-media information. In: O'Cass, A. (ed.) *Proceedings of the ANZMAC 2000 Conference*. Australian and New Zealand Marketing Academy, Gold Coast, Australia, pp. 182–187.

Cleaver, M. (2001) Psychological and demographic predictors of cognitive age among seniors: a contribution to theory and implications for the segmentation of the older traveller market. Unpublished PhD dissertation, Griffith University, Gold Coast, Australia.

Cleaver, M., Muller, T.E., Ruys, H.F.M. and Wei, S. (1999) Tourism product developments for the senior market, based on travel motive research. *Tourism Recreation Research* 24(1), 5–12.

Cleaver Sellick, M. (2004) Discovery; connection; nostalgia: Key travel motives within the seniors market. *Journal of Travel and Tourism Marketing* (in press).

Cohen, E. (1972) Toward a sociology of tourism. *Social Research* 39, 164–182.

Cohen, E. (1984) The sociology of tourism: approaches, issues and findings. *Annual Review of Sociology* 10, 373–392.

Cohen, G.D. (1989) *The Ageing Brain*. Springer, New York.

Crompton, J.L. (1979) Motivations for pleasure vacation. *Annals of Tourism Research* 6(4), 408–424.

Crotts, J.C. (1993) Personality correlates of the novelty seeking drive. *Journal of Hospitality and Leisure Marketing* 1(3), 7–29.

Dann, G.M.S. (1981) Tourist motivation: an appraisal. *Annals of Tourism Research* 8(2), 187–219.

Dann, G.M.S. (2001) Targeting seniors through the language of tourism. *Journal of Hospitality and Leisure* 8(3/4), 5–35.

Dychtwald, M.K. (1997) Marketplace 2000: riding the wave of population change. *Journal of Consumer Marketing* 14(4), 271–275.

Edgar, D. (1991) *Ageing: Everybody's Future*. Walter Murdoch Memorial Lecture, 17 September. Murdoch University, Perth, Australia.

Elderhostel (1999) *Elderhostel History* at http://www.elderhostel.org/EHORG/Ehhist.html (accessed 10 January 2000).

Engle, J. (2002) Online sites, books have tips for getting remaining discounts; senior travel. *Seattle Times* September 1, M3.

Erikson, E. (ed.) (1978) *Adulthood*. WW Norton, New York.

Etzel, M.J. and Wahlers, R.G. (1985) The use of requested promotional material by pleasure travellers. *Journal of Travel Research* 23(Spring), 2–6.

Gantz, W., Gantenberg, H.M. and Rainbow, C.K. (1980) Approaching invisibility: the portrayal of the elderly in magazines advertisements. *Journal of Communication* 30, 56–60.

Gay, J. (1999) A guide to tour designing for seniors. *Tourism Recreation Research* 24(1), 90–92.

George, L.K., Mutran, E.J. and Pennybacker, M.R. (1980). The meaning and measurement of age identity. *Experimental Ageing Research* 6(3), 283–298.

Gilbert, D.C. (1991) An examination of the consumer behaviour process related to tourism. In: Cooper, C.P. (ed.) *Progress in Tourism, Recreation and Hospitality Management*, Vol. 3. Belhaven, London, pp. 78–105.

Goggin, J.M. (1999) Elderhostel meets the "silent revolution". *Tourism Recreation Research* 24(1), 86–89.

Goodhead, V. (1991) Marketing to mature adults requires a state of being. *Marketing News* 25(25), 10.

Grabowski, C.P. (1999) Elder travellers and health. *Tourism Recreation Research* 24(1), 80–81.

Gustin, M.E. and Weaver, P.A. (1993) The mature market: underlying dimensions and group differences of a potential market for the hotel industry. *FIU Hospitality Review* 11(2), 49–59.

Hawkins, D.I., Best, R.J. and Coney, K.A. (2001) *Consumer Behaviour: Building Marketing Strategy*, 8th edn. Irwin McGraw-Hill, Boston, Massachusetts.

Horneman, L., Carter, R.W., Wei, S. and Ruys, H. (2002). Profiling the senior traveller: an Australian perspective. *Journal of Travel Research* 41(August), 23–37.

Hort, L. and Strickland, C.D. (1995) *University of the Third Age and Griffith University: An Evaluation of the Services Provided and the Guidelines on Best Practice*. Research Report, Griffith University Quality Assurance Round 1995, Gold Coast, Australia.

Hsu, C.H.C. (2000) Determinants of mature travellers' motorcoach tour satisfaction and brand loyalty. *Journal of Hospitality and Tourism Research* 24(2), 223–238.

Hubley, A.M. and Hultsch, D.F. (1994) The relationship of personality trait variables to subjective age identity in older adults. *Research on Ageing* 16(4), 415–439.

Japan Economic Newswire (2002) Travel agents launch drive to attract seniors. Available from *LexisNexis Academic Universe* at http://

web.lexis-nexis.com/universe (accessed 4 March 2003).

Kastenbaum, R., Derbin, V., Sabatini, P. and Artt, S. (1972) The ages of me: toward personal and interpersonal definitions of functional aging. *Aging and Human Development* 3(2), 197–211.

Kaufman, S.R. (1993) Values as sources of the ageless self. In: Kelly, J.R. (ed.) *Activity and Ageing: Staying Involved in Later Life*. Sage, Newbury, California, pp. 17–24.

Keng, K.A. and Cheng, J.L.L. (1999) Determining tourist role typologies: an exploratory study of Singapore vacationers. *Journal of Travel Research* 37(May), 382–390.

Kobey, R.W. (1980) Television and the aging: past, present, and future. *Gerontologist* 20, 24–28.

Leitner, M. (1999a) Promoting peace through intergenerational tourism. *Tourism Recreation Research* 24(1), 53–56.

Leitner, M. (1999b) Enabling tourism for low functioning elders and their spouses. *Tourism Recreation Research* 24(1), 77–79.

Leventhal, R.C. (1997) Ageing consumers and their effects on the marketplace. *Journal of Consumer Marketing* 14(4), 276–281.

Levinson, D., Darrow, C., Klein, E., Levinson, N. and McKee, B. (1978) *The Seasons of a Man's Life*. Knopf, New York.

Lewis, H.G. (1996) Another look at the seniors market. *Direct Marketing* March, 20–23.

Lloyd, K.M. and Auld, C.J. (2002) The role of leisure in determining quality of life: issues of content and measurement. *Social Indicators Research* 57, 43–71.

Lum, M. (2002) The age of travel *The Straits Times* (Singapore), 19 November. Available from *LexisNexis Academic Universe* at http://web.lexis-nexis.com/universe (accessed 4 March 2003).

Maslow, A.H. (1970) *Motivation and Personality*, 2nd edn. Harper and Row, New York.

McGuire, F.A. (1984) A factor analysis study of leisure constraints in advanced adulthood. *Leisure Sciences* 6(3), 313–326.

McLennan, W. (1999a) *Australian Social Trends 1999*. Cat. No. 4102.0, Australian Bureau of Statistics, Canberra.

McLennan, W. (1999b) *Year Book Australia*. Cat. No. 1301.0, Australian Bureau of Statistics, Canberra.

Mathur, A., Sherman, E. and Schiffman, L.G. (1998) Opportunities for marketing travel services to new-age elderly. *Journal of Services Marketing* 12(4), 265–277.

Mill, R.C. and Morrison, A.M. (1985) *The Tourism System: An Introductory Text*. Prentice Hall, Englewood Cliffs, New Jersey.

Mohl, B. (2002) Despite terror worries, tour opera-
tors find surge in travel by senior citizens.
Knight Rider Tribune Business News 14
February, 1.

Moldofsky, L. (2001) Traveller's advisory. *Time* 5
March, 6.

Morris, J. (1999) Seniors are on the go and tour
operators are rushing to meet their demands.
Boston Globe 1 August, M1.

Moschis, G.P. (1992) *Marketing to Older Consumers:
a Handbook of Information for Strategy
Development*. Quorum, Westport, Connecticut.

Moschis, G.P. (1996) *Gerontographics: Life-Stage
Segmentation for Marketing Strategy
Development*. Quorum, Westport, Connecticut.

Moschis, G.P., Lee, E. and Mathur, A. (1997)
Targeting the mature market: opportunities and
challenges. *Journal of Consumer Marketing*
14(4), 282–293.

Muller, T.E. (1995) The coming boom in education
travel: why North American's maturing baby
boomers will expand the world. In: Archiblad, J.
and Jolin, L. (eds) *Proceedings of the Third
Global Classroom Conference: Educational
Tourism and the Needs of Older Adults*.
Universitè du Quèbec á Montrèal, Montrèal,
Canada.

Muller, T.E. and Cleaver, M. (2000) Targeting the
CANZUS baby boomer explorer and adventure
segments. *Journal of Vacation Marketing* 6(2),
154–169.

Muller, T.E. and O'Cass, A. (2001) Targeting the
young at heart: seeing senior vacationers the
way they see themselves. *Journal of Vacation
Marketing* 7(4), 285–301.

Muller, T.E. and Strickland, C.D. (1995) Educational
and adventure tourism for older adults: assess-
ing the potential. In: Sogar, D.H. and Weber, I.
(eds) *Proceedings of the 1995 Marketing
Educators and Researchers International
Conference*, Griffith University, Gold Coast,
Australia, pp. 656–664.

Neugarten, B.L. (1976) *The Psychology of Aging:
An Overview*. American Psychological Association, Chicago, Illinois.

Neugarten, B.L. (1980) Personality and the aging
process. In: Williams, R.H., Tibbitts, C. and
Donahue, W. (eds) *Process of Aging: Social
and Psychological Perspectives,* Vol. 1. Arno,
New York, pp. 321–334.

Neugarten, B.L. and Neugarten, D.A. (1986)
Changing meanings and of age and aging. In:
Pifer, A. and Bronte, A. (eds) *Our Aging
Society: Paradox and Promise*. WW Norton,
New York, pp. 33–51.

Norman, W.C., Daniels, M.J., McGuire, F. and
Norman, C.A. (2001) Whither the mature

market: an empirical examination of the travel
motivations of neo-mature and veteran-mature
markets. *Journal of Hospitality and Leisure
Marketing* 8(3/4), 113–130.

Odyssey Ed-ventures (2003) *Odyssey Travel*.
Available from http://www.odysseytravel.com.
au (accessed 31 May 2003).

Oh, H.C., Uysal, M. and Weaver, P.A. (1995)
Product bundles and market segments based on
travel motivations: a canonical correlation
approach. *International Journal of Hospitality Management* 14(2), 123–137.

Ostroff, J. (1989) An aging market: how businesses
can prosper. *American Demographics* 11(5),
26–28, 33, 58–59.

Pearce, P.L. (1988) *The Ulysses Factor: Evaluating
Visitors in Tourist Settings*. Springer, New
York.

Pearce, P.L. (1993) Fundamentals of tourist motivation. In: Pearce, D.G. and York, R.W. (eds)
Fundamentals of Tourist Motivation. Routledge, London, pp. 113–134.

Pearce, P.L. and Singh, S. (1999) Senior tourism.
Tourism Recreation Research 24(1), 1–4.

Perkins, E. (2000) Millions of senior travellers can't
be wrong. *Times-Picayune* 20 February, E8.

Perlmutter, M. (1988) Cognitive potential throughout
life. In: Birren, J.E. and Bengtson, V.L. (eds)
Emergent Theories of Ageing, 3rd edn.
Springer, New York, pp. 247–268.

Peterson, R.T. and McQuitty, S. (2001) The depic-
tion of seniors in hotel and motel television
commercials. *Journal of Hospitality and
Leisure Marketing* 8(3/4), 37–49.

Pfeffer, M. and Green, D. (1997) The making of policies for the aged. In: Borrowski, A., Encel, S.
and Ozanne, E. (eds) *Ageing and Social Policy
in Australia*. Cambridge University Press,
Oakland, Australia, pp. 276–300.

Pitts, R.E., Jr and Woodside, A.G. (1986) Personal
values and travel decisions. *Journal of Travel
Research* 25(1), 20–25.

Prakash, I.J. (1999) Senior women's perceptions of
leisure in India. *Tourism Recreation Research*
24(1), 82–85.

Razzouk, N. and Seitz, V. (2003) Nude recreation in
the US: an empirical investigation. *Journal of
Hospitality and Leisure Marketing* 10(3/4),
145–157.

Russell, C. (1981) *The Aging Experience*. George
Allen and Unwin, Sydney.

Ruys, H. and Wei, S. (1998) Accommodation needs
of mature Australian travellers. *Australian
Journal of Hospitality Management* 5(1),
51–59.

Schiffman, L.G. and Sherman, E. (1991) Value orientations of new-age elderly: the coming of an

ageless market. *Journal of Business Research* 22(April), 187–194.

Schlueter, S. (1998) Maturing market offer an opportune niche. *Marketing News* 32(18), 12, 14.

SeniorDiscounts.com. (2001) *Discount Search*. Available from http://www.seniordiscounts.com (accessed 31 May 2003).

Shifflet, D.K. and Bhatia, P. (1999) Retired road warriors: senior leisure travellers fuel summer room-demand growth. *Hotel and Motel Management* 17 May, 26.

Silvers, C. (1997) Smashing old stereotypes of 50-plus America. *Journal of Consumer Marketing* 14(4), 303–309.

Snepenger, D.J. (1987) Segmenting the vacation market by novelty-seeking role. *Journal of Travel Research*(Fall), 8–14.

SRI International (2001) *Japan-VALS*. Available from http://www.sric-bi.com/VALS/JVALS.shtml (accessed 22 July 2003).

Stone, G.J. and Nicol, S. (1999) Older, single female holidaymakers in the United Kingdom: who needs them? *Journal of Vacation Marketing* 5(1), 7–17.

Szmigin, I. and Carrigan, M. (2001) Leisure and tourism services and the older innovator. *Service Industries Journal* 21(3), 113–129.

Szucs, F.K., Daniels, M.J. and McGuire, F.A. (2001) Motivations of Elderhostel participants in selected United States and European educational travel programmes. *Journal of Hospitality and Leisure Marketing* 9(1/2), 21–34.

Tornstram, L. (1989) Gero-transcendence: a reformulation of the disengagement theory. *Ageing* 1(1), 55–63.

Travel Industry Association of America (1998a) *The Adventure Travel Report, 1997*. Travel Industry Association of America, Washington, DC.

Travel Industry Association of America (1998b) *Not Just a Vacation, but an Adventure*. Available from http://www.tia.org/press/022098adven.stm (accessed 3 November 1999).

Underhill, L. and Cadwell, F. (1983) What age do you feel? Age perception study. *Journal of Consumer Marketing* 1, 19–21.

United Nations (1997) *1995 Demographic Yearbook*. United Nations, New York.

Western Mail (2003) Older tourists step out beyond the day trip by coach. *Western Mail* 25 January, 5.

Wolfe, D.B. (1990) *Serving the Ageless Market: New Strategies for Selling to the Fifty-Plus Market*. McGraw Hill, New York.

Wolfe, D.B. (1997) Older markets and the new marketing paradigm. *Journal of Consumers Marketing* 14(4), 294–302.

Wuest, B., Emenheiser; and Tas, R. (2001) Is the lodging industry serving the needs of mature consumers? A comparison of mature travellers' and lodging managers' perception of service needs. *Journal of Hospitality and Leisure Marketing* 8(3/4), 85–96.

Wylie, R.C. (1974) *The Self Concept*. University of Nebraska Press, Lincoln, Nebraska.

14 Volunteer Tourism: New Pilgrimages to the Himalayas

Shalini Singh[1] and Tej Vir Singh[2]

[1]Department of Recreation and Leisure Studies, Brock University, 500 Glenridge Avenue, St Catharines, Ontario, Canada L2S 3A1; [2]Centre for Tourism Research and Development, A-965/6 Indira Nagar, Lucknow – 226016, India

Introduction

All forms of social living are a reflection of prevailing times, and tourism is no exception. Through centuries of leisure and travel practices, tourism has metamorphosed fundamentally (Franklin and Crang, 2001) from being an exclusive privilege of a few to a 'right' of all; from incipient leisure and recreational activity to a cultivated habit; from elitism to mass consumerism; and from educational serendipities to extracting expectations. Having lost much of its flavour to capitalism (Cohen, 2003: 1), tourism has been compromised for mass appeal. The anomie is not restricted to the relatively traditional societies of the Third World alone, as may be understood from tourism literature – it is fairly pervasive throughout the world (Singh et al., 2003: 4). Materialism and economic growth has woefully besmirched the ennobling humanitarian spirit of tourism. Global events, such as the Earth Summit (1992) and the Social Summit (1995), need to be acclaimed for having raised the awareness of the masses on matters concerning consumption, production, resource use and accompanying issues. Without these events, post-material ideologies (Inglehart, 1977, 1997; Giddens, 1998) would have probably taken even longer to become widespread. Tourism literature, too, has gravitated towards addressing its controversies in the context of sustainability (e.g.

Mowforth and Munt, 1998; Singh and Singh, 1999).

Identified as an expedient opportunity for social exchange, mutual understanding, self-actualization and learning, tourism in all its alternative forms espouses such worthy causes as the generation of harmony, goodwill, amity and brotherhood among peoples. Irrespective of time and space, it is this integrity that renders tourism justified and meaningful, even today (Amman Declaration on Peace Through Tourism, 2000). Tourism studies have focused largely on the problem of retaining and reinstating the cardinal values of the phenomenon. In the process, many forms of tourism, such as 'green', 'alternative', 'appropriate', 'responsible', 'community', 'eco'-tourism and the like, have been proposed and experimented with. Each form, in its own right, is aligned with the ideology of sustainable development. It is interesting to observe that most of these alternative forms of tourism place special emphasis on tourists and their activities as an inevitable indicator of the emerging trends in post-modern tourism (see Table 14.1).

Tourism and Tourists: a Social Movements Perspective

Almost all accounts of tourism are complemented with a reference to (or a thorough

Table 14.1. Characteristics of the contemporary tourist.

Genus	Traits	Reference
Reborn	Seeker of personal growth through experiences in novelty, spontaneity, risk, simple living and independence; rejection of affluence	Vogt (1978)
Peacemaker	Messengers of understanding and reconciliation; cultural ambassador; promoter of 'one world'; harbinger of harmony	D'Amore (1988)
Humanist	New, all-round individuals; a humble human being; seeker of knowledge/self through inner journeys; willingness to learn and share	Krippendorf (1987)
Value-based	Seeker of humane bonds through understanding, awareness, honesty, modesty, tolerance; willingness to learn /adapt/ experiment; creative, respectful, sensitive, attitude of learning, self-inspired and responsible	Muller (1990)
Post-Fordist	Mature individuals with changeable demands; conscious avoidance of negative consequences; flexible and diverse	Wang (2000)
Moralist	Seeker of direction; new wave tourist who elevates host culture; self-disciplined and self-critical; sensitive, sophisticated and sustainable	Butcher (2003)
Post-tourist	Seasoned and contemporary, reflective, sceptical, open-minded, involutionary, participative, receptive	Cohen (2003)

examination of) concomitant tourist typology. Repetitive scholarly engagement with this theme is indicative of the truth that tourists and their activities are central to the concept of tourism (Tribe, 1999: 79), and that if any benign change is to be effected, it must be initiated by the tourist (Mastny, 2002: 124). In thinking this, researchers seem to have entrusted the tourist with the responsibility of realizing the 'blessings' of tourism. Hence, while certain types of tourist have been criticized on issues of insensitive interactions with the destination's environment and society (Urry, 2000; Mowforth and Munt, 1998), evidence of their 'mindfulness' has been less well acknowledged (Franklin and Crang, 2001; Feifer, 1985). These recent studies indicate a perceptible transformation in the mind of the tourist, over the years (Cohen, 2003; Harrison, 2003), largely in the context of the effect of their presence among and interactions with the locals. Recent documentations on social movements in tourism (e.g. Parrinello, 1996; Kousis, 1999, 2000; McGehee, 2002; Cohen, 2003; Smith, 2003; Mustonen, 2003) allude to this trend.

In this regard, the tourist appears to have progressed from being a seeker of meaningless 'change' (Smith, 1989: 1) to being a seeker of value-based 'exchange' (Edensor, 2001), and from fantasized internalization to rationalized internalization. In view of concerns regarding tourism's role in organizing modern life (Franklin and Crang, 2001), this group of tourists could be a promising genre in the evolution of post-modern tourism. Researchers have attempted to profile the contemporary tourist differentially (Table 14.1). Such works reconstruct the tourist from a post-modernist perspective. In general, the 'new tourist' appears to be an inward-looking individual who seeks out places and people with whom s/he can engage meaningfully, without the inhibiting barriers of colour, class, creed or caste. These tourists are portrayed as post-materialists/post-modernists, who are in search of opportunities that permit them to 'feel good' by 'doing good' (Beck, 1997, cited in Hustinx and Lammertyn, 2000). This rather abstract expression simply relates back to a need for self-actualization and learning through observing and involving the self with the 'other' and the other's environment (Harrison, 2003). The question that now arises is – what kind of environments and pursuits can best serve the intrinsic needs of the contemporary tourist?

Of late, volunteering has drawn the attention of tourism scholars as a purposeful recreational and learning activity. It is rationalized that, much like tourists, volunteers travel nationally and internationally with the objective of 'experiencing' other people and environments. However, this type of 'volunteering-tourism' has been little studied, and it will be some time before this omission is rectified. The knowledge-gap is essentially due to the novelty, obscurity and even lack of scholarly attention to such purposeful tourism pursuits. Studies on tourists as volunteers (Wearing, 2001; Singh and Singh, 2001; Uriely and Reichel, 2003; *Tourism Recreation Research*, 2003) have documented a few cases and aspects accruing from the practice and benefits of tourism from a social movements perspective. But these are indeed too few, and perhaps incipient, to safely deduce the power of volunteering in delivering the common good of benign tourism.

Volunteering: a Touristic Pursuit

Organizational volunteering, including national and international volunteering, has been traced back to the early 20th century (Wearing and Neil, 2001: 241; Beigbeder, 1991). Although voluntary initiatives have been undertaken in various sectors (see UNEP/IE, 1998), they seem to be particularly confined to addressing environmental concerns (Barde, 1998: 13). With respect to tourism, volunteering by guests is implied in some definitions of ecotourism. Ceballos-Lascurain's definition of ecotourism hints at voluntary and active participation of ecotourists in their experience (Wearing and Neil, 2001: 238). The overt conjunction of volunteering and tourism is a recent terminological reference placed alongside various forms of ecotourism and sustainable tourism. It is understood to be a quaint mix of leisure, recreation and work. This heterotopic amalgam of work into the larger frame of meaningful tourism finds congruency with Stebbins' (1979) concept of 'serious leisure'. Therefore, when tourists willingly engage themselves in recreative work while on vacation, it transpires into volunteer tourism. Wearing (2001) defines voluntary tourism more elaborately:

The generic term 'Volunteer Tourism' applies to those tourists who, for various reasons, volunteer in an organized way to undertake holidays that might involve aiding or alleviating the material poverty of some groups in society, the restoration of certain environments or research into aspects of society or environment.
(2001: 1)

While volunteer tourism is not proposed as yet another new form of tourism, it is made distinctive due to the specialized segment of tourers, who engage in volunteering as non-proletarians. Thus the work of volunteer tourers in destination areas during vacations, while being non-remunerative, is accomplished with responsibility to self.

T.V. Singh and S. Singh (2001) explain volunteer tourism:

. . . as being more of a conscientious practice of righteous tourism – one that comes closest to utopia. At best, it may be regarded as an altruistic form of tourism, which has the capacity to uphold the highest ideals intrinsically interwoven in the tourism phenomenon.

Such a form of participation is self-motivated and is guided by a self-developed mission (Searle and Brayley, 1993) for the ultimate gratification of higher intrinsic need (Maslowian thought) for self-actualization. In the process, the volunteer (helper) receives as much satisfaction from the task undertaken as the receiver (resident host), since they work together for the common cause of catalysing welfare among the less privileged. Volunteering in tourism focuses primarily on the gratification of subliminal human needs through cooperative and selfless employment. By virtue of the generic character of volunteering and the post-tourist experience, volunteer tourism acquires an exclusive set of qualities by which it may be recognized as a subtype of ecotourism and/or sustainable tourism (Fig. 14.1). The discussion now moves on to two empirical studies on the subject of volunteer tourism practices in the remote Himalayas. These examples of self-developed volunteer tourism are from two typically rural mountain villages in the lesser-known peripheries of the Indian Himalayas. A brief description of the methods used for data collection is thus pertinent at this juncture.

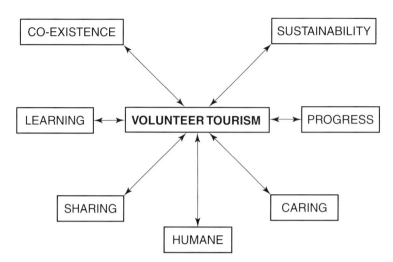

Fig. 14.1. Volunteer tourism: inputs and outputs.

Research Methodology

The two case studies discussed here are the outcome of a series of research investigations in community tourism in the Indian Himalayas.[1] The locations were identified on the basis of reliable secondary sources and personal communication with participants of the study. Having gathered information through primary and secondary sources, a planned on-site study was conducted at both locations at various times.[2] Evidently, the two cases reported are unique examples in volunteer tourism, inasmuch as the intrinsic aspects of the community tourism were the focus of study (Stake, 1995; Berg, 1998).

While on site, data were collected through various techniques. Unstructured interviews were the predominant method employed to gather information from community members and volunteers. This allowed a relatively wide representation from the community to participate in the process, thereby yielding a good range of opinions from its members. An open-ended questionnaire was also administered to the primary participants in each case to gain an in-depth understanding of their perceptions of specific externalities, such as volunteers, community and tourist involvement, and sustainability. In both the studies, the primary participants allowed access to documents which were in their sole possession, such as completed applications/forms, volunteer reports, photographs, audio-visual documentaries and official documents/records. Besides these, the researchers followed the daily lives of these participants (using a technique of unobtrusive observation) to obtain a deeper understanding of the processes under study.

The multiple methods thus adopted in data collection, for both cases, afforded triangulation in these studies. Multiple types of triangulation were thus employed in content analysis, namely person-specific data, methodological and investigator (Denzin, 1978).[3]

Tourism in the Indian Himalayas

Generally, the tourism ecology of the Himalayas is a sad narrative of negatives – losses of flora and fauna, degradation of mountain slopes, trail pollution with garbage, eutrophication of waters, and overburdening of landscape are commonplace (Singh, 1999). The ever-present conflicts between ecology and economy, dependency and autonomy are unresolved in the Himalayas (Brugger and Messerli, 1984). It is a pity that the Himalayas lost the noble art of religious travel and could not tame the modern tourism that threatens its grandiose and splendid environments. Marginalized by physical isolation, economic primitivism and nature's challenges, the simple Himalayan communities have silently suffered the burdens of impoverishing consumerism. Exploitative tourism, as with other destructive activities, such as indiscriminate logging, green-felling and widespread poaching, were identi-fied as the main culprits (Singh and Kaur, 1989). Thus afflicted, it was appropriate for the local people to work out solutions for them-selves and their habitats. Efforts to remedy problems at localized scales were initiated by individuals who either worked on their own accord or came together as a community group to undertake corrective action. Organized vol-untary efforts on a larger scale are few, though appreciably effective, for instance, the *Himalayan Tourism Advisory Board* (HIMTAB), which has emerged as a voluntary body of tourism practitioners supporting the cause of eco-development; *The People's Commission on Environment and Develop-ment in India* is an NGO and NFP group that engages in nationwide awareness pro-grammes, through forums, in the realms of socio-economic development and environmen-tal conservation; *Pragya* is yet another Himalaya-based NFP that devotes itself to appropriate development of vulnerable com-munities and sensitive ecosystems; the *Ladakh Ecological Development and Environmental Group* (LEDEG) is a well-known conservation group in Ladakh. Voluntary initiatives in the Himalayas usually find education and aware-ness-building to be the most effective and effi-cient approach to resolving the issues in the long term. Often, tourism seems to become an inevitable partner in the process. Such activities are better known as projects usually having international or national linkages: the *Himalayan Education Lifeline Programme* which, besides having international linkage, works with an educational approach; the *Gap Year Project* which uses tourism as a tool to educate travellers to be responsible while on their journeys; or the education programme of the *Jamyang Foundation* which provides opportunities for overseas volunteers to inter-act with women monks. These are select pro-jects in volunteering, through international tourism, over the Indian Himalayas. Of the few known cases, two are presented here as unique examples of volunteer tourism. Both these cases share commonalities with respect to: (i) remote and pristine locations, (ii) close proxim-ity to tourism honey-pots, (iii) local initiative and ownership, and (iv) volunteering as prime tourist engagement.

Ananda Project

Background

The Ananda Project was conceived in the sacred precincts of the Murlidhar Krishna Temple of Thawa, within the Kulu Valley, in the Himalayan State of Himachal Pradesh. The valley is extremely popular among domestic and international tourists. The local residents, the Kuluvians, however, look upon their valley with geo-pious sentiments. Thus, despite being acclaimed as the recreation corridor of Himachal, the valley remained particularly prized as a Hindu religious heritage. With the coming of modernity, and tourism in particular, this recreational corridor has been stripped of its delightful bucolic and ethnic charms, layer by layer. Ecologically, the natural system has been interrupted by indiscriminate use of the resource base, namely the forest cover, agricul-tural landscape and water systems. Culturally, the local community failed to prevent external forces from creeping into and interfering in their traditional patterns, resulting in a number of issues.

Perched on a forested ridge overlooking the river Beas, this hill-top temple receives a sprinkling of devotees, trekkers and tourists during the summer season (50 on average). The temple and its surroundings are owned and maintained by the local priest (*Pujari*) and his family. In keeping with pilgrims' needs, the temple extends elementary hospitality to its devotees and the sporadic visitors. In 1999, a visitor (Ben Heron) was welcomed by the *Pujari's* family. While at the temple's guest-house, Ben spent his time communicating with the people of the place and visitors, roaming around and trekking, reading, and picking up the vernacular language. In due time, this visi-tor developed a fondness for the place and the people. His fondness eventually translated into concern for the people and their future. Having grasped the milieu attributes of the valley, he envisaged a community development project within the framework of the Krishna Temple

Society (KTS). Later, this was registered as the Ananda Project in April 2002.

The Krishna Temple Society and the Ananda Project are the result of unsustainable practices that are destroying the place attributes of the Kulu Valley in general. Ananda is now a community-based organization (CBO) that works together with its members, coming from several villages located in and around the Krishna Temple, alongside other volunteers who find pleasure in participating. The Krishna Temple Society's Ananda Project is a typical example of locals and visitors volunteering physical, social, intellectual and creative acumen, entirely by choice. Each individual is a committed contributor, who simply enjoys his/her activity and opens doorways to enhanced personal introspection. Somewhere in their mind, each has the self-determination to uphold the well-being of others and a conscious desire to 'feel good' by 'doing good'.

Balancing tourism and volunteering

The Krishna Temple is the epicentre of people's commitment, religion, traditionality, knowledge and local influence. The *Pujari* (chief priest), his wife – *Devi*, their graduate son – *Pappu*, and a graduate daughter – *Bina*, have identified roles for themselves. The Pujari attends to the Temple chores and its related tasks of performing prayers and ceremonies, advising and loaning money to locals; the son assists Ben in the cause of social forestry besides guiding tourists on distant eco-treks; Bina involves herself with teaching yoga and meditation to travellers, as well as attending to household chores; and Devi looks after hospitality and oversees family and guest facilities. Volunteering tourists too, including Ben,[4] feel committed to the grassroots efforts regardless of its micro scale.

The Society (KTS) strongly disapproves of the idea of larger tourist numbers or even of adapting the project to permit tourism to occupy centre-stage. Tourism, for the KTS, performs a complementary function – that of bringing like-minded and proactive people together, without any discrimination. This policy is consciously practised in order to ensure that the local people and economy do

not become dependent upon tourism as a primary source of living. The Society has addressed value-based tasks that entail long-term planning towards poverty reduction, consumption pattern changes, conserving the environment and strengthening the local community. In pursuance of these goals, the KTS aims to raise awareness of ecological issues, encourage cooperation, and provide sustainable livelihoods to the local community. Thankfully, the location is not overwhelmed by droves of tourists, which is very important in view of its carrying capacity. On the contrary, the lukewarm response of potential visitors to the sequestered location is deemed extremely positive and encouraging.

Project outcomes

The KTS has had slow but definite progress, owing to the selfless devotion of its members, which may be considered as a fair achievement, considering the numerous impediments along its path. Ben, Pappu, Pujari and Bina, along with visiting volunteers, have managed to

- document several indigenous multi-purpose tree species and medicinal herbs and prepare a photographic database with a full description of their ethno-botanical uses, propagation methods, market values and current threats;
- facilitate communication between local self-help groups (SHGs) in neighbouring villages, scientists, members of the Forest Department and foreign volunteers, with a view to educating and raising awareness among locals;
- involve visiting volunteers and locals in collecting seeds and developing small private plant nurseries in their own properties for the afforestation project, help with the waste-management schemes, recycle, organize community waste-collecting sessions and raise awareness on environmental and health concerns regarding the increasing waste problem in the Kulu Valley;
- grow a large variety of organic vegetables on family-owned land;
- facilitate cooperation between the Forest Department and local SHGs, with special

emphasis on working with *Mahila Mundals* (women's groups) to organize community plantations;

- conduct guided treks – nature and culture – to the higher reaches for an enriching Himalayan experience;
- obtain the use of some land from forest officials to carry out an experiment on herbal agro-forestry for the possibility of fair trade in the future;
- host 15 guests (usually foreign volunteers) in the Temple's guest house, providing them with health-giving, locally and organically grown authentic cuisine prepared by the family, a clean hearth in a bucolic environment, and cool fresh water from the mountain spring.

One of the most appealing features of the Ananda Project is the voluntary contributions of the Kuluvians and tourists alike. A self-determined commitment on both sides is of course essential, and the nature of its enactment will have a profound bearing on the long-term viability of their current action. One feels greatly enriched by the environment created by man and nature, and one's experience of work among local groups, both men and women. Their common cause invokes caring and sharing among themselves as well as in the wider community. These outcomes are being invested for wider spin-offs. Ben and the Pujari's family are in constant consultation among themselves and some community folks for future actions, including:

- *Development of a medicinal plant-based agroforestry* on which *ex situ* cultivation of medicinal plants will be done to help reduce pressure on the plants in their natural habitat and help provide local people with a sustainable source of income. Most of the trees that provide fodder and fuel wood are being bred in nurseries to be planted on the perimeter of villages and agricultural land. By doing so, that pressure is taken off the trees in the forests; and the workload of the women, who normally collect the wood each day, will be reduced.
- *Creation of two central nurseries* – a high altitude nursery (2500 m) and a lower

nursery (Thawa, at 1800 m) as well as working in five other villages to cultivate medicinal herbs organically.

- *Working together with trained scientists* to gain a scientific understanding of herbs and their uses and also to educate local herb collectors on sustainable methods of harvesting apart from employing them for seed collection.
- *Establishing a small clay-pot industry* in nearby Chachogi village so as to discourage the use of polythene bags, provide employment and solve waste disposal issues.
- *Generation of funds* through endemically nurtured income-generating activities.
- *Conducting market research*, acquiring all necessary export licenses and obtaining organic certification for the medicinal herb nurseries.

Though on a small scale, the work initiated by the Krishna Temple Society is beginning to find appreciation among community members. Given the measure of success in their efforts so far, the chance of success in future programmes is indeed promising. The locals, and also the Pujari's family, are convinced that their work is blessed and divinely sanctioned by Lord Krishna. Equipped with devout conviction, perhaps this generation of Kuluvians will showcase their vision of blending traditionality with modernity in a viable format for the common good.

Volunteering: a binding force

The Ananda Project of the KTS reaffirms faith in humanity, due to the inspiring commitment of all to whom their concerns matter. Their practices rekindle fading hopes in human kindness, loyalty and self-offering. These qualities are fundamental to the success of the project. Here, volunteering seeks to serve at the grassroots as it sustains a cautious distance from the privileged sectors such as institutions of power, capitalism and governance (Wearing, 2001). Indeed, the simplicity and innocence of the mountain folks, the freshness of the place, the enlightening jubilation of community compensability and a divine omnipresence together create an idyllic effect. This 'society' of residents

Fig. 14.2. Volunteers from abroad with members of the local community preparing fields for organic farming in the Himalayas.

and volunteers seeks out alternatives by which people of the world may perceive the intrinsic joys of life in its organic form. They humbly accept it as a divine calling – 'Krishna's will' – which they fulfil each day through little acts.

Since individual volunteers attach a very personal meaning to their act of volunteering (Hustinx and Lammertyn, 2000), there is a possibility that not all volunteering tourists may experience similar levels of satisfaction. However, the degree of satisfaction may be visible in their behaviour patterns. Usually, those who fail to be satisfactorily engaged stay for a shorter duration, which is regarded as a positive outcome by all concerned. The KTS, along with all its supporters, form an arcadian community, basking in the blessings of human life. Here, the enlightening aura of peace, love, understanding and sustainability of real 'human progress', through volunteering in tourism, is experienced only through self-engagement.

Rural Organization for Social Elevation (ROSE)

Background

The *Rural Organization for Social Elevation* (ROSE), with its headquarters in Sonargaon (Kanda), is a project in 'self-developed rural tourism'. Kanda (1500 m) is a small rural settlement (of approximately 30 villages) in the recently formed Himalayan State of Uttaranchal (see Fig. 14.3). This hamlet is located in the periphery of the state's busiest summer resort of Nainital and its satellites, Bhimtal, Ranikhet, Almora, Binsar and Kausani. The Kanda settlement is a green micro-watershed, drained by the river Sarju and punctuated by numerous water springs that are the lifeline of the Kanda community. They pursue subsistence farming, forestry, horticulture, tea-gardening, handicrafts and, lately, mining for a livelihood. Youngsters usually join the armed forces, leaving behind their young wives and old parents to survive largely on the 'money-order economy' and scarce local resources. The village market place – *Parau* – is a developing rural service centre that caters to the needs of the Kanda community. It has tea-shops and grocery stores, small stores of readymade garments and beverages, besides three banks and one post office. The Kanda landscape is visually appealing in different aspects of terrace-farming, with an intercropping system that presents pleasing shades of colours to the eyes as much as it strengthens the soil fertility; rich afforested slopes all along the skyline where snow-covered mountain

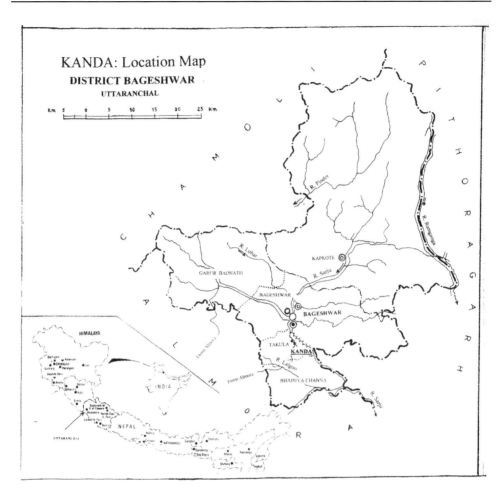

Fig. 14.3. Kanda location map.

peaks peep out from behind on any sunny day. Kanda's best asset, perhaps, is its human resources – the people of this place have a pleasing presence and are open, friendly and hospitable. The community is compact and resilient. Most of them are well-informed persons, a few have college and university education. The locals look rather sceptically at the tourist developments in their neighbourhood and perhaps are not very enthusiastic about encouraging the overspill. Nevertheless, the few who do come are offered basic amenities with openness. Jeevan, a local resident, was able to look beyond the malaise and chose to experiment with tourism as a vehicle for progress for the benefit of the village. He discussed the strategy of self-developed rural tourism with the community leaders, village chiefs (*Pradhans*) and other 'influentials' of the Kanda community who pledged their support. Thus an organization with the name of *Kurmanchal Seva Sansthan* (KSS Society) was registered (in 1983) with its headquarters in Sonargaon.

Creating a better world

The first and foremost item on Jeevan's agenda was to create space for hospitality with moderate home-stays and clean environment for which he deployed personal resources to provide necessary facilities and amenities. With the active support of his family, a paying-guest unit was created where 15 visitors could be accommodated at any given time. Here the guests, who are usually overseas tourists, experience a different world full of homeliness, health, nature and socially useful engagements. There is a good choice of activities to engage in – teaching, farming, construction, gardening, reading, playing, trekking, cooking and even lazing around. Since most of the visitors are altruistically motivated, they feel for their less-to-do, often penurious, Kanda brethren. Jeevan explores the issues with his guests to acquaint them with the place and the people. These foreign guests, who are invariably real ecotourists, mingle with Jeevan's family and learn about Himalayan people and their cultural life, fairs, festivals, rituals, manners and mores. They also learn that these highlanders have few economic opportunities and have to move out to the lowlands to earn their living.

Change for betterment

ROSE uses the skills of volunteers and local manpower for the good of the community. Many houses of the Kanda community are repaired, or even constructed, by the volunteers who come to ROSE. Jeevan has identified homes of such community seniors who are too old to walk to the fields for defecation. ROSE has constructed many toilets for them. With the help of volunteers and locals, ROSE was able to have 40 latrines constructed, with twin tank systems to recycle waste into liquid manure fertilizer, with the financial help of UNICEF and the Indian government. This has increased environmental quality and reduced the high level of excreta-borne disease in the population. Volunteers with an architectural background have experimented with constructing architecturally superior earthquake-proof houses using local materials and requiring minimum labour costs. This has encouraged other locals to have their houses built in this manner. This has created new job opportunities for the locals, and also instilled self-efficacy, courage and confidence in living in that seismic Himalayan zone. Another yeoman service that these foreign guests have rendered to the community is constructing pathways from the market to ROSE in which local people joined hands, symbolizing Kanda as a global village.

ROSE now has a bio-gas plant, a cattle shed, greenhouse and bee-keeping unit. Thus it has built up a fairly good infrastructure with the help of foreign volunteers and the assistance of the local community. It has been successful in forging positive links between tourism, dairy farming, agriculture, floriculture, horticulture and handicrafts. All these sectors are represented at the ROSE campus in their miniature form. During their stay, which lasts an average of 3 weeks, volunteers engage themselves in organic farming, paper-making, preparing greeting cards from recycled papers and dried flowers, and even cook Indian food, using biogas or solar cooker.

Lasting effects

Sonargaon, with a wide network of international participation and observation, has been transformed into a local microcosm where tourism is undergoing a new manifestation. Participant observation did not record any negative shades of opinion.

Interestingly, all the community members had a good word for ROSE and hoped to cooperate with its endeavour. Volunteers observed that they returned home enriched and better people, with unmatchable experience, and would like to return in furtherance of the noble cause. The Kanda nostalgia prompted them to send gifts and clothing for the poor children to whom they taught English or with whom they prepared home-made greeting cards while staying in Sonargaon. ROSE has the all-embracing broad vision of resolving socio-economic and ecological problems in the community; such as restricted availability of educational facilities for children of impoverished families, limited health and sanitation facilities, high unemployment, environmental degradation and dwindling cottage industries. Ecotourism blending with voluntary tourism remained in focus, both for economic gains and conservation of community resources.

ROSE may sound like a rustic initiative to capture the nuances of elusive and complex tourism, but it suits the demands of a peripheral mountain community that has a weak economy and scarce resources. It may be a small step

Fig. 14.4. Volunteers preparing infrastructure for installing a biogas plant in Kanda.

forward to transform a society for better goals, but certainly it is a bold move where guests care for the hosts – an example worth emulating. How little acts of love and kindness can make this world happier, more peaceful, and a better place to live – appears to be the message that emerges from the fascinating Himalayan landscapes. Indeed these are the new pilgrimages that the Himalayas need for the benefit of both host and guest and for their own conservation (Singh, 2002).

Lessons Learnt From Ananda and ROSE

The cases presented above are atypical of volunteer tourism. Certainly the uniqueness is borne out of the philosophy of altruism. Being devoid of ulterior motives of such volunteering activities of hosts and guests alike, the negative impacts of tourism are largely obliterated. An absence of any discussion on the 'not-so-benign' aspect of volunteering does not, however, imply that such effects were non-existent. Primary data provide evidence of limited conflicts, resentment and discontentment between the host and volunteers on specific issues such as lack of opportunities for volunteer engagements, absence of structured programmes for volunteering and out-of-context behaviours of

volunteers and hosts. Upon further examination of these issues, it was found that limited understanding of context (place, people and processes) perhaps led to occurrences of incompatibility. It is interesting to note that while such incompatibilities were reported by the participants, verbally (during the interview process) or through documentation, all efforts were made to avoid and or mitigate overt conflicts. These measures were justified and interpreted by the participants themselves as being in tune with the spirit of altruism.

Concluding Observations

Since the theme of peoples lies at the heart of the tourism phenomenon (Dann, 1988: 17), volunteer tourism appears to be an appropriate design to put people (hosts and guests) into the perspective. It is pertinent to understand that volunteering in tourism may acquire a spectrum of expressions that may range from the very subtle, such as volunteering to be minimally demanding (such as accepting Indian standards in everyday living), to the most visible form such as volunteering with skills and abilities for a proactive engagement. Assuming that the contemporary tourist is an indicator of social mobilization, it may not be long before tourism scholars begin documenting this 'spectrum' of manifestations in volunteer tourism.

Volunteer tourism provides ample opportunity for 'person-to-person encounters' to promote understanding, encourage sharing and appreciation of cultures through acceptance of realities. Such an approach mitigates 'culture shocks' and 'demands' prevalent in conventional *tourist–host encounters* as it diverts energies towards developing *tourist–host synergies*. Typified by reciprocation, sustenance and perpetuation, volunteer tourism is capable of generating these synergies through the underlying principle of symbiosis. In the above cases, symbiotic synergies between the visitor and the visited occur with fair equity. This uniqueness becomes the core element in altruistic volunteer tourism. An involving symbiosis is perceived as the quintessence of life as it is dedicated to the cause of fostering brotherhood among people of the world in their microcosms. It generates an interconnectedness of independents into a system that is emergent from the harmonious interplay of elements (Caan *et al.*, 1996).

Although it is still too early to comment on the nature of the interaction of volunteers with their destination environments, the element of symbiosis is prescribed as a precondition to benign tourism (Fennell and Butler, 2003). From among the wide array of tourism forms known to researchers, volunteer tourism deserves a fair trial. Nevertheless, one must be careful not to attempt positioning volunteer tourism as a suitable replacement for unsustainable mass tourism (Weaver, 2000; Uriely and Reichel, 2003). It is imperative to focus on the 'therapeutic' value of volunteer tourism, typically prescribed in order to restore health to ailing eco-cultural systems, particularly those similar to the cases from the remote Himalayas. This prescription invokes healing basically through the pursuit of its ideals by all stakeholders who are in any way affected by the land and its people. Time and again, these axioms have been emphasized to urge benign tourism.

Notes

1, These studies were conducted by the authors of this chapter and involved the collaborative efforts of the Brock University and the Centre for Tourism Research and Development, India, respectively.

2. The researchers stayed at the sites for approximately 1 week each during summer 2001 to gather primary and secondary data for the reported case studies.

3. It is relevant to note that the cases reported here have been written in a style that blends the manifest and latent content analysis techniques.

4. Ben Heron had been staying in India on a tourist visa until the year 2002. In 2003 he returned to this location on a volunteer worker's visa.

References

Amman Declaration on Peace Through Tourism (2000) *Global Summit on Peace Through Tourism*, Amman, Jordan. International Institute for Peace through Tourism (IIPT), Stowe, Vermont.

Barde, J. (1998) OECD work on the role of voluntary approaches in environmental policy. In: *UNEP/IE,* Vol. 21(1 and 2), p. 13.

Beigbeder, Y. (1991) *The Role and Status of International Humanitarian Volunteers and Organizations.* (Legal Aspects of International Organization, Vol. 12) Kluwer Legal, Dordrecht, The Netherlands.

Berg, B.L. (1998) *Qualitative Research Methods for the Social Sciences,* 3rd edn. Allyn and Bacon, Boston, Massachusetts.

Brugger, E.A. and Messerli, P. (1984) *The Problem: the Transformation of Swiss Mountains Regions.* Paul Haupt, Bern, Switzerland.

Butcher, J. (2003) *The Moralization of Tourism: Sun, Sand and Saving the World.* Routledge, London.

Caan, R., Handy, F. and Wadsworth, M. (1996) Defining who is a volunteer. *Social Policy and Administration* 30, 206–226.

Cohen, E. (2003) Contemporary tourism and the host community in less developed areas. *Tourism Recreation Research* 28(1), 1–9.

D'Amore, L. (1988) Tourism: the world's peace industry. In: D'Amore, L. and Jafari, J. (eds) *Tourism: a Vital Force for Peace.* D'Amore and Associates, Montreal, Canada, pp. 7–14.

Dann, G.M.S. (1988) Peoples: social, cultural and economic dimensions. In: D'Amore, L. and Jafari, J. (eds) *Tourism: a Vital Force for Peace.* D'Amore and Associates, Montreal, Canada, pp. 17–24.

Denzin, N.K. (1978) *The Research Act.* McGraw-Hill, New York.

Edensor, T. (2001) Performing tourism, staging tourism: (re)producing tourist space and practice. *Tourist Studies* 1(1), 59–81.

Feifer, M. (1985) *Going Places: The Ways of the Tourist from Imperial Rome to the Present.* Macmillan, London.

Fennell, D.A. and Butler, R.W. (2003) A human ecological approach to tourism interactions. *International Journal of Tourism Research* 5, 197–210.

Franklin, A. and Crang, M. (2001) The trouble with tourism and travel theory. *Tourist Studies* 1(1), 5–21.

Giddens, A. (1998) *The Third Way: The Renewal of Social Democracy.* Polity, Cambridge, UK.

Harrison, J. (2003) *Being a Tourist: Finding Meaning In Pleasure Travel.* UBC Press, Vancouver, Canada.

Hustinx, L. and Lammertyn, F. (2000) Solidarity and volunteering under a reflexive-modern sign: towards a new conceptual framework. *Paper presented to ISTR's Fourth International Conference International Society for Third-Sector Research,* 5–8 July, Dublin, Ireland.

Inglehart, R. (1977) *The Silent Revolution: Changing Values and Political Styles Among Western Publics.* Princeton University Press, Princeton, New Jersey.

Inglehart, R. (1997) *Modernization and Post-modernization: Cultural, Economic and Political Change in 43 Societies.* Princeton University Press, Princeton, New Jersey.

Kousis, M. (1999) Tourism: development or environment friendly? Comparing Corsica, Sardinia, Sicily, and Crete. In: Apostolopoulos, Y., Ioannides, D. and Sommez, S.F. (eds) *Mediterranean Islands and Sustainable Tourism Development.* Cassell Academic Publishers, London.

Kousis, M. (2000) Tourism and the environment: a social movements perspective. *Annals of Tourism Research* 27, 468–489.

Krippendorf, J. (1987) *The Holiday Makers: Understanding the Impact of Leisure and Travel.* Heinemann, London.

Mastny, L. (2002) Redirecting international tourism. In: Starke, L. (ed.) *State of The World 2002: Progress Towards a Sustainable Society.* Earthscan Publications, London, pp. 102–125.

McGehee, N.G. (2002) Alternative tourism and social movements. *Annals of Tourism Research* 29, 124–143.

Mowforth, M. and Munt, I. (1998) *Tourism And Sustainability: New Tourism In The Third World.* Routledge, London.

Muller, H. (1990) The case for developing tourism in harmony with man and nature. In: Bramwell, B. (ed.) *Shades of Green: Working Towards Green Tourism in the Countryside* (Conference Proceedings). English Tourist Board (ETB), London, pp. 11–20.

Mustonen, P. (2003) Environment as a criterion for choosing a holiday destination: arguments and findings. *Tourism Recreation Research* 28(1), 35–46.

Parrinello, G.L. (1996) Motivation and anticipation in post-industrial tourism. In: Apostopoulos, Y., Leivadi, S. and Yiannakis, A. (eds) *The Sociology of Tourism: Theoretical and Empirical Investigations.* Routledge, London/New York.

Searle, M.S. and Brayley, R.E. (1993) *Leisure Services in Canada: an Introduction.* Venture Publishing, State College, Pennsylvania.

Singh, S., Timothy, D. and Dowling, R. (2003) *Tourism in Destination Communities.* CAB International, Wallingford, UK.

Singh, T.V. (1999) Keep the sharks out of the mountains. In: *Our Planet* 10(1). UNEP, Nairobi, pp. 22–23.

Singh, T.V. (2002) Alturistic tourism – another shade of sustainable tourism: the case of Kanda Community. *Tourism* 50(4), 361–370.

Singh, T.V. and Kaur, J. (1989) (eds) *Studies in Himalayan Ecology,* 2nd edn. Himalayan Books, New Delhi, India.

Singh, T.V. and Singh, S. (1999) *Tourism Development in the Critical Environments.* Cognizant Communication Corp., New York

Singh, T.V. and Singh, S. (2001) Emergence of voluntary tourism in Uttaranchal Himalayas. *Paper Presented at the IAST Binneal Meeting, Macau, China,* 10–14 July.

Smith, M. (2003) Holistic holidays: tourism and the reconciliation of body, mind and spirit. *Tourism Recreation Research* 28(1), 103–108.

Smith, V. (1989) (ed.) *Hosts and Guests: the Anthropology of Tourism.* University of Pennsylvania Press, Pennsylvania.

Stake, R.E. (1995) *The Art of Case Study Research.* Sage, Thousand Oaks, California.

Stebbins, R. (1979) *Amateur: On the Margin Between Work and Leisure.* Sage, Beverly Hills, California.

Tourism Recreation Research (2003) *Volunteer Tourism* (special issue). Vol. 28 (3).

Tribe, J. (1999) The concept of tourism: framing a wide tourism world and broad tourism society. *Tourism Recreation Research* 24(2), 75–81.

UNEP/IE (1998) *Voluntary Initiatives* 21, 1 and 2, January–June.

Uriely, N. and Reichel, A. (2003) Working tourists and their attitudes to hosts. *Annals of Tourism Research* 27(2), 267–283.

Urry, J. (2000) *Consuming Places.* Routledge, London.

Vogt, J. (1978) Wandering: youth and travel behaviour. In: Zamora, M., Sutlive, V.M. and Altshuler, N. (eds) *Tourism and Behaviour Studies in Third World Societies*. Department of Anthropology, College of William and Mary, Williamsburg, Virginia, pp. 19–40.

Wang, N. (2000) *Tourism and Modernity: a Sociological Analysis*. Pergamon, Oxford.

Wearing, S. (2001) *Volunteer Tourism: Seeking Experiences that Make a Difference*. CAB International, Wallingford, UK.

Wearing, S. and Neil, J. (2001) Expanding sustainable tourism's conceptualization: ecotourism, volunteerism and serious leisure. In: McCool, S.F. and Moisey, R.N. (eds) *Tourism Recreation and Sustainability: Linking Culture and the Environment*. CAB International, Wallingford, UK, pp. 233–254.

Weaver, D.B. (2000) A broad context model of destination development scenario. *Tourism Management* 21, 217–224.

15 Will Travel Vanish? Looking Beyond the Horizon

Julio R. Aramberri

*Department of Hospitality Management, Drexel University, Academic Building,
Office 110, 33rd and Arch Streets, Philadelphia, PA 19104, USA*

An unexpected demise?

Most of the chapters in this volume describe a panorama that is difficult to ignore – the number of new tourist products and attractions seems to grow by the day. Only a few years ago, even though it was said with a touch of hype, tourism could be reduced to the four big 'S's – Sun, Sea, Sand and Sex (Bosker and Lencek, 1999; Lofgren, 1999; Phelts, 1997). Critical voices in the discipline would add a fifth 'S' – Subservience (Crick, 1996) – but this did not change the basic mix. In fact, most vacations were summer holidays and the favourite spot was the beach. Most holidaymakers just wanted a peaceful, passive holiday in the sun; the type of product that turned the western Mediterranean and the Caribbean into tourist Meccas and also made the fortunes of many European and American tour operators (Čavlek, 2004).

Even though a great number of holiday-makers still move within this dreamscape, in fact the proportion of sun/sea holidays has diminished in relative terms (Čavlek, 2002). Several factors seem to account for this trend. First, the main vacation period has shrunk, to be replaced by shorter breaks during the rest of the year (long weekends, spring breaks, winter holidays, etc.) and, in the same time-frame, the demand for new types of holiday have increased (from mini-trips to catch a cultural event to wine and gastronomy tours; from bird or whale watching to danger-zone visits; from religious travel to space, heritage or sex tourism to diving or trekking or cruise expeditions). When one talks to industry professionals, they usually tell you how demand has grown more sophisticated and taxing and that this trend is here to stay (Gartner, 2004). Today, as a result, the future of tourism and travel is rightly spelled in the plural – the *futures* of tourism and travel.

And most of those futures, the argument continues, are bright. Altogether the industry is in great shape and, as a whole, it will keep on breezing. The two main databases that keep track of global developments (WTO and WTTC) share this optimistic view for the long term. According to WTO (2003), using 1995 as baseline year, the number of international arrivals will roughly double by 2010 and treble in 2020 as shown in Table 15.1. Growth will not be even, though; while East-Asia Pacific (EAP) will reach nearly 400 million international arrivals, Africa, the Middle East and South Asia will still have a very limited market share; and while long-haul vacations will nearly triple in number, still they will only represent one in four of the total.

If we turn our attention to the rate of growth until 2020, WTO expects that the number of international arrivals worldwide will keep on an even keel of around 4% from 1995 to 2020, with the same unevenness already mentioned. EAP will exceed average growth by

Table 15.1. WTO Tourism 2020 Vision: Forecast of Inbound Tourism, World by Regions
International Tourist Arrivals by Tourist Receiving Region (million).

	Base year 1995	Forecasts		Average annual growth rate (%) 1995–2020	Market share	
		2010	2020		1995	2020
World	565.4	1,006.4	1,561.1	4.1	100	100
Africa	20.2	47.0	77.3	5.5	3.6	5.0
Americas	108.9	190.4	282.3	3.9	19.3	18.1
East Asia and the Pacific	81.4	195.2	397.2	6.5	14.4	25.4
Europe	338.4	527.3	717.0	3.0	59.8	45.9
Middle East	12.4	35.9	68.5	7.1	2.2	4.4
South Asia	4.2	10.6	18.8	6.2	0.7	1.2
Intraregional [a]	464.1	790.9	1,183.3	3.8	82.1	75.8
Long-haul [b]	101.3	215.5	377.9	5.4	17.9	24.2

Source: World Tourism Organization (WTO) 2003
[a] Intraregional includes arrivals where country of origin is not specified.
[b] Long-haul is defined as everything except intraregional travel.*

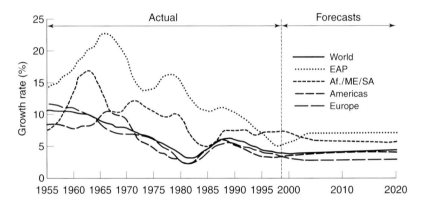

Fig. 15.1. International tourist arrivals by receiving region growth rate, 1955–2020.

2.5% and long-haul will increase at a quicker pace than intra-regional traffic (see Fig. 15.1).

WTTC does not count bodies but money. It includes not only international receipts but all tourism-related income, following its own Tourism Satellite Accounts (TSA) methodology, and providing estimates and forecasts for the global growth of the industry. Its conclusions, however, point in the same direction as those of WTO – a significant leap ahead of the industry within the next decade. Of special significance is the biggest magnitude of all, called Travel and Tourism (T&T) Demand in WTTC's own jargon. This category includes all income generated directly and indirectly by T&T and is expected to reach US$8.94 trillion in 2013, with an annualized real growth of 4.6%. In a narrower sense, the so-called T&T industry, that is, income directly generated by demand for T&T goods and services, will reach US$6.46 trillion and 3.6% annualized growth by the same year. WTTC also forecasts a big increase in Visitor Exports (more or less what WTO calls International Receipts), rising to US$1.33 trillion in 2013, with an annualized growth of 7.1% (WTTC, 2003a). Other magnitudes forecast also show upward trends, as shown in Table 15.2.

Table 15.2. World estimates and forecasts.

World	2003			2013		
	US$ bn	% of tot	Growth[1]	US$ bn	% of tot	Growth[2]
Personal travel and tourism	2.135.9	9.9	2.2	3,862.3	10.8	3.7
Business travel	488.8	—	0.6	871.7	—	3.7
Government expenditures	224.1	3.9	2.8	378.2	4.1	3.0
Capital investment	686.0	9.6	2.8	1,308.6	10.1	4.3
Visitor exports	530.9	5.9	3.0	1,332.1	6.0	7.1
Other exports	479.0	5.3	8.9	1,187.0	5.4	7.2
Travel and tourism demand	4,544.2	—	2.9	8,939.7	—	4.6
T&T industry GDP	1,280.4	3.7	1.1	2,279.2	3.8	3.6
T&T economy GDP	3.526.9	10.2	2.0	6,461.4	10.8	3.9
T&T industry employment	67,441.1	2.6	0.1	83,893.6	2.8	2.2
T&T economy employment	194,562.0	7.6	1.5	247,205.0	8.4	2.4

[1] WTTC (2003a) Real Growth Adjusted for Inflation (%); [2] 2004–2013 Annualized Real Growth Adjusted for Inflation (%); '000 of jobs.

Indeed, forecasts are just that – forecasts – and they may crumble due to unexpected causes and events. 2001 was an excellent tourist year until the terrorist attacks of 11 September forced the industry to nosedive. The recent war in Iraq made WTTC reduce its estimates for 2003, reckoning a slump of between US$3.52 billion in the base scenario, and more than US$30 billion in the worst-case projection (WTTC, 2003b). The outbreak of severe acute respiratory syndrome (SARS) in China, later extended to other regions of the world, also took its toll on the accuracy of forecasts. New unexpected events like these may shatter the best econometric crystal balls in the short term. However, in the long run, expectations remain intact. T&T is a resilient industry that should see its growth unabated.

Or is it? Up until now, we have been talking of exogenous factors. But would it be possible that T&T could reach saturation point because of reasons that remain below most researchers' radar screens? Of late, Dean MacCannell (2001) has raised this possibility. Tourism may be reaching its final days because of internal exhaustion, he says, and he reaches this diagnosis not from a consideration of factual trends such as those noted, but from the essence of modern tourism and its awkward nature.

In the following pages, we shall consider this argument. In order to do so, however, the discussion will have to adopt a theoretical twist that will take us far away from the matter-of-fact approach we have adopted until now. We will: (i) review the internal logic of MacCannell's arguments, (ii) test their mettle in the light of some empirical evidence, and (iii) defend our conviction that nothing in the nature of tourism and of the modern world suggests T&T's eventual demise. Perhaps those already discouraged to keep on reading will be grateful that I anticipate my final conclusion from the outset.

Chronicle of a Death Foretold

Sooner or later, every new and successful technology meets its nemesis. In 1950, nearly at the same time as television was about to become the most popular of the mass media, the late David Riesman and colleagues published *The Lonely Crowd* (Riesman et al., 1950). Their arguments are well-known by now. Modern US society, which might be taken as a developmental metaphor for the rest of what in the future would be called industrial societies, had suffered a recent transformation. Americans had stopped behaving as the inner-directed citizens of yore to become a crowd of other-directed individuals adapting their social behaviour to the expectations of their peer groups. In turn, those peer groups downloaded many of their views on themselves and their expectations about the world from the mass media. So, the mass media became the prime suspects for the lack of individual judgement and of free and critical thought. In today's terms, Riesman's book amounted to a critique of the media from a progressive or liberal point of view. From Vance Packard (1977, 1985) to Neil Postman (1985) to James Fallows (1997) and many others, the same criticisms of the mass media have been levelled, with particular stress on the harmful effects of TV.

Despite all the brouhaha that has accompanied its short life, no-one would imagine that the Internet could be capable of bucking this trend. Nie and Erbring (2000), from the Stanford Institute for the Quantitative Study of Society (SIQSS) published a preliminary report on the social effects of the Internet that purportedly confirmed the *Lonely Crowd* hypothesis. The SIQSS report was quickly touted by some elements of the media as evidence of an even lonelier American crowd. Among other salient conclusions, it was reported that the more time that people spend using the Internet, the more they lose contact with their social environment and the more they turn their backs on the traditional media (Nie and Erbring, 2000: 6). Perhaps this new trend will bring some comfort to the previously mentioned school of media critics, as between 27 and 65% of heavy Internet users reported a decrease in TV viewing (Nie and Erbring, 2000: 11, chart 7). At least it will make TV moguls feel part of a less lonely crowd, for now they have the company of the myriad Internet websites as additional suspects in crowd manipulation.

MacCannell (2001), for his part, did not think twice before jumping head-first into the new fad. In fact some might argue that he was already at the station before the train departed and simply added the Internet theme to update his previous theories. In his view, it is all a question of unrequited motives. We travel to places in search of otherness, looking for a different world away from home. In this version, the cognitive impulse is the prime mover of our nomadic ventures.

Let us stop for a moment to reflect that this is a clearly limited view of tourism motives.

Current surveys show that there are a rather indefinite number of reasons that tourists mention when asked about what made them travel or visit an attraction (Leiper, 1990; Richards, 2002). In order to make them more manageable, all those explanations have been clustered into bigger concepts such as the cognitive and behavioural models (Gnoth, 1997) or the push, pull and hedonistic factors (Goossens, 2000) and other matrices (McCabe, 2000). For my part, I will follow the old Parsonian model of social action and its four main motives – *cognitive*, *expressive*, *cathectic*, plus *status-oriented* (Parsons, 1959, 1967, 1970). To other classifications it adds the status dimension that is so crucial to modern social systems (Harrison, 2002). This marker laid down, one can go back to MacCannell.

Post-modernity constantly frustrates our quest for the real world or otherness, as the tourist experience pointedly shows, for

> [n]ow it is possible to travel around the world without leaving a globally unified protective envelope in which ticketing, banking, hotels, restaurants, airport lounges, shopping areas, tour buses, and the planes themselves are utterly uniform.
>
> (MacCannell, 2001: 382)

In this way, the tourist experience, even when it looks beyond rest and recreation in search of authenticity, adventure, risk, strenuousness, and the like, has been denuded of all magic. No matter where we go, thousands of other tourists have preceded us and millions will follow. Furthermore, there cannot be novelty in any of our tourist expeditions. Otherness has vanished and entire human habitats are fabricated as fake reminders of it.

> At the end of this drive, we predictably find the reproduction and redistribution of markers of locality to the point that the local is killed in the very desire to embrace it. The culture of tourism may eventually be seen as the millennial stage of colonialism and Empire.
>
> (MacCannell, 2001: 385)

One may wonder whether his extant evidence warrants such a sweeping conclusion, but there are no holds barred for MacCannell – tourism has become another form of entertainment at the service of a spurious cause. It is just part of a universal architecture of pleasure manipulated by a network of tightly knit corporations that hold sway over most human toils.

Why should one travel under those circumstances? Places increasingly resemble home and tourists spend their money just to reinforce a feeling of narcissism or of pure vanity – one only travels to have travelled (2001: 387). But in order to satisfy those needs one might as well stay at home. Not only does it get increasingly difficult to experience otherness; but in fact, virtual otherness, as peddled by the media and more recently by the Internet, is often superior to actual experience. 'Mickey Mouse on screen is enormously more entertaining than the actor in the Mickey Mouse suit at Disneyland' (2001: 388). So, stay at home, switch on your computer and there will be no need to move further than to the telephone to ask your broker to sell immediately any Amex shares you might still hold. Only couch potatoes need apply as future tourists.

MacCannell does not provide many clues as to the sources of this wisdom. One would wait in vain for even a shred of empirical evidence, but this should come as no surprise when he had previously claimed that there is really no difference between statistical surveys and symbolic analysis (1992: 89–90), whatever the latter may be. In a still more sweeping generalization he had already probed the many recesses of such an extensive category as *the tourist* (no further qualifications), with just the help of that fail-safe tool known as participant observation (MacCannell, 1999: 102) or, as wine experts have it, the nose.

He might be right, though. Why not? Aren't social phenomena essentially unpredictable? No serious social scientist could think otherwise. However, the whole purpose of scientific discovery lies in establishing, through rigorous discourse and intersubjectively legitimated procedures (Popper, 1992, 1993, 2002), a difference between the merely possible and the utterly probable. While we can always be surprised by the former, it is the latter that we must survey, at least until further evidence shows that we need to change our framework or, to use a trendy expression, our mindscape. Such is the evolution of scientific research (Kuhn, 1993; Popper, 2001).

The Virtues of Virtual Sex

The statistics quoted in the first section should give us some pointers to the future of tourism, beyond and opposed to MacCannell's hunch. However, he might still be right. Perhaps the introduction of Internet navigation and the corresponding information overload may leave us jaded about meeting the other, for the other is just like us. But if this is the predicament of tomorrow's tourism, one can expect that other human activities may also suffer the same plight. Let us focus for a change on the sex drive. Is recreational sex bound for extinction because of the increasing availability of information? Will the expansion of the Internet sex kill actual sex? Some statistical considerations should not be amiss here.

What is the contribution of the electronic sex trade in economic terms? The US Census Bureau carries out an ongoing series of measurements that provide a rough idea of the economic volume of e-commerce in general (US Census Bureau, 2003). Of the four economic sectors it studies (*manufacturing, merchant wholesalers, retail trades* and a grouping of *selected service industries* or SSI), the last is the one that applies to our purposes. Within this group of SSI, in 2001 e-commerce contributed 0.8% of the total value to an amount of US$37 billion.

> Four groups account for 49 percent of total Selected Service e-revenues. Travel Arrangement and Reservation Service account for 17 percent of total Selected Service e-revenues, and Publishing, including newspaper, periodical, book, and software publishers, accounts for an additional 13 percent. Securities and Commodity Contracts Intermediation and Brokerage and Computer Systems Design and Related Services are each 10 percent of total e-revenues.
> (US Census Bureau, 2003: 3)

Therefore e-commerce in publishing, with its 13% share of all activity in this industry, produced US$4.81 billion in 2001.

It is not easy to estimate the total amount of erotic and pornographic materials within this amount, but the numbers usually provided, as we shall see, are out of step with this modest sum. The figures commonly quoted for Internet sex seem overly exaggerated. The zeal of the opponents of porn to expose the avalanche of smut produced in our increasingly heathen societies goes hand in glove with the interests of the industry to lionize itself. For the former, overblown data show the alleged need to limit free speech. The latter use them to buttress their goal of becoming legitimate. Therefore, caution is mandatory. However, even so, Internet sex is not just a matter of a few trifling dollars.

Some media speak of an industry with annual profits of US$10–12 billion (see quotes in Richards, 2002), clearly exceeding, for instance, the profits of Microsoft. Others (Rich, 2001) provide the same number, but this time the talk is of estimated revenues. On the other hand, there are more sober evaluations of the smut industry that take those guesses significantly downwards. *Forbes* talks of revenues between US$2.6 and 3.9 billion (*Forbes*, 2001) for the whole industry, including e-porn, which is closer to the figure offered by Micklethwaite and Wooldridge (2001) of about US$5 billion. The same magazine breaks down this total into adult video (US$500 million to US$1.8 billion), the Internet (US$1 billion), pay-per-view in homes and hotels (US$128 million), and magazines (US$1 billion). In this way, porn e-commerce would be around 20% of the total e-commerce in the Publishing category of the US Census Bureau. This seems both a high amount and a high percentage, but it is the best educated guess. At any rate, the industry seems to have grown significantly since 30 years ago, when a federal study put its total retail value at US$5–10 million (Egan, 2000).

Even if we settle for the lower range, the electronic sex trade in the USA is big business. Compared with revenues of US$6.29 billion for travel e-commerce, the biggest e-industry in 2001, it totals about 14% of it. If one bears in mind that pornography is cheaper than travel products, one can reach the conclusion that the purported US$1 billion revenue covers a very significant number of consumers. Some accounts, again to be taken with a large pinch of salt, speak of 60 million visitors per year to the estimated 50,000 porn sites on the Internet (Hazen, 2001). Among other advantages, Internet porn is easily accessible and saves the consumer the need to venture into seedy adult shops. Apparently it has already punched an increasingly big hole in the profits of many glossy sex publications (Lane, 2001: 219–223; Carr, 2003).

It is possible that the increased availability of pornography on the Internet may have quenched the actual practice of sex. This would be in keeping with MacCannell's hypothesis that growing information and global uniformity decrease the novelty and attraction of any object of desire in late capitalism and, for the time being, I know of no surveys to disprove this point. However, there is no evidence to the contrary either. While the jury is out, one could safely bet the ranch that all that pent-up sexual energy that surrounds Internet sex sites must somehow find an outlet for discharge, be it individual or companionable. In this way, the expansion of e-porn, far from being a harbinger of the death of recreational sex, instead seems to be a stimulus in the opposite direction.

Internet sex is playing another role that we should stress – it is turning the black market of upmarket prostitution in all its dimensions (heterosexual, homosexual and sexually in between – or liminal as a Turnerian might put it) into a global grey zone. Except in the few places where it is lawful, prostitution is a risky business. Usually it is shrouded in a cloud of legal indeterminacy and factual limbo that makes enforcement erratic at best. Risks rise significantly in those places (like most US states) where legal sanctions are not only meted out to pimps and prostitutes, but also to the consumer. These policies have been successful in taking prostitution out of the streets of most American cities, but obviously have not rooted out the love-for-sale business lock, stock and barrel. They just put a premium on the activity that both providers and consumers must bear. The arrival of the Internet, however, has changed the picture considerably.

A quick search in Google, Yahoo, AltaVista or any other search engine under the keyword *escorts* shows a singular landscape. The profusion of sites, many of them with overlapping offers, is such that it discourages attempts at a head count. The offers include services both in the USA and abroad. If we limit our scope to the USA, there is plenty of information on this otherwise illegal activity that can assuage most consumers' fears. First of all, there are some guides that detail providers of different sexual services in a great number of towns. Take, for instance, the *Eros Guide* (2003). At the last count it provided information for 37 towns in the USA plus other areas of Canada, the UK and Ireland. I refer here, as an example, to the first page of the guide for Philadelphia, the city where I work; hardly an overachiever in any vice ranking.

The guide contains a sizeable amount of information on the providers by categories (regular escorts, massage, fetish/fantasy, BDSM (bondage/domination, sadism/masochism), dancers, TV/TS (transvestite/transsexual), *Eros* men and gadgets). At last count, for Philadelphia, it included 72 in the regular *escorts* category. The guide includes photos for most of them that allegedly represent the image of the real person.

Some providers are locally based, but the guide shows an increasing number of transients who travel to different locations at given times well publicized in advance. There are also different categories among the providers. Beyond the non-credentialled, it is possible to find special offers by porn stars who are already known to the clients by their appearances in magazine pictorials or adult movies. These are carefully noted in the details attached to their photo displays. Indeed, these two categories have different pricing strategies, and usually porn stars can charge three times as much for their time than the others.

Money, of course, changes hands, and this is the tricky part of the exchange. However, most sites and individual adverts usually carry a disclaimer to avoid prosecution. Here is an example:

> Money exchanged in legal adult personal services for modeling is simply for time and companionship. Anything else that may or may not happen is a matter of personal choice and personal preference between two or more consenting adults of a legal age, and is not contracted for, nor is it requested to be contracted for, or compensated for in any manner.
>
> (*Completely Elite*, 2003)

On the other hand, many escorts also advertise their willingness to travel anywhere in the world, expenses paid as a premium, thus making in fact moot any attempt at policing the prostitution network by local authorities. In the new global economy, services may be contracted and paid for in places where they are legal or, at least, opaque, while being performed elsewhere.

In this way, the upscale prostitution market, even in the USA, nowadays has better visibility than in the past. As explained, the Internet facilitates the old requirements for secure business, product diversification, value for money, and aggressive marketing. It also provides etiquette rules and quality control. The first comes in the form of do's and don'ts for the sexual encounter with an escort. A search in Yahoo yielded 2860 sites that offered some kind of advice on the issue. An attempt at quality control can be seen in websites like the *Erotic Review* or *Escort Finder* (2003), where clients post their views on services provided as well as vivid descriptions of their experiences, with access to the latter usually reserved for paying members of the site.

Will easy access to sex sites on the Internet diminish the collective sex drive, as MacCannell's logic might lead us to think? Actually there is reason to expect the opposite – that increased information, even in late capitalism, will lead to more instead of less demand for this type of services. Of course, there is still the vexing issue of whether those services have become so uniform and predictable in our post-modern world that they have lost any novelty value. This is an experimental nut that this lay researcher has not tried to crack, although reading through the previously mentioned escort reviews, doctored as they undoubtedly are, he would not dare say that this is in effect the case. In spite of our still scant information on the real effects of the Internet on sexual or travel or any other drives, there seems to be no evidence to conclude that those needs are on the wane because of an information overdose.

Information Overdose?

Rather, it is MacCannell's theory of motivation that does not seem up to scratch. Most of his work endeavours to prove that the expansion of modernity – which, unlike other members of the same fraternity, he insists in labelling as post-modernity – is either an automatic drive or a purposeful goal (this point is never clearly made) of some dark forces described in different occasions as late capitalism (2001), white culture (1992: 121–145), modern cannibalism (1992: 47–52), anal-sadistic homosexuality (1992: 58) and the like. This cultural construct, we are told, can only create uniformity, at the same time that it controls work, leisure, and knowledge of the world and the place of the individual (2001: 388) ever more. It feeds on the death wish, the single architecture of pleasure and so on. Even if MacCannell is right, we only have his word for it.

In fact, there are other hypotheses about why consumer society partially thrives on uniformity, standards, or the bulk, as people in the industry say. One of these, in markets that are increasingly global and anonymous, is that uniformity (a.k.a. brands) provides the imperfectly informed consumer with some clue to the quality and reliability of a product or service at a given price level. Brands, in spite of Naomi Klein's (2002) efforts to reduce them to a consumer trap, do play an effective informative role. Such is the driving force behind the global rush to franchising which McDonald's and Holiday Inn started in the hospitality business (Halberstam, 1994). It has simple names – informed consumer, economies of scale – concepts usually learned in basic-level economics classes.

In economic terms, MacCannell's reviled uniformity is the price we pay to make travel (and many other commodities) affordable to the increasing numbers of people who now find them to be within the reach of their disposable income, unlike the pipe-dreams that they were for most consumers just a couple of generations ago. Far from carrying out Dr Evil's sinister designs, modern tourism instead looks like another support to Bentham's ideal of the greatest happiness for the greatest number. If this sounds too cheerful, one should look at the alternative. Uniformity could easily be reduced by a nostalgic return to the good old days when only people of substance had the means to travel and indulge in conspicuous consumption. That is, the well-heeled clientele that elite travel agencies still cater for today, a legitimate niche in the market. But if one preaches the come-back of elite travel as a broad strategy, one

must indeed be prepared for its likely consequence – T&T would become much more expensive – which sounds a bit odd as part of a critique of late capitalism or post-modernity or white culture or whatever, according to which only the latter frustrates the real needs of the people. Would those needs be better served by a reduction in tourism when the hoi polloi see it as an integral part of their quality of life?

In fact, MacCannell once again shows a cavalier disregard for the data. Uniformity does not necessarily increase with market development; rather, the latter gradually veers away from it. Modern industry, including tourism, faces markets that have become more and more segmented. Perhaps the first company to successfully understand this fact was General Motors, which since its inception has used a diversified mix of price strategy and branding (Halberstam, 1986) to cater for different clusters of consumers. Alongside the mass-marketed products easily affordable by the greater number, there is also a growth of specialized or niche services available at a premium. More than ever, in order to be successful, global supply essentially means widely differentiated supply.

One can raise moral or legal issues as to whether the unequal access that this trend elicits is wise or fair, and they are no doubt meaningful, but the discussion should avoid getting entangled in a maze of unlikely conspiracy theories. In the real world, uniformity is not the future – nor even the present – while brands or quality markers are recognized and accepted by consumers for solid economic reasons. Portending that consumers are misled in their choices requires either a higher wisdom not easily found within the purview of humans, or an uncommon stubbornness. In a nutshell, MacCannell's vision of the future of tourism not only disregards well-proven data, not only blows some facts out of proportion; it also relies heavily on an impoverished notion of motivation. No surprise, then, that he winds up his argument with an unexpected about-face. After all, tourism may be here to stay for

> [w]hat better way of marking status differences in a world in which we must 'stay in our places' than having visited just about every place?
> (MacCannell, 2001: 389)

He may have hit pay dirt, but if taken seriously this new idea would force him to discard his narrow view of modernity altogether.

A Touch of Class

Talcott Parsons is seldom quoted these days. However, he knew a couple of things about the way in which modern market societies work. One of them, coming in a straight line from Max Weber's notion of honour (1972), is the centrality of dynamic status to the social order. Weber had already warned that honour is a different stratification dimension than social class; '[o]n the contrary, it normally stands in sharp opposition to the pretensions of sheer property' (Gerth and Mills, 1970: 187). Parsons reinforces this notion in his convoluted analysis of the four main types of social structure (1959: chapter 5).

For our purposes, we will just focus on the axis 'acquisition/universalism'. In this societal type, which is another name for modern market societies, rewards are openly related to occupational positions, the open system of social stratification is based on differential lifestyles, and a high degree of individualistic values predominate. At any rate, if the Weber–Parsons model is right, dynamic status or lifestyles have become the key dimension of modern societies and, by the same token, MacCannell's *Das-Kapital*-meets-Austin-Powers version of late capitalism and tourism is dubious. Among other things, far from threatening the expansion of tourism, the development of market societies would demand its sustained growth. Not only because, in spite of the increased flow of information made possible by the Internet and the media, people will still think that Bergson's *le vécu* (2001) or Dilthey's *Erlebniss* (1991) or, in plain English, the lived experiences of how the other half lives, are worth a million images, but also because they will want to prevent the Joneses from keeping up with them. As disposable income increases, T&T and other leisure-related activities become one of the major available symbolic rewards.

But before we come to such a conclusion, two previous questions – one theoretical, the other factual – need to be discussed. To start with theories, we will select Bourdieu's ideas on distinction. Then we will explore a factual issue: the real direction that taste and distinction are taking in modern market societies.

It is difficult to explain why human beings are so badly in need of marking the differences between them (Pinker, 1997, 2002; Epstein, 2002), even within social groups that are otherwise collectively subject to discrimination, as African-Americans were before the Civil Rights era (Graham, 1999), but the fact seems to be here to stay. The hunger for status, for instance, particularly hit the assimilated natives in all parts of the British empire. To wit:

> [p]rotocol in India was strictly governed by the 'warrant of precedence', which in 1881 consisted of no fewer than seventy-seven separate ranks.
>
> (Ferguson, 2002: 208–209)

It may even reach the furthest confines of credibility. In the days of the SARS outbreak, some people in Hong Kong were wearing protective masks with fake Louis Vuitton logos embossed on them, creating serious consternation at the company's headquarters (Bradsher, 2003).

Marx did not pay much attention to the issue, absorbed as he was with finding the laws of capitalist development and of the inexorable ascent of the proletariat. Some remarks may be found in his unpublished 1844 philosophical drafts (Marx, 1973a) about political economy, but they are confined to the dualistic notion that the modern worker cannot really even think of distinction and good taste in a world of private property. As humans, workers are capable of enjoying the wealth of human sensitivity; but when their senses are the prisoners of need, as under the regime of private property, food or even the finest of plays cannot be appreciated in themselves, but only as 'objectified powers of the human essence' (Marx, 1975: 354). If alienation from his own labour denies a human sensuality to the worker, capitalists fare no better in their subservience to money and greed. The reciprocal alienation of workers and capitalists is a point also made in the treatment of commodity fetishism (Marx, 1972: 85–98). In the 1875 critique to the programme that the nascent German social democrats drafted at Gotha, there is a more positive formulation. Some day, alienation will wither away for good, but only when the division in classes and between manual and intellectual labour is abolished, abundance becomes the norm, and communist society unbolts mankind's real history (Marx, 1973c).

One can legitimately question whether this morality tale of reciprocal alienation was *ever* true in the past (Thompson, 1966), but it would undoubtedly be a stretch of the imagination to describe the situation of salaried workers in today's market societies as one of absolute deprivation (Goldthorpe, 1987). In fact, by the 1920s, consumer or mass society was already alive and kicking in the USA, and from there it would spread out to Europe and other regions of the world. How to reconcile the real evolution of those societies with the tenets of such an influential theory as Marxism? Marx himself had been well aware in his journalistic and historical writings that reality was messier than his capitalist/proletariat divide. There were peasants, traders, nobilities of the sword and of the robe, large landowners, kulaks, *zamindari* – the works; the petit-bourgeoisie had more incarnations than *Vishnu*; even owners and workers were split at the core by conflicting interests. However, some Gnostic faith made Marx believe that the Armageddon *du jour* would come in the form of a proletarian revolution.

As time went by and real societies became less and less amenable to dualistic chasms, *ad hoc* accommodations had to be devised. Gramsci's notion of hegemony (1949, 1967, 1971) came first. The ruling-class hypothesis should be ruled out. Power everywhere was wielded by social coalitions that in modern times the big bourgeoisie had been able to steer, though many times at the cost of its own immediate goals. Then, another assumption was grafted on – that hybrid of a three-tiered, rather than a dualistic, social order. Although it retains Marx's two main classes, it adds a trump card in direct provenance from the French *Annales* school. In most historical societies, besides rulers and ruled, there is a nondescript third social group with a changing constituency through the ages (Duby, 1973, 1982; Dumézil, 1968, 1969, 1973, 1978). Poulantzas (1975, 1978) adapted it to late capitalism, now defined as a new social structure made of capitalists, petit-bourgeois (increasingly split between the traditional and the new middle classes) and

workers, where the former succeed in imposing their hegemony. An adaptation of the thesis to the USA can be found in Wright's writings (1978, 1989, 1997).

The new formula has found many followers among post-modern academics. In fact, two features recommend it. The first is what might be called the marginal utility function of Marxism to the post-modern, and can be represented like this:

$$f_{pmm}(\Sigma \ mrs - 11tf)$$

where f is the function, *pmm* post-modern Marxism, $\Sigma \ mrs$ the Marxian repertoire selected according to personal taste, and $11tf$ the 11th thesis on Feuerbach (Marx, 1973b). As the latter fades, users are exonerated from that old brainteaser of accommodating theory and practice. There is another helpful trait – hegemony does not convey the same straightlaced image as class polarization. But this is only an impression. To misquote Groucho Marx, Marxian post-moderns may talk like pluralists, they may mumbo-jumbo as pluralists, they may pose as pluralism lovers; but beware – they are unredeemed devotees of the old dualist canon. This is even so when, beyond the framework of politics or social structure, they venture into the less rigid landscape of tastes, distinction, lifestyles and, by extension, T&T.

Dualist Die-hards

In the realm of culture and art, Bourdieu's work epitomizes the new shift. Cultures, tastes and lifestyles are not chosen at random by individuals – they correspond to their inherited social capital and are defined by a range of probable trajectories that lead to more or less equivalent social positions.

> The dialectics of conditions and habitus [in Bourdieu's parlance, a generative code of distinctive signs. *J.A.*] is the basis of an alchemy which transforms the distribution of capital, the balance-sheet of a power relation, into a system of perceived differences.
> (Bourdieu, 1984: 172)

Taste reflects conditions of existence that, at their root (the opposition of 'distinguished' and 'vulgar'), coincide with the polarity of classes under market conditions.

Are we back, then, to the old gospel according to St Marx? No and yes. On the one hand, we should discard Occam's razor, as 'the different fractions of the dominant class are oriented towards cultural practices so different' but, on the other, we may keep on shaving, for one should not 'forget that they are variants of the same fundamental relationship to necessity' (Bourdieu, 1984: 176). From such premises, conclusions flow with ease. Lifestyles reflect three broad class positions – those of the bourgeoisie (to which the old *noblesse* is usually assimilated), the petit bourgeoisie and the proletariat. Legitimate or distinguished culture is usually the playground where the former flaunt their lifestyles. They consume a range of the 'proper' goods and services with the 'appropriate' attitude – withdrawal from economic necessity, disinterestedness, pedigreed detachment, profligacy at times. The working class, on its side, dwells in the opposite region – it has been forced to develop a taste for the necessary. Conformity becomes the only explicit norm of popular taste. What happens in between? Bourdieu professes a charming distaste for the petit bourgeoisie, or middle class. Along with the bourgeoisie it shares a taste for detached culture and education, but it also lacks the self-assurance that only capital can bestow. Insecurity and deference are the rules of its game, a game made of vicarious order, restraint and propriety that shows in choices of food, drink, habitat, body care, dress, travel, sport, and any other dimension of its lifestyles.

One might think that, after all, Bourdieu's classification does not stray from the well-known notions of high-, middle- and lowbrow that are commonplace in discussing modern cultural life (Boorstin, 1973; Levine, 1990; Gans, 1999). There is a big difference, though. While the 'brow' notions usually reflect broad categories that only haphazardly overlap with social classes, Bourdieu, on his side, goes into often pointless detail to develop a class cartography in which given consumption patterns can be adjudged to only one given class fraction or subfraction. 'Small industrial and commercial employers, the incarnation of the 'grocer' [. . .] say they change into carpet slippers every day before dinner' (1984: 187); 'a taste for

elaborate casserole dishes (pot-au-feu, *blanquette*, *daube*) [. . .] is linked to a traditional concept of woman's role' (1984: 185) particularly adapted to the working class; workers refrain from fish, because it 'has to be eaten in a way which totally contradicts the masculine way of eating' (1984: 190); and so on. Even specific musical pieces can be allocated to every given social position (Bourdieu, 1984: 15). It looks as though his many occupations had prevented Bourdieu from frequenting malls and other shopping centres, where the consumer crowd forms a rather undifferentiated group, not easily pinned down into class fractions.

There is an additional red thread that ties Bourdieu to the old Marxian class dualism. In spite of their internal diversity, the formal oppositions (i.e. distinguished/vulgar; spiritual/material, light/heavy) that characterize the social mythology of taste:

> refer back, more or less discreetly, to the most fundamental oppositions within the social order: the opposition between the dominant and the dominated, which is inscribed in the division of labour.
>
> (Bourdieu, 1984: 469)

Bourdieu does not need to be spurred to reach the conclusion that his three-tiered scheme is but a *trompe-l'oeil* beyond which there is a homology between the space of the dominant class and that of the middle classes (1984: 123).

Bourdieu's book was based on a two-stage survey. The first part was completed in 1963 and included a sample of 692 subjects in Paris, Lille and a small provincial town. In the second, carried out in 1967–1968, a complementary sample raised the total number of respondents to 1217 (see Appendix I in Bourdieu, 1984: 503–518). The merits of his sampling techniques and questionnaires deserve an in-depth discussion that cannot be pursued here; if we bring up those figures, it is in order to highlight something different – the dates of the survey. During the 1960s, France (as well as other European countries) gradually became a fully fledged consumer society.

Consumer or mass societies induce the emergence of a wide range of new social services and positions that cannot easily be jumbled in with the old or traditional middle class of teachers, shopkeepers, low-rank professionals, bank employees, civil servants, etc. If order, rank, restraint and correctness defined the traditional middle class, the so-called new middle classes are a different beast. Mighty beastly at that, for it shows no respect, as Tony Soprano would say. They are made of occupations involving 'presentation and representation' that mainly deal with 'providing symbolic goods and services' (1984: 359) filled by all those free agents so much touted in new-economy lingo. They ape the mores of the high class; they thrive on credit; they have no other goal than conspicuous consumption; they are avant-garde when it comes to attitudes about sex, family values, gender, generational relations; they have relinquished the old repressive morality and adopted fun and hedonism as categorical imperatives. They might as well have read Susan Sontag's notes on *camp* (2001: 275–292).

No wonder Bourdieu pelts them with a torrent of scorn. Not only are they shrinking the traditional working class, as Bell (1973) predicted a while ago; the emergence of the new professions has created a multidimensional social structure that can no longer be rammed through a dualistic logic and, at the same time, endangers the original blueprint of domination by a single ruling class. As Bourdieu nonchalantly remarks in passing, the new petit bourgeoisie:

> can itself only be understood in terms of changes in the mode of domination, which, substituting seduction for repression, public relations for policing, advertising for authority, the velvet glove for the iron fist, pursues the symbolic integration of the dominated classes by imposing needs rather than inculcating norms.
>
> (1984: 154)

How can he be so sure that this new type of social compact is but a legatee of the old domination, when apparently it has turned upside down all the expected tenets of ruling class governance? The surprising fact is not that the notion of class, together with its accoutrements (the three-dimensional social order, hegemony), has to wither away, but that it took him so long to realize it.

Not Classy, Just Sassy

Now we will have to face a factual issue. Have classes effectively vanished from the real world? Not exactly, but that's what some people are saying (Kingston, 2000; Sørensen, 2001), meaning that social research needs not exchange permanent marital vows with Marxism. Classes in the traditional Marxian sense have mostly been ministered to from a theoretical, and often even normative, perspective at the expense of factual studies, although:

> [a]ny depiction of class structure—with typically related imputations of exploitation, domination, alienation, and the like—becomes meaningful only if it reflects concrete class formations.
>
> (Kingston, 2000: 24)

In the absence of micro-level analysis, macro-level theorizing becomes stale. Add that on the analytical stage traditional theories of class require some degree of hierarchy that modern occupational categories (the real positions occupied by individuals in particular job structures) usually lack. Occupation and class, therefore, are not univocal or coextensive concepts. So, in order to improvise upon the prevailing theory, one has to throw into the mix some fuzzy concepts such as inequality. Classes are validated as analytical tools by the pervading presence of perceived social differences. But, as Kingston notes:

> [a]t least hypothetically, any particular level of inequality can be accompanied by varying levels of class structuration.
>
> (2000: 53)

While one can find evidence of unrelenting and substantial inequality, for instance, in the USA, it does not mean that class is the prevalent dimension in the American social compound. If, at all, Kingston argues, low class structuration seems to be the norm. Classes have found their nemesis in a very dynamic mobility process. He goes on to show that class in present-day American society is not the significant factor in a number of fields such as politics, family, residence, friendship and, of course, lifestyles. In raising children, musical taste, the performing arts, reading, religious belief:

> Americans appear remarkably divided in their moral orientations, but these differences are also remarkably unrelated to class cleavages.
>
> (Kingston, 2000: 145)

One should accordingly conclude: (i) that social hierarchies are multidimensional, and (ii) that ranking along those dimensions is not tightly structured. This does not necessarily mean that history or, more modestly, social conflict, has come to an end, even on income distribution issues. As we have seen in the USA over the last decades, cultural conflicts based on race, sex or religion may become quite virulent.

Could that, however, be but another instance of American exceptionalism with no consequences for the rest of the world? Already in 1906, Werner Sombart was asking why there was no socialism in the USA. Even though this was not exactly the case (Lipset and Marks, 2000), at no time was socialism ever a powerful alternative in the USA, especially after the 1920s. However, it is quite possible that American exceptionalism in terms of social classes will become the norm in most advanced and some developing market societies (Lipset, 1996). The USA was exceptional in that it became the first mass or consumer society in the world, but the path has been followed by many others since. This may not be a Vicoan, Comtian or Spencerian mandatory rung in the ladder of progress, but it seems a well-established trend, sorely missed by the great intellectuals of Old Europe, from Weber to Ortega y Gasset; from the Frankfurters to Isaiah Berlin; from Derrida to, as we just saw, Pierre Bourdieu.

In the realm of lifestyles, all that array of complex and ever-changing new social categories such as the baby boomers, generation X-ers, hippies, yuppies, buppies, dinks, yucas, bobos (Brooks, 2001), radical chics, neocons, born-again whatever, redneck intellectuals or any of the endless sociographic categories that can be built for the USA (Weiss, 2000) or Europe (Jupiter Media, 2003), well shows that wide-ranging categories such as ruling class, or late capitalism, or domination/hegemony have to be taken with a large pinch of salt and with an eye on the fast-moving occupational ball. Even the useful and flexible concepts of high-, middle- and lowbrow seem unable to reflect this fast-changing reality (Rubin, 1992). It has cred-

ibly been argued (Seabrook, 2000) that they are just the flotsam of outdated ways of thinking, clinging to a static social order with clearly delimited boundaries. Even the notion of *camp*, in spite of its open disregard for the high/low dichotomy in culture, dangerously makes room for the old status system. Today, though, the brows have morphed into the single category of 'nobrow'.

> In Nobrow, subculture was the new high culture, and high culture had become just another subculture.
>
> (Seabrook, 2000: 66)

Old distinctions based on a rigid cultural divide such as avant-garde and mass aesthetics, including well-known tactics such as *épater le bourgeois* or provocation or guerrilla art have become obsolete. There are no bourgeois around and, even if we can find some, they have long ago learned how to insulate themselves from shock and awe. When one sees white Ivy-League college students singing and dancing to the gangsta rap and hip-hop rhythms blaring on MTV and its clones the world over, or the invasion of reality shows on TV, or the universal audience that blockbusters have to aim at (*Economist*, 2003), the feeling that MacCannell, Bourdieu and Co. are barking up the wrong tree becomes more than just a hunch. In multidimensional social structures, status overlaps and overwhelms class as the main signifier of our multiple identities.

> Taste is the act of making the thing part of your identity. Stripped of the legitimacy that the old cultural hierarchy gave to them, acts of taste are acts of appetite, whether applied to art, furniture, or food [. . .] In the cultural marketplace of Nobrow any number of possible identities are on offer.
>
> (Seabrook, 2000: 170–171)

One no longer needs to be classy, just sassy.

These reflections apply to T&T as well. After all T&T is part of culture and is affected by the same trends that move and shake it. T&T opens an immense world of possibilities to shine in Nobrowland. Status is conferred by the way one travels, the places selected and the attractions one goes after, with no hierarchical compass to help navigation. Backpackers, for instance, carefully create a world of subtle lin-guistic and narrative practices (Elsrud, 2001; Murphy, 2001) to mark differences between rookies and old hands; or clearly distance them-selves from the yuppies who imitate their ways of travel (Harrison, 2002) or continuously look out for yet unexplored destinations (Wilson, 1997). It is their way of establishing a pecking order of status.

Since Dennis Tito's space jaunt in 2001, new vistas have opened up for space tourism. Indeed the US$20 million allegedly paid for his star trek by the millionaire might be seen as another sign that only the very rich may carve their names in a minor hall of fame. However, Tito's trip created a lot of excitement among some consumer segments that an eager travel industry is ready to satisfy at considerably cheaper prices. Space tourism may become one of the hot buttons for status-oriented tourists in the not so distant future (Crouch, 2004; Smith, 2001).

What is better, to spend one's time attend-ing Donald Duck's birthday party and making friends with Goofy and Minnie along America's Main Street, Orlando, or to get acquainted with the danger-zone, as some young tourists have been doing lately? Aren't travels to perilous Asian destinations (Timor, Indonesia, Kashmir, Sri Lanka, even Afghanistan) *the real thing*, a third, wilder dimension of authenticity, 'which includes the sense of heightened awareness (on a very physical level) experienced during endangerment' (Adams, 2001: 275). Though she does not say so, one has the impression that Kathleen Adams has no straight answers to this question. However, after an excellent analysis of danger-zone tourists' experiences and goals, she suggests with an enviable flair that the point in travel, as in any other con-spicuous consumption, is not the act itself, but the fact of preventing the Joneses from keep-ing up with us. For isn't collecting unique expe-riences and objects unavailable to the rest of our circle, of our class, or of our society the ulti-mate attribute of distinction?

At present, Reinhold Messner happens to be a member of the Green fraction of the European parliament. But:

[s]ince 20 years ago, [Messner] has been a member of the most successful group of world

mountaineers. He has participated in over 3500 mountain treks, ascending over 100 of them for the first time. He has been to the top of all 14 peaks higher than 8000 metres. He explored on foot Antarctica, Greenland, the whole of Tibet and the deserts of Takla and Makan.

(Messner, 2003)

Messner has inspired with his books (Messner, 1999, 2002) and his philosophy (Caysa and Schmid, 2002) many imitators who, even if unable to duplicate his feats, have turned mountaineering into their main tourist activity. During my last visit to Nepal, I met a 75-year-old Spanish gentleman on his way to the base camp for Sagarmatha or Chomolungma or Everest (your choice of the politically correct name). He had just read Messner and was going to join a few hundred other climbing fans. Admittedly, not many people of his age or nationality will be able to tell the same story, although boundless examples of similar branch-ing out of T&T activities can be described. Status seeking, the search for identities, a thirst for knowledge or selective experiences are their driving force. They do not of necessity follow the class template.

Conclusion

This has been a long journey, but we have reached our announced conclusion. If the future of T&T may one day darken, it will not be because of endogenous factors, as MacCannell suggested. We have offered evi-dence that, far from killing T&T, the evolution of modern market societies seems to breathe new life into it every day. We have argued that this is not a haphazard trend, but that it belongs to the essence of their evolution. It is easy to agree with MacCannell's view that T&T is mainly motivated by a desire to know and to experience other worlds and other people. However, nothing seems to warrant his conclusion that this goal cannot be reached in late capitalism. On the other hand, we con-tended that the latter has been clearly benefi-cial to T&T as it has increased the range of options at the disposal of ever larger numbers of consumers. All the extant empirical evi-dence for T&T, recreational sex and, as one might show in each individual case, many other forms of leisure, runs counter to MacCannell's predictions of gloom and doom. As José Zorrilla, a 19th-century Spanish playwright, put it in his version of the Don Juan saga, 'the corpses of those you killed / enjoy an enviable health'.

We have also made the case that T&T's enviable health springs from other sources. Although we have not explored them at all, desires and emotions play important roles in the decision to travel (Riley *et al.*, 1998; Ryan, 1998). However, the status dimension appears at least as important as the cognitive impulse to engage in T&T. In order to show its real importance, we had to get rid of some baggage close to the hearts of classical Marxism and postmodern cultural studies. Understanding the proper importance of status, taste and distinction in modern market societies and its impact on T&T is in no way helped by their insistence on an outdated idea of social classes as prime movers of social action – the main marginal utility function of today's Marxism.

So, as my practically oriented friends keep asking, should we hold on to those Amex shares in our portfolios after all? That's a tough one, but straight questions require straight answers. For the long term – yes, hold on to them. Wars, plagues, earthquakes and other exogenous phenomena will come, but they will also go. Beware, though, for even when T&T may remain as unyielding as Stonewall Jackson, Amex may misinterpret the mysterious but quickly changing tastes of the nobrow crowd that only some visionary trend-spotters will be able to anticipate.

References

Adams, K. (2001) Danger-zone tourism: prospects and problems for tourism in tumultuous times. In: Teo, P., Chang, T.C. and Ho, K.C. (eds) *Interconnected Worlds: Tourism In Southeast Asia.* Pergamon, Cambridge, pp. 265–281.

Bell, D. (1973) *The Coming of Post-Industrial Society: a Venture in Social Forecasting.* Basic Books, New York.

Bergson, H. (2001) *Time and Free Will: an Essay on the Immediate Data of Consciousness.* Translated by F.L. Pogson. Dover Publications, New York.

Boorstin, D. (1973) *The Americans: the Democratic Experience.* Random House, New York.

Bosker, G. and Lencek, L. (1999) *The Beach: a History of Paradise on Earth.* Penguin, New York.

Bourdieu, P. (1984) *A Social Critique of the Judgment of Taste.* Translated by R. Nice. Harvard University Press, Cambridge, Massachusetts.

Bradsher, K. (2003) Economies sickened by a virus, and fear. *New York Times* 21 April.

Brooks, D. (2001) *Bobos in Paradise: the New Upper Class and How They Got There.* Touchstone Books, New York.

Carr, D. (2003) Can an old leopard change its silk pajamas? *New York Times* 21 April.

Čavlek, N. (2002) Tour operators and destination safety. *Annals of Tourism Research* 29(2), 478–496.

Čavlek, N. (2004) The impact of tour operators on tourism development: a sequence of events. In: Aramberri, J. and Butler, R. (eds) *Tourism Development: Issues for a Vulnerable Industry.* Channel View Publications, London.

Caysa, V. and Schmid, W. (2002) *Reinhold Messners Philosophie.* Suhrkamp Verlag, Frankfurt-am-Main, Germany.

Completely Elite (2003) See http://www.complete-lyelite.com/ (accessed 21 April 2003).

Crick, M. (1996) Representations of international tourism in the social sciences: sun, sex, sights, savings and servility. In: Apostolopoulos, Y., Leivadi, S. and Yiannakis, A. (eds) *The Sociology of Tourism: Theoretical and Empirical Investigations.* Routledge, London.

Crouch, G. (2004) After Tito, where to from here? Marketing issues in the development of space tourism. In: Aramberri, J. and Butler, R. (eds) *Tourism Development: Issues for a Vulnerable Industry.* Channel View Publication, London.

Dilthey, W. (1991) Selected works. In: Makkreel, R.A. and Rodi, F. (eds) *Introduction to the Human Sciences,* Vol.1. Princeton University Press, Princeton, New Jersey.

Duby, G. (1973) *Guerriers et Paysans.* Gallimard, Paris.

Duby, G. (1982) *The Three Orders: Feudal Society Imagined.* University of Chicago Press, Chicago.

Dumézil, G. (1968) *Mythe et Épopée I.* Gallimard, Paris.

Dumézil, G. (1969) *Le Destin du Guerrier.* Presses Universitaires de France, Paris.

Dumézil, G. (1973) *From Myth to Fiction: The Saga of Hadingus.* University of Chicago Press, Chicago.

Dumézil, G. (1978) *Déesses Latines et Mythes Védiques.* Ayer, New York.

Economist (2003) How to manage a dream factory. 16 January.

Egan, T. (2000) Wall Street meets pornography. *New York Times* 23 October.

Elsrud, T. (2001) Risk creation in traveling: backpacker adventure narration. *Annals of Tourism Research* 28, 597–617.

Epstein, J. (2002) *Snobbery: The American Version*. Houghton Mifflin, New York.

Eros Guide (2003) (Philadelphia) *The Ultimate Guide to Erotic Entertainment* at http://www.eros-philly.com/eros.htmhttp://www.eros-philly.com/eros.htm (accessed 21 April 2003).

Escort Finder (2003) See http://www.escort-finder.com/ (accessed 21 April 2003).

Fallows, J. (1997) *Breaking the News: How the Media Undermine American Democracy*. Vintage Books, New York.

Ferguson, N. (2002) *Empire: The Rise and Demise of British World Order and the Lessons for Global Power*. Basic Books, New York, pp. 208–209.

Forbes (2001) How big is porn? *Forbes Magazine* 25 May.

Gans, H.J. (1999) *Popular Culture and High Culture: an Analysis and Evaluation of Taste*. Basic Books, New York.

Gartner, W.C. (2004) A synthesis of tourist trends. In: Aramberri, J. and Butler, R. (eds) *Tourism Development: Issues for a Vulnerable Industry*. Channel View, London.

Gerth, H.H. and Mills, C.W. (eds) (1970) *From Max Weber: Essays in Sociology*. Translated, selected and with an introduction by the editors. Routledge and Kegan Paul, London.

Gnoth, J. (1997) Tourism motivation and expectation formation. *Annals of Tourism Research* 24(2), 283–204.

Goldthorpe, J. (1987) *Social Mobility and Class Structure in Modern Britain*, 2nd edn. Clarendon, Oxford.

Goossens, C. (2000) Tourism information and pleasure motivation. *Annals of Tourism Research* 27(2), 301–321.

Graham, L.O. (1999) *Our Kind of People: Inside America's Black Upper Class*. Harper-Collins, New York.

Gramsci, A. (1949) Il moderno principe: noterelle sulla politica del Machiavelli. In: *Quaderni del Carcere*. Einaudi, Turin, Italy.

Gramsci, A. (1967) *Scritti Politici*. A Cura di Paolo Spriano. Editori Riuniti, Rome.

Gramsci, A. (1971) *Selections from the Prison Notebooks*. International Publishers, New York.

Halberstam, D. (1986) *The Reckoning*. Avon Books, New York.

Halberstam, D. (1994) *The Fifties*, reprint edn. Fawcett Books, New York.

Harrison, J. (2002) *Being a Tourist: Finding Meaning in Pleasure Travel*. University of British Columbia Press, Vancouver.

Hazen, D. (2001) All porn, all the time. *AlterNet* at http://www.alternet.org/story.html?StoryID=10778 (accessed 24 April 2003).

Jupiter Media (2003) *Jupiter Consumer Survey Report: European Attitudinal Consumer Clusters 2002*. http://www.jup.com/bin/home.pl (accessed 21 April 2003).

Klein, N. (2002) *No Logo: No Space, No Choice, No Jobs*. Picador, New York.

Kingston, P.W. (2000) *The Classless Society*. Stanford University Press, Stanford, California.

Kuhn, T. (1993) *The Structure of Scientific Revolutions*, 6th edn. University of Chicago Press, Chicago.

Lane, F.S. (2001) *Obscene Profits: The Entrepreneurs of Pornography in the Cyber Age*. Routledge, New York.

Leiper, N. (1990) Tourist attractions systems. *Annals of Tourism Research* 17, 367–384.

Levine, L.W. (1990) *Highbrow/Lowbrow: the Emergence of Cultural Hierarchy in America*. Harvard University Press, Cambridge, Massachusetts.

Lipset, S.M. (1996) *American Exceptionalism: a Double-Edged Sword*. W.W. Norton, New York/London.

Lipset, S.M. and Marks, G. (2000) *It Didn't Happen Here: Why Socialism Failed in the United States*. W.W. Norton, New York/London.

Lofgren, O. (1999) *On Vacation: a History of Vacationing*. University of California Press, Berkeley, California.

MacCannell, D. (1992) *Empty Meeting Ground: the Tourist Papers*. Routledge, London/New York.

MacCannell, D. (1999) *The Tourist: a New Theory of the Leisure Class*. New edition with a Foreword by L.R. Lippard and an Epilogue by the author. University of California Press, Berkeley and Los Angeles, California.

MacCannell, D. (2001) Remarks on the commodification of cultures. In: Smith, V.L and Brent, M. (eds) *Hosts and Guests Revisited: Tourism Issues of the 21st Century*. Cognizant Communication, New York.

Marx, K. (1972) Das Kapital, Erster Band. In: *Marx und Engels Werke, Band 23*. Dietz Verlag, Berlin.

Marx, K. (1973a) Ökonomisch-philisophische Manuskripte. In: *Marx und Engels Werke, Ergänzungsband, Erster Teil*. Dietz Verlag, Berlin.

Marx, K. (1973b) Thesen über Feuerbach. In: *Marx*

und Engels Werke, Band 3. Dietz Verlag, Berlin.

Marx, K. (1973c) Kritik des Gothaer Programms. In: *Marx und Engels Werke, Band 19*. Dietz Verlag, Berlin.

Marx, K. (1975) Early Writings. Translated by R. Livingstone and G. Benton. Penguin Books, Harmondsworth, UK.

McCabe, A.S. (2000) Tourism motivation process. *Annals of Tourism Research* 27(4), 1049–1052.

Messner, R. (1999) *Überlebt. Alle Achttausender mit Chronik*. BLV, Berlin.

Messner, R. (2002) *Der Nackte Berg. Nanga Parbat: Bruder, Tod und Eisamkeit*. Malik Verlag, Berlin.

Messner, R. (2003) *Reinhold Messner* website at http://www.reinhold-messner.de/ (accessed 21 April 2003).

Micklethwaite, J. and Wooldridge, A. (2001) *A Future Perfect: the Challenge and Promise of Globalization*. Random House, New York.

Murphy, L. (2001) Exploring social interactions of backpackers. *Annals of Tourism Research* 28, 50–67.

Nie, N. and Erbring, L. (2000) *Internet and Society. A Preliminary Report*. See http://www.stanford.edu/group/siqss/Press_Release/Preliminary_Report-4–21.pdf (accessed 21 April 2003).

Packard, V. (1977) *The People Shapers*. Little Brown and Co, New York.

Packard, V. (1985) *The Hidden Persuaders* (updated edn). Pocket Books, New York.

Parsons, T. (1959) *The Social System*, 3rd edn. Free Press of Glencoe, New York.

Parsons, T. (1967) *The Structure of Social Action*, 2nd edn. Free Press of Glencoe, New York.

Parsons, T. (1970) *Social Structure and Personality*. Free Press of Glencoe, New York.

Phelts, M.D. (1997) *An American Beach for African Americans*. University Press of Florida, Gainesville, Florida.

Pinker, S. (1997) *How the Mind Works*. W.W. Norton, New York.

Pinker, S. (2002) *The Blank Slate: The Modern Denial of Human Nature*. Viking, New York.

Popper, K. (1992) *Conjectures and Refutations: The Growth of Scientific Knowledge*, 5th edn. Routledge, London.

Popper, K. (1993) *Realism and the Aim of Science* (Postscript to *The Logic of Scientific Discovery*). Edited by W.W. Bartley. Routledge, London.

Popper, K. (2001) *All Life Is Problem-Solving*. Routledge, London.

Popper, K. (2002) *The Logic of Scientific Discovery*, 15th edn. Routledge, London.

Postman, N. (1985) *Amusing Ourselves to Death: Public Discourse in the Age of Show Business*. Viking, New York.

Poulantzas, N. (1975) *Political Power and Social Classes*. Prometheus Books, New York.

Poulantzas, N. (1978) *Classes in Contemporary Capitalism*. Schocken Books, New York.

Rich, F. (2001) Naked capitalists: there is no business like porn business. *New York Times Magazine* 18 May.

Richards, G. (2002) Tourism attraction systems: exploring cultural behavior. *Annals of Tourism Research* 29(4), 1048–1064.

Riesman, D., Glazer, N. and Denney, R. (1950) *The Lonely Crowd: a Study of the Changing American Character*. Yale University Press, New Haven, Connecticut.

Riley, R., Baker, D. and Doren, C.S.V. (1998) Movie induced tourism. *Annals of Tourism Research* 25, 919–935.

Rubin, J.S. (1992) *The Making of Middlebrow Culture*. University of North Carolina Press, Chapel Hill, North Carolina.

Ryan, C. (1998) The travel career ladder: an appraisal. *Annals of Tourism Research* 25, 936–957.

Seabrook, J. (2000) *Nobrow: The Culture of Marketing—the Marketing of Culture*. Alfred A. Knopf, New York.

Smith, V. (2001) Space tourism. *Annals of Tourism Research* 28, 238–240.

Sombart, W. (1976) *Why Is There No Socialism in the United States?* International Arts and Sciences Press, Ithaca, New York.

Sontag, S. (2001) *Against Interpretation: and Other Essays*. Originally published in 1966. Picador, New York.

Sørensen, A.B. (2001) The basic concepts of stratification research: class, status and power. In: Grusky, D.B. (ed.) *Social Stratification: Class, Race and Gender in Sociological Perspective*. Westview Press, Boulder, Colorado.

Thompson, E.P. (1966) *The Making of the English Working Class*. Random House, New York.

US Census Bureau (2003) *E-Commerce 2001 Highlights*. http://www.census.gov/eos/www/papers/2001/2001estatstext.pdf (accessed 19 March 2003).

Weber, M. (1972) *Wirtschaft und Gesellschaft. Fuenfte, revidierte Auslage*. J.C.B. Mohr (Paul Siebeck), Tübingen, Germany.

Weiss, M. J. (2000) *The Clustered World: How We Live, What We Buy, and What It All Means About Who We Are*. Little, Brown and Co, Boston, Massachusetts.

Wilson, D. (1997) Paradoxes of tourism in Goa. *Annals of Tourism Research* 24, 52–75.

Wright, E.O. (1978) *Class, Crisis and the State.* Verso, New York.

Wright, E.O. (1989) *Classes.* Verso, London.

Wright, E.O. (1997) *Class Counts: Comparative Studies in Class Analysis.* Cambridge University Press, Cambridge, UK.

WTO (2003) *Tourism Vision 2020.* See http://www.world-tourism.org/market_research/facts &figures/menu.htm (accessed 12 April 2003).

WTTC (2003a) World travel and tourism: a world of opportunity. *2003 Travel and Tourism Economic Research* at http://wttc.org/measure/PDF/World.pdf (accessed 21 April 2003).

WTTC (2003b) The potential impact of an Iraq war on travel and tourism. See http://wttc.org/News6.htm (accessed 21 April 2003).

Index

Note: page numbers in *italics* refer to boxes, figures and tables.